THE CONTEMPORARY SCIENCE SERIES

EDITED BY HAVELOCK ELLIS

THE EVOLUTION OF MODERN CAPITALISM

THE EVOLUTION OF
MODERN CAPITALISM

A Study of Machine Production

BY

JOHN A. HOBSON, M.A.

Author of
" Conditions of Industrial Peace"
" Free Thought in the Social Sciences"

LONDON: GEORGE ALLEN & UNWIN LTD
NEW YORK: CHARLES SCRIBNER'S SONS

FIRST PUBLISHED, MAY 1894
REPRINTED, MARCH 1901
REVISED EDITION, OCTOBER 1906
REVISED EDITION, DECEMBER 1916
REPRINTED, SEPTEMBER 1919
REPRINTED, MARCH 1921
REVISED EDITION, MAY 1926
REPRINTED, FEBRUARY 1927
REPRINTED, SEPTEMBER 1928
REPRINTED, AUGUST 1930

PREFACE TO NEW AND REVISED EDITION.

IN the long Supplementary Chapter added to this new edition of *The Evolution of Modern Capitalism* I have endeavoured to trace and illustrate the chief movements of trade and industry which are distinctive of the opening quarter of the twentieth century. In the first part of the chapter I have dealt chiefly with the movements prior to the Great War, though in some cases I have brought the statistical record of events up to the present time. It is, however, evident that the War period (1914–1918) makes a definite cleavage in economic as in general history, and that the mode, the direction, and the pace of capitalist development have undergone great changes in consequence of the War and its political and economic sequelæ. The period has been one of disturbance, recovery, and readjustments.

The redistribution of political boundaries and controls, not only in Europe, but in Africa, Asia, and the Pacific, have affected industrial development and trade routes.

State policies during the War and after have had important reactions upon the relative growth of industries and upon the structure of businesses, stimulating in no ordinary degree the combinations and associations which always modify and often displace the competitive system.

The new development of electric power, for transport,

industry, and domestic purposes, is already producing changes not only of industrial structure but of the relative importance of the industrial areas of the world. Water power and oil are seen to be determinants of economic strength. Assessments of current economic strength, in terms of coal, iron, foreign trade, etc., give some valuable indications of the changing wealth of the advanced industrial nations—in particular, the new place taken by the United States as a financial and economic power. Post-war difficulties and disturbances have ripened old problems and disclosed new ones in the field of international finance, the control of backward countries with rich natural resources, and the relations between capital and labour within the several countries and in the international sphere. I offer some brief settling of these problems, in terms of fact and figure, as a contribution towards a speculative forecast of the capitalism of the near future.

J. A. HOBSON.

May, 1926.

PREFACE TO THE REVISED EDITION.

THIS new and enlarged edition of *The Evolution of Modern Capitalism* contains additions and alterations so great as to constitute it in effect a new book.

The chapters dealing with the concentrative forces in modern industry, the growth of industrial Combinations, Trusts, Cartels, etc., are entirely rewritten. Large use has been made of recent English and American material, and much attention is given to new developments of capitalism in the transport and manufacturing industries of the United States.

In Chapter X. an analysis of the position occupied by the financier in modern industry is presented, with illustrations from recent developments in South Africa and America.

While most of the matter of the earlier historical chapters in the first edition is retained, numerous emendations and additions have been made, and an introductory chapter on the Origin of Modern Capitalism, based largely upon the researches in Professor Sombart's great work, *Der Moderne Kapitalismus*, has been inserted.

For material relating to capitalistic combinations in Great Britain I desire to express my deep indebtedness to the writings of Mr. W. H. Macrosty, whose collection and analysis of instances form the best single fund of information. For recent American material relating to Trusts I have made large use of the reports of the Industrial Commission and the writings of Professor Richard Ely and Professor Jeremiah Jenks.

J. A. HOBSON.

August, 1906.

CONTENTS.

CHAPTER I.

CHAPTER II.

CHAPTER III.

CHAPTER IV.

CHAPTER V.

CHAPTER VI.

CHAPTER VII.

CHAPTER VIII.

CHAPTER IX.

CHAPTER X.

CHAPTER XI.

CHAPTER XII.

CHAPTER XIII.

CHAPTER XIV.

CHAPTER XV.

CHAPTER XVI.

CHAPTER XVII.

SUPPLEMENTARY CHAPTER.

PART I.

PART II.

THE EVOLUTION
OF MODERN CAPITALISM.

CHAPTER I.

THE ORIGIN OF MODERN CAPITALISM.

§ 1. *The first conditions of Capitalism.*
§ 2. *Mediæval repositories of Wealth.*
§ 3. *Rents the origin of early Capital.*
§ 4. *"Treasure" as the monetary basis.*
§ 5. *Nobles, burghers, and officials the first "Business Men."*
§ 6. *The beginnings of Colonial Exploitation and "Forced Labour."*
§ 7. *The rise of a British proletariat of dispossessed cultivators.*
§ 8. *Similar movement in Continental Europe.*
§ 9. *Slow growth of use of Machinery.*
§ 10. *The Spirit of Economic Rationalism.*
§ 11. *Causes of England's priority in Capitalism.*

§ 1. Capitalism may provisionally be defined as the organisation of business upon a large scale by an employer or company of employers possessing an accumulated stock of wealth wherewith to acquire raw materials and tools, and hire labour, so as to produce an increased quantity of wealth which shall constitute profit. Wherever in the course of history a conjunction of certain essential economic and moral forces has appeared, capitalist industry in some form

and size has existed.   These essential conditions may be
thus enumerated:—

> First, a production of wealth not required to satisfy the
> current wants of its owners, and therefore saved.

> Second, the existence of a proletariat or labouring class
> deprived of the means of earning an independent
> livelihood by putting their productive labour-power
> into materials which they can freely appropriate,
> purchase, or hire, consuming or selling the product
> for their own advantage.

> Third, such a development of the industrial arts as enables
> indirect methods of production to afford profitable
> employment to organised group-labour using tools
> or machinery.

> Fourth, the existence of large, accessible markets with
> populations willing and economically able to con-
> sume the products of capitalist industry.

> Fifth, the capitalist spirit, or the desire and the capacity
> to apply accumulated wealth to profit-making by the
> organisation of industrial enterprise.

These are, of course, no series of wholly independent
conditions.   On the contrary, they are closely inter-related.
The causes which favour an accumulation of wealth in one
class of a nation, or other social aggregate, will commonly
assist the formation of a proletariat labour class.   The
existence of a population capable of generating new wants
will help not only to stimulate accumulation, by offering the
possibility of large profitable sales, but will also arouse the
development of industrial arts, which in their turn will re-act
upon the consuming public by provoking new wants.   Such
an atmosphere of technical progress, alike in the arts of
production and of consumption, will educate the desire and
the capacity of capitalist organisation.

§ 2. The forms which capitalist enterprise takes differ
widely according to the relative development of these constituent forces or conditions.

Unless we regard as capitalist enterprises the military and
naval expeditions for pillage, to which so large a share of
the accumulations in the ancient world and throughout the
Middle Ages was applied, the area of older capitalism was

virtually confined to certain public or semi-public works,
such as palaces, temples, tombs, castles, and other edifices
for ostentation or defence; the making of roads, water-
courses, and other permanent improvement of transport;
mining, chiefly for precious metals; and certain expensive
and hazardous branches of commerce with distant parts.
Slave or serf labour applied to the cultivation of the soil
may also be accounted a species of capitalism in ancient
times. Of the most characteristic branch of modern capitalism, large-scale manufacture, the ancient world contains few
traces.

Until the close of what we call the Middle Ages none of
the conditions we have named as essential to a wide general
development of capitalism was present, and two at least did
not assume considerable dimensions until the eighteenth
century.

As we briefly trace the emergence of these forces in the
modern world, we shall bring into prominence the distinctive
features of modern as distinguished from ancient capitalism,
as well as furnish an explanation of the rapid growth of th
capitalist economy.

In his elaborate research into the sources of accumulation
in the Middle Ages, Sombart finds five principal repositories
of accumulated wealth :—

1. The papal treasury at Rome, fed by the contributions
   of the faithful, and enormously enhanced during the
   period of the Crusades.

2. The knightly orders, foremost among them the
   Templars, whose establishments extended over the
   entire known world, from Greece to Portugal, from
   Sicily to Scotland.

3. The royal treasuries of France and England.

4. The higher grades of the feudal nobility.

5. The city funds of the important commercial centres,
   Venice, Milan, Naples, ranking first, followed by
   Bologna and Florence in Italy, Paris, London,
   Barcelona, Seville, Lisbon, Bruges, Ghent (later
   Antwerp), Nürnberg, and Köln.[1]

---

[1] *Der moderne Kapitalismus*, Zweites Buch. Zehntes Kap.

If we seek the actual origins of these early accumulations we run them "to earth" in rents of agricultural and city lands, in the working of mines, and the discovery or pillage of ancient treasures of the East. In the Middle Ages the home trade and the industrial crafts were never anything else than means of "livelihood," their scale and the conditions under which they were conducted furnishing no scope for considerable accumulations. Though in the later periods of the Middle Ages large profits were made out of Colonial trade and money-lending, these processes implied the pre-existence of large accumulations which were essential to their operations; moreover, further analysis of Colonial trade and money-lending drive down to labour on the land as the prime source of their profits.

§ 3. The historical foundation of capitalism is rent, the product of labour upon land over and above what is requisite to maintain the labourers; this surplus accrues by political or economic force to the king, feudal superior, or landowner, and can be consumed or stored by him.

By taxes and tolls, fines, rents, or even by voluntary contributions, the king, the Church, the landlord, was able to draw from the cultivation of the land the surplus product of the more fertile soil, and most of the increment of the productivity of agriculture due to improved methods of cultivation. Systems of taxation and of land tenure were evolved in order to extract as much as possible of these natural surpluses for the benefit of the political or economic superior. This power, however, to draw from the cultivators a large amount of the produce, though conferring on the landowner or feudal superior a large command over surplus wealth for his personal consumption and that of a body of idle retainers, would not in itself enable him to accumulate, for the wealth he thus received would consist almost wholly of perishable goods; even the forced labour he sometimes extorted in lieu of produce was of necessity applied chiefly to the production of buildings, roads, bridges, etc., which, though of more permanent utility, could contribute little to such accumulation as is required for capitalism.

To the surplus product of agriculture must be added the rents of town lands. Though the small town trader or craftsman under primitive conditions was seldom able to make sufficient savings out of his profits to become even a local usurer, the growth of the smallest sort of town yielded to the owner of the ground on which it stood a number of little rents whose growth became a considerable source of wealth. As from his country estates the feudal noble was able to squeeze from the peasants the fruits of improved agriculture and more settled government, so from his town lands he could take the value of improvements of the industrial arts. The beginnings of the wealth of cities are accumulated ground rents.[1]

Investigations into the records of the early history of rising cities show that in nearly all cases the early capitalists are representatives of the families originally in possession of the ground on which the town is built. The landowners necessarily controlled the laying out of streets; the mill, the smithy, the markets were made or controlled by them; houses, booths, and workshops were often built by them. The increments of city values came to them in hereditary or life leases, or in time leases; while sales of these town lands and redemptions put large sums into the hands of the territorial aristocracy, who as early as the thirteenth century in Italy and Flanders are found in the position of large "capitalists."

"It was a slow, gradual, and for the working population an unobserved draining of small particles of labour which in course of time was destined to serve as the foundation of the capitalist economy."[2] The important point to recognise is that whether the industry whose surplus profits (the excess over the subsistence of the worker) is agriculture, or town handicrafts and trading, the first instrument of appropriation is the ownership of land.

§ 4. But we must look to another sort of labour on the land to furnish the technical condition of effective accumulation. Payment of rents for country or town lands in kind could not found capitalism. The discovery and appropriation of the precious metals are essential to this achievement. It is necessary that the original power of drawing rents should be monetised before the possession of capital can become itself a basis of profit. Until "treasure" could be obtained and retained in Western Europe modern capitalism could make no really considerable start. The

---

[1] Cf. Sombart, vol. i. p. 291.   [2] *Ibid.*, vol. i. p. 268.

earlier treasure-houses were in the East, and during the
early Middle Ages Western intercourse with these older
civilisations meant a constant suckage of the precious
metals eastwards to pay for the goods which came into
Europe through the Levant trade. Though Germany and
Austro-Hungary turned out considerable quantities of gold
and silver, these passed through the hands of the Italian
merchants into the East. Not until the collapse of the
Byzantine empire opened the Ægean and the Asiatic coast
to the plunder and exploitation of Italian rulers and
merchants did the tide begin to turn and Western Europe
obtain the supply of money required as a basis of
capitalism.

Economic historians often misrepresent the part played
by money. The development of mines and a large output
of the precious metals assist the rise of capitalism in that
they give to the possessors of these precious metals a power
to divert into channels of indirect production the surplus industrial energy drawn from the producers in taxes, tolls, rents,
etc. A sufficient development of agriculture and of other
industrial arts to furnish such a surplus is a pre-requisite.
The existence of the precious metals in a community enables the type known as "the business man" to arise and
function by directing the flow of "superfluous industrial
energy" from the production of immediate to that of mediate
goods; or in other words, from the direct production of consumers' wealth to the production of industrial and commercial capital-goods. This does not necessarily occur as
a result of the discovery of gold and silver even in a fairly
civilised state. The owners of wealth got from mines
may, often do, use it chiefly for ostentation and for decorative consumption. But blended with this use is the recognition of another use of precious metals and jewels as
a store of value which on occasion may give the owner a
command over other forms of wealth and over the energy of
men.

This storage of treasure in the hands of kings, nobles, and
of cities is first conceived with the design of providing for
defensive or offensive warfare. For defence or attack it is
necessary to maintain and equip quickly large bodies of
men, to furnish weapons, ships, and other expensive apparatus of war, and the earliest forms of large enterprise

which resemble capitalist industry are the equipment of land and sea expeditions for conquest and plunder. The early funds not only of monarchs but of the Italian cities in the Middle Ages were chiefly designed and used for war.

So long as the surplus-product of labour passed, in forms of tax, toll, and rent, into the hands of kings and nobles, the Church, the orders, and city funds, whether to be consumed in luxury or to be accumulated as treasure, it could not give rise to capitalism.

§ 5. It was essential that masses of this surplus wealth should pass into the hands of "business men," who should seek to make it a basis of "profitable" use. Now, records seem to point to two chief origins of such a class.

The rise of the great mercantile power of the Italian cities clearly indicates one origin—the entrance of members of the landed aristocracy into city life and burgher occupations. With the growth of more settled order in the country, and of a softer, more luxurious habit of life, some of the landed nobility came to settle in the cities, bringing with them their rent-rolls and buying more city lands. Especially the younger branches of the nobility, no longer wholly occupied with war, came into town life. This merging of the landed nobility with city life was earlier and freer in the Italian and Flemish states than in France or Germany, and the larger quantity of money thus brought into the cities by the "monetisation" of the rents of their estates contributed not a little to the earlier development of large commercial undertakings by Italian and Flemish merchant-houses. In England also from the thirteenth century the lower nobles began to mix more easily with burgher life, and "the younger sons of the country knight sought wife, occupation, and estate in the towns."[1] "A large proportion of the London apprentices were drawn from the houses of rural gentry"[2] in the time of Elizabeth, the cleavage between the landed and the moneyed interests not having yet begun to display itself. So, too, in Germany the early commercial prosperity of such towns as Augsburg, Nürnberg, Basel, and Köln was fed from a similar source. Unfortunately, the history of Germany in the later Middle Ages tended more

[1] Stubbs, 197.
[2] Cunningham, *Growth of English Industry*, vol. i. p. 126 (8vo, 1903).

and more to estrange the landed nobility from the peaceful life and pursuits of towns, a fact which greatly contributed to retard the commercial and industrial development of that country.

While many of the great business men of the Middle Ages in Italy, Flanders, Germany thus sprang from the landed aristocracy, possessing agricultural rents, tolls, and fines as their commercial nest-egg, the smaller owners of city-grounds, the original burgher-families, played an equally important part in cases where the town-lands were not closely held by noble or by church. These original settlers, small farmers at the start, extending their holdings, often encroaching on or dividing by agreement common lands, formed strong local oligarchies, sucking the rising land values to form the capital which they afterwards employed in commerce.

To these nobles or small land-holders who passed into commerce with accumulations directly derived from ground-rents, must be added the officials who, under the feudal system, were quartered upon the public resources in lucrative offices of state, or were entrusted with the collection and farming of taxes and tolls. Not only were the salaries of chancellors, marshals, and other high officers extremely large, but all officials connected with the raising and expenditure of public moneys had opportunities for peculation which were freely exercised. The ruling families in the cities could thus add to their private ground-rents a share of the city funds. So large shares of the original accumulations of royal and papal treasuries, and of the rents and endowments of monasteries and cities passed into the hands of the business men, who were agents for these great public sources of income.[1]

The management of the estates and the finances of the private land-owners, lay and spiritual, was largely entrusted to a class of business officials, who, as rent collectors, stewards, bailiffs, reeves, intendants, came to share the riches of the landlords. But it must be remembered that in whatever form incomes came to these public or private officers and agents, as salaries, fees, profit, or peculation, land-rents were the almost exclusive origin.

[1] So the Spini, Spigliati, Bardi, Cerchi, Pulci, Alfani, and later the Medici, became the great bankers of the Papacy. (Sombart, vol. i. p. 251.)

Given a class of business-men with such sources of
accumulation in their hands, it is not difficult to perceive
the chief profitable use to which they could put this
"capital." The most important branch of primitive
capitalism is "usury" or "money-lending," and the part
this played in converting feudal into burgher wealth was
noteworthy.[1] The great spiritual landlords were driven to
borrowing money in order to forward to Rome the increasing monetary contributions which the "age of faith"
called forth; the temporal lords, embarrassed by the growing expenses of war and of building (the two chief uses of
money), were drawn more and more into debt to the
"banking-houses" in Italy, Flanders, and Germany. The
Crusades form a chief landmark in this growing power of
the new business class, compelling the Crusaders to borrow
for their expenses of equipment and travel, giving increased
power to their stewards and agents, and bringing back a
new influx of luxurious habits of life from the East which
led them into further extravagances. In Italy and elsewhere increasing quantities of land were thus alienated from
their aristocratic owners, forfeited for debt. When the
period of the Renaissance brought the fuller influence of the
East to bear upon "barbarous" Europe, and cities began to
assume an air of luxury and to exercise influence as "social
centres," the country nobility and gentry wishing to enter
this new life, found themselves short of money and compelled to borrow from the rich burghers. Beginning in
Italy as early as the thirteenth century, this movement
reached Germany in the fifteenth, and England in Elizabeth's reign showed that the "money-lending" business
was so large and profitable as to tempt not only Continental
capital but Dutch settlers from Amsterdam and elsewhere
to compete with the Jewish and Lombard houses in
London.[2]

Extravagance of dress was itself a considerable factor in
the borrowing habits which built the wealth of the city
financiers.

§ 6. But all these modes by which capital has passed
from the ownership of landlords into that of business men
furnish an inadequate explanation of the rapid increase of

[1] Cf. Sombart, vol. i. p. 255. [2] Cunningham, vol. i. p. 324.

wealth in Western Europe. Without far larger access to
monetary treasures as instruments of concentrated accumulation, without larger opportunities of gathering the various
material resources for the development of the industrial arts,
modern capitalism would have been impossible in its existing dimensions. Western Europe supplied no adequate
output of precious metals from the mines: her agricultural
population afforded no increase of production in the form of
rents large enough to furnish a great stream of accumulating
wealth, nor could the productiveness of the industrial arts of
the towns yield a rapid growth of profit. The economy
of mediæval Europe did not expose a large landless proletarian population to the free exploitation of profit-seeking
masters. The labour basis of modern capitalism was
lacking.

The exploitation of other portions of the world through
military plunder, unequal trade, and forced labour has been
one great indispensable condition of the growth of European
capitalism. "The riches of the Italian cities is quite incon-
ceivable apart from the exploitation of the rest of the
Mediterranean; just as the prosperity of Portugal, Spain,
Holland, France, and England is unthinkable apart from the
previous destruction of the Arab civilisation, the plundering
of Africa, the impoverishment and desolation of Southern
Asia, and its island world, the fruitful East Indies, and the
thriving states of the Incas and Astecs."[1]

The Italian republics were the first to take this work in
hand. The close of the Crusades saw them in virtual control of numerous cities in Syria, Palestine, the Ægean, and
the Black Sea. From the beginning of the twelfth century,
Genoa, Pisa, and Venice fastened their economic fangs into
the towns of Arsof, Cæsarea, Acre, Sidon, Tyre, etc. The
break up of the Eastern empire gave Venice a vast colonial
power, not less than three-eighths of that empire falling
under her single sway; while her rival, Genoa, also acquired
large possessions among the Ionian islands and on the main-
land. Asia Minor and the Ægean islands were full of rich
natural resources, with large civilised populations inheriting
arts of skilled industry as yet unknown to the Western
world. The Italian cities did not pretend to colonise in any

[1] Sombart, vol. i. p. 326.

labourers required as one condition of great profitable capitalism. It is for this reason that colonial economy must be regarded as one of the necessary conditions of modern capitalism. Its trade, largely compulsory, was in large measure little other than a system of veiled robbery, and was in no sense an equal exchange of commodities. Trading profits were supplemented by the industrial profits representing the "surplus-value" of slave or forced labour, and by the yield of taxation and plunder.

"The particular significance of the colonial economy is that it affords undertaker's profits before the conditions of true capitalism are ripe, before the required accumulation of money has taken place, before there is a proletariat, and before free land has disappeared."[1]

§ 7. The growth of a large proletariat in Western Europe was an essential condition for capitalist industry. That meant an increase of rural population beyond the means of subsistence on the soil, according to current modes of agriculture and land tenure, and an increase of town population incapable of earning a livelihood as independent artificers or craftsmen. Now this condition was long delayed by the slow growth of population in the European nations. Famine, plague, and war kept down the population through the Middle Ages: the death-rate of children was enormous, and the effective life for the mass of the people was very short. Though no really reliable statistics are available, it is pretty well established that up to the eighteenth century the rate of increase of population for Europe as a whole was very slow, and even during the eighteenth century showed no great expansion. In Germany for a long time after the Thirty Years' War the population actually fell off, recovering only in the eighteenth century. France about the middle of the eighteenth century reached again the numbers she had attained in the first half of the fourteenth century, and still stood below the 18,000,000 she had attained after the death of Louis XIV. Holland and Belgium seem hardly to have increased for three centuries. From the last half of the sixteenth century to the beginning of the eighteenth century Italy was stagnant at

[1] Sombart, vol. i. p. 358.

about 11,000,000. In Spain the population showed an extraordinary decline during the sixteenth and seventeenth centuries.

The English population estimated at nearly 2,000,000 at the time of Doomsday, seems to have grown very slightly for three centuries, reaching not more than two and a half millions by 1377, in the last year of Edward III. During the following two centuries and a quarter the pace of growth was more rapid, for at the end of Elizabeth's reign it is estimated at some 5,000,000. From this time the rate of growth again declined, and 6,000,000 was not attained until nearly the middle of the eighteenth century.[1]

Mere growth of population, however, in lands, large parts of which were uncultivated or poorly cultivated, does not in itself explain the formation of a proletariat. As we traced the beginnings of "capital" to the accumulated ground-rents, so we must trace the beginnings of a mobile wage-earning class to agricultural and industrial changes which detached large numbers of the rural population from their earlier status as small owners or holders of land, or as labourers with some stake in the profits of the farm they helped to work. Agricultural reforms, involving more pro-ductive utilisation of land and better business methods, were the chief instruments of change. In Great Britain and upon the Continent the primitive agriculture of feudal

---

[1] Mr. Cunningham gives the following selected estimates of the population of England and Wales from 1688 onwards (*Growth of English Industry*, vol. iii. p. 935):—

1688	...	5,500,520	G. King, in *Davenant Works*, vol. ii. p. 184.
1700	...	5,475,000	
1710	...	5,240,000	
1720	...	5,565,000	
1730	...	5,796,000	
1740	...	6,064,000	*Statistical Journal*, vol. xliii. p. 462.
1750	...	6,467,000	
1760	...	6,736,000	
1770	...	7,428,000	
1780	...	7,928,000	
1790	...	8,675,000	
1801	...	8,892,536	
1811	...	10,114,226	
1821	...	12,000,237	*Accounts and Papers*, 1852-53, lxxxv.-xxxiii.
1831	...	13,896,798	
1841	...	15,914,146	
1851	...	17,927,609	

society required little "capital," and afforded no play for the "business" spirit. The "landowner" was not much concerned to exact money rents or to get considerable profits out of the land; his tenants and the cottagers or other workers on the farm enjoyed fixity of tenure and of status, tilled the soil according to custom for their livelihood, sharing the produce and living a nearly self-sufficing existence.

Trade in agricultural produce, bringing an increased use of money into the agricultural economy and stimulating owners and tenants to a more careful and intensive cultivation, so as to earn money rents and profits, was the chief channel of the innovating current. It was the Flemish demand for wool, which, coming upon England in the Tudor age when political and social conditions were favourable, afforded a large profitable use of pasture, leading to the enclosure of great quantities of common lands and wastes, and the formation of large pasture farms under new proprietors who, entering into the estates of the decayed baronial families and the confiscated church and guild lands, administered them by their agents in the spirit of a modern rent-receiver. This foreign market for wool, and the growing market for grain afforded by the increase of London and other centres of population and by a certain sporadic export trade, began that process of converting the small yeoman and cottager into the mere wage-earner which reached its fullest pace in the enclosures at the end of the eighteenth and the beginning of the nineteenth centuries. Whereas in the earlier period of this movement it was enclosure for pasture that was the chief propeller, in the later period it was enclosure for tillage.

Though the earlier enclosures involved much injustice in depriving small farmers and labourers of their legal or customary rights in the use of the land, and set afloat a considerable number of landless folk who lived as "rogues and vagabonds," or found a settlement in the towns, the mass of the villagers and rural workers seem to have retained until the eighteenth century some stake, however slender, in the soil, that differentiates them from the pure proletariat which modern capitalism requires as a condition. The simultaneous improvements in tillage, cattle-breeding, and sheep-farming of the eighteenth century found an England one-third of which still remained in common fields with the slovenly and wasteful cultivation involved in this system. A large part of the country was in the hands of small yeomen, farming their own land, cottagers or crofters, renting small holdings and enjoying not only a share in the common fields, but other rights of pasture, forest, and waste. The wage-work for farmers was partly performed by these, partly by farm-labourers who, if single, "lived in," and, if married, were supplied with a cottage on the farm, and were allowed certain small rights of pasturage for a cow, etc. Again, farmers in many parts of the country let patches of land to sub-tenants, who were primarily engaged in weaving or other domestic industry, and worked on the land in their spare time.

The conditions of enclosure and the new farming changed all this. Scientific rotation of crops, deep cultivation, the use of artificial manures, the increasing employment of machinery, involved a capital outlay and a business administration with which the small farmer could not cope.

The yeomen and other small owners or holders were unable to keep their grip upon the land: the legal and other expenses of acts of enclosure, the cost of fencing and other adjustments ruined many of them, and they were unable to stand up against the large landowners in the defence of doubtful legal or customary rights. The speculative business of growing for markets, with fluctuating prices, was unsuited alike to their means and their intelligence. Many of this class, thus failing to maintain an independent footing, came to recruit the new industrial army of the towns.

The cottagers, crofters, and other labourers were still less able to retain whatever rights custom yielded them in the beneficial use of the land. The old patriarchal farm life, which preserved elements of a profit-sharing character, gave way before the new business pressure, the supplementary wages in kind disappeared or were commuted into a trifling addition to a money-wage which the Poor Law in the later eighteenth century reduced to a degraded level.

The new wheat-farming economy had the further effect of diminishing winter employment. An even more serious consideration was the effect of the introduction of machinery in destroying the supplementary industries which helped the small peasants to pay their money rents, and made even the labourers greatly independent of the farmer. Though it cannot be supposed that the increased quantity and improved tillage which followed the enclosures, the increase of agricultural land by drainage and occupation of wastes, and the other agricultural improvements, diminish the aggregate demand for labour, they do not seem to have increased it sufficiently to absorb the rapid increase of the rural population; for already in the last decade of the eighteenth century there arose numerous complaints of over-population in rural parts as well as in towns, and this condition notoriously prevailed through the first half of the following century.

The new economy of large farming which had shaken from all ownership or stake in the land the great mass of the rural population, did not then become sufficiently intensive to absorb them as mere wage-earners in the new system. On the other hand, the forces drawing the superfluous labour into the towns or into foreign emigration were not yet fully operative. The Napoleonic war had retarded for a while the development of machine industry and the demand for labour in the industrial towns; transport was too feeble and too expensive for any large stream of emigration to the colonies or to America; the shackles of the Poor Law and the Law of Settlement greatly impaired the mobility of the working population.

It is, however, to this growth of a large rural population deprived of any ownership or security of tenure in the soil, that we must look for the chief explanation of the "proletariat" required for modern capitalism. This class, gradually loosened from its economic and legal settlement upon the soil, was drawn faster and faster into the new industrialism of the factory, the mine, the city shop, and warehouse. There it fused with a town-bred, wage-earning population, representing the journeymen who from the fifteenth century on had been excluded more and more persistently from the guild organisations, and formed a town proletariat which was later reinforced by small masters[1] unable to hold their independence against the closing monopoly of the craft-guilds, and by skilled workmen from

---

[1] Unwin, *Industrial Organisation in the Sixteenth and Seventeenth Centuries*, ch. viii.

the Continent, religious or political refugees, and in the earlier era of the industrial revolution by large migrations of unskilled labourers from Ireland.

§ 8. In Germany the same origin of an industrial proletariat is plainly traceable. The same survival of the patriarchal farm-family, in which the labourers held a small legal or customary share in the land, cattle, and product of the farm, receiving part of their payment in a share of the harvest, broken up, partly by the agrarian reform of 1811-16, partly by the Schlesian Law of 1845, the enclosure of the common fields, the restriction and gradual disappearance of the labourers' rights, and the subsequent conversion of a class of little profit-sharing farmers into hired labourers. The same compelling forces were operative here as half-a-century earlier in England—the growth of more intensive cultivation, use of machinery, diminished winter employment in agriculture or in supplementary industries.[1]

In Italy, France, Belgium, Switzerland, in fact throughout Western Europe, the same general movement has been discernible, its pace determined partly by the growth of population, partly by the size of the estates, and partly by the condition of agricultural arts. The rapid rise of land values in Belgium from the middle of the nineteenth century, together with the decay of village industries, broke up the economy of a distinctively peasant tenure; the same holds alike of the small peasant districts of Central Italy and the larger estates of South Italy. The prevalence of small holdings in these countries and in France, though doubtless retarding the adoption of capitalistic agriculture and the displacement of rural population, has not prevented the constantly increasing flow of a redundant labouring proletariat into town industrial life. Everywhere a farm-labouring class, shaken from its earlier hold upon the land, has been accompanied in its townward trend by the children of the small peasant proprietors who, finding the economic conditions of the old patriarchal farm-family no longer tolerable, seek the better livelihood and larger independence of industrial life.

---

[1] More work for summer, less for winter, resulted from (α) increased arable, diminished pasture, especially reductions of sheep and flax-growing; (β) machine-threshing in place of the hand-flail; (γ) diminished work in forestry. (Cf. Sombart, ii. 126.)

§ 9. The existence of accumulated wealth, and of a large population dependent on the sale of their labour power could not, however, generate the system of modern industrial capitalism unless the industrial arts had attained a high development. The capitalism of the ancient, and even of the mediæval world, exhibiting a few rare instances of large organisation of workers under a single control, working on wages for the profit of their employers, differed in one important respect from modern industrial capitalism. Whether in the great serf agriculture of the early Roman Empire, or in the mines of Thrace or Sicily, or still earlier in the great building operations of Egypt, Babylon, or India, the element of "fixed" capital was very small, consisting of simple tools or relatively slight and unimportant "machinery": the capital by which employment was afforded consisted of food and raw materials, which were "advanced" to the labourers.

Early accumulations of "capital" consisted in (a) treasure, (β) raw materials and a store of food; or from the standpoint of the individual capitalist, in either a or β.

Though the financial capitalism of the money-lender or banker making loans or advances to farmers and artificers, and the commercial capitalism of merchants giving out raw materials to workers, collecting, purchasing, and marketing their manufactured products, are, as we shall see, important stages in the evolution of the capitalist structure, the business organisation they imply differs essentially from the structure of the great factory, ironworks, railroad, mine, or shipping firm in which modern industrial capitalism finds its typical expression.

The concrete basis of modern industrial capitalism is its large complex structure of "fixed" factors, plant and machinery, the mass of expensive instruments to assist labour in furthering processes of production. The economy of expensive machinery, and the development of indirect or "roundabout" methods of production were the chief instruments in the industrial revolution of manufactures. It is strange how slow this discovery and application of machinery was, and how little progress was made from ancient times up to the middle of the eighteenth century. To those who regard evolution as essentially the product of "accidental variations," the inventions of industrial machinery may appear attributable to the "chance" which assigns to some ages and countries a large crop of inventive geniuses, and denies it to other ages and countries. A more scientific view of history explains the slow growth of mechanical invention by the presence of factors unfavourable to, and the absence of factors favourable to, the application of human intelligence to definite points of mechanical progress. The vested interests and conservative methods of existing industrial castes and their guild organisations rendered the mediæval city poor soil for the introduction of "labour saving" machinery or other revolutionary experiments: the small dimensions of markets, confined partly by political, partly by natural restrictions, presented no opportunities for the profitable disposal of large outputs. No great "free" labour market existed in the mediæval town; the ambition and the trained capacity of the business organiser had little opportunity of discovering and asserting themselves in an age when education was almost wholly confined to classes who regarded with disdain the useful arts and crafts. In times when the early thirst for gold and the zest of physical inquiry absorbed men of "science" and intellectual ingenuity in "alchemy" and problems of perpetual motion, there was no "conduction" of intelligence along the humbler paths of detailed mechanical improvement in the useful arts.

The force of these unfavourable factors is made more manifest by the fact that single examples of successful capitalist organisation upon a tolerably large scale did actually occur in the later Middle Ages in a few instances, where machinery had come into play. The printing trade showed an early tendency to concentration in large capitalist businesses, attributable to the expensive "fixed" capital in presses. At the end of the fifteenth century we find in Nürnberg a large printing business with twenty-four presses and a hundred employees—type-setters, printers, correctors, binders, etc. So likewise in the fourteenth and fifteenth centuries we find paper-mills in Nürnberg and Basel on a capitalistic basis. In Bologna, as early as 1341, we find accounts of large spinning-mills worked by water-power, and even where no non-human power was available, the comparative expensiveness of the distaffs and looms helped to establish mills in which large bodies of workers were employed in Genoa and other Italian cities.[1] A large capitalist silk manufacture was formed in Ulm, in which the loom played a distinctive part. In the early development of capitalism in the metal industries, the importance of plant and tools is discernible, and the introduction of the blast-furnaces in the first half of the fifteenth century with the use of coal and of water-power to work stamps, hammers, etc., was a conspicuous advance towards modern conditions.

Difficulties of transport and the slight irregular structure of markets were largely responsible for the retardation of mechanical inventions and capitalistic enterprise in the manufactures. The early beginnings noted above are confined to articles at once costly, portable, and durable; and even for such commodities as books, silk and woollen cloth, and hardware, the narrow limits of a distant market, in which packmen and annual fairs were important links between producer and consumer, offered little encouragement to enterprise.

§ 10. Under such conditions the evolution of the business man, and in particular the application of the organising mind to manufacture, was necessarily slow. It is difficult to realise how modern is the capitalist spirit, the disposition to employ accumulated wealth in furthering production for the sake of profit. The early accumulations of money were animated by no such motive. King, nobles, knightly orders, church, sought wealth in order to spend it on war, personal display, and largesse or almsgiving. Neither to the getting nor the spending of money were any steady rational motive and method applied. The quick attainment of treasure by rapine, extortion, and adventure, its quick squandering in the "unproductive consumption" which such a life involved, marked the spirit of the powerful classes in the Middle Ages. Even when the craving for money spread more widely by the introduction of luxuries into city life, the idea of industry or trade as a regular instrument for obtaining money was slow to make its way. Freebooting, the squeezing of peasants or townsmen by rents, aids, or taxes, or the more romantic, though less productive adventures of treasure-digging and alchemy, had earlier vogue. Only as the lust of

---

[1] Cf. Sombart, vol. i. p. 405.

accumulation spread among lower and more peaceful sorts of men did money-lending and commerce begin to be recognised as means to get money by the use of money. "Economic Rationalism" is the suggestive name which Sombart gives to the change of spirit from the romantic, adventurous money-hunting of the Middle Ages to the pursuits of modern commercialism. In this process he assigns a very significant part to the discovery and use of technical business methods in account-keeping, the application of exact calculation to Industry. Two names mark the early advances towards modern book-keeping—Leonardo Pisano, whose *Liber Abbaci*, published in 1202, may be said to indicate the beginning of modern industry, coinciding as it did with the Venetian assault upon Constantinople; and Fra Luca, whose completed system of double entry was essential to capitalistic account-keeping. The development of book-keeping, accompanied as it was by a wide general application of rational and mathematical system throughout commerce, in the shape of exact measurement of time and place, forms of contract, land surveying, modern methods of weights and measures, city plans, public accounts, was at once an indispensable tool and an aspect of modern industry. It rationalised business, releasing it from caprice and chance, and giving it a firm objective character from the profit-making standpoint. This was the most definite and direct contribution to industry of the Renaissance, with its emphasis on individual interests, personal responsibility, and free competition—the same spirit which wrought in art, literature, religion, and politics.

Such were the technical conditions for the development of the modern business spirit, the rationale of the *entrepreneur* approximating to the type known as "the economic man." Such a man was first found in the banking and merchant class of the Italian and German cities of the later Middle Ages. Of the great Jacob Fugger it was told that, when a rich competitor, wishful to retire from business in advancing years, approached the old banker with the suggestion—"Let us both retire, now we have led a long career of profit-making, and give others a chance," his reply was that "he had quite a different mind. He wanted to go on making profit as long as he could."

This spirit, then new, and confined to a few merchant-bankers, was destined to spread until it became the life of modern industry, absorbing the greater part of the intelligence and will-power of the directing classes in the modern world. The warrior-noble, the sportsman, the churchman, the landed-gentleman, who gave example and direction to the feelings, thoughts, and activities of our ancestors in the Middle Ages, had no feeling for "profit," and gave no regular accumulative impulse to the production of wealth. The mental and moral equipment of the *entrepreneur*, required for the conduct of modern capitalist industry, demands a special valuation and outlook upon life, possible to very few even in the more developed industrial cities of the fourteenth and fifteenth centuries. Not until the eighteenth century was his character sufficiently evolved to enable him to take full advantage of the new industrial conditions:[1] not until that period did there arise in all advanced industrial countries large numbers of men who set themselves to administer commercial and manufacturing businesses on a basis of large capital, and to employ large masses of labour for profit.

§ 11. This brief statement of the main conditions essential to modern capitalism enables us to understand England's priority in the adoption of new industrial methods, and the retardation of the Industrial Revolution upon the Continent of Europe and in America; for most of the conditions we have named were better fulfilled for Great Britain than for any other nation by the middle of the eighteenth century.

At that time Great Britain was indeed second to Holland in the existing development of industrial and commercial resources. Adam Smith accounted Holland, "in proportion to the extent of the land and the number of its inhabitants, by far the richest country in Europe," and he ascribed to her "the greatest share of the carrying trade of Europe."[2]

---

[1] Hume, *Essays*, vol. ii. p. 57, gives a clear-cut image of the new *entrepreneur*:—"If the employment you give him be lucrative, especially if the profit be attached to every particular exertion of industry, he has gains so often in his eye, that he acquires by degrees a passion for it, and knows no such pleasure as that of seeing the daily increase of his fortune. And that is the reason why trade increases frugality, and why, among merchants, there is the same overplus of misers over prodigals as among the possessors of land there is the contrary."

[2] *Wealth of Nations*, Book II., chap. v.

Her command of capital was attested by the low rate of interest for public and private borrowing, and her wage-level was said to be higher than in England.[1]   But Great Britain, larger in land and population, and already gaining upon Holland in the possession of capital, the control of colonies and of the carrying trade, was in other respects best fitted for industrial development upon new lines.   The absolute amount of capital and of labour available for new industrial enterprise in England was greater than elsewhere. The rise of land-values alike in country and in town, the profits from colonial trade, the beginnings of large businesses at home in banking, brewing, mining, and the woollen trade, etc., afforded larger accumulated funds than were to be found elsewhere.   The great capacity of growth exhibited by the working-class population of Great Britain was assisted by freer immigration from Ireland and the Continent, while the earlier and more complete reforms of the agricultural system drove larger numbers into the new industrial centres. This larger supply of capital and labour available for new industries coincided with a great development of the industrial arts, which indeed they served to stimulate, and the discovery of rich deposits of coal and iron in various parts of the country furnished a solid material basis for the new machine economy.

Finally, the minds of British business men were directed more sharply and continuously to the cultivation of business methods in the organisation of capital and labour and the development of markets, and the opportunity of taking a profitable part in this enterprise was open to a larger proportion of the population than was the case elsewhere.

[1] *Wealth of Nations*, Book I., chap. ix.

CHAPTER II.

THE INSTRUMENTS OF CAPITALISM.

§ 1. *Scientific inventions and economic direction.*
§ 2. *The meaning of the term Capital.*
§ 3. *Place of Machinery in Capitalism.*
§ 4. *The financial aspect of Capitalism.*

§ 1. While the conditions laid down in our introductory chapter offer a variety of approaches to the study of capitalism, the efficient causation of the evolutionary process may be found in the application of scientific inventions to the industrial arts, and in the new art of economic direction as expressed in the methods of the modern *entrepreneur*. From these two standpoints we may most profitably study the evolution of the structure and functions of capitalist business. Following the history of the application of new scientific methods, we shall be kept in close touch with the changes of productive processes which give increased importance to "fixed" capital in the form of machinery and power, involving radical changes in the use of labour-power and indirectly in the structure of markets and the life of industrial communities. Following the other route, our study of the changing rationale of business enterprise will yield its primary results in a fuller understanding of the shifting relations between the persons whose intelligences and voluntary efforts contribute—as employers, capitalists,[1] labourers to the several processes of production, and of the capitalist business regarded as an organic co-operation of humanly ordered activities. The latter study would also keep us in closer contact with the financial or account-keeping side of business, that exact register of

[1] Including landowners.

buying and selling in which all economic processes mirror and record themselves in terms of quantity.

The close relation between what, without serious misunderstanding, may be called the objective and the subjective aspects of the industrial order is obvious. A complete study of modern capitalism will be continually engaged in passing from one aspect to the other, and dwelling upon the constant interaction between the concrete industrial changes and the changes of mental direction and disposition which are involved. A new invention of machinery or a new application of chemistry, displacing a domestic system of simple tool labour by a factory system, alters not only the mode of production but the direction of producing power: the quantities, qualities, and the composition of the human efforts involved in the industry are changed.

Every simplification of the study of this complex interaction involves some sacrifice of accuracy, but in every elementary treatise some such sacrifice is required. It is here proposed to pursue as our main line of inquiry the concrete development of capitalism as expressed in the growing part taken by the material forms of capital in the operations of modern business, contenting ourselves with a more general consideration of the subjective aspects of business enterprise as affected by capitalist control.

§ 2. Writers upon Political Economy have brought much metaphysical acumen to bear upon definitions of Capital, and have reached very widely divergent conclusions as to what the term ought to mean, ignoring the clear and fairly consistent meaning the term actually possesses in the business world around them. The business world has indeed two views of Capital, but they are consistent with one another. Abstractly, money or the control of money, sometimes called credit, is Capital. Concretely, capital consists of all forms of marketable matter which embody labour. Land or nature is excluded except for improvements: human powers are excluded as not being matter: commodities in the hands of consumers are excluded because they are no longer marketable. Thus the actual concrete forms of capital are the raw materials of production, including the finished stage of shop goods; and the plant and implements used in the several processes of industry, including the monetary implements of exchange. Concrete business capital is composed of these and of nothing but these.[1] In taking modern industrial phenomena as the subject of scientific inquiry it is better to accept such terminology as is generally and consistently received by business men, than either to invent new terms or to give a private significance to some accepted term which shall be different from that given by other scientific students, and, if we may judge from past experience, probably inferior in logical exactitude to the current meaning in the business world.

§ 3. The chief material factor in the evolution of Capitalism is machinery. The growing quantity and complexity of machinery applied to purposes of manufacture and conveyance, and to the extractive industries, is the great special fact in the narrative of the expansion of modern industry.

It is therefore to the development and influence of machinery upon industry that we shall chiefly direct our attention, adopting the following method of study. It is first essential to obtain a clear understanding of the structure of industry or "the industrial organism" as a whole, and of its constituent parts, before the new industrial forces had begun to operate. We must then seek to ascertain the laws of the development and application of the new forces to the different departments of industry and the different parts of the industrial world, examining in certain typical machine industries the order and pace of the application of the new machinery and motor to the several processes. Turning our attention again to the industrial organism, we shall strive to ascertain the chief changes that have been brought about in the size and structural character of industry, in the relations of the several parts of the industrial world, of the several trades which constitute industry, of the processes within these trades, of the businesses or units which comprise a trade or a market, and of the units of capital and labour comprising a business. It will then remain to undertake closer studies of certain important special outcomes of

---

[1] Professor Marshall regards this restricted use of capital as "misleading," rightly urging that "there are many other things which truly perform the services commonly attributed to capital" (*Principles*, Bk. II., chap. iv.). But if we enlarge our definition so as to include all these "other things" we shall be driven to a political economy which shall widely transcend Industry as we now understand the term, and

machinery and factory production. These studies will fall
into three classes. (1) The influences of machine-production upon the size of the units of capital, the intensification
and limitation of competition, the natural formation of
Trusts and other forms of economic monopoly of capital;
trade depressions and grave industrial disorders due to dis-
crepancies between individual and social interests in the
working of modern methods of production. (2) Effects of
machinery upon labour, the quantity and regularity of
employment, the character and remuneration of work. (3)
Effects upon the industrial classes in the capacity of consumers, the growth of the large industrial town and its
influences upon the physical, intellectual, moral life of the
community. Lastly, an attempt will be made to summarise
the net influences of modern capitalist production in their
relation to other social progressive forces, and to indicate
the relations between these which seem most conducive to
the welfare of a community measured by generally accepted
standards of character or happiness.

§ 4. Since every industrial act in a modern community
has its monetary counterpart, and its importance is commonly estimated in terms of money, it will be evident that
the growth of capitalism might be studied with great advantage in its monetary aspect. Corresponding to the changes
in productive methods under mechanical machinery we
should find the rapid growth of a complex monetary system
reflecting in its international and national character, in its
elaborate structure of credit, the leading characteristics
which we find in modern productive and distributive industry. The whole industrial movement might be regarded
from the financial or monetary point of view. But though
such a study would be capable of throwing a flood of light
upon the movements of concrete industrial factors at many
points, the intellectual difficulties involved in simultaneously
following the double study, in constantly passing from the

shall comprehend the whole science and art of life so far as it is concerned with human effort and satisfaction. If it is convenient and
justifiable to retain for certain purposes of study the restricted connota-
tion of Industry now in vogue, the confinement of Capital as above to
Trade Capital is logically justified. For a fuller treatment of the question of the use of the term Capital in forming a terminology descriptive
of the parts of Industry the reader is referred to Chapter VII.

more concrete to the more abstract contemplation of industrial phenomena, would tax the mental agility of students too severely, and would greatly diminish the chance of a substantially accurate understanding of either aspect of modern industry. We shall therefore in this study devote our attention chiefly to the concrete aspect of capitalism, describing in a single chapter the main outlines of the recent development of the financial mechanism and the place it occupies in the structure and working of modern capitalism.

CHAPTER III.

THE STRUCTURE OF INDUSTRY BEFORE MACHINERY.

§ 1. In order to get some clear understanding of the laws of the operation of the new industrial forces which prevail under machine-production it is first essential to know rightly the structure and functional character of the "industrial organism" upon which they were destined to act. In order to build up a clear conception of industry it is possible to take either of two modes of inquiry. Taking as the primary cell or unit that combination of labour and capital under a single control for a single industrial purpose which is termed a Business, we may examine the structure and life of the Business, then proceed to discover how it stands related to other businesses so as to form a Market, and, finally, how the several Markets are related locally, nationally, internationally so as to yield the complex structure of Industry as a whole. Or reversely, we may take Industry as a whole, the Industrial Organism as it exists at any given time, consider the nature and extent of the cohesion existing between its several parts, and, further, resolving these parts into their constituent elements, gain a close understanding of the extent to which differentiation of industrial functions has been carried in the several divisions.

Although in any sociological inquiry these two methods are equally valid, or, more strictly speaking, are equally balanced in virtues and defects, the latter method is here to be preferred, because by the order of its descent from the whole to the constituent parts it brings out more definitely the slight cohesiveness and integration of industry beyond the national limits, and serves to emphasise those qualities of nationalism and narrow localism which mark the character of earlier eighteenth century industry. We are thus enabled better to recognise the nature and scope of the work wrought by the modern industrial forces which are the central object of study.

While the Market or the Trade is less and less determined or confined by national or other political boundaries in modern times, and nationalism is therefore a factor of diminishing importance in the modern science of economics, the paramount domination of politics over large commerce in the last century, acting in co-operation with other racial and national forces, obliges any just analysis of eighteenth century industry to give clear and early emphasis to the slight character of the commercial interdependency among nations. The degree of importance which statesmen and economists attached to this foreign commerce as compared with home trade, and the large part it played in the discussion and determination of public conduct, have given it a prominence in written history far beyond its real value.[1]

It is true that through the Middle Ages a succession of European nations rose to eminence by the development of navigation and international trade, Italy, Portugal, Spain, France, Holland, and England; but neither in size nor in

[1] A. Smith, *Wealth of Nations*, Bk. iv., chap. i.

character was this trade of the first importance. Even in the case of those nations where it was most developed it formed a very small proportion of the total industry of the country, and it was chiefly confined to spicery, bullion, ornamental cloths, and other objects of art and luxury.

It is important to recognise that in the first half of the eighteenth century international trade still largely partook of this character. Not only did it bear a far smaller proportion to the total industry of the several countries than does foreign trade to-day, but it was still engaged to a comparatively small extent with the transport of necessaries or prime conveniences of life. Each nation, as regards the more important constituents of its consumption, its staple foods, articles of clothing, household furniture, and the chief implements of industry, was almost self-sufficing, producing little that it did not consume, consuming little it did not produce.

In 1712 the export trade of England is officially estimated at £6,644,103,[1] or considerably less than one-sixth of the home trade of that date as calculated by Smith in his *Memoirs of Wool*. Such an estimate, however, gives an exaggerated impression of the relation of foreign to home trade, because under the latter no account is taken of the large domestic production of goods and services which figure in no statistics. A more instructive estimate is that which values the total consumption of the English people in 1713 at forty-nine or fifty millions, out of which about four millions covers the consumption of foreign goods.[2] In 1740 imports amounted to £6,703,778, exports to £8,197,788. In 1750 they had risen respectively to £7,772,339 and £12,699,081,[3] and ten years later to £9,832,802 and £14,694,970. Macpherson, whose *Annals of Commerce* are a mine of wealth upon the history of foreign commerce in the eighteenth century, after commenting upon the impossibility of obtaining a

---

[1] Macpherson, *Annals of Commerce*, vol. ii. p. 728.

[2] Smith, *Memoirs*, vol. ii., chap. iii. As the approximate calculation of a very competent business man these figures are more reliable than the official figures of imports and exports, the value of which throughout the eighteenth century is seriously impaired by the fact that they continued to be estimated by the standard of values of 1694.

[3] Whitworth's *State* quoted, Macpherson, vol. iii. p. 283.

just estimate of the value of home trade, alludes to a
calculation which places it at thirty-two times the size of
the export trade.   Macpherson contents himself with con-
cluding that it is "a vast deal greater in value than the

PROGRESS OF FOREIGN TRADE IN ENGLAND.

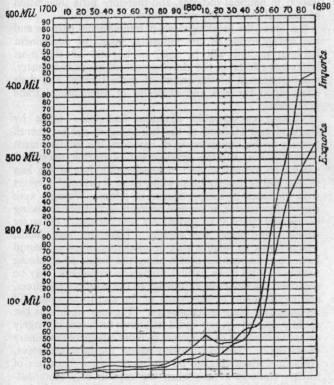

whole of the foreign trade."[1]   There is every reason to
believe that in the case of Holland and France, the only
two other European nations with a considerable foreign
trade, the same general conclusion will apply.

[1] *Annals*, vol. iii. p. 340.

The smallness of the part which foreign trade played in industry signifies that in the earlier part of the eighteenth century the industrial organism as a whole must be regarded as a number of tolerably self-sufficing and therefore homogeneous national forms attached to one another by bonds which are few and feeble. As yet there was little specialisation in national industry, and therefore little integration of national parts of the world-industry.

§ 2. Since the breaking-down of international barriers and the strengthening of the industrial bonds of attachment between nations will be seen to be one of the most important effects of the development of machine-industry, some statement of the nature of these barriers and their effect upon the size and character of international trade is required.

Though considerable advances had been made by England and Holland at the beginning of the eighteenth century in the improvement of harbours, the establishment of lighthouses, and the development of marine insurance,[1] navigation was still subject to considerable risks of the loss of life and of investments, while these "natural" dangers were increased by the prevalence of piracy. Voyages were slow and expensive, commerce between distant nations being necessarily confined to goods of a less perishable character which would stand the voyage. Trade in fresh foods, which forms so large a part of modern commerce, would have been impossible except along the coasts of adjoining nations. With these natural barriers to commerce may be reckoned the defective knowledge of the position, resources, and requirements of large parts of the earth which now fill an important place in commerce. The new world was but slightly opened up, nor could its known resources be largely utilised before the development of more adequate machinery of transport. We can scarcely realise the inconveniences, costs, and risks entailed by the more distant branches of foreign trade at a time when the captain of a merchant-ship still freighted his vessel at his own expense, and when each voyage was a separate speculation. Even in the early nineteenth century the manufacturer commonly shipped his surplus produce at his own risk, employing the merchant

---

[1] *Annals,* vol. iii. p. 340. For estimates of import and export values between 1613 and 1832, see Cunningham, *Growth of English Industry,* p. 931, Appendix F.

upon commission, and in the trade with the Indies, China, or South America he had frequently to lie out of his money or his return freight of indigo, coffee, tea, etc., for as long as eighteen months or two years, and to bear the expense of warehousing as well as the damage which time and tide inflicted on his goods.

§ 3. Next come a series of barriers, partly political, partly pseudo-economic, in which the antagonism of nations took shape, the formation of political and industrial theories which directed the commercial intercourse of nations into certain narrow and definite channels.

Two economic doctrines, separate in the world of false ideas, though their joint application in the world of practice has led many to confuse them, exercised a dominant influence in diminishing the quantity, and determining the quality of international trade in the eighteenth century. These doctrines had reference respectively to the construction and maintenance of home industries and the balance of trade. The former doctrine, which was not so much a consciously-evolved theory as a short-sighted, intellectual assumption driven by the urgent impulse of vested interests into practical effect, taught that, on the one hand, import trade should be restricted to commodities which were not and could not with advantage be produced at home, and to the provision of cheap materials for existing manufactures; while export trade, on the other hand, should be generally encouraged by a system of bounties and drawbacks. This doctrine was first rigidly applied by the French minister, Colbert, but the policy of France was faithfully copied by England and other commercial nations and ranked as an orthodox theory of international trade.

The Balance of Trade doctrine estimated the worth of a nation's intercourse with another by the excess of the export over the import trade, which brought a quantity of bullion into the exporting country. This theory was also widely spread, though obviously its general application would have been destructive of all international commerce. The more liberal interpretation of the doctrine was satisfied with a favourable balance of the aggregate export over the aggregate import trade of the country, but the stricter interpretation, generally dominant in practice, required that in the case of each particular nation the balance should be favourable. In regarding England's commerce with a foreign nation, any excess in import values over export was spoken of as "a loss to England." England deliberately cut off all trade with France during the period 1702 to 1763 by a system of prohibitive tariffs urged by a double dread lest the balance should be against us, and lest French textile goods might successfully compete with English goods in the home markets. On the other hand, we cultivated trade with Portugal because "we gain a greater balance from Portugal than from any other country whatever." The practical policy prevalent in 1713 is thus summarised by one of its enthusiastic upholders—"We suffer the goods and merchandises of Holland, Germany, Portugal, and Italy to be imported and consumed among us; and it is well we do, for we expect a much greater value of our own to those countries than we take from them. So that the consumption of those nations pays much greater sums to the rents of our lands and the labour of our people than ours does to theirs. But we keep out as much as possible the goods and merchandises of France, because our consumption of theirs would very much hinder the consumption of our own, and abate a great part of forty-two millions which it now pays to the rents of our lands and the labour of our people."[1] Thus our policy was to confine our import trade to foreign luxuries and raw materials of manufacture which could not be here produced, drawn exclusively from countries where such trade would not turn the balance against us, and, on the other hand, to force our export trade on any country that would receive it Since every European nation was largely influenced by similar ideas and motives, and enforced upon their colonies and dependencies a like line of conduct, many mutually profitable exchanges were prevented, and commerce was confined to certain narrow and artificial grooves, while the national industrial energy was wasted in the production of many things at home which could have been more cheaply obtained from foreign countries through exchange.

The following example may suffice to illustrate the intricacy of the legislation passed in pursuance of this policy. It describes a change of detailed policy in support and regulation of textile trade :—

[1] Smith, *Memoirs of Wool*, vol. ii. p. 113.

" A tax was laid on foreign linens in order to provide a fund for raising hemp and flax at home; while bounties were given on these necessary articles from our colonies, the bounty on the exportation of hemp was withdrawn. The imposts on foreign linen yarn were withdrawn. Bounties were given on British linen cloth exported; while the making of cambricks was promoted, partly by prohibiting the foreign and partly by giving fresh incentives, though without success, to the manufacture of cambricks within our island. Indigo, cochineal, and logwood, the necessaries of dyes, were allowed to be freely imported." [1]

The encouragement of English shipping (partly for commercial, partly for political reasons) took elaborate shape in the Navigation Acts, designed to secure for English vessels a monopoly of the carrying trade between England and all other countries which sent goods to English or to colonial shores. This policy was supported by a network of minor measures giving bounties to our colonies for the exportation of shipping materials, pitch, tar, hemp, turpentine, masts, and spars, and giving bounties at home for the construction of defensible ships. This Navigation policy gave a strong foundational support to the whole protective policy. Probably the actuating motives of this policy were more political than industrial. Holland, the first to apply this method systematically, had immensely strengthened her maritime power. France, though less successfully, had followed in her wake. Doubtless there were many clearthinking Englishmen who, though aware of the damage done to commerce by our restrictive regulations about shipping, held that the maintenance of a powerful navy for the defence of the kingdom and its foreign possessions was an advantage which outweighed the damage. [2]

The selfish and short-sighted policy of this protective system found its culminating point in the treatment of Ireland and the American plantations. The former was forbidden all manufacture which might either directly or indirectly compete with English industry, and was compelled to deal exclusively with England; the American colonies were forbidden to weave cloth, to make hats, or to

[1] Chalmers, *Estimates*, p. 148.
[2] Cf. Cunningham, *Growth of English Industry*, vol. ii. p. 292.

forge a bolt, and were compelled to take all the manufactured goods required for their consumption from England.

The freedom and expansion of international commerce
was further hampered by the policy of assigning monopolies
of colonial and foreign trade to close Chartered Companies.
This policy, however, defensible as an encouragement of
early mercantile adventure, was carried far beyond these
legitimate limits in the eighteenth century. In England
the East Indian was the most powerful and successful of
these companies, but the assignment of the trade with
Turkey, Russia, and other countries to chartered companies
was a distinct hindrance to the development of foreign
trade.

Our foreign trade at that period might indeed be classed
or graded in accordance with the degree of encouragement
or discouragement offered by the State.

Imports would fall into four classes.

1. Imports forbidden either (*a*) by legislative prohibition, or (*b*) by prohibitive taxation.
2. Imports admitted but taxed.
3. Free imports.
4. Imports encouraged by bounties.

Exports might be graded in similar fashion.

1. Prohibited exports (*e.g.*, sheep and wool, raw
   hides, tanned leather, woollen yarn, textile implements,[1] certain forms of skilled labour).
2. Exports upon which duties are levied (*e.g.*,
   coals[2]).
3. Free exports.
4. Exports encouraged by bounties, or by drawbacks.

The unnatural and injurious character of most of this
legislation is best proved by the notable inability to
effectively enforce its application. The chartered companies were continually complaining of the infringement of
their monopolies by private adventurers, and more than one
of them failed through inability to crush out this illegal
competition. A striking condemnation of our policy to-

---

[1] Smith, *Wealth of Nations*, Bk. iv., chap. viii.   [2] *Ibid.*

wards France consisted in the growth of an enormous illicit trade which, in spite of the difficulties which beset it, made a considerable part of our aggregate foreign trade during the whole of the century. The lack of any clear perception of the mutuality of advantage in foreign and colonial trade was the root fallacy which underlay these restrictions. Professor Cunningham rightly says of the colonial policy of England, that it "implied that each distinct member should strengthen the head, and not at all that these members should mutually strengthen each other."[1]

So, as we tried to get the better of our colonies, still more rigorously did we apply the same methods to foreign countries, regarding each gain which accrued to us as an advantage which would have wholly gone to the foreigner if we had not by firmness and enterprise secured it for ourselves.

The slight extent of foreign intercourse was, however, partly due to causes which are to be regarded as genuinely economic. The life and experience of the great mass of the population of all countries was extremely restricted; they were a scattered and rural folk whose wants and tastes were simple, few, home-bred, and customary. The customary standard of consumption, slowly built up in conformity with local production, gave little encouragement to foreign trade. Moreover, to meet the new tastes and the more varied consumption which gradually found its way over this country, it was in conformity with the economic theory and practice of the day to prefer the establishment of new home industries, equipped if necessary with imported foreign labour, to the importation of the products of such labour from abroad. So far as England, in particular, is concerned, the attitude was favoured by the political and religious oppression of the French government which supplied England in the earlier eighteenth century with a constant flow of skilled artisan labour. Many English manufacturers profited by this flow. Our textile industries in silk, wool, and linen, calico-printing, glass, paper, and pottery are specially beholden to the new arts thus introduced.

Among the economic barriers must be reckoned the

slight development of international credit, and of the machinery of exchange.

§ 4. These barriers, natural, political, social, economic, against free international intercourse, throw important light upon the general structure of world-industry in the eighteenth century.

In this application they determined and strictly limited not only the quantity but the nature of the international trade. The export trade of England, for example, in 1730 was practically confined to woollen goods and other textile materials, a small quantity of leather, iron, lead, silver, and gold plate, and a certain number of re-exported foreign products, such as tobacco and Indian calicoes. The import trade consisted of wine and spirits, foreign foods, such as rice, sugar, coffee, oil, furs, and some quantity of foreign wool, hemp, silk, and linen-yarn, as material for our specially favoured manufactures. Having regard to the proportion of the several commodities, it would not be much exaggeration to summarise our foreign trade by saying that we sent out woollen goods and received foreign foods. These formed the great bulk of our foreign trade.[1] Excepting the woollen goods and a small trade in metals, leather is the only manufactured article which figured to any appreciable extent in our export of 1730. At that time it is clear that in the main English manufacture, as well as English agriculture, was for the supply of English wants. The same was true of other industrial countries. Holland and France, who divided with England the shipping supremacy, had a foreign trade which, though then deemed considerable, bore no greater proportion to the total industry of these countries than in the case of England. Germany, Italy, Russia, Spain, and even Portugal were almost wholly self-sustained.

Regarding, then, the known and related world of that time in the light of an industrial organism, we must consider it as one in which the processes of integration and of differentiation of parts has advanced but a little way, consisting as yet of a number of homogeneous and incoherent national cells.

This homogeneity is of course qualified by differences in production and consumption due to climate, natural pro-

---

[1] Macpherson, *Annals*, vol. iii. pp. 155, 156.

ducts, national character and institutions, and the development of industrial arts in the several nations.

§ 5. This consideration of the approximate homogeneity of the national units of world-industry gives a higher scientific value to the analysis of a single typical industrial nation such as England than would be the case in modern times, when the work of differentiation of industrial functions among the several nations has advanced much further.

Taking, therefore, the national industry of England as the special subject of analysis, we may seek to obtain a clear conception of the size, structure, and connections of the several branches of industry, paying special regard to the manufactures upon which the new industrial forces were chiefly to operate.

It is not possible to form a very accurate estimate of the relative importance of the different industries as measured either by the money value of their products, or by the amount of labour engaged in producing them. Eighteenth century statistics, as we saw, furnished no close estimate of the total income of the nation or of the value of home industries. Since no direct census of the English population was taken before 1805, the numbers were never exactly known, and eighteenth century economists spent much time and ingenuity in trying to ascertain the growth of population by calculations based upon the number of occupied houses, or by generalising from slender and unreliable local statistics, without in the end arriving at any close agreement. Still less reliable will be the estimates of the relative size and importance of the different industries.

Two such attempts, however, one slightly prior to the special period we are investigating, and one a little later, may be taken as general indications of the comparative importance of the great divisions of industry, agriculture, manufacture, distribution or commerce.

The first is that of Gregory King in the year 1688. King's calculation, however, can only be regarded as roughly approximate. The quantity of combined agriculture and manufacture, and the amount of domestic industry for domestic consumption, renders the manufacturing figures, however carefully they might have been collected, very deceptive. The same criticism, though to a less degree, applies to the estimate of Arthur Young for 1769.

KING'S ESTIMATE OF THE POPULATION 1688.

Agricultural Classes (Freeholders, Farmers, Labourers, Outservants, Cottagers, Paupers)
4,265,000

Commerce
246,000

Manufacture
240,000

YOUNG'S ESTIMATE 1769

Agricultural Classes 3,600,000

Manufacturing Classes 3,000,000

Commerce 700,000

Professional 200,000

Paupers 600,000

Military & Official 500,000

If to Young's estimate of the population dependent upon agriculture we add the class of landlords and their direct dependents and a proper proportion of the non-industrious poor, who, though not to be so classed in a direct measurement of occupations, are supported out of the produce of agriculture, we shall see that in 1769 we are justified in believing that agriculture was in its productiveness almost equivalent to the whole of manufactures and commerce.

In turning to the several branches of manufacture, the abnormal development of one of them, viz. the woollen, for purposes of foreign trade, marks the first and only considerable specialisation of English industry before the advent of steam machinery. With the single exception of woollen goods almost the whole of English manufactures were for home consumption. At the opening of the eighteenth century, and even as late as 1770, no other single manufacture played any comparable part in the composition of our export trade.

According to Chalmers,[1] in the period 1699-1701, the annual value of woollen exports was over two and a half million pounds, or about two-fifths of the total export trade, while in 1769-71 it still amounted to nearly one-third of the whole, giving entire or partial employment to no fewer than "a million and a half of people," or half of the total number assigned by Young to manufacture.

Next to the woollen, but far behind in size and importance, came the iron trade. In 1720 England seems to have developed her mining resources so imperfectly as to be in the condition of importing from foreign countries 20,000 out of the 30,000 tons required for her hardware manufactures.[2] Almost all this iron was destined to home consumption with the exception of hardware forced upon the American colonies, who were forbidden to manufacture for themselves. In 1720 it is calculated that mining and manufacture of iron and hardware employed 200,000 persons.[3]

Copper and brass manufactures employed some 30,000 persons in 1720.[4]

Silk was the only other highly developed and consider-

---

[1] Chalmers, *Estimate*, p. 208. See, however, Baines, who gives a slightly smaller estimate, *History of the Cotton Manufacture*, p. 112.
[2] Macpherson, *Annals*, vol. iii. p. 114.
[3] *Ibid.*, vol. iii. p. 73.   [4] *Ibid.*, vol. iii. p. 73.

able manufacture. It had, however, to contend with Indian competition, introduced by the East India Company, and also with imported calicoes.[1] In 1750 there were about 13,000 looms in England, the product of which was almost entirely used for home consumption. Cotton and linen were very small manufactures during the first half of the eighteenth century. At the beginning of the century the linen trade was chiefly in the hands of Russia and Germany, although it had taken root in Ireland as early as the close of the seventeenth century, and was worked to some extent in Lancashire, Leicestershire, and round Darlington in Yorkshire, which districts supplied the linen-warp to the cotton weavers.[2] As for cotton, even in 1760 not more than 40,000 persons were engaged in the manufacture, and in 1764 the cotton exports were but one-twentieth of the value of the woollen exports.[3] The small value of the cotton trade and an anticipatory glance at its portentous after-growth is conveyed in the following figures :—

	Home Market.		Export Trade.
1766	£379,241	...	£220,759 (Postlethwayte)
1819–21	13,044,000	...	15,740,000 } (Ellison[4])
1829–31	13,351,000	...	18,074,000 }

The many other little manufactures which had sprung up, such as glass, paper, tin-plate, produced entirely for home consumption, and employed but a small number of workers.

§ 6. If we turn from the consideration of the size of English industry and the several departments to the analysis of its structure and the relation to the several trades, we shall find the same signs of imperfect organic development which we found in the world-industry, though not so strongly marked. Just as we found each country in the main self-sufficing, so we find each district of England (with a few significant exceptions) engaged chiefly in producing for its own consumption. There was far less local specialisation in industry than we

---

[1] Smith, *Memoirs on Wool*, vol. ii. pp. 19, 45.

[2] Smith, *ibid.*, vol. ii. p. 270; cf. also Cunningham, *Growth of English Industry*, vol. ii. p. 300.

[3] Toynbee, *Industrial Revolution*, p. 50.

[4] Schulze-Gaevernitz, *Der Grossbetrieb*, p. 77. The estimates of the annual importation of cotton wool during the eighteenth century, cf. Cunningham, vol ii. p. 624.

find to-day.   The staple industries, tillage, stock-raising, and those connected with the supply of the common articles of clothing, furniture, fuel, and other necessaries were widespread over the whole country.

Though far more advanced than foreign intercourse, the internal trade between more distant parts of England was extremely slight.   Defective facilities of communication and transport were of course in large measure responsible for this.

The physical obstructions to such freedom of commerce as now subsists were very considerable in the eighteenth century.   The condition of the main roads in the country at the opening of the century was such as to make the carriage of goods long and expensive.   Agricultural produce was almost entirely for local consumption, with the exception of cattle and poultry, which were driven on foot from the neighbouring counties into London and other large markets.[1] In the winter, even round London, bad roads were a great obstacle to trade.   The impossibility of driving cattle to London later than October often led to a monopoly of winter supply and high prices.[2]   The growth of turnpike roads, which proceeded apace in the first half of the century, led to the large substitution of carts for pack horses, but even these roads were found " execrable " by Arthur Young, and off the posting routes and the neighbourhood of London the communication was extremely difficult.   " The great roads of England remained almost in this ancient condition even as late as 1752 and 1754, when the traveller seldom saw a turnpike for two hundred miles after leaving the vicinity of London."[3]

Rivers rather than roads were the highways of commerce, and many Acts were passed in the earlier eighteenth century for improving the navigability of rivers, as the Trent, Ouse, and Mersey, partly in order to facilitate internal trade and partly to enable towns like Leeds and Derby to engage directly in trade by sea,[4] and to connect adjoining towns such as Liverpool and Manchester.   In 1755 the first canal was constructed, and in the latter part of the century the part played by canals in the development of the

[1] Defoe, *Tour*, vol. ii. p. 371.
[2] *Ibid.*, vol. ii. p. 370.
[3] Chalmers, pp. 124, 125.
[4] Defoe, *Tour*, vol. iii. p. 9, etc.

new factory system was considerable. But in spite of these efforts to improve methods of transport in the earlier eighteenth century, it is evident that the bulk of industry was engaged in providing articles for local consumption, and that the area of the market for most products was extremely narrow.

The facile transport of both capital and labour, which is essential to highly specialised local industry, was retarded not merely by lack of knowledge of the opportunities of remunerative investment, but also by legal restrictions which had the influence of checking the free application and migration of labour. The Statute of Apprentices by requiring a seven years' apprenticeship[1] in many trades, and the Law of Settlement by impairing mobility of labour, are to be regarded as essentially protective measures calculated to prevent that concentrated application of capital and labour required for specialisation of industry.

Within the nation we had for the most part a number of self-sufficing communities, or, in other words, there was little specialisation of function in the several parts, and little integration in the national industry. With the single exception of Holland, whose admirable natural and artificial water communication seemed to give unity to its commerce, the other countries of Europe, France, Germany, Italy, Spain, Russia, were still more disintegrated in their industry.

§ 7. In regarding those districts of England in which strong indications of growing industrial specialisation showed themselves, it is important to observe the degree and character of that specialisation.

We find various branches of the woollen, silk, cotton, iron, hardware, and other manufactures allocated to certain districts. But if we compare this specialisation with that which obtains to-day we shall observe wide differences.

In the first place, it was far less advanced. The woollen industry of England, though conveniently divided into three districts—one in the Eastern Counties, with Norwich, Colchester, Sandwich, Canterbury, Maidstone, for principal centres; one in the West, with Taunton, Devizes, Bradford (in Wilts), Frome, Trowbridge, Stroud, and Exeter; and the third, in the West Riding, is in reality distributed over

---

[1] Smith, *Wealth of Nations*, vol. i., chap. x., part 2.

almost the whole of England south of the Thames, and over a large part of Yorkshire, to say nothing of the widespread

INDUSTRIAL ENGLAND IN 1730.

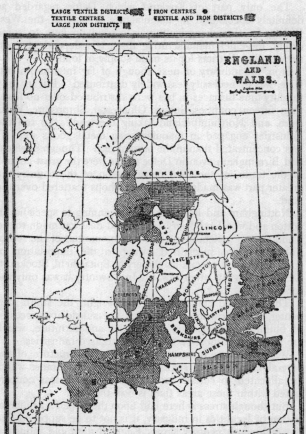

production, either for private consumption or for the market, in Westmoreland, Cumberland, and indeed all the North of England. Where the land was richer in pasture or with easier access to large supplies of wool, the clothing manufactures were more flourishing and gave more employment, but over all the southern and most of the northern counties some form of woollen manufacture was carried on.

The only part of England which Defoe regarded as definitely specialised in manufacture is part of the West Riding, for though agriculture is carried on here to some extent, the chief manufacturing district is dependent upon surrounding districts for its main supply of food.[1]

Iron, the industry of next, though of far inferior importance, was of necessity less widely distributed. But in 1737 the fifty-nine furnaces in use were distributed over no fewer than fifteen counties, Sussex, Gloucester, Shropshire, Yorkshire, and Northumberland taking the lead.[2] So too the industries engaged in manufacturing metal goods were far less concentrated than in the present day. Though Sheffield and Birmingham even in Defoe's time were the great centres of the trade, of the total consumption of the country the greater part was made in small workshops scattered over the land.

Nottingham and Leicester were beginning to specialise in cotton and woollen hosiery, but a good deal was made round London, and generally in the woollen counties of the south. Silk was more specialised owing to the importation of special skill and special machinery to Spitalsfield, Stockport, Derby, and a few other towns. In Coventry it was only the second trade in 1727.[3]

The scattered crafts of the wheelwright, the smith, carpenter, turner, carried on many of the subsidiary processes of building, manufacture of vehicles and furniture, which are now for the most part highly centralised industries.

When we come presently to consider the structure of the several industries we shall see that even those trades which are allocated to certain local areas are much less concentrated within these areas than is now the case.

But though stress is here laid upon the imperfect differentiation of localities in industry, it is not to be supposed that the eighteenth century shows England a simple industrial community with no considerable specialisation.

---

[1] Defoe, *Tour*, vol. iii. p. 84.
[2] Scrivener, *History of the Iron Trade*.
[3] Defoe, *Tour*, vol. ii. p. 323.

Three conditions of specialised industry are clearly discernible in the early eighteenth century — conditions which always are among the chief determinants.

1. *Physical aptitudes of soil*—*e g.*, since timber was still used almost entirely for smelting, iron works are found where timber is plentiful or where river communication makes it easily procurable. So the more fertile meadows of Gloucester and Somerset led these districts to specialise in the finer branches of the woollen trade. A still more striking example is that of South Lancashire. By nature it was ill-suited for agriculture, and therefore its inhabitants employed themselves largely in the cotton and woollen trades. The numerous little streams which flowed from the hills to the neighbouring sea gave plenty of water-power, and thus made this district the home of the earlier mills and the cradle of machine-industry.[1] The "grit" of the local grindstones secured the supremacy of Sheffield cutlery, while the heavy clay required for the "seggars," or boxes in which pottery is fired, helped to determine the specialisation of Staffordshire in this industry.[2]

2. *Facility of Market.*—The country round London, Bristol, and other larger towns became more specialised than the less accessible and more evenly populated parts, because the needs of a large town population compelled the specialisation in agriculture of much of the surrounding country; cottagers could more easily dispose of their manufactures; improved roads and other facilities for conveyance induced a specialisation impossible in the purely rural parts.

3. *The Nature of the Commodity.*—When all modes of conveyance were slow the degree of specialisation depended largely upon the keeping quality of the goods. From this point of view hardware and textiles are obviously more amenable to local specialisation than the more perishable forms of food. Where conveyance is difficult and expensive a commodity bulky for its value is less suitable for local

[1] Schulze-Gaevernitz, *Der Grossbetrieb*, p. 52.
[2] Cf. Marshall, *Principles*, p. 328. In the case of Staffordshire, however, there existed an early trade in wooden platters dependent on quality of timber and traditional skill. When the arts of pottery came in, the new trade taken up in the same locality ousted the old, though there was no particular local advantage in materials.

specialisation in production than one containing a high value in small weight and bulk. So cloth is more suitable for trade than corn ;[1] and coal, save where navigation is possible, could not be profitably taken any distance.[2]

The common commodities consumed, as food, fuel, and shelter, were thus excluded from any considerable amount of specialisation in their production.

§ 8. Turning from consideration of the attributes of goods and of the means of transport which served to limit the character of internal trade and determine the size of the market, let us now regard the structure of the market, the central object in the mechanism of internal commerce.

The market, not the industry, is the true term which expresses the group of organically related businesses. How far did England present a national market? How far was the typical market a district or purely local one?

The one great national market town was London. It alone may be said to have drawn supplies from the whole of England, and there alone was it possible to purchase at any season of the year every kind of produce, agricultural or manufactured, made anywhere in England or imported from abroad. This flow to and from the great centre of population was incessant, and extended to the furthermost parts of the land. Other large towns, such as Bristol, Leeds, Norwich, maintained close and constant relations with the neighbouring counties, but exchanged their produce for the most part only indirectly with that of more distant parts of the country.

The improving communication of the eighteenth century enabled the clothiers and other leading manufacturers to distribute more of their wares even in the remotest parts of the country, but the value paid for their wares reached the vendors by slow and indirect channels of trade, passing for the most part through the metropolis.

But while London was the one constant national market-place, national trade was largely assisted by fairs held for several weeks each year at Stourbridge, Winchester, and other convenient centres. At the most important of

---

[1] Smith, *Wealth of Nations*, Book III., chap. iii.
[2] Westmoreland coal did not compete in the Newcastle market.— *Wealth of Nations*, Book I., chap. xi. p. 2.

these the large merchants and manufacturers met their customers, and business was transacted between distant parts of the country, including all kinds of wares, English and foreign. Thus we had one constant and two or three intermittent avenues of free national trade. The great bulk of markets, however, were confined within far smaller areas.

In the more highly developed and specialised textile trades certain regular market-places were established of wide local importance. The largest of these specialised district markets were at Leeds, Halifax, Norwich, and Exeter. Here the chief local manufacturers of cloth, worsted, or crape met the merchants and factors and disposed of their wares to these distributing middle-men.

It was, however, in the general market-places of the county town or smaller centres of population that the mass of the business of exchange was transacted. There the mass of the small workers in agriculture and manu-facture brought the product of their labour and sold it, buying what they needed for consumption and for the pursuance of their craft. Only in considerable towns were there to be found in the earlier eighteenth century any number of permanent shops where all sorts of wares could be bought at any time. The weekly market in the market-town was the chief medium of commerce for the great mass of the population.

Regarding the general structure of Industry we see that not only are international bonds slight and unessential, but that within the nation the elements of national cohesion are feeble as compared with those which subsist now. We have a number of small local communities whose relations, though tolerably strong with other communities in their immediate neighbourhood, become greatly weakened by distance. For the most part these small communities are self-sufficing for work and life, producing most of their own necessaries, and only dependent on distant and unknown producers for their comforts and luxuries.

Trade is for the most part conducted on a small local basis with known regular customers; markets are less fluctuating in quantities of supply and in prices than in modern days.

Outside of agriculture the elements of speculation and fluctuation are almost entirely confined to foreign trade.

Capital and labour are fixed to a particular locality and a particular business.[1]

§ 9. Turning to the structure of the several industries we find that different employments are not sharply separated from one another. In the first place, agriculture and manufacture are not only carried on in the same locality but by the same people. This combined agriculture and manufacture took several forms.

The textile industries were largely combined with agriculture. Where spinning was carried on in agricultural parts there was, for the most part, a division of labour within the family. The women and children spun while the men attended to their work in the fields.[2] Every woman and child above the age of five found full employment in the spinning and weaving trades of Somerset and the West Riding.[3]

This method prevailed more generally in the spinning than in the weaving trades, for before the introduction of the spinning-jenny the weaving trade was far more centralised than the other. For example, a large quantity of weaving was done in the town of Norwich while the earlier process was executed in the scattered cottages over a wide district. But even these town workers were not specialised in manufacture to the extent which prevails to-day. Large numbers of them had allotments in the country to which they gave their spare time, and many had pasture rights and kept their cattle on the common lands. This applied not merely to the textile but to other industries. At West Bromwich, a chief centre of the metal trade, agriculture was still carried on as a subsidiary pursuit by the metal workers.[4] So too the cutlers of Sheffield living in the outskirts of the town had their plot of land and carried on agriculture to a small extent, a practice which has lasted almost up to the present day. The combined agriculture and manufacture often

---

[1] Adam Smith, writing later in the century, observes with some exaggeration, "A merchant, it has been said very properly, is not necessarily the citizen of a particular country. It is in a great measure indifferent to him from what place he carries on his trade, and a very trifling disgust will make him remove his capital, and together with it all the industry which it supports, from one country to another."— Book III., chap. iv.

[2] Defoe, vol. ii. p. 37.   [3] *Ibid.*, vol. ii. p. 17.
[4] *Annals of Agriculture*, chap. iv. p. 157.

took the form of a division of labour according to season. Where the weaving was not concentrated in towns it furnished a winter occupation to many men who gave the bulk of their summer time to agriculture. Generally speaking, we may take as fairly representative of the manufacturing parts of England the picture which Defoe gave of the condition of affairs in the neighbourhood of Halifax. He found "the land divided into small enclosures from two acres to six or seven acres each, seldom more; every three or four pieces of land had a house belonging to it—one continued village, hardly a house standing out of speaking distance from another—at every house a tenter, and on almost every tenter a piece of cloth or kersie or shalloon—every clothier keeps a horse—so every one generally keeps a cow or two for his family."[1]

Not only were agriculture and many forms of manufacture conjoined, but the division of labour and differentiation of processes within the several industries was not very far advanced. The primitive tillage of the common-fields which still prevailed in the early eighteenth century, though the rapid enclosure of commons was effecting a considerable, and from the wealth-producing point of view, a very salutary change, did not favour the specialisation of land for pasture or for some particular grain crops. Each little hamlet was engaged in providing crops of hay, wheat, barley, oats, beans, and had to fulfil the other purposes required by a self-subsisting community. This arose partly from the necessity of the system of land tenure, partly from ignorance of how to take advantage of special qualities and positions of soil, and partly from the self-sufficiency imposed by difficulties of conveyance. As the century advanced, the enclosure of commons, the increase of large farms, the application of new science and new capital led to a rapid differentiation in the use of land for agricultural purposes. But in the earlier part of the century there was little specialisation of land except in the West Riding and round the chief centres of the woollen trade, and to a less extent in the portions of the counties round London whose position forced them to specialise for some particular market of the metropolis.

[1] Defoe, vol. iii. pp. 78, 79.

§ 10. As the small agriculturist on a self-sufficing farm must perform many different processes, so the manufacturer was not narrowed down to a single process of manufacture. A large part of the ruder manufactures were home productions for home consumption, and the same hands tended the sheep which furnished the wool, and spun and wove the wool for family use. The smith was in a far fuller sense the maker of the horse-shoe or the nail or bolt than he is to-day; the wheelwright, the carpenter, and other handicraftsmen performed a far larger number of different processes than they do now. Moreover, each household, in addition to its principal employments of agriculture and manufacture, carried on many minor productive occupations, such as baking, brewing, butter-making, dressmaking, washing, which are now for the most part special and independent branches of employment.

In the more highly-developed branches of the textile and metal trades the division of processes appears at first sight more sharply marked than to-day. The carder, spinner, weaver, fuller in the cloth trade worked in the several processes of converting raw wool into finished cloth, related to one another only by a series of middlemen who supplied them with the material required for their work and received it back with the impress of their labour attached, to hand it out once more to undergo the next process.[1] But though modern machine-production will show us these various processes drawn together into close local proximity, sometimes performed under the same roof and often making use of the same steam power, we shall find that a chief object and effect of this closer local co-ordination of the several processes is to define and narrow more precisely the labour of each worker and to make the spinner and the weaver confine himself to the performance of a fractional part of the full process of spinning or weaving. Thus we find that English industry in the early eighteenth century is marked on the one hand by a lack of clear differentiation as regards industries, and on the other hand by a lack of minute differentiation of processes within the industry.

§ 11. Upon the area and structure of the market depends the size and character of the unit of Industry—the Business.

---

[1] Cf. Burnley, *Wool and Wool-combing*, p. 417.

"Thus the handicraft or guild system is associated with the *town economy*, the domestic or commission system with the *national economy*, and the factory system with the world economy."[1]

In the study of the composition of capital, labour, and direction in a business, the following are points of dominant importance :—

Capital.
- α. The ownership of the raw material.
- β.   ,,   ,,   tools (and sources of non-human power).
- γ.   ,,   ,,   workplace.

- δ. The labour-power.
- ε. The work of superintendence and management.
- ζ. The work of marketing.

In other words, in the operation of an industrial Business, an employer organises and directs the application of labour-power working with tools upon raw materials in a workshop or factory, and sells the product. Now all these six functions may be combined in a single person or family, or they may be divided in various ways among two or many persons. The simplest form of manufacturing business would be one in which an industrial family, growing or buying the materials and tools, and working with the power of their own bodies in their own home, under the direction of the head of the household, produce commodities, partly for their own consumption, partly for a small local market.

Omitting all consideration of the virtually self-sufficing economy of the farmers and cottagers who, producing food, clothing, etc., for their own consumption, cannot rank as business-units for our purposes, we find even in eighteenth-century England a large number of town and rural industries in which the differentiation from the primitive type has only just begun.

The simplest structure of "domestic" manufacture is that in which the farmer-manufacturer is found purchasing his

[1] *Industrial Organisation in the Sixteenth and Seventeenth Centuries.* Unwin, p. 10.

own material, the raw wool or flax if he is a spinner, the warp and weft if he is a weaver, and, working with his family, produces yarn or cloth which he sells himself, either in the local market or to regular master-clothiers or merchants. The mixed cotton weaving trade was in this condition in the earlier years of the eighteenth century. "The workshop of the weaver was a rural cottage, from which, when he was tired of sedentary labour, he could sally forth into his little garden, and with the spade or the hoe tend its culinary productions. The cotton-wool which was to form his weft was picked clean by the fingers of his younger children, and was carded and spun by the elder girls, assisted by his wife, and the yarn was woven by himself, assisted by his sons."[1]

The weak point in this economy lay in the trouble and uncertainty of marketing the product. It was here that the merchant, who represents the earliest form of industrial capitalism, presses in upon the self-employing artisan-capitalist. Taking from the small producer his product, paying him for it, and undertaking the trouble, delay, and risk of finding consumers to purchase it at a price which will yield him a profit, the merchant relieves him of the function which he is least competent to perform.

From the habit of selling his product to a specialist middleman, it is a small step to receiving "orders" from the latter. But where, as is usual, the raw material, or some of it, has to be bought by the producer, the latter is apt to find that this buying is almost as troublesome as selling, and so he is easily induced to receive his warp and woof, or other materials, from the same merchant who takes from him his product.

So the ownership of the raw material often passes from the "independent" small workman into the hands of the organising merchant or middleman, who, as early as the seventeenth century, in the clothing trade is found usurping the title "manufacturer."

This stage, where the workman receives his "orders" and his "materials" from another, while retaining the disposal of his labour-power and working with his own tools in his

---

[1] Ure, *History of the Cotton Manufacture*, vol. i. p. 224.

own home or workplace, prevailed widely in the textile industries of rural England.

The condition of the cotton-trade in Lancashire about 1750 illustrates most clearly the transition from the independent weaver to the dependent weaver. So far as the linen warp of his fabric was concerned he had long been in the habit of receiving it from the larger "manufacturer" in Bolton or in Manchester, but the cotton yarn he had hitherto supplied himself, using the yarn spun by his own family or purchased by himself in the neighbourhood. The difficulty of obtaining a steady, adequate supply, and the waste of time involved in trudging about in search of this necessary material, operated more strongly as the market for cotton goods expanded and the pressure of work made itself felt.[1] It was this pressure which we shall see acting as chief stimulus to the application of new inventions in the spinning[2] trade. In the interim, however, the habit grew of receiving not only linen warp but cotton weft from the merchant or middleman. Thus the ownership of the raw material entirely passed out of the weaver's hands though he continued to ply his domestic craft as formerly.[3] This had grown into the normal condition of the trade by 1750. The stocking-trade illustrates one further encroachment of the capitalist system upon domestic industry. In this trade not only was the material given out by merchants, but the "frames" used for weaving were likewise owned by them, and were rented out to the workers, who continued, however, to work in their own homes.

But this stage of business organisation, where the material is provided and the product taken by an outsider, a merchant or other customer, is by no means confined to the country weaver. It is frequently to be traced as a stage in the decline of a town trade-guild. When, for example, the processes of the cloth manufacture became specialised, the weaver, fuller, bureller, finisher, and dyer becoming separate trained handicrafts, it happened sometimes that one or other of these related crafts became strong enough to set up as

[1] Baines, *History of the County Palatine of Lancashire*, vol. ii. p. 413.
[2] Ure, *History of Cotton Manufacture*, vol. i. p. 224, etc.
[3] Dr. Aikin, *History of Manchester* (quoted Baines, p. 406).

employers of the others, and gave out work for them to do. So it seems that in the later thirteenth century a number of the burellers in London gave out work to the weavers, while among the weavers themselves large masters sprang up, who gave out yarn to the poorer masters, and employed fullers and dyers.[1]

When the raw material is given out to an artisan by a merchant or another manufacturer there is a clear loss of independence, especially when this step is followed by the letting out of tools or machines. In London, as early as the thirteenth century, big master-weavers seem to have hired out looms to small weavers.[2] Similarly in the stocking-trade, at a much later period, "frames" as well as material were let out by merchants to the workers, who continued to work in their own homes.[3]

§ 12. Two further steps remained to be taken in the transition from the "domestic" to the "factory" system, the one relating to the ownership of "power," the other to the workplace. (a) The substitution of extra-human power owned by the employer for the physical power of the worker; (b) the withdrawal of the workers from their homes, and the concentration of them in factories and workplaces owned by the capitalists.

Although these steps were not completely taken until the age of steam had well set in, before the middle of the eighteenth century there were found examples of the factory, complete in its essential character, side by side and in actual competition with the earlier shapes of domestic industry.

Capitalist ownership of extra-human industrial "power" was of course narrowly restricted before the age of steam. Water-power, horse-power, and to a much smaller extent, wind-power, were utilised. But the most important services water rendered to industry prior to the great inventions were in facilitating the transport of goods, and in certain subsidiary processes of manufacture such as dyeing. Though a considerable number of water-mills existed early in the century, they played no large part in manufacture. A natural force so strictly confined in quantity and in local application, and subject to such great waste from the back-

[1] Unwin, pp. 27, 29.   [2] Ibid., p. 29.
[3] Cooke Taylor, *The Modern Factory System*, p. 69.

ward condition of mechanical arts, was not able to serve to any great extent as a substitute for or aid to the muscular activity of man.

But although the economy of mechanical power was not yet operative to any appreciable extent in concentrating labour, certain other notable economies of large-scale production were beginning to assert themselves in all the leading manufactures. Indeed so powerful are some of the economies of division of labour and co-operation even in a primitive condition of the industrial arts, that Professor Ashley considers it not improbable that the great manufactory might have become an important or even a dominant feature of the woollen trade as early as the sixteenth century, if legislative enactments had not stood in the way.[1] As it was, these earlier centralising forces, while they drove the workers to work and live in closer and compacter masses, did not at first dispose them in factories to any great extent. They continued for the most part to work in their own houses, though for material and sometimes for the implements of their craft they were dependent upon some merchant or large master-manufacturer. This was the condition of industry in the neighbourhood of Leeds in 1725. "The houses are not scattered and dispersed as in the vicarage of Halifax, one by one, but in villages, and those houses thronged with people and the whole country infinitely populous."[2] In the more highly-developed branches of the cloth trade, however, where the best looms were a relatively costly form of capital, the foundation of the factory system was clearly laid. In Norwich, Frome, Taunton, Devizes, Stourbridge, and other clothing centres, Defoe found the weaving industry highly concentrated, and rich employers owning considerable numbers of looms. Some of this work was put out by the master-manufacturers, but other work was done in large sheds or other premises owned by the master. This large organised "business," half factory, half domestic, continued to prevail in the important West of England clothing industry up to the close of the eighteenth century. "The master clothier of the West of England buys his wool from the importer, if it be foreign, or in the fleece if it be of domestic growth; after which, in

[1] *Economic History*, vol. ii. p. 237.
[2] Defoe, *Tour*, vol. iii. p. 89.

all the different processes through which it passes, he is under the necessity of employing as many distinct classes of persons; sometimes working in their own houses, sometimes in that of the master clothier, but none of them going out of their proper line. Each class of workman, however, acquires great skill in performing its particular operation, and hence may have arisen the acknowledged excellence, and, till of late, the superiority of the cloths of the West of England." [1]

So again, in the cotton industry of Lancashire, the hold which the merchants had got over the weavers by supplying them with warp and weft led in some cases, before the middle of the century, to the establishment of small factories containing a score or two of looms, in which hired men were employed to weave. A little later, though long before steam power, Arthur Young finds a factory at Darlington with over fifty looms, a factory at Boynton with 150 workers, and a silk mill at Sheffield with 152 workers. In the more developed branches of the textile industry this transformation of business structure was tolerably complete by the end of the eighteenth century. Improved means of communication were beginning to expand the area of the market, enlarged businesses enabled labour to be profitably divided, and required a more effective control over the workers than could be obtained over a scattered population of agricultural manufacturers.

Thus by a series of economic changes the several functions of the independent craftsman have been taken from him, until he is left in possession of his labour-power alone, which he must sell to an employer who furnishes materials, tools and machinery, workplace, and superintendence, and who owns and markets the production of his labour. From a free craftsman he has passed into a " hired hand."

In this growth of capitalistic structure there have, of course, been various halting places, temporary or lasting. The small craftsman or other producer working in his own premises with his own tools and machinery, sometimes with his own power, using his own labour or that of a few hired workers, has survived in many departments of industry.

[1] *Report of the Commission on the Woollen Manufacture of England* (1806).

From early times many sorts of craftsmen have received their "orders" and material directly from the consumer. In the country the weaver, miller, baker. cobbler, tailor, smith, were mostly engaged in working at materials supplied by customers. Even till quite recent days in many parts of Germany and Switzerland cobblers, tailors, coopers, sometimes saddlers, carpenters, wheelwrights, were a nomad folk, not only working on material supplied by others, but working in the houses of their customers. In mediæval times it was chiefly where some sort of fixed plant or machinery were required, such as mills, ovens, forges, looms, that customers gave out the material to be made up in the workplace of the artisan.[1]

Even in the most advanced countries, where tools or machines are easily capable of transport, the itinerant craftsman still survives—e.g. tinkers and coopers, and among women's work that of the dressmaker and seamstress. In the less advanced European countries a great deal of work remains in this stage. "In Russia and the southern Slav countries there are hundreds of thousands of wage-workers, belonging especially to the building and clothing trades, who lead a continuous migratory life, and who, on account of the great distances travelled, often remain away from home half a year or more."[2]

While the receipt of raw materials and "orders" from merchants or other producers has commonly been the first stage in the breakdown of an independent business, this is by no means universally the case. There are many instances where all the factors of an independent business survive except the ownership of the raw material. In the textile trades great capitalist businesses, engaged in dyeing, bleaching, printing, etc., survive in this stage, while in shipping yards and in the metal and machine manufactures large numbers of repairing trades stand on this footing.

A further variety is furnished in the food and drink trades. The maltster, brewer, miller was in mediæval times the owner of kilns, brewing-house, or mill, to which the customer not only brought his own materials, but where he

---

[1] Cf. Bücher, *Industrial Evolution*, p. 63.
[2] Bücher, p. 164.

personally superintended their manufacture, the owner of the plant and premises looking to the working of his machinery, and supplying the power and other technical conditions of the process.

§ 13. Regarding the Business as a combination of Labour and Capital, we perceive that one strongly distinctive characteristic of the pre-machinery age is the small proportion which capital bears to labour in the industrial unit. It is this fact that enabled the "domestic" worker to hold his own so long in so many industries as the owner of a separate business. So long as the mechanical arts are slightly developed and tools are simple, the proportion of "fixed capital" to the business is small and falls within the means of the artisan who plies his craft in his home. So long as tools are simple, the processes of manufacture are slow, therefore the quantity of raw material and other "circulating capital" is small and can also be owned by the worker. The growing divorcement in the ownership of capital and labour in the industrial unit will be found to be a direct and most important result of those improvements in mechanical arts which, by continually increasing the proportion of capital to labour in a business, placed capital more and more beyond the possession of those who supplied the labour power required to co-operate in production.

In the middle of last century there were very few instances of a manufacturing business in which a large capital was engaged, or in which the capital stood to the labour in anything like modern proportion. It was indeed the merchant and not the manufacturer who represented the most advanced form of Capitalism in the eighteenth century. Long before Dr. Johnson's discovery that "an English merchant is a new species of gentleman," Defoe had noted the rise of merchant-princes in the Western clothing trades, observing that "many of the great families who now pass for gentry in these counties have been originally raised from and built out of this truly noble manufacture."[1] These wealthy *entrepreneurs* were sometimes spoken of as "manufacturers," though they had no claim either upon the old or the new signification of that

---

[1] *Tour*, vol. ii. p. 35.

name. They neither wrought with their hands nor did they own machinery and supervise the labour which worked with it. They were, as has been shown above, merchant-middlemen. The clothing trade being the most highly developed, evolved several species of middlemen, including under that term all collectors and distributors of the raw material or finished goods.

(*a*) One important class of "factors" engaged themselves in buying wool from farmers and selling it to clothiers, and appear to have sometimes exercised an undue and tyrannous control over the latter by an unscrupulous manipulation of the credit system which was growing up in trade.[1]

(*b*) The "clothiers" themselves must be regarded in large measure as middleman-collectors, analogous in function to the distributors, who still rank as one of the grades of middlemen in the cheap clothing trade of London to-day.[2]

(*c*) After the cloth was made three classes of middlemen were engaged in forwarding it to the retailer—(1) travelling merchants or wholesale dealers who attended the big fairs or the markets at Leeds, Halifax, Exeter, etc., and made large purchases, conveying the goods on pack-horses over the country to the retail trader; (2) middlemen who sold on commission through London factors and warehousemen, who in their turn disposed of the goods to shopkeepers or to exporters; (3) merchants directly engaged in the export trade.

With the exception of shipping and canal transport (which became important after the middle of the century) there were no considerable industries related to manufacture where large capitals were laid down in fixed plant. Even the capital sunk in permanent improvements of land, which played so important a part in the development of agriculture, belonged chiefly to the latter years of the eighteenth century. Almost the only persons who wielded large capitals within the country were those merchants, dealers, or middlemen whose capital at any given time consisted of a large stock of raw material or finished

---

[1] For an interesting account of the cunning devices of "factors" see Smith's *Memoirs of Wool*, vol. ii. p. 311, etc.

[2] Cf. Booth, *Labour and Life of the People*, vol. i. p. 486, etc.

goods. Even the latter were considerably restricted in the magnitude of their transactions by the imperfect development of the machinery of finance and the credit system. In 1750 there were not more than twelve bankers' shops out of London.[1] Until 1759 the Bank of England issued no notes of less value than £20.

Joint-ownership of capital and effective combination of the labour units in a business were only beginning to make progress. The Funded Debt, the Bank of England, the East India Company were the only examples of really large and safe investments at the opening of the eighteenth century. Joint-ownership of large capitals for business purposes made no great progress before the middle of the eighteenth century, except in the case of chartered companies for foreign trade, such as the East India Company, the Hudson's Bay Company, the Turkish, Russian, Eastland, and African companies. Insurance business became a favourite form of joint-stock speculation in the reign of George I. The extraordinary burst of joint-stock enterprise culminating in the downfall of the South Sea Company shows clearly the narrow limitations for sound capitalist co-operation. Even foreign trade on joint-stock lines could only be maintained successfully on condition that the competition of private adventurers was precluded.

Joint-capital had yet made no inroad into manufacture, one of the earliest instances being a company formed in 1764 with a capital of £100,000 for manufacturing fine cambrics.[2]

The limits of co-operative capitalism at the opening of the period of Industrial Revolution are indicated by Adam Smith in a passage of striking significance:—"The only trades which it seems possible for a joint-stock company to carry on successfully, without an exclusive privilege, are those of which all the operations are capable of being reduced to what is called a routine, or to such a uniformity of method as admits of little or no variation. Of this kind is, first, the banking trade; secondly, the trade of insurance from fire and from sea risk and capture in time of war; thirdly, the trade of making and maintaining a navigable

[1] Toynbee, *Industrial Revolution*, p. 55.
[2] Cunningham, vol. ii. p. 350.

cut or canal; and fourthly, the similar trade of bringing water for the supply of a great city."[1]

In other words, the businesses amenable to joint-stock enterprise are those where skilled management can be reduced to a minimum, and where the scale of the business or the possession of a natural monopoly limits or prohibits competition from outside.

[1] *Wealth of Nations*, Bk. V., chap. i., part 3.

CHAPTER IV.

THE ORDER OF DEVELOPMENT OF MACHINE INDUSTRY.

§ 1. It appears that in the earlier eighteenth century, while there existed examples of various types of industrial structure, the domestic system in its several phases may be regarded as the representative industrial form. The object of this chapter is to examine the nature of those changes in the mechanical arts which brought about the substitution of machine-industry conducted in factories or large workshops for the handicrafts conducted within the home or in small workshops, with the view of discovering the economic bearing of these changes.

A full inductive treatment would perhaps require this inquiry to be prefaced by a full history of the inventions which in the several industries mark the rise of the factory system and the adoption of capitalist methods. This, however, is beyond the scope of the present work, nor does it strictly belong to our scientific purpose, which is not to write the narrative of the industrial revolution, but to bring such analysis to bear upon the records of industrial changes as shall enable us clearly to discern the laws of those changes.

The central position occupied by machinery as the chief material factor in the modern evolution of industry requires that a distinct answer should be given to the question, What is machinery?

In distinguishing a machine from a mere tool or handicraft implement it is desirable to pay special attention to two points, complexity of structure and the activity of man in relation to the machine. Modern machinery in its most developed shape consists, as Karl Marx points out, of three parts, which, though mechanically connected, are essentially distinct, the motor mechanism, the transmitting mechanism, and the tool or working machine.

"The motor mechanism is that which puts the whole in motion. It either generates its own motive power, like the steam-engine, the caloric engine, the electro-magnetic machine, etc., or it receives its impulse from some already existing natural force, like the water-wheel from a head of water, the windmill from wind, etc. The transmitting mechanism, composed of fly-wheels, shafting, toothed wheels, pullies, straps, ropes, bands, pinions, and gearing of the most varied kind, regulates the motion, changes its form where necessary, as, for instance, from linear to circular, and divides and distributes it among the working machines. These two first parts of the whole mechanism are there solely for putting the working machines in motion, by means of which motion the subject of labour is seized upon and modified as desired."[1]

Although the development of modern machinery is largely concerned with motor and transmitting mechanisms, it is to the working machine we must look in order to get a clear idea of the differences between machines and tools. A tool may be quite simple in form and action as a knife, a needle, a saw, a roller, a hammer, or it may embody more complex thought in its construction, more variety in its movement, and call for the play of higher human skill. Such tools or implements are the hand-loom, the lathe, the potter's-wheel. To these tools man stands in a double relation. He is handicraftsman in that he guides and directs them by his skill within the

[1] Karl Marx, *Capital*, p. 367.

scope of activity to which they are designed. He also furnishes by his muscular activity the motive force with which the tool is worked. It is the former of these two relations which differentiates the tool from the machine. When the tool is removed from the direct and individual guidance of the handicraftsman and placed in a mechanism which governs its action by the prearranged motion of some other tool or mechanical implement, it ceases to be a tool and becomes part of a machine. The economic advantage of the early machines consisted chiefly in the economy of working in combined action a number of similar tools by the agency of a single motor. In the early machine the former tool takes its place as a central part, but its movements are no longer regulated by the human touch.[1] The more highly evolved modern machinery generally represents an orderly sequence of processes by which mechanical unity is given to the labour once performed by a number of separate individuals, or groups of individuals with different sorts of tools. But the economy of the earlier machines was generally of a different character. For the most part it consisted not in the harmonious relation of a number of different processes, but rather in a multiplication of the same process raised sometimes to a higher size and speed by mechanical contrivances. So the chief economic value of the earlier machinery applied to spinning consisted in the fact that it enabled each spinner to work an increased number of spindles, performing with each the same simple process as that which he formerly performed with one. In other cases, however, the element of multiplication was not present, and the prime economy of the machine consisted in the superior skill, regularity, pace, or economy of power obtained by substituting mechanical direction of the tool for close and constant human direction. In modern machinery the sewing-machine illustrates the latter, as the knife-cleaning machine illustrates the former.

The machine is inherently a more complex structure than the tool, because it must contain within itself the mechanical means for working a tool, or even for the combined working of many tools, which formerly received their direction from man. In using a tool man is the direct agent, in using a working machine the transmitting

---

[1] Marx points out how in many of the most highly evolved machines the original tool survives, illustrating this from the original power-loom. (*Capital*, vol. ii. p. 368.)

mechanism is the direct agent, so far as the character of the several acts of production is not stamped upon the form of the working machine itself. The man placed in charge of a machine determines whether it shall act, but only within very narrow limits how it shall act. The two characteristics here brought out in the machine, complexity of action and self-direction or automatic character, are in reality the objective and subjective expression of the same factor—namely, the changed relation of man towards the work in which he co-operates.

Some of the directing or mental effort, skill, art, thought, must be taken over, that is to say, some of the processes must be guided not directly by man but by other processes, in order to constitute a machine. A machine thus becomes a complex tool in which some of the processes are relatively fixed, and are not the direct expression of human activity. A machinist who feeds a machine with material may be considered to have some control over the pace and character of the first process, but only indirectly over the later processes, which are regulated by fixed laws of their construction that make them absolutely dependent on the earlier processes. A machine is in the nature of its work largely independent of the individual control of the "tender," because it is in its construction the expression of the individual control and skill of the inventor. A machine, then, may be described as a complex tool with a fixed relation of processes performed by its parts. Even here we cannot profess to have reached a definition which enables us in all cases to nicely discriminate machine from tool. It is easy to admit that a spade is a tool and not a machine, but if a pair of scissors, a lever, or a crane are tools, and are considered as performing single simple processes, and not a number of organically relative processes, we may by a skilfully arranged gradation be led on to include the whole of machinery under tools. This difficulty is of course one which besets all work of definition.

But while it is not easy by attention to complexity of structure always to distinguish a tool from a machine, nothing is gained by making the differentia of a machine to consist in the use of steam or other non-human motor.

A vast amount of modern machinery is of course directed not to combining tools or series of productive processes upon which the productive skill of man is closely engaged, but to substituting other motors for the muscular power of man. But though certain tools as well as certain forms of human effort are here replaced by machines, these tools are not commonly embodied in the machinery for generating and transmitting the new force, so that the mere consideration of the different part played by the worker in generating productive force does not assist us to distinguish a machine from a tool. A type-writer, a piano, which receive their impulse from the human muscles, must evidently be included among machines. It is indeed true that these, like others of the same order, are exceptional machines, not merely in that the motive power is derived more essentially from human muscles, but in that the *raison d'être* of the mechanism has been to provide scope for human skill and not to destroy it. But though it is true that a high degree of skill may be imparted to the first process of the working of a piano or type-writer, it is none the less true that the "tool," the implement which strikes the sound or makes the written mark, is not under immediate control of human touch. The skill is confined to an early process, and the mechanism as a whole must be classed under machinery. Nothing would indeed be gained in logical distinctness if we were to abandon our earlier differentia of the machine and confine that term to such mechanical appliances as derived their power from non-human sources—the fact which commonly marks off modern from earlier forms of machine production. For we should find that this substitution of non-human for human power was also a matter of degree, and that the most complex steam-driven machinery of to-day cannot entirely dispense with some directing impulse of human muscular activity, such as the shovelling of coal into a furnace, though the tendency is ever to reduce the human effort to a minimum in the attainment of a given output.

This consideration of the difficulties attending exact definitions of machinery is not idle, for it leads to a clearer recognition of the nicely graded evolution which has changed the character of modern industry, not by a catastrophic substitution of radically different methods, but by the continuous steady development of certain elements, common to all sorts of industrial activity, and a corresponding continuous degeneration of certain other elements.

§ 2. The growth of machine-industry then may be measured by the increased number and complexity of the processes related to one another in the mechanical unit or machine,

and by a corresponding shrinkage of the dependence of the
product upon the skill and volition of the human being
who tends or co-operates with the machine.[1] Every product
made by tool or machine is quâ industrial product or commodity the expression of the thought and will of man;
but as machine-production becomes more highly developed, more and more of the thought and will of the
inventor, less and less of that of the immediate human
agent or machine-tender is expressed in the product.
But it is evidently not enough to say that the labour-
saving machine has merely substituted the stored and concentrated effort of the inventor for that labour of the
handicraftsman which is saved. This would be to ignore
the saving of muscular power due to the substitution of
forces of nature—water, steam, electricity, etc., for the
painful effort of man. It is the thought of the inventor,
plus the action of various mechanical and other physical
forces, which has saved the labour of man in the production of a commodity. The further question—how far this
saving of labour in respect of a given commodity is compensated by the increased number of commodities to which
human labour is applied—is a consideration which belongs
to a later chapter

In tracing the effect of the application of modern
machinery to English industry there appear two prominent
factors, which for certain purposes require separate treatment—the growth of improved mechanical apparatus, and
the evolution of extra-human motor power.

We speak of the industry which has prevailed since the
middle of the eighteenth century as machine-production,
not because there were no machines before that time, but
firstly, because a vast acceleration in the invention of complex machinery applied to almost all industrial arts dates

[1] This does not imply a corresponding growth in the mechanical
complexity of the machine itself, for, as Adam Smith observed, "All
machines are generally, when first invented, extremely complex in
their principles, and there is often a particular principle of motion for
every particular movement which it is intended they should perform.
Succeeding improvers observe that the principle may be so applied as
to produce several of these movements, and thus the machine becomes
gradually more and more simple, and produces its effects with fewer
wheels and fewer principles of motion."—*Moral Sentiments*, quoted
Hirst, "Adam Smith," p. 64.

from that period, and secondly, because the application upon an extensive scale of non-human motor powers manifested itself then for the first time.

One important external effect and indication of the momentous character of these changes is to be found in the quickening of that operation, the beginning of which was observable before the great inventions, the substitution of the Factory System for the Domestic System.

The peculiar relation of Machinery to the Factory System consists in the fact that the size, expensiveness, and complexity of machinery on the one hand, and the use of non-human power on the other hand, were forces which united to drive labour from the home workshop to the large specialised workshop—the Factory.

"The water frame, the carding engine, and the other machines which Arkwright brought out in a finished state, required both more space than could be found in a cottage, and more power than could be applied by the human arm. Their weight also rendered it necessary to place them in strongly-built walls, and they also could not be advantageously turned by any power then known but that of water. Further, the use of machinery was accompanied by a greater division of labour, and therefore a greater co-operation was requisite to bring all the processes of production into harmony and under a central superintendence."[1]   Hence the growth of machine-production is to a large extent synonymous with the growth of the modern Factory System.

§ 3. Man does his work by moving matter.   Hence machinery can only aid him by increasing the motive power at his disposal.

(1) Machinery enables forces of man or nature to be more effectively applied by various mechanical contrivances composed of levers, pulleys, wedges, screws, etc.

(2) Machinery enables man to obtain the use of various motor forces outside his body—wind, water, steam, electricity, chemical action, etc.[2]

Thus by the provision of new productive forces, and by the more economical application of all productive forces, machinery improves the industrial arts.

[1] Cooke Taylor, *History of the Factory System*, p. 422.
[2] Cf. Babbage, p. 15.

Machinery can increase the scope of man's productive
ability in two ways. The difficulty of concentrating a large
mass of human force upon a given point at the same
time provides certain quantitative limits to the productive
efficiency of the human body. The steam-hammer can
perform certain work which is quantitatively outside the limit
of the physical power of any number of men working with
simple tools and drawing their motor power from their own
bodies. The other limit to the productive power of man
arises from the imperfect continuity of human effort and
the imperfect command of its direction. The difficulty of
maintaining a small, even, accurate pressure, or a precise
repetition of the same movement, is rather a qualitative
than a purely quantitative limit. The superior certainty and
regularity of machinery enables certain work to be done
which man alone could not do or could do less perfectly.
The work of the printing machine could not be achieved by
man. Machinery has improved the texture and quality of
certain woollen goods;[1] recent improvements in milling
result in improved quality of flour and so on. Machinery
can also do work which is too fine or delicate for human
fingers, or which would require abnormal skill if executed
by hand. Economy of time, which Babbage[2] accounts a
separate economy, is rightly included in the economies just
named. The greater rapidity with which certain manufacturing processes—e.g., dyeing—can be achieved arises from the
superior concentration and continuity of force possible
under machinery. All advantages arising from rapid transport are assignable to the same causes.

The continuity and regularity of machine work are also
reflected in certain economies of measurement. The faculty
of self-registering, which belongs potentially to all machinery,
and which is more utilised every day, performs several
services which may be summed up by saying that they
enable us to know exactly what is going on. When to self-
registration is applied the faculty of self-regulation, within
certain limits a new economy of force and knowledge is
added. But machinery can also register and regulate the
expenditure of human power. Babbage well says :—" One
of the most singular advantages we derive from machinery

---

[1] Burnley, *Wool and Wool-combing*, p. 417.
[2] *Economy of Machinery*, p. 6.

is in the check which it affords against the inattention, the idleness, or the knavery of human agents."[1] This control of the machine over man has certain results which belong to another aspect of machine economy.[2]

These are the sources of all the improvements of economies imputed to machine-production. All improvements in machinery, as applied to industrial arts, take therefore one of the following forms:—

(1) Re-arrangement or improvement of machinery so as to utilise more fully the productive power of nature or man. Improvements enabling one man to tend more spindles, or enabling the same engine at the same boiler-pressure to turn more wheels, belong to this order of improvement.

(2) Economies in the source of power. These will fall under four heads—

   1. Substitution of cheaper for dearer kinds of human power. Displacement of men's labour by women's or children's.

   2. Substitution of mechanical power for human power. Most great improvements in the "labour-saving" character of machinery properly come under this head.

   3. Economies in fuel or in steam. The most momentous illustration is the adoption of the hot blast and the substitution of raw coal for coke in the iron trade.[3]

   4. The substitution of a new mechanical motor for an old one derived from the same or from different stores of energy—e.g., steam for water power, natural gas for steam.

(3) Extended application of machinery. New industrial arts owing their origin to scientific inventions and their practice to machinery arise for utilising waste products. Under "waste products" we may include (a) natural materials, the services of which were not recognised or could not be utilised without machinery—e.g., nitrates and other "waste" products of the soil; (b) the refuse of manufacturing processes which figured as "waste" until some unsuspected use was found for it. Conspicuous examples of this economy are found in many trades. During the interval between great

---

[1] *Economy of Machinery*, p. 39.
[2] *Vide infra*, p. 340.
[3] Scrivener, *History of the Iron Trade*, pp. 296, 297.

new inventions in machinery or in the application of power many of the principal improvements are of this order. Gas tar, formerly thrown into rivers so as to pollute them, or mixed with coal and burnt as fuel, is now "raw material for producing beautiful dyes, some of our most valued medicines, a saccharine substance three hundred times sweeter than sugar, and the best disinfectants for the destruction of germs of disease." "The whole of the great industries of dyeing and calico-printing have been revolutionised by the new colouring matters obtained from the old waste material gas tar."[1] These economies both in fuel and in the utilisation of waste material are largely due to the increased scale of production which comes with the development of machine industry. Many waste products can only be utilised where they exist in large quantities.

§ 4. If we trace historically the growth of modern capitalist economies in the several industries we shall find that they fall generally into three periods—

1. The period of earlier mechanical inventions, marking the displacement of domestic by factory industry.
2. The evolution of the new motor in manufacture. The application of steam to the manufacturing processes.
3. The evolution of steam locomotion, with its bearing on industry.

As these periods are not materially exclusive, so also there are close economic relations subsisting between the development of machinery and motor, and between the improvements in manufacture and in the transport industry. But in order to understand the nature of the irregularity which is discernible in the history of the development of machinery, it is essential to consider these factors both separately and in the historical and economic relation they stand to each other. For this purpose we will examine two large staple industries, the textile and the iron industries of England, in order that we may trace in the chief steps of their progress the laws of the evolution of modern machinery.

The textile industry offers special facilities to such a study. The strongest and most widespread of English manufactures, it furnishes in the early eighteenth century the

---

[1] Sir Lyon Playfair, *North American Review*, Nov. 1892.

clearest examples of the several forms of industry. To the several branches of this industry the earliest among the great inventions were applied. This start in industrial development has been maintained, so that the most advanced forms of the modern factory are found in textile industry. Moreover, the close attention which has been given to, and the careful records which have been kept of certain branches of this work, in particular the Lancashire cotton industry, enable us to trace the operation of the new industrial forces here with greater precision than is the case with any other industry. As Schulze-Gaevernitz, in his masterly study, says of the cotton industry—— " The English cotton industry is not only the oldest, but is in many respects that modern industry which manifests most clearly the characteristics of modern industrial methods, both in their economic and their social relations." [1]

The iron industry has been selected on the ground of its close connection with the application of steam-driven machinery to the several industries. It is in a sense the most fundamental industry of modern times, inasmuch as it furnishes the material environment of the great modern economic forces. Moreover, we have the advantage of tracing the growth of the iron manufacture *ab ovo*, for, as we have seen, before the industrial revolution it played a most insignificant part in English commerce.

Lastly, a study of the relations between the growth of the iron and the textile industries will be of special service in assisting us to realise the character of the interaction of the several manufactures under the growing integration of modern industry. [2]

§ 5. In observing the order of inventions applied to textile industries, the first point of significance is that cotton, a small industry confined to a part of Lancashire, and up to 1768 dependent upon linen in order to furnish a complete cloth, should take the lead.

The woollen trades, in the first half of the eighteenth

---

[1] *Der Grossbetrieb*, p. 85.
[2] The important part which the cotton and iron industries play in the export trade of England entitles them to special consideration as representatives of world-industry. Out of £283,000,000 value of English exports in 1903, cotton comprised £72,000,000; iron and steel, £35,000,000.

century, as we saw, engaged the attention of a vastly larger number of persons, and played a much more important part in our commerce. The silk trade had received new life from the flow of intelligent French workers, and the first modern factory with elaborate machinery was that set up for silk throwing by Lombe. Yet by far the larger number of the important textile inventions of the eighteenth century were either applied in the first instance to the cotton manufacture and transferred, sometimes after a lapse of many years, to the woollen, worsted, and other textile trades, or being invented for woollen trades, proved unsuccessful until applied to cotton.[1]

Although the origin and application of inventive genius is largely independent of known laws, and may provisionally be relegated to the domain of "accident," there are certain reasons which favoured the cotton industry in the industrial race. Its concentration in South Lancashire and Staffordshire, as compared with the wide diffusion of the woollen industries, facilitated the rapid acceptance of new methods and discoveries. Moreover, the cotton industry being of later origin, and settling itself in unimportant villages and towns, had escaped the influence of official regulations and customs which prevailed in the woollen centres and proved serious obstacles to the introduction of new industrial methods.[2] Even in Lancashire itself official inspectors regulated the woollen trade at Manchester, Rochdale, Blackburn, and Bury.[3]

The cotton industry had from the beginning been free from all these fetters. The shrewd, practical business character which marks Lancashire to-day is probably a cause as well as a result of the great industrial development of the last hundred years.

Moreover, it was recognised, even before the birth of the great inventions, that cotton goods, when brought into free competition with woollen goods, could easily undersell them and supplant them in popular consumption. This knowledge held out a prospect of untold fortune to inventors who should, by the application of machinery, break through the limitations imposed upon production

[1] Cunningham, chap. ii. p. 450.
[2] Schulze-Gaevernitz, *Der Grossbetrieb*, p. 34.
[3] Ure, *The Cotton Manufacture*, p. 187.

by the restricted number of efficient workers in some of the processes through which the cotton yarn must pass.

But the stimulus which one invention afforded to another gave an accumulative power to the application of new methods. This is especially seen in the alternation of inventions in the two chief processes of spinning and weaving.

Even before the invention of John Kay's Fly Shuttle, which doubled the quantity of work a weaver could do in a day, we found that spinners had great difficulties in supplying sufficient yarn to the weavers. This seems to have applied both to the Lancashire cotton and to the Yorkshire woollen manufactures. After the fly-shuttle had come into common use this pressure of demand upon the spinners was obviously increased, and the most skilful organisation of middleman-clothiers was unable to supply sufficient quantities of yarn. This economic consideration directed more and more attention to experiments in spinning machinery, and so we find that, long before the invention of the jenny and the water-frame, ingenious men like John Kay of Bury, Wyatt, Paul, and others had tried many patents for improved spinning. The great inventions of Hargreaves, Arkwright, and Crompton enabled spinning to overtake and outstrip weaving, and when, about 1790, steam began to be applied to considerable numbers of spinning mills, it was no longer spinning but weaving that was the limiting process in the manufacture of woollen and cotton cloths.

This strain upon weaving, which had been tightening through the period of the great spinning improvements, acted as a special incentive to Cartwright, Horrocks, and others to perfect the power-loom in its application, first to woollen, then to cotton industries. Not until well into the nineteenth century, when steam power had been fully applied by many minor improvements, were the arts of spinning and weaving brought fully into line. The complete factory, where the several processes of carding, spinning, weaving (and even dyeing and finishing), are conducted under the same roof and worked in correspondence with one another, marks the full transition from the earlier form of domestic industry, where the family performed with simple tools their several processes under the domestic roof.[1]

§ 6. The history of these textile inventions does a good deal to dispel the "heroic" theory of invention—that of an idea flashing suddenly from the brain of a single genius and effecting a rapid revolution in a trade. No one of the inventions which were greatest in their effect, the jenny, the water-frame, the mule, the power-loom, was in the main attributable to the effort or ability of a single man; each represented in its successful shape the addition of many successive increments of discovery; in most cases the successful invention was the slightly superior survivor of many similar attempts. "The present spinning machinery which we now use is supposed to be a compound of about eight hundred inventions. The present carding machinery is a compound of about sixty patents."[2] This is the history of most inventions. The pressure of industrial circumstances direct the intelligence of many minds towards the comprehension of some single central point of difficulty, the common knowledge of the age induces many to reach similar solutions: that solution which is slightly better adapted to the facts or "grasps the skirts of happy chance" comes out victorious, and the inventor, purveyor, or, in some cases, the robber is crowned as a great inventive genius. It is the neglect of these considerations which gives a false interpretation to the annals of industrial invention by giving an irregular and catastrophic appearance to the working of a force which is in its inner pressure much more regular than in its outward expression. The earlier increments of a great industrial invention make no figure in

[1] Modern economy now favours the specialisation of a factory and often of a business in a single group of processes—e.g., spinning or weaving or dyeing, both in the cotton and woollen industries. This, however, is applicable chiefly to the main branches of textile work. In minor branches, such as cotton thread, the tendency is still towards an aggregation of all the different processes under a single roof, both in England and in the United States.

[2] P. R. Hodge, civil engineer—evidence before House of Lords Committee in 1857.

In Germany a spinning-wheel had been long in use for flax-spinning, which in effect was an anticipation of the throstle (cf. Karmarch, Technologie, vol. ii. p. 844, quoted Schulze-Gaevernitz, p. 30), and machine-weaving is said to have been discovered in Danzig as early as 1579.

the annals of history because they do not pay, and the final increment which reaches the paying-point gets all the credit, though the inherent importance and the inventive genius of the earlier attempts may have been as great or greater.

There is nothing fortuitous or mysterious in inventive energy. Necessity is its mother, which simply means that it moves along the line of least resistance. Men like Kay, Hargreaves, Arkwright, Cartwright, set their intelligence and industry to meet the several difficulties as they arose. Nearly all the great textile inventors were practical men, most of them operatives immersed in the details of their craft, brought face to face continually with some definite difficulty to be overcome, some particular economy desirable to make. Brooding upon these concrete facts, trying first one thing then another, learning from the attempts and failures made by other practical men, and improving upon these attempts, they have at length hit upon some contrivance that will get over the definite difficulty and secure the particular economy. If we take any definite invention and closely investigate it, we shall find in nearly every case it has thus grown by small increments towards feasibility. Scientific men, strictly so called, have had very little to do with these great discoveries. Among the great textile inventors, Cartwright alone was a man leading a life of thought.[1] When the spinning machinery was crippled in its efficiency by the crude methods of carding, Lees and Arkwright set themselves to apply improvements suggested by common sense and experience; when Cartwright's power-loom had been successfully applied to wool, Horrocks and his friends thought out precisely those improvements which would render it remunerative in the cotton trade.

Thus in a given trade where there are several important processes, an improvement in one process which places it in front of the others stimulates invention in the latter, and each in its turn draws such inventive intelligence as is required to bring it into line with the most highly-developed process. Since the later inventions, with new knowledge and new power behind them, often overshoot the earlier ones, we have a certain law of oscillation in the several

[1] Cf. Brentano, *Uber die Ursachen der heutigen socialen Not; Der Grossbetrieb*, p. 30.

processes which maintains progress by means of the stimulus constantly applied by the most advanced process which "makes the pace." There is nothing mysterious in this. If one process remains behind in development each increment of inventive effort successfully applied there brings a higher remuneration than if applied to any of the more forward processes. So the movement is amenable to the ordinary law of "Supply and Demand" enforced by the usual economic motives. As the invention of the fly-shuttle gave weaving the advantage, more and more attention was concentrated upon the spinning processes and the jenny was evolved; the deficiency of the jenny in spinning warp evolved the water-frame, which for the first time liberated the cotton industry from dependence upon linen warp: the demand for finer and more uniform yarns stimulated the invention of the mule. These notable improvements in spinning machinery, with their minor appendages, placed spinning ahead of weaving, and stimulated the series of inventions embodied in the power-loom. The power-loom was found to be of comparatively little service until the earlier processes of dressing and sizing had been placed on a level of machine development by the efforts of Horrocks and others. Not until after 1841 was an equilibrium reached in the development of the leading processes. So likewise each notable advance in the machinery for the main processes has had the effect of bringing an increase of inventive energy to bear upon the minor and the subsidiary processes —bleaching, dyeing, printing, etc. Even now the early process of "ginning" has not been brought fully into line in spite of the prodigious efforts, made especially in the United States, to overcome the difficulties involved in this preparatory stage of the cotton industry.

The following schedule will serve to show the relation of the growth of the cotton industry as measured by consumption of raw cotton to the leading improvements of machinery.

Cotton Imported. lbs.		Inventions &c.
1730	1,545,472	1730 Wyatt's roller-spinning (patented 1738).
		1738 Kay's fly-shuttle.
1741	1,645,031	1748 Paul's carding-machine (useless until improved by Lees, Arkwright, Wood, 1772-74).

6

	Cotton Imported. lbs.		Inventions, &c.
1764	3,870,392	1764	Hargreave's spinning-jenny (patented 1770), for weft only.
		1764	Calico-printing introduced into Lancashire.
		1768	Arkwright perfects Wyatt's spinning-frame (patented 1769), liberating cotton from dependence on linen warp.
1771 to 1775	4,764,589	1771	Arkwright's mill built at Cromford.
		1775	Arkwright takes patents for carding, drawing, roving, spinning.
		1779	Crompton's mule completed (combining jenny and water-frame, producing finer and more even yarn).
1781	5,198,775		
1785	18,400,384	1785	Cartwright's power-loom. Watt and Boulton's first engine for cotton-mills.
1792	34,907,497	1792	Whitney's saw-gin.
1813	51,000,000	1813	Horrocks' dressing-machine.
1830	261,200,000	1830	The "Throstle" (almost exclusively used in England for spinning warp).
1832	287,800,000	1832	Roberts' self-acting mule perfected.
1841	489,900,000	1841	Bullough's improved power-loom. Ring spinning (largely used in U.S.A., recently introduced into Lancashire).

From this schedule it is evident that the history of this trade may be divided with tolerable accuracy into four periods.

(1) The preparatory period of experimental inventions of Wyatt, Paul, etc., to the year 1770.

(2) 1770 to 1792 (*circa*), the age of the great mechanical inventions.

(3) 1792 to 1830, the application of steam power to manufacture and improvements of the great inventions.

(4) 1830 onward, the effect of steam locomotion upon the industry (1830, the opening of the Liverpool and Manchester railway).

If we measure the operation of these several industrial forces within these several periods, as they are reflected on the growing size of the cotton industry, we shall realise the accumulative character of the great industrial movement, and form some approximately accurate conception of the relative importance of the development of mechanical inventions and of the new motor-power.

§ 7. The history of the cotton industry is in its main outlines also the history of other textile industries. We do not possess the same means of measuring statistically the growth of the woollen industries in the period of revolution ; but since, on the one hand, many of the spinning and weaving inventions were speedily adapted into the woollen from the cotton industry, while the application of steam to manufacture and the effects of steam locomotion were shared by the older manufacture, the growth of the trade in the main conforms to the same divisions of time. The figures of imported wool are not so valuable a register as in the case of cotton, because no account is taken of home-produce, but the following statistics of foreign and colonial wool imported into England serve to throw light upon the growth of our woollen manufactures.

STATISTICS OF WOOL IMPORTED INTO ENGLAND.

	lbs.		lbs.
1766	1,926,000	1830	32,305,000
1771	1,829,000	1840	49,436,000
1780	323,000	1850	74,326,000
1790	2,582,000	1860	151,218,000
1800	8,609,000	1870	263,250,000
1810	10,914,000	1880	463,309,000
1820	9,775,000	1890	635,340,110
		1902	647,204,376

In the silk industry the influence of machinery is complicated by several considerations especially affecting this manufacture. Although the ingenuity and enterprise of the Lombes had introduced complex machinery into silk throwing many years before it was successfully applied to any other branch of textile industry, the trade did not grow as might have been expected, and the successive increments of great mechanical invention were slowly and slightly applied to the silk industry. There are special reasons for this, some of them connected with the intrinsic value of the commodity, others with the social regulation of the trade.

The inherent delicacy of many of the processes, the capricious character of the market for the commodities, the expensive production of which renders them a luxury and especially amenable to the shifts of taste and fashion, have preserved for artistic handicraft the production of many of the finer silk fabrics, or have permitted the application of machinery in a far less degree than in the cotton and woollen industries.

Moreover, the heavy duties imposed upon raw and thrown silk, which accompanied the strict prohibition of the importation of manufactured silk goods in 1765, by aggravating the expenses of production and limiting the market at the very epoch of the great mechanical inventions, prevented any notable expansion of consumption of silk goods, and rendered them quite unable to resist the competition of the younger and more enterprising cotton industry, which, after the introduction of colour-printing early in the nineteenth century, was enabled to out-compete silk in many markets.

Even in the coarser silk fabrics where weaving machinery was successfully applied at an early date, the slow progress in "throwing" greatly retarded the expansion of the trade, and after the repeal of the duty on imported silk in 1826 the number of throwing mills was still quite inadequate to keep pace with the demands of the weavers.[1] Subsequent improvements in throwing mills, and the application of the ingenious weaving machinery of Jacquard and later improvers, have given a great expansion to many branches of the trade in the last fifty years.

But the following statistics of the consumption of raw and thrown silk from 1765 to 1844 indicate how slight and irregular was the expansion of the trade in England during the era of the great inventions and the application of the steam-motor, and how disastrously the duties upon raw and thrown silks weighed upon this branch of manufacture.

---

[1] Porter, *Progress of the Nation*, p. 219.

AVERAGE IMPORTATION.[1]

lbs.			lbs.
1765		1823	2,468,121
1766 } 715,000		1824	4,011,048[2]
1767		1825	3,604,058
1785		1826	2,253,513
1786 } 881,000		1827	4,213,153
1787		1828	4,547,812
1801		1829	2,892,201
to } 1,110,000		1830	4,693,517
1812		1831	4,312,330
1814	2,119,974	1832	4,373,247
1815	1,475,389	1833	4,761,543
1816	1,088,334	1834	4,522,451
1817	1,686,659	1835	5,788,458
1818	1,922,987	1836	6,058,423
1819	1,848,553	1837	4,598,859
1820	2,027,635	1838	4,790,256
1821	2,329,808	1839	4,665,944
1822	2,441,563	1840	4,819,262

In the linen industry the artificial encouragement given to the Irish trade, which, bounty-fed and endowed with a monopoly of the British markets, was naturally slow to adopt new methods of production, and the uncertain condition of the English trade, owing to the strong rivalry of cotton, prevented the early adoption of the new machine methods. Although Adam Smith regarded linen as a promising industry, it was still in a primitive condition. Not until the very end of the eighteenth century were flax spinning mills established in England and Scotland, and not until after 1830 was power-loom weaving introduced, while the introduction of spinning machinery into Ireland upon a scale adequate to supply the looms of that country took place a good deal later.

We see that the early experimental period in the cotton industry produced no very palpable effect upon the volume of the trade. Between 1700 and 1750 the manufacture was

[1] Selected from Porter, p. 218.

[2] In 1824 Mr. Huskisson introduced the principle of free trade, securing a reduction of the duties on raw and thrown silks, and in 1825, 1826, considerable further reductions were made. (Cf. Ure, *Philosophy of Manufacture*, p. 454, etc.) But protection of English silk manufactured goods was maintained until the French Treaty of 1860.

stagnant.[1]   The woollen manufacture, owing largely to
the stimulus of the fly-shuttle, showed considerable expansion.   The great increase of cotton production in 1770-90
measures the force of the mechanical inventions without the
aid of the new motor.   The full effects of the introduction
of steam power were retarded by the strain of the French
war.   Though 1800 marks the beginning of a large continuous expansion in both cotton and woollen manufactures,
it was not until about 1817, when the new motor had established itself generally in the large centres of industry and
the energy of the nation was called back to the arts of
peace, that the new forces began to fully manifest their
power.   The period 1840 onwards marks the effect of the
revolution in commerce due to the application of the new
motor to transport purposes, the consequent cheapening of
raw material, especially of cotton, the opening up of new
markets for the purchase of raw material and for the sale of
manufactured goods.   The effect of this diminished cost of
production and increased demand for manufactured goods
upon the textile trades is measured by the rapid pace of the
expansion which followed the opening of the early English
railways and the first establishment of steam-ship traffic.

§ 8. The development of the textile trades, and that of
cotton in particular, arose from the invention of new
machinery.   This machinery was quickened and rendered
effective by the new motor.   The iron trade in its development presents the reverse order.   The discovery of a new
motor was the force which first gave it importance.   The
mechanical inventions applied to producing iron were
stimulated by the requirements of the new motor.

In 1740 the difficulty of obtaining adequate supplies of
timber, and the failure of attempts to utilise pit-coal, had
brought the iron trade to a very low condition.   According
to Scrivener, at this time "the iron trade seemed dwindling
into insignificance and contempt."[2]

The earlier steps in its rise from this degradation are
measured by the increased application of pit-coal and the
diminished use of charcoal.

The progress may be marked as follows :—

[1] Cf. Ure, *History of the Cotton Manufacture*, vol. i. p. 223.
[2] Scrivener, *History of the Iron Trade*, p. 56.

(1) The application of Watt's earlier improvements upon Newcomen's engines, patented 1769, was followed by a rise in the average output for furnaces worked with charcoal. The average output of 294 tons in 1750 was increased to 545 tons in 1788.

(2) The substitution of coke for charcoal proceeding *pari passu* with improved methods of smelting yielded an average output for coke-fed furnaces of 903 tons in 1788. To this epoch belong also Cort's inventions for puddling and rolling (patented 1783-84), which revolutionised the production of bar-iron.

(3) The introduction of Watt's double-power engine in 1788-90. In 1796 the production of pig-iron was double that of 1788, and the average output per furnace raised to 1048 tons.

(4) The substitution of hot for cold blast in 1829, effecting an economy of coal to the extent of 2 tons 18 cwt. per ton of cast-iron.

(5) The adoption of raw coal instead of coke in 1833, effecting a further reduction of expenditure of coal from 5 tons 3½ cwt. to 2 tons 5¼ cwt. in producing a ton of cast-iron.

These were the leading events in the establishment of the iron industry of this country. The following table indicates the growth of the production of English iron from 1740 to 1840 :—

Year.	No. of Furnaces.	Average Output. Tons.	Total Produce. Tons.
1740	59	294	17,350
1788	77	909 coke ⎱ 545 charcoal ⎰	61,300
1796	121	1048	125,079
1806	133	1546	258,206
1825	364 (261 in blast)	2228	703,184
1828	365 (277 in blast)	2530	
1839	378	3592	1,347,790

Here we see that economy of power rather than improved machinery is the efficient cause of the development of industry, or more properly, that economy of power precedes and stimulates the several steps in improvement of machinery.

The substitution of coke for charcoal and the application of steam power not merely increased enormously the volume of the trade, but materially affected its localisation. Sussex and Gloucester, two of the chief iron-producing counties when timber was the source of power, had shrunk into insignificance by 1796, when facilities of obtaining coal were a chief determinant. By 1796, it is noteworthy that the four districts of Stafford, Yorkshire, South Wales, and Salop were to the front.

The discovery of the hot blast and substitution of raw coal for coke occurring contemporaneously with the opening of railway enterprise mark the new interdependence of industries in the age of machinery.

Iron has become a foundation upon which every machine-industry alike is built. The metal manufactures, so small in the eighteenth century, attained an unprecedented growth and a paramount importance in the nineteenth.

The application of machinery to the metal industries has led to an output of inventive genius not less remarkable in this century than the textile inventions of the eighteenth century.

"In textile manufacture it was improved machinery that first called for a new motor; in metal manufacture it was the new motor which rendered necessary improved machinery. . . . For all modern purposes the old handi-craft implements were clearly obsolete. The immediate result of this requirement was the bringing to the front a number of remarkable men, Brindley, Smeaton, Maudsley, Clements, Bramah, Nasmyth, etc., to supply mechanism of a proportionate capacity and nicety for the new motive-power to act upon and with, and the ultimate result was the adoption of the modern factory system in the larger tool-making and engineering workshops, as well as in metal manufactories proper. Thus there gradually grew up," says Jevons, "a system of machine-tool labour, the substitution of iron hands for human hands, without which the execution of engines and machines in their present perfection would be impossible."[1]

In the later era of machine development an accumulative

---

[1] Cooke Taylor, *Modern Factory System*, p. 164; cf. also Karl Marx, *Capital*, p. 381.

importance is attached to the improvements in the machine-making industries. The great inventions associated with the names of Maudsley and Nasmyth, the cheapening of steel by the Bessemer process, and the various steps by which machines are substituted for hands in the making of machinery, have indirect but rapid and important effects upon each and every machine-industry engaged in producing commodities directly adapted to human use. The economy of effort for industrial purposes requires that a larger and larger proportion of inventive genius and enterprise shall be directed to an interminable displacement of handicraft by machinery in the construction of machinery, and a smaller proportion to the relatively unimportant work of perfecting manufacturing machinery in the detailed processes of each manufacture engaged in the direct satisfaction of some human want.

A general survey of the growth of new industrial methods in the textile and iron industries marks out three periods of abnormal activity in the evolution of modern industry. The first is 1780 to 1795, when the fruits of early inventions are ripened by the effective application of steam to the machine-industries. The second is 1830 to 1845, when industry, reviving after the European strife, utilised more widely the new inventions, and expanded under the new stimulus of steam locomotion. The third is 1856 to 1866 (*circa*), when the construction of machinery by machinery became the settled rule of industry.

§ 9. Bearing in mind how the invention of new specific forms of machinery in the several processes of manufacture proceeds simultaneously with the application of the new motor-power, we find ourselves quite unable to measure the amount of industrial progress due to each respectively. But seeing that the whole of modern industry has thus been set upon a new foundation of coal and iron, it is obvious that the bonds connecting such industries as the textile and the iron must be continually growing closer and stronger. In earlier times the interdependency of trades was slight and indirect, and the progress in any given trade was almost wholly derived from improvements in specific skill or in the application of specific mechanical invention. The earlier eighteenth century did indeed display an abnormal activity in these specific forms of invention. For examples of these it is only necessary to allude to Lombe's silk mill at Derby, the pin factory made famous by Adam Smith, Boulton's hardware factory at Soho, and the renowned discoveries of Wedgwood. But all increased productivity due to these specific improvements was but slight compared with that which followed the discovery of steam as a motor and the mechanical inventions rendering it generally applicable, which marked the period 1790 to 1840. By this means the several specific industries were drawn into closer unity, and found a common basis or foundation in the arts of mining, iron-working, and engineering which they lacked before.

From these considerations it will follow that the order in which the several industries has fallen under the sway of modern industrial methods will largely depend upon the facility they afford to the application of steam-driven machinery. The following are some of the principal characteristics of an industry which determine the order, extent, and pace of its progress as a machine industry:—

(*a*) *Size and complexity of Structure.*—The importance of the several leading textile manufactures, the fact that some of them were highly centralised and already falling under a factory system, the control of wealthy and intelligent employers, were among the chief causes which enabled the new machinery and the new motor to be more quickly and successfully applied than in smaller, more scattered, and less developed industries.

(*b*) *Fixity in quantity and character of demand.*—Perfection of routine-work is the special faculty of machine-production. Where there is a steady demand for the same class of goods, machinery can be profitably applied. Where fashion fluctuates, or the individual taste of the consumer is a potent factor, machinery cannot so readily undertake the work. In the textile industries there are many departments which machinery has not successfully invaded. Much lace-making, embroidery, certain finer weaving is still done by human power, with or without the aid of complex machinery. In the more skilled branches of tailoring, shoe-making, and other clothing trades, the individual character of the demand—*i.e.*, the element of irregularity— has limited the use of machinery. A similar cause retains human motor-power in certain cases to co-operate with ınd control complex machinery, as in the use of the sewing-machine.

Uniformity of demand is a first essential of that "standardisation" which enables a process to be performed by machinery. In many industries where mechanical methods have made great advance, complete standardisation remains impracticable. "There is some doubt as to the possibility of standardising ships, at least to such an extent as we have already attained in building bridges, railway engines, and stationary engines. A modern steamship is a much more complex agency than a bridge or a locomotive engine, and while standardising may apply much more largely than is at present the case in the production of certain features, it is certain that a present practice of standardising does not generally prevail in the manufacture of hull and ship-machinery, except as ships are built to a standard for record and to come under low rates of insurance.[1]

(c) *Uniformity of material and of the processes of production.*—Inherent irregularity in the material of labour is adverse to machinery. For this reason the agricultural processes have been slow to pass under steam-power, especially those directly concerned with work on the soil, and even where steam-driven machines are applied their economy, as compared with hand labour, is less marked than in manufacturing processes. To the getting of coal and other minerals steam and other extra-human power has been more slowly and less effectively applied than in dealing with the matter when it is detached from the earth. The displacement of a less uniform material, wood, by the more uniform steel for building-structures, railroad cars, barges, ships, furniture, etc., marks a great advance for machine-production.

(d) *Durability of valuable properties.*—The production of quickly perishable articles being of necessity local and immediate demands a large amount of human service which cannot economically be replaced or largely aided by machinery. The work of the butcher and the baker have been slow to pass under machinery. Where butchering has become a machine-industry to some extent, the direct cause

---

[1] Chapman, *Foreign Competition*, p. 106.

has been the discovery of preservative processes which have diminished the perishability of meat. So with other food industries, the facility of modern means of transport has alone enabled them gradually to pass under the control of machinery. Until quite recently cakes and the finer forms of bakery were a purely local and handicraft product.

(*e*) *Ease or simplicity of labour involved.*—Where abundance of cheap labour adequate to the work can be obtained, and particularly in trades where women and children are largely engaged, the development of machinery has been generally slower. This condition often unites with (*b*) or (*c*) to retain an industry in the "domestic" class. A large mass of essentially "irregular" work requiring a certain delicacy of manipulation, which by reason of its narrowness of scope is yet easily attained, and which makes but slight demands upon muscular force or intelligence, has remained outside machine-production. Important industries containing several processes of this nature have been slower to fall into the complete form of the factory system. The slow progress of the power-loom in cotton and wool until after 1830 is explained by these considerations. The stocking-frame held out against machinery still longer, and hand work still plays an important part in several processes of silk manufacture. Even now, in the very centre of the factory system, Bolton, the old hand-weaving is represented by a few belated survivors.[1]

(*f*) *Skilled Workmanship.*—High skill in manipulation or treatment of material, the element of art infused into handicraft, gives the latter an advantage over the most skilful machinery, or over such machinery as can economically be brought into competition with it. In some of the metal trades, in pottery and glass-making there are many processes which have not been able to dispense with human skill. In these manufactures, moreover, more progress is attributable to specific inventions than to the adoption of the common machinery and motor-power which are not largely available in the most important processes.

§ 10. The new industrial forces first applied to the cotton

[1] Schulze-Gaevernitz, p. 140.

spinning of South Lancashire, and rapidly forcing their
way into other branches of the textile manufactures, then
more gradually transforming the industrial methods of
the machinery, hardware, and other staple English manufactures, passed into the Western Continent of Europe
and America,[1] destroying the old domestic industry and
establishing in every civilised country the reign of steam-
driven machinery. The factors determining the order and
pace of the new movement in the several countries are
numerous and complex. In considering the order of
machine-development, it must be remembered that the
different nations did not start from an equal footing at
the opening of the age of great inventions. By the beginning of the eighteenth century England had established
a certain supremacy in commerce. The growth of her
colonial possessions since the Revolution and the drastic
and successful character of her maritime policy had enabled
her to outstrip Holland. Although, as we have seen, the
actual amount of foreign trade done in the eighteenth
century by the most advanced commercial nations bore a
very small proportion to their domestic trade, the expansion
of England's export trade in textiles was so rapid as to play
an important part in stimulating not only the new machine
processes in these trades, but indirectly the development
of iron and shipbuilding. In 1729 by far the greater part
of the Swedish iron exported from Gothenburg went to
England for shipbuilding purposes.[2] At the close of the
seventeenth century Gregory King placed England, Holland, and France at the head of the industrial nations with
regard to the productivity of their labour.[3] Italy and

---

[1] "It was not until about 1840 that the factory method of manufacture extended itself widely to miscellaneous industries, and began
rapidly to force from the markets the hand-made products with
which every community had hitherto chiefly supplied itself. It
seems probable that until about the year 1850, the bulk of general
manufacturing done in the United States was carried on in the
shop and the household, by the labour of the family or individual
proprietors, with apprentice assistance." (*Twelfth Census*, vol. vii.
p. 53.)

[2] Yeats, *The Growth and Vicissitudes of Commerce*, p. 284.

[3] The average income for England in 1688 he puts at £7 18s.;
for Holland, £8 1s. 4d.; France, £6—p. 47. Such an estimate,
however, has little value.

Germany were little behind in the exercise of manufacturing
arts, though the naval superiority and foreign possessions
of the above-named nations gave them the commercial
superiority. By 1760 England had strengthened her position as regards foreign commerce, and her woollen industry
was the largest and most highly-developed industry in the
world. But so far as the arts of manufacture themselves
were concerned there was no such superiority in England
as to justify the expectation of the position she held at the
opening of the nineteenth century. In many branches of
the textile arts, especially in silk spinning and in dyeing, in
pottery, printing, and other manufactures, more inventive
genius and more skill were shown on the Continent, and
there seemed *à priori* no reason why England should outstrip so signally her competitors.

The chief factors in determining the order of the development of modern industrial methods in the several countries
may be classified as natural, political, economic.

(*a*) NATURAL. (1) *The structure and position of the several
countries.* — The insular character of Great Britain, her
natural facilities for procuring raw materials of manufacture
and supplies of foreign food to enable her population to
specialise in manufacture, the number and variety of easily
accessible markets for her manufactures, gave her an immense
advantage. Add to this a temperate climate, excellent internal communication by river (or canal), and an absence
of mountain barriers between the several districts. These
advantages were of greater relative importance before steam
transport, but they played a large part in facilitating the
establishment of effective steam transport in England.
Extent of sea-board and good harbourage have in no small
measure directed the course of modern industry, giving to
England, Holland, France, Italy an advantage which the
levelling tendency of modern machinery has not yet been
able to counteract. The slow progress of Germany until
recent years, and the still slow progress of Russia, is
attributable more to these physical barriers of free communication, internal and external, than to any other single cause
that can be adduced. Inherent resources of the soil,
quality of land for agriculture, the proximity of large supplies of coal and iron and other requisites of the production
of machinery and power rank as important determinants

of progress. The machine development of France in particular has been retarded by the slow discovery of her natural areas of manufacture, the districts where coal and iron lie near to one another in easily accessible supply. The same remark applies to Germany and to the United States. At the close of last century, when the iron trade of England was rapidly advancing, the iron trade of France was quite insignificant, and during the earlier years of the nineteenth century the progress was extremely slight.[1]

(2) *Race and National Character.*—Closely related to climate and soil, these qualities of race are a powerful directing influence in industry. Muscular strength and endurance, yielding in a temperate climate an even continuity of vigorous effort; keen zest of material comfort stimulating invention and enterprise; acquisitiveness, and the love of external display; the moral capacities of industry, truth, orderly co-operation; all these are leading factors determining the ability and inclination of the several nations to adopt new industrial methods. Moral qualities in English workmanship have indisputably played a large part in securing her supremacy. "A British trade-mark was accepted as a guarantee of excellence, while the products of other countries were viewed with a suspicion justified by experience of their comparative inferiority."[2] The more highly civilised nations have thus gained by this civilisation, and have widened the distance which separates them from the less civilised. England, France, Germany, Holland, and the United States are in wealth and in industrial methods far more widely removed from Spain and Russia than was the case a hundred years ago.

(*b*) POLITICAL.—Statecraft has played an important part in determining the order and pace of industrial progress. The possession of numerous colonies and other political attachments in different parts of the world, comprising a large variety of material resources, gave to England, and in a less measure to France, Holland, Spain, a great advantage. The tyrannical use these nations made of their colonies for

---

[1] In 1810 the total produce was 140,000 tons.
   „ 1818   „   „   „   114,000 „
   „ 1824   „   „   „   164,000 „
   (Scrivener, *History of the Iron Trade*, p. 153.)
[2] Yeats, *Growth and Vicissitudes of Commerce*, p. 285.

the purpose of building up home manufactures enabled them to specialise more widely and safely in those industries to which the new methods of production were first applied. Even after the North American colonies broke loose, the policy of repression England had applied to their budding manufactures enabled her to retain to a large extent the markets thus created for her manufactured goods.

The large annexations England made during the eighteenth and early nineteenth centuries gave her a monopoly of many of the finest markets for the purchase of raw materials and for the sale of manufactured goods. The large demand thus established for her textile and metal wares served not only to stimulate fresh inventions, but enabled her to utilise many improvements which could only be profitably applied in the case of large industries with secure and expanding markets.

But the most important factor determining the priority of England was the political condition of continental Europe at the very period when the new machinery and motor-power were beginning to establish confidence in the new industrial order. When Crompton's mule, Cartwright's power-loom, Watt's engines were transforming the industry of England, her continental rivals had all their energies absorbed in wars and political revolutions. The United States and Sweden were the only commercial nations of any significance who, being neutral, obtained a large direct gain from the European strife. Yet England, in spite of the immense drain of blood and money she sustained, under the momentum of the new motor-power far outstripped the rivalry of such states. Though she had to pay a heavy price for her immunity from invasion, she thereby secured an immense start in the race of modern machine-production. Until 1820 she had the game in her own hands. In European trade she had a practical monopoly of the rapidly advancing cotton industry. It was this monopoly which, ruthlessly applied to maintain prices at a highly remunerative rate, and to keep down wages to starvation point, built up, in an age of supreme and almost universal misery for the masses, the rapid and colossal fortunes of the cotton kings. Not until peace was established did the textile and other factories begin to take shape upon the Continent, and many

years elapsed before they were able to compete effectively
with England. Switzerland was the first continental country
to actively adopt the new methods. The large supply of
water-power stood her in good stead, and the people took
more willingly to the factory system than in other countries.[1]
France was slower in her development, in spite of the strong
protective system by which she strove, though not very
successfully, to exclude English cotton goods. The fall of
English prices and profits in the cotton trade between 1820
and 1830 marks clearly the breakdown of the English
monopoly before the cheap labour of Alsace and the cheap
raw material of the United States, now organised in the
factory system with the new machinery.[2] In this, the most
advanced trade, the world-competition which now is operative
in a thousand different industries, measuring and levelling
economic advantages, first clearly shows itself, and in 1836
Ure finds the continental nations and America competing
successfully with England in markets which had hitherto
been entirely her own.

(c) ECONOMIC CONDITIONS.—The transformation of English agriculture, the growth of large farms, drove great
numbers of English peasants into the towns, and furnished
a large supply of cheap labour for the new machinery.

This movement was accelerated by the vices of our land
tenure. In France and Germany, where the agricultural
workers had a stronger interest and property in their land,
they were less easily detached for factory purposes. But
in England, where the labourer had no property in the land,
reformed methods of agriculture and the operation of the
Poor Law combined to incite the large proprietors and
farmers to rid themselves of all superfluous population in
the rural parts and accelerated the migration into the towns.

[1] Schulze-Gaevernitz, *Der Grossbetrieb*, p. 48.
[2] Ellison, *History of the Cotton Trade*, presents the following interesting table (yarn, 40 hanks to the lb.) :—

	1779.		1784.		1799.		1812.		1830.		1882.	
	s.	d.	s.	d.	s.	d.	s.	d.	s.	d.	s.	d.
Selling price .	16	0	10	11	7	6	2	6	1	2½	0	10½
Cost of Cotton (18 oz.) .	2	0	2	0	3	4	1	6	0	7¾	0	7⅛
Labour & Capital	14	0	8	11	4	2	1	0	0	6¾	0	3⅜

Here the population bred with a rapidity hitherto unknown.
The increase of population in England and Wales during
the thirty years from 1770 to 1800 is placed at 1,959,590,
or 27$\frac{1}{10}$ per cent., while during the next thirty years, 1800
to 1830, it amounted to 5,024,207, or 56$\frac{3}{8}$ per cent.[1] This
large supply of cheap labour in the towns enabled the
Lancashire and Yorkshire factories to grow with startling
rapidity. The exhaustion left by the Napoleonic wars, the
political disorder and insecurity which prevailed on the
Continent, retarded until much later the effective competition of other European nations who were behind England
in skill, knowledge, and the possession of markets. The
American manufactures which had sprung up after the
revolution had made considerable strides, but the conquest
and settlement of vast new areas of land, and the immense
facilities afforded for the production of raw material, retarded
their rate of growth until long after the opening of this
century. It was, indeed, not until about 1845 that the
cotton manufacture made rapid strides in the United States.
During the twenty years previous the progress had been
very slight, but between 1845 and 1859 a very substantial
and, making allowance for fluctuations in the cotton crops,
a very steady growth took place.[2]

Another great economic advantage which assisted England was the fact that she, more than any other European
nation, had broken down the old industrial order, with its
guilds, its elaborate restrictions, and conservative methods.
Personal freedom, security of property, liberty to work and
live where and how one liked, existed in England to an
extent unknown on the Continent before the French Revolution. The following account of the condition of the
cotton manufacture in Germany in the eighteenth century
will serve to indicate the obstacles to the reformed methods
of industry:—"Everything was done by rule. Spinning
came under public inspection, and the yarn was collected
by officials. The privilege of weaving was confined to the
confraternity of the guild. Methods of production were
strictly prescribed; public inspectors exercised control.
Defects in weaving were visited with punishment. Moreover,

---

[1] Porter, *Progress of the Nation*, p. 13. Eighteenth century figures
are, however, not trustworthy. The first census was in 1801.
[2] Ure, *Philosophy of Manufactures*, p. 531.

the right of dealing in cotton goods was confined to the
confraternity of the merchant guild: to be a master-weaver
had almost the significance of a public office. Besides
other qualifications, there was the condition of a formal
examination. The sale also was under strict supervision; for a long time a fixed price prevailed, and a
maximum sale was officially prescribed for each dealer.
The dealer had to dispose of his wares to the weaver,
because the latter had guaranteed to him a monopoly of
the export trade."[1]

Under such conditions the new machine-industry could
make little advance. Excepting in the case of the woollen
industries, England had for the most part already shaken
off the old regulations before 1770. In particular, the
cotton trade, which was in the vanguard of the movement,
being of recent growth and settling outside the guild towns,
had never known such restrictions, and therefore lent itself
to the new order with a far greater facility than the older
trades. Moreover, England was free from the innumerable
and vexatious local taxes and restrictions prevalent in
France and in the petty governments of Germany.
Although the major part of these foolish and pernicious
regulations has been long swept away from Germany and
other continental nations, the retarding influence they
exercised, in common with the wider national system of
protection which still survives, kept back the cotton
industry, so that in Germany it still stands far behind its
place in England.[2]

The following figures show how substantial was the lead
held by England in the cotton manufacture a little before
the middle of the century.

---

[1] Schulze-Gaevernitz, *Der Grossbetrieb*, p. 34.

[2] In 1882 42 per cent. of the German textile industry was still conducted in the home or domestic workshop, while only 38 per cent. was
carried on in factories employing more than 50 persons. More weavers
were still engaged with hand-looms than with power-looms, and the
latter was so little developed that the hand-loom could still hold its own
in many articles. Knitting, lace-making, and other minor textile industries are still in the main home industries.—(*Social Peace*, p. 113.)
"While in England in 1885 each spinning or weaving mill had an
average of 191 operatives, each spinning mill in Germany in 1882
employed an average of 10 persons only."—(Brentano, *Hours, Wages,
and Production*, p. 64.)

NUMBER OF SPINDLES WORKING IN COTTON MILLS IN 1846.[1]

	Spindles.
England and Wales . . .	15,554,619
Scotland	1,727,871
Ireland	215,503
Austria and Italy . . .	1,500,000
France	3,500,000
Belgium	420,000
Switzerland	650,000
Russia	7,585,000
United States	3,500,000
States of the Zollverein .	815,000
	35,467,993

Making due allowance for the necessary inexactitude of such a table, it remains reasonable to suppose that Great Britain in the middle of the century was doing half the cotton spinning for the civilised world.

Lastly, the national trade policy of England was of signal advantage in her machine development. Her early protective system had, by the enlargement of her carrying trade and the increase of her colonial possessions, laid the foundation of a large complex trade with the more distant parts of the world, though for a time it crippled our European commerce. While we doubtless sacrificed other interests by this course of policy, it must be generally admitted that " English industries would not have advanced so rapidly without Protection."[2] But as we built up our manufacturing industries by Protection, so we undoubtedly conserved and strengthened them by Free Trade—first, by the remission of tariffs upon the raw materials of manufacture and machine-making, and later on by the free admission of food stuffs, which were a prime essential to a nation destined to specialise in manufacture. France, our chief national competitor, weakened her position by a double protective policy, not merely refusing admittance to foreign manufactures in her markets, but retaining heavy duties upon the importation of foreign coal and iron, the foundational constituents of machine-production. This protective policy, adopted by nations whose skill, industry, and natural resources would have rendered them formidable competitors

[1] Ure, *Philosophy of Manufactures*, p. 515.
[2] Toynbee, *Industrial Revolution*, p. 79.

to English manufacturers, has hindered considerably the operation of those economic forces which impel old and thickly-peopled countries to specialise in manufacture and trade, and so has retarded the general development of modern machine-production. But while protective tariffs indisputably operate in this way, it is not possible to determine the extent of their influence. In a large country of rich resources a high degree of specialisation in manufacture is possible in spite of a protective policy. The pressure of high wages is an economic force more powerfully operative than any other in stimulating the adoption of elaborate machinery.[1] Both in the textile and the iron industries the United States present examples of factory development more advanced even than those of England. Certain processes of warping and winding are done by machinery in America which are still done by hand labour in England.[2] The chain and nail-making trades, which employ large numbers of women in South Stafford-shire and Worcestershire, are conducted more cheaply by machinery in America.[3] Moreover, the high standard of living and the greater skill of the American operatives enables them to tend more machines. In German factories a weaver tends two, or rarely three looms; in Lancashire women weavers undertake four, and in Massachusetts often six looms, and sometimes eight.[4]

Thus we see how the new industrial forces were determined in the order of their operation by the character and conditions of the several countries, their geographical position and physical resources, the elements of racial character, political and industrial institutions, deliberate economic policies, and, above all, by the absorbing nature of the military and political events contemporary with the outburst of inventive ingenuity. The composition of these forces determined the several lines of less resistance along which the new industry moved.

The exact measurement of so multiform a force is

[1] The highly elaborate American machine industry of watch-making is a striking example of this influence of high wages. Cf. Schulze-Gaevernitz, *Social Peace*, p. 125.

[2] Schoenhof, *Economy of High Wages*, p. 279.

[3] *Ibid.*, pp. 225, 226.

[4] Schulze-Gaevernitz, p. 66 (note). This six and eight-loom weaving is, however, at a lower speed.

impossible. It seems desirable, however, to make some comparative statement of the level of modern industrial development attained by the chief civilised nations of the world. With this object certain criteria of material progress have been selected, the principal branches of the mining industry, the iron and steel trade, and the most important of the textile trades; transport is best represented by the statistics of railroads and shipping. In regard to the true industrial development of a country, consumption is, however, in reality more instructive than production; we have therefore added certain figures measuring the comparative consumption of certain staple commodities by the chief industrial nations. Finally, a selection has been made of comparative statistics of occupations made from recent official publications of the Board of Trade. The appended tables and diagrams, however, will serve to indicate (1) the comparative development of the chief industrial nations in certain leading branches of industry and of consumption; (2) the absolute size of certain national industries :—

COMPARATIVE TABLE, PRODUCTION AND CONSUMPTION.[1]

(Per caput of the respective populations.)

	Exports (domestic merchandise).	Railways (mileage per 10,000).	Steel (production tons per caput).	Wheat (consumption lbs. per caput).	Pig Iron (consumption tons per caput).	Coal (per tons caput).	Raw Cotton (bales).
United Kingdom .	£6.8	5.28	0.12	350	0.18	3.89	39
Russia . . .	0.6	—	0.014	145	0.02	0.15	3
U.S.A. . .	3.9	25.52	0.17	274	0.20	3.30	26
Austria-Hungary .	1.7	4.66	0.03	223	0.03	0.40	6
France . .	4.1	7.46	0.04	473	0.06	1.15	10
Italy . . .	1.7	—	—	283	—	0.15	9
Germany . .	3.9	6.4	0.11	200	0.14	2.70	13
Belgium . .	10.5	6.03	0.10	418	0.13	2.79	11

[1] Selected from Table in Cd. 1761, xxviii.

COMPARATIVE TABLE, PRODUCTION AND CONSUMPTION
PER CAPUT OF THE RESPECTIVE POPULATIONS.

EXPORTS, DOMESTIC MERCHANDISE, PER CAPUT.

U.Kingdom 6·8
Russia 0·6
U.S.A. 3·9
Austria Hungary 1·7
France 4:1
Italy 1·7
Germany 3·9
Belgium 10·5

RAILWAYS MILEAGE, PER 10,000 POPULATION.

U. Kingdom 5·28
U.S.A. 25·52
Austria Hungary 4·66
France 7·46
Germany 6·4
Belgium 6·03

STEEL PRODUCTIONS, TONS PER CAPUT.

U. Kingdom 0·12	
Russia 0·014	
U.S.A. 0·17	
Austria Hungary 0·03	
France 0·04	
Germany 0·11	
Belgium 0·10	

WHEAT CONSUMPTION, LBS. PER CAPUT.

U.Kingdom 350.
Russia 145.
U.S.A. 274.
Austria.Hungary 223.
France 473.
Italy 283.
Germany 200.
Belgium 418.

PIG IRON CONSUMPTION, TONS PER CAPUT.

U.Kingdom 0·18 Russia 0·02 U.S.A. 0·20 Austria.Hungary 0·03 France 0·06 Germany 0·14 Belgium 0·13

COAL, TONS PER CAPUT.

U.Kingdom 3·89
Russia 0·15
U.S.A 3 30
Austria.Hungary 0·40
France 1 15
Italy 0 15
Germany 2·70
Belgium 2·79

RAW COTTON (LBS.).

U. Kingdom 39 lbs
Russia 3 ..
U.S.A. 26 ..
Austria Hungary 6 ..
France 10 ..
Italy 9 ..
Germany 13 ..
Belgium 11 ..

TABLE OF OCCUPATIONS.[1] (000 OMITTED.)

	Cotton.	Woollen.	Mining.	Iron, Steel, Engineering.	Leather.	Paper.	Glass.	Bricks, Pottery.	Chemicals.	Population (000 omitted).
Great Britain, 1901	606	252	872 (1903)	1,198	384	74	33	136	58	41,455
U.S.A., 1900	331	135	518[2] (1902)	1,150	329	72	61	122	141	77,647
Germany, 1895	255	262	609 (1902)	1,115	555	85	58	223	97	57,086
France, 1896	187	214	181 (1902)	573	323	52	39	80	43	38,962
Russia, 1897	360	151	377 (1900)	432	37	47	36	88	32	135,000
Holland, 1899	23	8	—	62	40	4	3	7	3	5,263
Belgium, 1896	20	23	136 (1902)	119	58	9	23	23	12	6,800
Switzerland, 1901	26	4	—	35	9	7	1	7	4	3,335
Austria, 1900	111	53	74 (1902)	370	238	17	41	70	13 (1890)	26,151
Sweden, 1901	11	11	—	60	6	14	6	70	9	—
Italy, 1901	171	78	63 (1902)	324	407	20	8	13	16	32,475
Japan, 1902	72	11	—	33 (imperfect)	—	7	—	37	—	44,710
India, 1903	178	3	—	—	—	5	—	—	—	—

[1] Compiled from Memorandum XVII. in Cd. 2337.   [2] Coal only.

GROWTH OF WORLD'S PRODUCTION OF COAL.[1]

	Average Annual Increase of Coal Production. Short tons of 2000 lbs. (000 omitted).			Actual Total Quantity in 1900.	Percentage Rate of Increase.		
	1870 to 1880	1880 to 1890	1890 to 1900		1870 to 1880	1880 to 1890	1890 to 1900
U.S.A. ...	3,468	8,623	11,191	269,683	94	121	71
Great Britain	4,092	3,880	4,879	252,203	33	24	24
Germany[2] ...	2,767	3,322	6,641	164,805	74	51	67
France ...	682	741	806	36,812	47	35	28
Austria ...	711	1,401	1,269	43,011	77	86	42
Belgium ...	352	384	340	25,856	23	21	15
Russia ...	283	306	1,117	17,799	385	85	168
Japan ...	—	292	526	8,187	—	—	180
Spain ...	—	1,336	134	2,947	—	—	120
Italy ...	9	26	11	530	137	170	27
India ...	1,000[3]	144	244	6,853	—	144	189
Canada ...	1,425[3]	143	312	5,322	—	119	71
New S. Wales	67	179	274	6,168	69	109	80
N. Zealand ...	336[3]	38	51	1,225	—	142	72
Queensland ...	4	31	18	557	160	483	47
Other Countries }	176	389	422	4,082	—	121	8

COAL.—Quantity of tons produced in 1900:—

Great Britain ...	...	252,000,000
U.S.A.	...	...	270,000,000
Germany	...	...	165,000,000
France	...	...	37,000,000
Austria	...	...	43,000,000
Belgium	...	...	26,000,000
Japan	...	...	8,000,000

STEEL.—Quantity of tons produced in 1901:—

Great Britain ...	...	4,904,000
U.S.A.	...	...	13,474,000
Germany	...	...	6,394,000
France	...	...	1,425,000
Austria	...	...	1,500,000
Belgium	...	...	653,000

[1] *British Industries under Free Trade* (edited Harold Cox), p. 351. Fisher Unwin.   [2] Including lignite.
[3] Total production in 1890; not increase over the decade.

SHIPBUILDING.—Tonnage of vessels of 100 tons and over, built 1900, as recorded in Lloyd's Register Book:—

U.K.	... ...	1,459,407
U.S.A.	... ...	297,931
Germany	... ...	211,850
France	... ...	101,318
Austria	... ...	14,945
Belgium and Holland	...	39,793
Japan	... ...	13,335

MERCHANT NAVIES OF THE CHIEF MARITIME NATIONS.

In millions of tons (steam and sailing tons together).

Year.	U.K.	Brit. Poss'ns.	Germany.	U.S.A.	France.	Norway.	Italy.	Japan.
1850	3.6	0.7	—	1.6	0.7	0.3	—	—
1860	4.6	1.0	—	2.5	1.0	0.5	—	—
1870	5.7	1.4	0.9	1.5	1.1	1.0	1.0	—
1880	6.6	1.9	1.2	1.3	0.9	1.5	1.0	0.1
1890	8.0	1.7	1.4	0.9	0.9	1.7	0.8	0.1
1900	9.3	1.4	1.9	0.8	1.0	1.5	0.9	0.8
1901	9.6	1.5	2.1	0.9	1.1	1.5	1.0	0.9
1902	10.0	1.5	—	0.9	—	—	—	—

MERCHANT STEAMSHIPS OF CHIEF NATIONS IN 1901.

			Tons.
U.K.	...	...	7,617,793
British Possessions	...	...	571,836
Germany	...	...	1,506,659
U.S.A.	...	...	429,722
France	...	...	546,541
Norway	...	...	531,142
Italy	...	...	424,711
Japan	...	...	583,067

[Chiozza-Money, *Elements of the Fiscal Question*, pp. 166, 167.]

CHAPTER V.

SIZE AND STRUCTURE OF THE MODERN BUSINESS.

§ 1. *General measure of growth of Business-structure.*
§ 2. *Evidence of the relative Economy of large and small Businesses in United States.*
§ 3. *Testimony from Great Britain, Germany, and France.*
§ 4. *Concentration in Transport Industry.*
§ 5. *Concentration in Banking and Insurance.*
§ 6. *Concentration in Distributive Processes.*
§ 7. *Concentration in Agriculture.*
§ 8. *Survival of small Farms.*
§ 9. *Summary of mechanical tendencies.*
§ 10. *Economies of Productive Power in large Businesses.*
§ 11. *Economies of Competitive Power.*
§ 12. *Survival of small Businesses.*
§ 13. *The morbid survival of small Sweating Businesses.*
§ 14. *General Summary of the opposed tendencies.*
§ 15. *The typical magnitude of a Business.*

§ 1. How far can we trace in modern industry a general tendency to the formation of larger business-units in which capital plays a relatively more important part than labour, and which tend to displace competition by various forms of trade agreement or by amalgamation?

Of the growth in the size of businesses, the increasing importance of capital, and the diminishing number of businesses in a trade, we have statistical evidence relating to certain fields of industry.

The largest mass of evidence is presented in the Comparative Summary taken of the Twelfth Census of the United States relating to manufactures. We have there a comparison of the general conditions of manufacturing development during recent decades and of the several departmental and local divisions of manufacture. Although

8

certain changes in modes of enumeration on the one hand, and difficulties of accurate ascertainment on the other hand, impair the exactitude of the figures,[1] these errors are not large enough to invalidate the general results of the investigation.

Year.	Number of Establishments.	Capital.	Number of Wage-earners.	Value of Products.
1900	512,191	$9,813,834,310	5,306,143	$13,000,149,159
1890	355,405	6,525,050,759	4,251,535	9,372,378,843
1880	253,852	2,790,272,606	2,732,595	5,369,579,191

From this table it appears that in the United States the average size of a business alike in capital and labour is growing, that the factor of capital is growing faster than that of labour, while the value of the product though larger per business unit[2] barely keeps pace with the growth of labour and falls far short of the growth of capital.

It is quite evident that these figures do not support any general judgment of the rapid concentration of capital throughout the manufacturing industries of America. Bearing in mind the growth of industrial combination which has given a few huge businesses command of a large proportion of the market in many manufactures, we must recognise in this growth of the number of separate establishments, a growth twice as fast as that of the American population,[3] a striking proof of the increase of small manufacturing establishments.

§ 2. If in the group analysis of manufactures[4] we turn to the groups where capitalist methods have made most advance, the textile, food, iron, steel and metal industries,

---

[1] Comparisons between the Censuses of 1890 and 1900 are more valid than those between 1880 and 1890, especially as regards capital. A new method of computing the number of employees in 1900 results in some variation of the average numbers as between the two censuses. Moreover, classes of "overseers and foremen" included in 1890 are excluded from "wage-earners" in 1900.

[2] The total number of manufacturing establishments increased by 101.8 per cent. between 1880 and 1900, while the total value of the product increased 142.2 per cent.

[3]   PERCENTAGE OF INCREASE.

	Population.	Manufacturing Businesses.
1890 to 1900 ...	20.7 ...	44.1
1880 to 1890 ...	24.9 ...	40.0

Abstract of the Twelfth Census.   Table 156.

leather, paper and printing, chemicals and vehicles, we still find that, while the amount of capital per business is considerably greater, and the amount of labour somewhat greater, the aggregate increase of establishments grows at least as fast as the population (except in the leather trades), while the growth of the value of the product, though somewhat greater than the growth in the number of businesses, fails in every such group to keep pace with the growth of capital.

In these pre-eminently capitalistic industries there is overwhelming testimony to a strong survival and growth of small plants as a counter-tendency to concentrative capitalism. The textile industries, to which machine-industry and capitalist methods were earliest applied, exhibit in a marked degree these cross-tendencies, as the following statistics indicate :—

	Number of Establishments.	Capital.	No. of Workers.	Value of Product.
1900	30,048	$1,366,604,058	1,029,910	$2,273,880,877
1890	16,847	1,008,050,268	824,138	1,636,197,191
1880	14,137	594,922,734	710,493	1,171,165,325

If instead of taking the entire area of the United States we confine ourselves to the North Atlantic division, which contains the largest proportion of developed manufactures, there is no marked difference in the tendencies.

	Number of Establishments.	Capital.	No. of Workers.	Value of Product.
1900	204,265	$5,299,725,076	2,772,117	$6,498,058,774
1890	162,796	3,548,288,553	2,317,736	4,896,743,650
1880	112,680	1,719,212,222	1,692,016	3,106,053,580

Narrowing our inquiry yet further to the most manufacturing of all the States, Massachusetts, we still find that, in spite of the large growth of capital per business, the number of establishments grows apace, increasing in fact faster than the number of employees, and exhibiting a smaller average value of product per business-unit.

	Number of Establishments.	Capital.	No. of Workers.	Value of Product.
1900	29,180	$823,264,287	499,448	$1,035,198,989
1890	26,923	630,032,341	447,270	888,160,403
1880	14,352	303,806,185	352,255	631,135,284

Finally, if we accept Mr. Edward Atkinson's analysis of

the Census results relating to the typical manufactures of textiles, boots and shoes, in Massachusetts, we have a measure of the relative status of large and small establishments, which is certainly unfavourable to the economy of the former, indicating as it does the superior economy both of capital and labour in the smaller plants.

TEXTILES, BOOTS AND SHOES.

	Collective.		Individual.
No. of establishments	1,078	...	28,102
Machinery and tools (per establishment)	$76,400	...	$4,200
Average number of workers ...	186	...	10.37
Average earnings	$393	...	$503
Average product per person ...	$1,528	...	$2,500

Taking the manufacturing industries of the United States as a whole, there seems overwhelming proof that no general tendency exists favourable to the substitution of great factories for small workshops and home industry.

In many particular industries, or branches of industries, the law of the economy of large establishments is doubtless plainly operative. But in the textile and shoe trades, as in many others where the factory system has been fully developed, this system only absorbs a certain section of the trade, leaving to smaller workshops or individual workers much of the best and the worst work, the former consisting in special orders or finishing processes where individual skill and care are required, the latter in low-grade routine work where "sweated" labour can undersell factory products.

If from such industries we turn to those which are entirely confined to factories we find strong testimony to the superior economy of large-scale production. Agricultural implements, a typical American machine-industry, will serve as an example. Here with an increasing capital and labour and a corresponding increase in value of product we find a diminishing number of establishments.

AGRICULTURAL IMPLEMENTS.

	No. of Establishments.	Capital.	No. of Workers.	Value of Product.
1900	715	$157,707,951	46,582	$101,207,428
1890	910	145,313,997	38,827	81,271,651
1880	1,943	62,109,668	39,580	65,640,486

In almost all the industries connected with iron and steel, the metal and machine-making manufactures, the same tendencies are visible; the number of establishments does not show any considerable increase, sometimes declines, while both capital and product are much larger than before.

The single great instance of iron and steel must suffice to illustrate this truth.

IRON AND STEEL.

	No. of Establishments.	Capital.	No. of Workers.	Value of Product.
1900	668	$573,391,663	222,490	$803,965,273
1890	645	372,678,018	148,715	430,954,348
1880	1,005	230,971,884	140,978	296,557,685

Almost all departments of brass work, cutlery, foundry supplies, hardware, the special iron and steel trades, jewellery, musical instruments, sewing machines, fire-arms, shipbuilding, come under this economy of large production; other trades conforming in a very marked degree to the same law are boots and shoes (factory products), bricks and tiles, carriages and cars, chemicals, clocks, cooperage, leather, saddlery, malt liquors, paper and wood pulp, pottery, soap and candles, smoking tobacco, umbrellas.

§ 3. In Great Britain, though no such large volume of ordered testimony is available, a large variety of evidence attests the operation of the same forces in the staple manufactures. In the fundamental textile and metal industries, in milling, brewing, chemicals, the leather, glass, pottery, paper and other machine industries, the size of a single plant and still more the size of a business has been growing, while the growth of the capital factor in the business exceeds that of the labour factor. Under domestic textile manufacture the value of the tools was, as a rule, equivalent only to a few months' wages. In 1845 McCulloch estimated that the fixed capital in well-appointed English cotton mills amounted to about two years' wages of an operative.[1] In 1890 Professor Marshall assigns a capital in plant amounting to about £200, or five years' wages, for every man, woman, or child engaged in a fully-equipped spinning mill.[2] The actual growth in the capital-size of a mill in the

---

[1] Porter, *Progress of the Nation*, p. 216.
[2] *Principles of Economics* (second edition), p. 282.

typical modern industry, the cotton trade, is illustrated by
the following estimate of the increase of the average number
of spindles and looms to a single factory between 1850 and
1885, though these figures take no account of the increased
speed and efficiency of the machines:—

		Spindles.		Looms.
1850	...	10,858	...	155
1885	...	15,227	...	213

Even these statistics do not fully represent the facts, for
they include a considerable number of mills of the older
sort, where spinning and weaving are carried on together.
Taking the more highly specialised spinning mills in the
Oldham district, Dr. Schulze-Gaevernitz found (1892) an
average of 65,000 spindles per mill, while the largest contained as many as 185,000. So also the average number of
power looms per mill in North Lancashire is placed at 600,
the largest number in a single mill being 4,500.

The growth of joint-stock enterprise here as elsewhere
has caused the size of the business to grow at a far faster
pace than that of the single plant.

The brewing trade, which within the last two generations
has passed almost entirely into the "company" business,
exhibits the concentrative tendency in a remarkable degree.

The following figures show the number of common
brewers, or "brewers for sale," as they are called, since
1850:—

1850	...	...	...	...	44,300
1860	...	...	...	...	39,948
1870	...	...	...	...	32,682
1880	...	...	...	...	21,346
1890	...	...	...	...	11,364
1900	...	...	...	...	6,447
1903	...	...	...	...	5,692

In Germany the brewing industry exhibits a similar
tendency to concentration, the number of breweries decreasing from 1,400 in 1872 to 1,050 in 1885, though a
large increase in production took place during this period.[1]

The comparative statistics of the Industrial Censuses of
Germany in 1882 and 1895 throw light upon the broad

[1] Cf. Ely, *Monopolies and Trusts*, p. 188.

tendencies in manufacture, showing that while the larger businesses grow at a faster pace the small businesses by no means tend to disappear, but on the contrary occupy an increasing proportion of the population.

While the growth of the population in this period amounted to 13.5 per cent. the comparative increase of small, moderate, and large establishments was as follows:—

	1882.	1895.	Increase per cent.
Small establishments (1 to 5 persons)	2,457,950	3,056,318	24.3
Moderate - sized establishments (6 to 10 persons)...	500,079	833,409	66.6
Large establishments (10 to 50 persons)	896,230	1,620,848	81.8

While no figures measuring recent tendencies in France are available, the Industrial Census of 1896 shows that "la grande industrie" has not made any great advance in general manufacture. Out of a total of 575,531 establishments, 461,354, or four-fifths of the whole number, comprised not more than three employees, while the number of great establishments with more than 500 employees amounted to no more than 446.

The distribution over the three main branches of employment runs as follows:—

	Agriculture Percentage.	Industry Percentage.	Commerce Percentage.
1 to 4 wage-earners ...	92.09 ...	85.03 ...	90.00
5 to 50 „ ...	7.89 ...	13.68 ...	9.82
50 to 500 „ ...	0.02 ...	1.21 ...	0.18
Over 500 „ ...	— ...	0.08 ...	—
	100	100	100

§ 4. It is, however, not to manufacture but to transport industry that we must look for the most conspicuous results of the concentrative influence of machinery. The substitute of the railroad for the pack-wagon and the stage-coach, of the steamship for the sailing-vessel, exhibits the largest advance of modern capitalism. "The cost of a steamship is perhaps equivalent to the labour of ten years or more of those who work her, while a capital of about £900,000,000 invested in railways in England and Wales is equivalent to the work of about twenty years of the 400,000 people employed on them."[1]   The fact that all privately-managed railroads, steam or electric, are joint stock enterprises, and that all sea-transport, with the exception of a diminishing proportion of the coast and river trade, has adopted the same typically capitalist form, testifies to the concentrative tendency in this department of industry.

§ 5. Next to transport the department of business where the concentrative forces are in strongest and most general operation is finance, using that term to cover banking and insurance, stockbroking, bill-broking, and money-lending of every kind.

These monetary businesses formed the cradle of modern capitalism: they were the earliest to adopt the form of joint stock enterprise, and to assume an international area of operation, capital expands in them out of all relation to labour, and the advantage of a large capital over a small capital is normally greater than in any other business operation.

The spread of an elaborate credit-system throughout the business world is in such close connection with improved machinery of communication that the whole of modern finance may be considered to rest upon a mechanical basis. In the creation and mobilisation of credit, by which the great mass of modern business transactions is conducted, the large financial business enjoys an obvious superiority. Large financial operations for governments and for industrial corporations can only be undertaken by great financial houses, and though detailed local or trade knowledge may form the basis for the survival of the small money-lender and the small broking-firm, the amount of financial independence enjoyed by smaller firms is always diminishing, so that they pass into the form of agencies or branches of some great finance company.

Bagehot, writing a generation ago, emphasised this tendency: " A large bank always tends to become larger, and a small bank to become smaller."   Since he wrote, the private bank has largely disappeared in Great Britain before the great joint stock banks, whose branches spread all over the country.   The deposits in British banks are estimated to

[1] Marshall (2nd ed.), p. 283.

have increased from £350,000,000 in 1875 to £859,000,000 in 1903, an increase of 147 per cent. in 27 years.[1] Between 1858 and 1903 the number of bank offices has grown from 2,008 to 6,592, entirely due to the extension of branch banking. Scotland, the earliest country to develop a general use of banking facilities, exhibits the closest concentration of banking industry. In 1883 she had ten banks with 912 branches, in 1896 ten banks with 1,015 branches. In England amalgamation is rapidly exterminating private and proprietory banks. Barclay's Bank has taken over 24 other businesses, Parr's as many, while Lloyd's has absorbed 38 other banking-houses.

A similar concentration of insurance business is everywhere discernible. Nowhere is the economic advantage of a large over a small capital so obvious as in the insurance business. The number of American life insurance offices has been steadily diminishing during the last quarter of a century, the smaller number doing an immensely larger business. In 1873 the number was 56, with an income of $118,396,502; and in 1897 the number was 35, with an income of $301,268,179.

§ 6. The concentrative forces in commerce are less easily ascertained; but, as regards wholesale operations, there can be no doubt that an increasing proportion of the distributive business is passing into the hands of large and growing firms. Over a considerable area of wholesale trade the separate mercantile stage has been eliminated, especially where the goods in question are raw materials or unfinished manufactures. Either the manufacturer purchases his materials direct from the producers by regular process of contract, or sets up producing plants of his own, as where jam manufacturers own fruit plantations or ironworks acquire collieries. In many other cases the producer supplies the retailer direct, as in the case of most patent or packet goods and over a large part of the clothing businesses; or undertakes the entire wholesale and retail distribution, as do certain shoe factories, collieries, etc. Most ordinary articles of manufacture are supplied to-day directly from the factories to the retailers. Where the wholesale merchant still remains as a distinct distributive

---

[1] *British Industries*, p. 91.

stage, he is usually either an importer of foreign produce or a collector of foods and other perishable home produce. Such businesses partake more and more of a speculative character, involving more largely the element of credit and becoming in most instances an appanage of finance. For successful business upon these lines, large capital is essential, and while the enormous growth of the commercial classes in all countries attests the mass of business done, this increase is in clerks, agents, commercial travellers, etc., not in the number of employers.

The application of joint stock enterprise to retail trading goes on apace. Gigantic stores, tending to become "universal providers," like Whiteley's and Barker's, or covering a wide area of wants, like Maple's or Spiers & Pond, spring up in the large cities, taking an increasing proportion of retail business. Other companies, more specialised, extend their business through numerous branches, as in the grocery and provision trades, milk, restaurants, fish, and game trades. In some of these cases the retail companies strengthen themselves by entering the productive processes of farming and manufacture; more frequently the manufacturers themselves acquire retail stores or operate through "tied" shops, as in the shoe, jewellery, and tobacco trades.

§ 7. All general measurements of the concentrative forces of capitalism as applied to agriculture are extremely difficult to compass.

In such countries, however, as the United States, where agricultural machinery has been very fully applied, it is clearly established that the size and value of farms increase in those departments of agriculture where machinery can be most largely utilised, and that the capital value of these farms as well as the value of the product increases more rapidly than the increase of labour employed upon them.

A careful monograph upon American agriculture recently published[1] shows that in the North Central States, which are most largely devoted to field crops, in the cultivation of which machinery is most developed, a considerable increase in the size of farms (including improved land only) has resulted, amounting to 26.4 per cent. for the decennium

---

[1] *The Influence of Farm Machinery on Production and Labour,* by H. W. Quaintance. Nov. 1904.

1880-90, and 41.8 per cent. for the two decennia 1880-1900.
In other divisions of the United States, where either a large
multiplication of negro farming, ensuant on the breaking of
plantations, has taken place, as in the South Atlantic and
South Central States, or where market-gardening and orchard
products form important and growing features, as in parts
of the North Atlantic and Western divisions, the tendency
of machinery to increase the area of the farm is either
entirely or partially counterbalanced by these forces making
for small culture.

But while these tendencies have kept the improved area
of an average farm for the United States as a whole from
increasing,[1] the capital value of an American farm and the
value per acre of its product are increasing tolerably fast.
The following table indicates this growth, and makes it
quite evident that American agriculture as a whole is being
brought by machinery into a form where capital performs a
more important and labour a relatively less important
part:—[2]

	Base.	1880.	1890.	1900.
Average value of all farm property . . .	$3,515 =	100	138.2	185.8
Average value of farms (land and improvements) . .	$2,835 =	100	138.6	189.0
Average value of implements and machines . . .	$136 =	100	111.0	152.9
Farmers, planters, and overseers	828,800 =	100	—	127.4
Agricultural labourers .	352,765 =	100	—	173.6

The fact that the employed or dependent class has increased 73.6 per cent. during the period 1880-1900, while
the employing or independent class has increased only 27.4
per cent., is a strong corroborative testimony to the growth
of the concentrative process.

[1] The actual size of farms (including unimproved lands) shows a
marked increase since 1880 as compared with a decline in the several
preceding decades.

[2] This decline in the importance of labour is made clearer by the
following figures from the Census:—

	1900.	1890.	1880.
Agricultural labourers . .	612,418	359,894	352,565
Farmers, planters, and overseers .	1,056,237	1,091,867	828,800
	1,668,655	1,451,761	1,181,365

Though much of the improvements in agriculture is due to better methods of cultivation, the use of fertilisers, irrigation, improved rotation, better seeds, etc., most of these are closely related to the use of modern machinery, which must be regarded as the representative agency of capitalism.[1]

The following table contains an estimate of the economy achieved in producing the crops where machinery is most largely used, expressed in units of time of man-labour:—

Unit No. 1.	Name and quantity of crop produced, and description of work done.	Year of Production.		Time Worked.			
				Hand.		Machine.	
		Hand.	Machine.	Hrs.	Min.	Hrs.	Min.
3	Barley: 30 bushels (1 acre) barley .	1829-30	1895-96	63	35.0	2	42.8
9	Corn : 40 bushels (1 acre) yellow corn, husked; stalks left in field	1855	1894	38	45.0	15	7.8
10	Cotton: By hand, 750 pounds; by machine, 1000 pounds (1 acre) seed cotton . .	1841	1895	167	48.0	78	42.0
12	Hay: Harvesting 1 ton (1 acre) timothy hay . . .	1850	1895	21	5.0	3	56.5
13	Oats: 40 bushels (1 acre) oats . . .	1830	1893	66	15.0	7	5.8
16	Potatoes: 220 bushels (1 acre) potatoes	1866	1895	108	55.0	38	—
17	Rice: 2,640 pounds (1 acre) rough rice	1870	1895	62	5.0	17	2.5
18	Rye: 25 bushels (1 acre) rye . . .	1847-48	1894-95	62	58.9	25	10.0
26	Wheat: 20 bushels (1 acre) wheat .	1829-30	1895-96	61	5.0	3	19.2

[1] Quaintance, p. 20.

The increased effectiveness of labour thus indicated varies from 150 per cent. in the case of rye to 2,244 per cent. in the case of barley, yielding an average increased productivity of about 500 per cent.[1]

§ 8. But while this concentrative force of machinery has been so strong in certain kinds of agriculture as to raise the average size of the farm as a unit of value and of productivity, it by no means follows that small farming everywhere tends to disappear. The reduced area of improved land per farm in every division except the North Central shows at any rate that capitalism in American agriculture does not generally imply large farms. In fact intensive and scientific as distinguished from merely mechanical cultivation everywhere makes for small farms, though involving in many cases an increased use of capital per acre. Uniform shape and character of land, a soil not so rich or so well-situated with regard to markets as to repay garden-culture, and yet sufficiently good and accessible to be worth cultivation by machinery, such are the conditions most favourable to large farming. In proportion as markets for the finer fruits, flowers, poultry, and other farm products which involve minute individual care and skill become relatively more important than the markets for staple crops and ordinary cattle, the forces making for large farms, or even for large capitalism in farming, will probably be diminished. Indeed, though in almost every branch of agricultural work machinery and other labour-saving contrivances are used to an increasing extent, this does not involve the elimination of the small, independent farmer. Though the great grain farm or ranche, worked with machinery and hired labour, is growing at such a pace as to weight the "average" for agriculture as a whole in this direction, this is quite consistent with a large growth of small farmers.

Recent evidence from Belgium throws an interesting light upon the conflicting tendencies in agriculture. While large estates have increased in number and in the proportion of the whole area of the country which they embrace, the number and the proportion of very small estates have grown still faster: the diminution has occurred in the intermediate sizes of property.[2] These small plots, however, it is main-

---

[1] Quaintance, p. 23.   [2] E. Vandevelde, *Modern Socialism*, p. 204.

tained, are not farms of small peasants, but strips of land
cultivated by industrial proletarians, who work them as
supplementary means of livelihood, either varying summer
work in agriculture with town wage-work in winter, or using
the land for allotments to be cultivated after a day's work
in the town.

While machinery favours the large as compared with the
middling farms, taken along with modern means of transport in a small, thickly-populated country like Belgium, it
drives the small peasant more and more into town industries.
The movement is thus summarised by M. Vandevelde:—
"What cannot be disputed is the progressive intensification
of agriculture, the development of the use of machinery—in
a word, the increase of fixed capital in comparison with
circulating (*i.e.*, in comparison with capital for paying manual
labour); agriculture is becoming industrialised; arable land
is turned into pasture; we see the multiplication of agricultural industries—distilling, sugar-making, the manufacture
of chicory, of syrups, etc.; and in consequence of this transformation, more and more of the population of the rural
districts is splitting into two quite distinct classes. You see
there a growing proletariat, made up of agricultural labourers,
who are the minority; industrial labourers, who go off daily
to work elsewhere; and what may be called half-and-half
labourers, half agricultural, half industrial, working in the
sugar factories at certain periods, harvesting at others, going
to the collieries in winter, to resume work in the fields in
the spring."[1]

§ 9. It is thus quite evident that economies of machinery
and power are operating in many fields of industry—

(1) To increase the size of the individual "plant" and
    "establishment," employing a larger co-operative
    unit of capital and labour to produce a larger
    "output."

(2) To increase the size and importance of capital in
    comparison with labour.

(3) To produce greater differentiation and specialisation
    of capital and labour, so as to give increased com-
    plexity to the business-unit.

This economy of machinery is furthest advanced in the

[1] *Modern Socialism*, p. 213.

staple manufactures where a large, regular demand for the same products exists, and where materials and methods are most capable of standardisation. A large and increasing share of the transport trades, where steam and electric power are utilised, comes under this same economy. The same tendency, less advanced, is operative over large parts of the mining industries, and over certain portions of agriculture. Wholesale trade is less amenable to the concentrative force of machine-economy, except so far as it involves the physical handling of large quantities of goods, while retail trade makes the smallest use of mechanical methods.

But this merely mechanical economy does not carry us very far in interpreting the concentrative tendency of capitalism. The increased size and complexity and "capitalist" nature of a single "plant" is represented by the growing cost and productivity of a modern textile or flour mill, as compared with the more primitive mill it displaces, or the superior carrying capacity of a modern railway train or steamship as compared with primitive vehicles. Now the true economic unit of capitalism is not the technical unit of a "plant," but the industrial and financial unit of the "business."

Except in a few instances, merely mechanical economy does not go very far towards explaining the larger development of the "business." Upon this mechanical economy is superimposed a series of other industrial, commercial, and financial economies favourable to the big business. Where and in proportion as these are operative we find a number of technically complete plants or establishments bound by a common control and ownership, and worked as a single business.

The great and growing size of many commercial, financial, and even retail distributive businesses makes it quite evident that machine-economy is not essential to the concentrative tendency of capitalism. Not only do vast businesses spring up, destitute of this foundation, but, as we have seen, in some manufactures a tolerably complex machine-plant forms the basis of small businesses.

While therefore it is important to enter upon an analysis of the economy of the large business by way of a study of mechanical efficiency, we must treat this as one element in a complex of economies favouring the large business. It is now necessary to make a formal statement of these elements, and to set against them other elements favouring the maintenance or increase of small businesses.

§ 10. The forces which are operating to drive capital to group itself in larger and larger masses, and the consequent growth of the business-unit, require special study in relation to changes effected in the character of competition in the market and the establishment of monopolies. The economies which give to the large business an advantage over the small business may be divided into two classes— economies of productive power, and economies of competitive power.

In the first class will be placed those economies which arise from increased subdivision of labour and increased efficiency of productive energy, and which represent a net saving in the output of human energy in the production of a given quantity of commodities, from the standpoint of the whole productive community. These include—

(*a*) The effort saved in the purchase and transport of raw materials in large quantities as compared with small quantities, and a corresponding saving in the sale and transport of the goods, manufactured or other. Under this head would come the discovery and opening up of new markets for purchase of raw materials and sale of finished goods, and everything which increases the area of effective competition and co-operation in industry.

(*b*) The adoption of the best modern machinery. Much expensive machinery will only "save labour" when it is used to assist in producing a large output which can find a tolerably steady market. The number of known or discoverable inventions for saving labour which are waiting either for an increase in the scale of production or for a rise in the wages of the labour they might supersede, in order to become economically available, may be considered infinite. With every rise in the scale of production some of these pass from the "nonpaying" into the "paying" class and represent a net productive gain in saved labour of the community.

(*c*) The performance of minor or subsidiary processes upon the same premises or in close organic connection with the main process, the establishment of a special workshop for repairs, various economies in storage, which attend large-scale production.

(*d*) Economies consisting in saved labour from increased efficiency of management, superintendence, clerical and other non-manual work, which follow each increase of size in a normally constructed business. These are often closely related to (*b*), as where clerical work is economised by the introduction of type-writers or telephonic communication, and to (*c*), as by the establishment of more numerous and convenient centres of distribution.

(*e*) Economy of place and space. The ability of a large business to utilise a given ground-area advantageously for productive work and for storage is often a great practical economy, measured financially by the smaller part rent occupies in establishment expenses. In retail trade where superficial "display" of goods, storage, and elbow-room are of prime importance, this is one of the chief factors favouring the large "store."

(*f*) The utilisation of waste-products, one of the most important practical economies in large-scale production.

(*g*) The capacity to make trial of new experiments in machinery and in industrial organisation.

§ 11. To the class Economies in Competitive Power belong those advantages which a large business enjoys in competing with smaller businesses, enabling it either to take trade away from the latter, or to obtain a higher rate of profits without in any way increasing the net productiveness of the community. This includes—

(1) A large portion of the economy in advertising, travelling, local agents, and the superiority of display and touting which a large business is able to afford. In most cases by far the greater part of this publicity and self-recommendation is no economy from the standpoint of the trade or the community, but simply represents a gain to one firm compensated by a loss to others. In not a few cases the "trade" may be advantaged to the damage of other trades or of the consumer, as when a class of useless or deleterious drugs is forced into consumption by persistent methods of self-appraisal which deceive the public.

(2) The power of a large business to secure and maintain the sole use of some patent or trade secret in machinery or method of manufacture which would otherwise have gone

9

to another firm, or would have become public property in the trade, represents no public economy, and sometimes a public loss. Where, however, such improvement is due solely to the skill and enterprise of a business man, and would not have passed into use unless the sole right were secured to his business, this economy belongs to the productive class.

(3) The superior ability of a large business to depress wages by the possession of a total or partial monopoly of local employment, the corresponding power to obtain raw material at low prices, or to extort higher prices from consumers than would obtain under the pressure of free competition, represent individual business economies which may enable a large business to obtain higher profits.

The better facilities of credit enjoyed as a rule by large firms must be accounted a separate economy. This economy is partly a productive advantage, implying a greater facility of expansion in business operations, partly a competitive advantage imparting greater freedom in processes of buying and selling and greater power in tiding over difficulties.

This particular economy is, of course, most important in financial businesses, next in large commercial businesses, playing however a considerable part in mining and manufacturing businesses, in proportion as the "speculative" factor is inherent in their conduct.

§ 12. When, as we perceive to be the case over large areas of industry, commerce, and other employments, the small business survives, this survival may be traced partly to the absence of some of these leading tendencies towards concentration, partly to the action of countervailing tendencies, positively favourable to the small form of business.

In considering the physical and economic limitations to the effective application of machinery we have already indicated certain economies of the small business. (1) Where the nature of the raw material or of the process of handling it is incalculably and greatly irregular this irregularity renders the full application of machinery and routine labour impossible. The kind or degree of this irregularity may be such as to make success in the business dependent so largely upon the skill, genius, character of the operator, or upon chance, as to preclude the use of machinery or of any sort of "routine" economy. The irregularity of material, if it relates to cheap products, may not suffice to defeat the net economy of the large business, though precluding the full use of machine methods. The irregularity in the shape, texture, etc., of hides does not prevent tanning from becoming an industry of big-businesses; nor does the irregular shape and quality of fruit keep the "canning" and "jam" trades in small businesses. But jewel cutting and setting, the most artistic grades of the clothing or dressmaking trades, of watchmaking and many other luxury trades where the choice and careful manipulation of fine qualities of expensive materials are concerned, tend to remain in small businesses. The most striking instance is in gold-mining, where individual digging remains for alluvial deposits while "banket" gold is mined by great companies.

The largest application of this principle is of course in agriculture. Small farms tend to survive in proportion to (a) the irregularity of soil, seed, climate, etc., and the consequent amount of detailed care and skill involved in the agricultural processes; (β) the absolute market value of the products, vegetable or animal, raised under such conditions.

Bonanza farms for growing great quantities of some single crop and applying machine methods may afford to disregard minor irregularities of soil, etc.; large cattle ranches, or even fruit farms, may for similar reasons be made to pay. But in raising the more delicate and costly plants or fruits, or in breeding the finest types of birds and animals, the factor of individual skill and interest is so important as commonly to outweigh all economies of large production.

(2) When the individuality of the consumer impresses himself upon an industry through demand for the satisfaction of particular needs, an "art" economy is substituted for a "routine" or "machine" economy. It is this force which, in large measure, gives importance to differences of materials, and evokes skill in dealing with them. But even where complete standardisation or regularity of materials exists, the demand of consumers for goods exactly accommodated to their individual fit or fancy involves skilled workmanship, and prohibits the use of machinery or routine method. This does not necessarily imply the execution of such orders by small businesses. A large pottery company often employs a number of designers and skilled craftsmen

in order to stimulate and supply the more refined demands of high-grade customers, just as a large firm of tailors or drapers may keep a special order department and a "fancy goods" department. But where the skill of some final process of production forms the chief element of use and of cost in a commodity, and especially when this output of skill approaches the nature of close personal service, the small unit of business is apt to survive. Though the ordinary work of photography may be passing to large companies, the more artistic work remains in the hands of independent artists. In London the best part of the clock-making, the saddlery and cabinetmaking trades remains in small businesses. Even when it is the "particular" demands not of consumers but of producers that are in question, the small business often holds its own, as in many of the minor metal trades of Birmingham.

Though the standardisation of machinery releases much work of repair from dependence on skilled engineers and smiths, while many large businesses keep repairing shops of their own, this essentially irregular work forms the basis of many small independent workshops in large manufacturing centres. Though the building and the printing trades are in the main large capitalist undertakings, jobbing builders, carpenters, plumbers, and printers exist in considerable numbers for special and emergency work.

In retail trade, as we have seen, the survival of the personal relation with "customers," the adhesion of some final productive process to the art of retail distribution, sometimes the importance of mere proximity, enable the small storekeeper to hold his own.

It is natural that the productive energy which functions for the production and distribution of material and immaterial wealth in the professions, the finer arts, and in the recreative and personal services, should be least amenable to the concentrative forces of capitalism. Though there is a sense in which the schools of law, medicine, theology, and pedagogy in our universities may be regarded as large capitalist enterprises—factory-plants for turning out and distributing legal, medical, religious, and other services—while the trade-organisations of the bar, the churches, the medical councils, etc., limit the liberty of professional men in their "practices," these considerations do not materially

impair the "business" independence of the ordinary clergy-
man or physician. The tendency towards the large
capitalist structure, though discernible in the teaching, the
legal, the medical, and especially the dental professions, does
not cover any large proportion of these professions and
reaches within a moderate compass a maximum economy.
In the recreative arts large capitalism has obtained a
stronger hold over some departments which involve a large
outlay of capital and a high order of business management.
Perhaps the intellectual art or profession in which the
centralising force is most powerful is journalism, though
even there the large capitalistic machinery of the press is
fed by an increasing number of small jobbers not closely
attached to any particular press.

All these small businesses in agriculture, the mechanical
trades, mining, retail trade, the arts and professions survive
because of certain features in the materials or processes
involved which give importance to those personal qualities
of skill, care, judgment, and character incapable of being
evoked, controlled, and applied effectively under the routine
economy of the large business. To these inherent advantages of the small business in the production and distribution
of certain high qualities of material and immaterial wealth,
must be added the independent spirit of the genuine artist
or craftsman, which, even in such largely routine work as
carpentry, shoemaking, or retail shopkeeping, is often
strong enough to induce a man to remain a small independent producer with a precarious unlucrative business
rather than become a mere cog in the capitalist machine.

§ 13. From these genuine economic survivals of the small
business-unit must be distinguished the numerous forms of
small sweat-shop and sweating home industry which are
found everywhere in the industrial lowlands. The characteristic of such small sweating businesses is the production
of low-grade routine goods by subdivided labour under
conditions of low wages, low rent, and evasion of sanitary
and other industrial restrictions which make this mode
of production cheaper than production in a factory by
machinery or by properly accommodated and protected
hand labour. Much of the production of the sweat-shop
consists of ill-made or shoddy goods which would not be
made at all except for the "demands" of the poorest class,

kept in poverty by the same economic maladies which furnish to these sweating trades their supply of cheap, inefficient labour; much of it would otherwise be done by machinery in factories, where the pay is higher, the hours shorter, and all the terms of employment better. This is the case, for instance, with most of the clothing and shoe manufactures of the sweat-shops. The rest, which though simple and not high skilled elude the full application of the machine by certain irregularities of detail—*e.g.*, flower-making, fur-pulling, packing, etc.—would become subsidiary departments of the major trades to which they belong. Though these sweating trades are rightly spoken of as "morbid" survivals of small businesses, as "parasitic" growths, they are natural products of the present stage of capitalism; for all the economic supports of these "low organisms"—the existence of a large margin of low-skilled "unemployed," the high rents which form a leading element of economy and the market for the debased products of the sweat-shop—can be traced to the unregulated operation of capitalist forces.

With the gradual development of a sounder social policy, expressed through public opinion and legislative action, these morbid growths may be excised from the industrial body. In this work of extirpation economic considerations are even more potent than philanthropic or sanitary ones, and it is probable that in England and America the proportion of these morbid to the healthy survivals of small businesses is diminishing, especially in the clothing trades, where machinery has made such large recent advances. At the same time, so long as cheap labour in considerable quantities is available, these parasitic trades will continue to appear anew, particularly in those industries to which season and fashion impart irregularity and where one economy of the sweat-shop consists in saving the waste incurred in factories by keeping machinery idle or half-used over considerable periods.

§ 14. But assuming that the sweating trades be left out of consideration, what general conclusion are we justified in forming as to the relative strength of the centripetal and centrifugal forces making respectively large and small businesses?

The industrial department in which the large capitalist business is most prevalent and where a growing tendency to concentration is most general is Transport. In all advanced industrial nations the carriage of persons, goods, news by railroads, steamships, pipe lines, telegraphic and telephonic services, has passed into the control of large companies: as the horse is more and more displaced by electric or oil traction for the subsidiary Transport services in town and country, this further mechanisation of transport favours the displacement of the small carrier and the private tradesman by the large company. Moreover, the relative importance of the transport trades, as indicated both by the quantity of capital and the quantity of labour employed, is growing rapidly and generally.

Among the extractive industries mining has become almost entirely a great capitalist business, and the increased use of machinery upon the one hand, the development of corporation finance upon the other, favour the absorption of this branch of industry by large company enterprise. The survival of small businesses in agriculture is widespread and persistent wherever small ownership or security of tenure prevails. The permanence of the small holding must, however, depend more and more upon the abandonment of certain elements of self-sufficiency, or otherwise upon the grafting of processes of large co-operative or corporate business upon the small farming economy. In Denmark, Switzerland, Belgium, Ireland, co-operation for dairying and other collecting and manufacturing processes, for the use of machinery, marketing, mutual credit, and education, are seen to be essential to the maintenance of small holdings. Without this co-operation the economic strength of the small holder or the tenant farmer is undermined by the carrying companies, the merchant-middlemen, and the money-lender, and in time he either is displaced by some large-farm system or becomes the mere dependent of one or other of the capitalist classes just named.

The fishing industry still continues to some considerable extent in small shapes, though the steam trawler and the large fish-merchant are bringing it more and more under large capitalism.

Most of the manufactures engaged upon the processes of making the foods, clothes, houses, and other prime necessaries and conveniences of life have passed or are passing into big capitalist businesses. While these staple manufactures employ an increasing proportion of capital, they do not, save in the less advanced nations, engage an increasing proportion of labour. Attached to each of them is a large quantity of manufacturing industries which remain in small businesses, and though the application of mechanical and other sciences continually displaces old handicrafts by large machine industries, while new industries arise capitalistic from their start, a large quantity of new irregular and highly skilled trades come into being, employing a large quantity of labour. It is by no means proved that an increasing proportion of manufacturing labour is employed in large businesses, or that the "labour-saving" economy of machinery is attended by so large a general expansion of manufacturing industry as to provide employment for all the labour that is "saved."[1]

While the concentrative forces are strong in wholesale commerce, the small dealer survives and even multiplies in most countries, though his economic independence is sapped in many trades by dependence on some large manufacturing or "furnishing" firm. Bearing in mind the growth of retail trading companies with many branches and the various forms of "tied" houses, it seems probable that a larger share both of the capital and the labour engaged is passing under large capitalism.

Banking, insurance, and other financial business is seen to be peculiarly adapted to the play of concentrative forces. In the civil arts, professions, and services which are growing so rapidly in the proportion of employment they afford, the small business very generally holds its own. The increase of labour and of capital employed in public services must, however, be accredited to the side of the large business.

It may then be concluded:—

(1) That an increasing proportion of the aggregate wealth (goods and services) in modern communities is produced in large and expanding businesses.

(2) That this concentrative tendency is particularly operative in the making and carrying of the goods which constitute the necessaries and prime conveniences of life of the people.

(3) That in the aggregate production of wealth capital

[1] On this point see Chapter XI.

plays a part of increasing importance as compared with labour.

(4) That the increasing importance of capital is greatest in the production of the most fundamental and essential forms of material wealth.

(5) That it is probable that an increasing proportion of the number of persons employed is employed in large or expanding business-forms, though the concentrative forces are less powerful in the case of labour than in the case of capital.

§ 15. But while a larger number of processes and industries are constantly brought under the operation of the concentrative forces which make for large business-units, there is no reason to regard the economy of large-scale production, as unlimited in any branch of production or transport.

Reverting to the recognised economic formula, there is no industry where the law of increasing returns permanently and absolutely overrides the law of diminishing returns. In any country in any given condition of industrial development there is for each industry a size of business where the maximum net economy is reached, and beyond which, unless supported by a legal or a natural basis of monopoly, it cannot grow.

In many manufacturing processes which have attained a high degree of mechanical development the maximum economy is soon reached, the unit of cheapest production representing a comparatively small annual output in tons, gallons, or other standard: the mere advantages of machinery and division of labour are soon exhausted. This limitation of the size of an individual plant is generally recognised. Of course where other economies besides those of the manufacturing process are taken into account, economies of purchase and of sale, of rent, establishment expenses, administration, advertising, etc., the profitable size of such a business may be considerably raised. But even the aggregate of these economies does not evade the law of diminishing returns. Not only for mechanical production but for administration of a business there is a point of maximum growth.[1]

[1] An experienced accountant in a large English midland manufacturing town writes to me as follows:—

"So far as I am able to judge from businesses I have been connected

Throughout industry businesses may be regarded as gravitating towards "a typical magnitude," which yields for the time being the maximum economy.

The final limits of this growth are described by a recent economist [1] as functions of:

(1) The internal complexity of arrangements.
(2) The importance of quality in the output.
(3) The expensiveness of the machinery used.
(4) External relations depending on the nature of the markets touched.
(5) Stability in the demand for the output.
(6) The stationary character of the industry in relation to methods or otherwise.
(7) The extent of the economies to be secured by producing on a large scale. [2]

If, however, we examine more closely the limits upon the economy of the large business, thus indicated, we shall perceive that they ultimately rest upon a law of diminishing returns, applied not to the mechanics but to the administration of business. Although there must be conceived to be an ultimate limit to the economy of large production dependent on the necessity of having recourse to inferior or more expensive sources of raw materials or power, this, save in rare instances, is not an actual limit. So, likewise, though the practical limits set upon the elaboration of machinery and the division of labour may fix the maximum size of an individual plant, it does not limit the size of a

with for years, and which are systematically increasing their output, far from its being possible to formulate a general rule that standing expenses diminish proportionately in relation to the output, I am inclined to think that they increase. I think there is a certain size (quickly attained in many businesses) at which everything is done most cheaply, and that, as the product goes on increasing, there is a slight relative increase in expense, due to the fact that mere size necessitates the doing of everything by rule, and the formation of separate departments, and a complicated system of checking and accounting generally, which tends to counterbalance, and which does in fact more than counterbalance, the advantage gained by size. There is also the intangible loss caused by the removal of direct responsibility, and this, I think, must account for a good deal."

[1] Professor S. J. Chapman, *The Lancashire Cotton Industry*, p. 169.
[2] This last economy is not separate from the rest, but appears to summarise them.

CHAPTER VI.

THE STRUCTURE OF TRADES AND MARKETS.

§ 1. *Differentiation of the Business Structure.*
§ 2. *Integration of Processes.*
§ 3. *Horizontal and Lateral Integration.*
§ 4. *Structure and Size of different Markets.*
§ 5. *Machinery a direct Agent in expanding Market Areas.*
§ 6. *Expanded Time-area of the Market.*
§ 7. *Interdependency of Markets.*
§ 8. *Sympathetic and Antagonistic Relations between Trades.*
§ 9. *National and Local Specialisation in Industry.*
§ 10. *Influences determining Localisation of Industry.*
§ 11. *Impossibility of Final Settlement of Industry.*
§ 12. *Specialisation in Districts and Towns.*
§ 13. *Specialisation within the Town.*

§ 1. In those industries where the business-unit grows in size it generally grows also in complexity of structure. This increased complexity is due partly to a process of differentiation within the business-unit, partly to a process of integration by which productive activities which formerly constituted separate businesses become departments of a single business.

The increasing differentiation or division of capital and labour due to the greater size and technical improvements of modern businesses is easily recognised. In a modern shoe factory there are about sixty distinct processes. Grain, in the elaborate machinery of the modern flour-mill, passes through a score of different stages, cleaning, winnowing, grinding, etc. The American machine-made watch is said to be the product of 370 separate actions. In an up-to-date textile factory a dozen different processes contribute to the spinning or weaving of cotton or silk, and new improvements or refinements of cleaning or finishing are always being added.

This process of differentiation is continually fed by the increased variety of demand due to an expanding market, involving larger variety in size, quality, and character of goods. Special classes of goods must be manufactured for Australia, Egypt, or Burma. New customers in China or Persia insist upon their cloth or hardware goods being made-up or packed in some familiar form long after the use or convenience of this form has passed away. The exigencies of keen competition requires constant experimentation in new lines of goods to touch the fancy of a newly opened market or to get away the trade of a competitor.

This differentiation of a business from within is often accompanied by a double course of integration, involving the absorption of various minor or subsidiary processes by some business performing a major process of production; or the expansion of some manufacturing or mercantile business taking on the production or sale of new kinds of goods which lay previously outside the limits of its business activity.

§ 2. Every industry is connected with a number of other industries engaged upon processes anterior to, subsequent to, or subsidiary to, the operation with which it is itself concerned : this creates a stable bond of common interest which forms a basis of integration. The most strongly organised and best developed of a series of business processes thus related tends frequently to absorb the others. So a modern steel-mill will often own its own smelting works and its own supply of iron-ore and coal, together with its own railway or line of boats for carrying the raw material. A cocoa or jam manufactory will own its own fruit plantations. In other cases the wholesale or the retail merchant takes the initiative, as when the English Co-operative Wholesale Society sets up cloth and shoe factories and imports its groceries on its own ships; or when a retail store like Whiteley's supplies fruits and dairy produce from its own farms. A railroad, as for instance the London and North Western, sometimes expands so as to be almost entirely self-sufficing, manufacturing its rails, rolling stock, etc., from its own stocks of materials, and making almost all the articles required for its service down to the wooden legs for the use of its crippled employees.

In the textile industries this integration is widely visible. In the woollen manufactures the preliminary processes of sorting and cleansing, carding or combing, as well as the main processes of spinning and weaving, fulling, dyeing, and finishing, each of which was at one time committed to a separate and independent group of workers, are frequently found going on simultaneously in a single factory.[1] This integration is, however, often qualified or crossed by a tendency to differentiation so strong as to detach a particular process and to set it up in business for itself. So in the Yorkshire woollen trade, whereas spinning and weaving are usually under the same roof, combing and fulling are often distinct, and "finishing" is usually done separately. The same conflicting tendencies are seen in the Lancashire cotton industry: all processes up to spinning are always united; twining is sometimes separate; spinning and weaving are sometimes united, sometimes not; dyeing is sometimes under the same management as spinning and manufacturing, sometimes committed to a dyer. Calico printing forms a separate business.[2]

In fact throughout the textile and metal manufactures we see clear signs of a double process of business differentiation opposing the process of integration in one direction, while assisting its advance in another. In the woollen trade, where strong differences of quality occur, there arises much specialisation, many businesses confining themselves to a particular class of goods, and absorbing all the processes involved in this special trade. Opposed to this specialisation of quality is the specialisation of processes exhibited in the "fulling" or "finishing" businesses which take work for a large number of the specialised mills. The cotton trade, as we shall see, develops in similar fashion by local differentiation of firms and coarser "counts" and various grades and types of manufacture.

The modern bicycle trade exhibits the conflict of the two tendencies most clearly in the struggle between the techni-

[1] A good deal of the cleansing and combing in the cloth and worsted trades is, however, done separately on commission by large firms such as Lister's (cf. Burnley, p. 417). In Germany "finishing" still remains a separate business process (cf. Chapman, *Foreign Competition*, p. 197).

[2] Chapman, *The Lancashire Cotton Industry*, p. 165.

cally complete factory turning out a whole machine of a particular type, and the factory confined to the production of a single part, suited for the structure of many types of machine.

So far as minor subsidiary processes are concerned, much integration is visible in all large manufactures. Wherever the demand is large and regular there is a tendency for packing, printing, box-making, etc., to be done on the premises; while engineering shops, carpenters' shops, chemical laboratories, are frequent appendages to a large modern factory.

Thus a number of small, relatively simple business-units, representing the various stages in the production and distribution of a commodity, come to group themselves into a large, complex business-unit.

§ 3. Though, as we see, there is in many trades a tendency to specialisation in quality of manufacture, a business confining itself to the many processes contributory to a single sort of commodity, in others the integration proceeds horizontally as well as laterally, a manufacturer or merchant extending the number of commodities in which he deals. This often happens where some community of raw material or of method of manufacture connects two different commodities. Hence a biscuit manufactory, like Messrs. Huntley & Palmer, expands its activity until it has absorbed a great variety of other food products, while a watchmaking business takes up electrical or surgical apparatus.

In retail trade this integrative tendency is widely operative. The modern grocer sells tinned meats, cakes, wine, teapots, and Christmas cards; the draper sells all sorts of ornamental wares; the stationer, oil-man, and china store set out an increasing miscellaneous lot of wares, advancing towards the position of "general dealer." The "Stores" and the Universal Provider represent the culmination of this movement in the retail business, returning to a more enlarged and complex form of the primitive "general shop" of the village.[1] Here, however, as elsewhere, the differentiating

---

[1] A similar reversion to a general primitive type is observed in some manufacturing businesses, e.g. cotton. "The weaver's cottage with its rude apparatus of jug-warping, hand-cards, hand-wheels, and imperfect looms, was the steam-loom factory in miniature." (Guest, *History of the Cotton Manufacture*, p. 47.)

tendency is sometimes dominant: fashionable shops devote themselves to special grades of gloves, hats, cigars or furs, while manufacturing or mercantile companies set up numerous branch shops for selling some single commodity, such as watches, bicycles, shirts, ready-made clothing, coffee, etc.

Wherever we turn in the industrial world we find the business-unit changing its form under the pressure of the integrating and the differentiating forces, sometimes taking on a wider range of activities, sometimes a narrower. As in manufacture and commerce, so in banking and finance. A modern bank has added various processes of money-lending and discounting which were alien to its early functions, while the modern bill-broker tends continually to become more highly specialised in the kind of bills which he discounts.

While, then, over a large field of business enterprise there exists a strong tendency towards increasing complexity of business structure, it is clear that this tendency is not of universal application even in distinctively capitalistic fields. Increasing size generally implies further division of labour and other increased differentiation even where no new lines of work are taken on. If a growing business, on the one hand, expands the variety of its products, and, on the other, takes on various antecedent or subsidiary processes hitherto independent, it may easily reach a stage of complexity which introduces larger risks of dislocation and waste from defective central control. We must therefore conclude that as for every class of business there exists at any given time a normal size of maximum efficiency, so there exists a normal degree of complexity.

Increased complexity generally proceeds with increasing size: where the capitalist forces are making for the production of routine goods and services upon a large-scale there we find the business-unit more heterogeneous and more highly integrated, partly as the result of differentiation from within, partly through taking on new lines of business activity from outside.

§ 4. Ascending from the business-unit to the larger unit in the structure of industry, the Market, or groups of directly competing businesses, we find similar changes have taken place. In considering these changes the relation between Market and Trade should be clearly grasped. The mere fact that two persons or groups of persons in different places are engaged in similar processes of production, that is to say, belong to the same trade, has no significance for us. The trade or aggregate of productive units of a particular sort receives industrial unity only in so far as there is competition of the units in buying the raw materials, tools, and labour for carrying on their trade, and in selling the results of their activity. Weavers of cotton goods in Central China belong to the same trade as weavers in Lancashire, and conduct their craft with similar implements to those which still prevail in the cottage industries of France and Germany, but such competition as may exist between them is so indirect and slight that it may be neglected in considering industrial structure. It is in the competition of a market that businesses meet and are vitally related. In a trade there may be several markets whose connection is distant and indirect. Market is the name given to a number of directly competing businesses. "Economists understand by the term market not any particular market-place in which things are bought and sold, but the whole of any region in which buyers and sellers are in such free intercourse with one another that the prices of the same goods tend to equalise easily and quickly."[1]

A single competitive price is then the essential feature and the test of a market. Businesses in such close relation with one another that the prices at which they buy and sell are the same, or differ only by reason of and in correspondence with certain local advantages or disadvantages, are members of a single market. The money market is a single market throughout the world. The price of money in London, Rome, Rio de Janeiro, may differ, but this difference will correspond to certain differences of risk. There will be a tendency towards a single price, or, putting the case in other words, wherever in the world £100 of money represents the same commodity the same price will be paid for its use, while any difference in its value as a commodity will be accurately reflected in the difference of price.

[1] Cournot, *Recherches sur les Principes Mathématiques de la Théorie des Richesses* (quoted Marshall, *Principles of Economics*, p. 384).

Absolute freedom of intercourse is not essential to the establishment of a common market. Market tariffs and other advantages and disadvantages may place the competitors on an unequal footing. Moreover, in order to form part of a market as helping to determine the price, a business need not actively enter the field of competition. Fear of the potential competition of outsiders often keeps down prices to a level above which they would rise were it not for the belief that such a rise would bring into active, effective competition the outsider. England had until recently a monopoly of the market for cotton goods in certain Eastern countries, but the price at which she sold was determined by the possibility of rival French or German merchants, as well as by the direct competition of the several English firms. In certain commodities the market is conterminous with the trade, that is, we have a world-market. This is the case with many of the forms of money, the most abstract form of wealth, and the most highly competitive.

Dealers in Stock Exchange securities and in the precious metals, are in active, constant competition at all the great commercial centres of the world. Other staple commodities, whose value is great, durable, and portable, such as jewels, wheat, cotton, wool, have to all intents and purposes a single market.

This world-market represents the fullest expansion due to modern machinery of transport and exchange, the railway, steamship, newspaper, telegraph, and the system of credit built up and maintained by the assistance of these material agents.

The market-area for various commodities varies with the character of these commodities, from the world-market for stock exchange securities down to the minimum market consisting of a few neighbouring farmers competing to sell their over-ripe plums or their skim-milk. The chief qualities which determine the market-area are—

(a) *Extent of demand.* — Things in universal or very wide demand, which are at the same time durable, such as money, wool, wheat, compete over very wide areas. Things specially accommodated to the taste or use of a particular locality or a small class of individuals will have a narrow market. This is the case with clothes of a particular cut, and with many kinds of fabrics out of which clothes are made. The market for certain classes of topographical books will be confined to the limits of a county, though the book market for some books is a world-market.

(*b*) *Portability.*—Even where the demand is far from a general one, the market-area may be very wide where high value is stored in small bulk. Smoking tobacco and more highly valued wines and liqueurs are examples of this order. The market for common bricks is local, though Portland marble finds a national market.

(*c*) *Durability.*—Durable objects and objects which can easily be brought within reach of modern means of rapid transport have a wide market. Perishable goods, as, for example, many fruits and vegetables, have for these reasons a narrow market.

§ 5. Modern machinery has in almost all cases raised the size of the market. The space-area of competition has been immensely widened, especially for the more durable classes of goods. It is machinery of transport—the transport of goods and news—that is chiefly responsible for this expansion. Cheaper, quicker, safer, and more calculable journeys have shrunk space for competing purposes. Improved means of rapid and reliable information about methods of production, markets, changes in price and trade have practically annihilated the element of distance.

Machinery of manufacture as well as of transport has a levelling tendency which makes directly for expansion of the area of competition. As the spread of knowledge places each part of the industrial world more closely *en rapport* with the rest, the newest and best methods of manufacture are more rapidly and effectively adopted. Thus in all production where less and less depends on the skill of the workers, and more and more upon the character of the machinery, every change which gives more prominence to the latter tends to equalise the cost of production in different countries, and thus to facilitate effective competition.

§ 6. Modern methods of production have also brought about a great expansion in the time-area of the market. Competition covers a wider range of time as well as of space. Production is no longer directed by the quantity and quality of present needs alone, but is more and more dependent upon calculation of future consumption. A larger proportion of the brain power of the business man is devoted to forecasting future conditions of the market, and a larger proportion of the mechanical and human labour to providing future goods to meet calculated demands. This expansion of the time-market, or growth of speculative production, is partly cause, partly effect of the improved mechanical appliances in manufacture and in transport. The multiplication of productive power under the new machinery has in many branches of industry far outstripped the requirements of present known consumption at remunerative prices, while increased knowledge of the widening market has given a basis of calculation which leads manufacturers to utilise their spare productive power in providing against future wants. So long as industry was limited by the labour of the human body, assisted but slightly by natural forces and working with simple tools, the output of productive energy could seldom outstrip the present demand for consumable goods.

But machinery has changed all this. Modern industrial nations are able to produce consumables far faster than those who have the power to consume them are willing to exercise it. Hence there is an ever-increasing margin of productive power redundant so far as the production of present consumptive goods is concerned. This excess of productive power is saved. It can only be saved by being stored up in some material forms which are required not for direct consumption but for assisting to increase the rate at which consumables may be produced in the future. In order to make a place for these new forms of saving it is necessary to interpose a constantly increasing number of mechanical processes between the earliest extractive process which removes the raw material from the earth and the final or retailing process which places it in the consumer's hands. New machinery, more elaborate and costly, is applied; special workshops, with machines to make this machinery— other machinery to make these machines; there is an expansion of the mechanism of credit, the system of agents and representatives is expanded, new modes of advertising are adopted. Thus an ever-widening field of investment is provided for the spare energy of machine-production. The change is commonly described by saying that production is more "roundabout."[1] A larger number of steps are inserted in the ladder of production. This increased complexity in the mechanism of production is not, however, the central point of importance. We must realise that the change is one which is essentially an increase in the "speculative" character of commerce. The "roundabout" method of production signifies a continual increase in the proportion of productive forces devoted to making "future goods" as compared with those devoted to making "present goods." Now future goods, plant, machinery, raw material of commodities, are essentially "contingent goods" : their worth or waste depends largely upon conditions yet unborn : their social utility and the value based upon it depend entirely upon the future powers and desires of those unknown persons who are expected to purchase and consume the commodities which shall come into existence as results of the existence and activity of these future goods.

The actual time which elapses between the extractive stage and the final retail stage of a commodity may not be greater and is in many cases far less under the new methods of industry. The raw cotton of South Carolina gets on the wearer's back more quickly than it did a century and a half ago. But when we add in the time-elements involved in the provision of the various forms of intricate plant and machinery whose utility entirely consists in forwarding these cotton goods, and whose existence in the industrial mechanism depends upon them, we shall perceive that the "roundabout" method signifies a great extension of the speculative or time-element in the market.[2]

§ 7. The growing interdependency of trades and markets, the ever closer sympathy which exists between them, the increased rapidity with which a movement affecting one communicates itself to others, are other striking characteristics of modern trade. This interdependency is in large measure one of growing structural attachment between trades

---

[1] It ought, however, to be kept in mind that the application of the "roundabout" method is only economically justified by a continual increase in consumption. So far as a given quantity of consumption is concerned the result of the "roundabout" method is to diminish the quantity of capital which assists to produce it.

[2] Professor Böhm Bawerk shows this increased time of production to be the essential characteris⸺ ⸺ capitalist production. Cf. *Positive Theory of Capital.*

and markets formerly in faint and distant sympathetic relationship. Formerly, agriculture was the one important foundational industry, and from the feebleness of the transport system the vital connections and the unity it supplied was local rather than national or international. Now the agricultural industries no longer occupy this position of prominence. The coal and iron industries engaged in furnishing the raw material of machinery and steam-motor, the machine manufacture, and the transport services, are the common feeders and regulators of all industries, including that of agriculture. They form a system corresponding to the alimentary system of the human body, any quickening or slackening of whose functional activities is directly and speedily communicated to the several parts. Any disturbance of price, of efficiency, or regularity of production in these foundational industries is reflected at once and automatically in the several industries which are engaged in the production and distribution of the several commodities. The mining and metal industries, shipbuilding, and the railway services are recognised more and more as furnishing the true measure and test of modern trade; their labour enters in ever larger proportion into the production of all the consumptive goods.

Besides the general integration or unification of industry implied by the common dependency of the specific trades upon these great industries, there are other forces engaged in integrating groups of trades. Foremost is the "roundabout" method of production, to which our attention has been already directed. Not merely does this capitalist system bring a number of trades and processes under the control of a single capital, as a single complex business, but it establishes close identity of trade-life and interests among businesses, trades, and markets which remain distinct so far as ownership and management are concerned.

§ 8. If we take the mass of capital and labour composing one of our staple productive industries, we shall find that it is related in four different ways to a number of other industries.

(1) It has a number of trades which are directly co-ordinate—*i.e.*, engaged in the earlier or later processes of

producing the same consumptive goods. Thus the manufacture of shoes is related co-ordinately to the import
trades of hides and bark, to tanning, to the export trade
in shoes, and to the retail shoe trade. A common stream
of produce is flowing through these several processes, and
though from the point of view of ownership and management there may be no connection, there is a close identity
of trade interest and a quick sympathy of commercial life
at these several points.

(2) Each important manufacturing industry has a number
of industries which in their relation to it are secondary,
although in some cases, having similar relations to a number
of other trades, they may in themselves be large and important. In the large textile centres are found a number of
minor industries, planers, sawyers, turners, fitters, smiths,
engaged in irregular work of alteration and repairs upon the
plant and machinery of the textile factories. The same
holds of all important manufactures, especially those which
are closely localised.

A somewhat similar relation appertains between those
manufactures engaged in producing the main body of any
product and the minor industries, which supply some slighter
and essentially subsidiary part. In relation to the main
textile and clothing industries, the manufacture of buttons,
of tape, feathers, and other elements of ornament or
trimmings may be regarded as subsidiary. In the same
way the manufacture of wall-papers or house paint may be
considered subsidiary to the building trades, that of black-
ing to the shoe manufacture. These subsidiary trades are
related to the primary one more or less closely, and are
affected by the condition of the latter more or less powerfully in proportion as the subsidiary elements they furnish are
more or less indispensable in character. The fur and feather
trades are far more dependent upon direct forces of fashion
than upon any changes of price or character in the main
branches of the clothing trade. On the other hand, any
cause which affected considerably the price of sugar would
have a great and direct influence on the jam manufacture,
while the rise in price of tin due to the M'Kinley tariff
caused serious apprehension to the Chicago manufacturers
and exporters of preserved meats.

(3) The relations between one of the great arterial

industries, such as coal-mining, railway transport, or machine-making, and a specific manufacture may be regarded as auxiliary. The extent to which the price of coal, railway rates, etc., enters into the price of the goods and affects the condition of profits in the trade measures the closeness of this auxiliary connection. In the case of the smelting industries or in the steam transport trades, even in the pottery trades, the part played by coal is so important that the relation is rather that of a primary than an auxiliary connection—*i.e.*, coal-mining must be ranked as co-ordinate to smelting. But where heat is not the direct agent of manufacture, but is required to furnish steam-motor alone, as in the textile factories, the connection may be termed auxiliary.

(4) The relationship between some industries is "sympathetic" in the sense that the commodities they produce appeal to closely related tastes, or are members of a group whose consumption is related harmoniously. In foods we have the relations between bread, butter, and cheese ; the relation in which sugar and salt stand to a large number of consumables. Some of these are natural relations in the sense that one supplies a corrective to some defect of the other, or that the combination enhances the satisfaction or advantage which would accrue from the consumption of each severally. In other cases the connection is more conventional, as that between alcohol and tobacco. The sporting tastes of man supply a strong sympathetic bond between many trades. The same is true of literary, artistic, or other tastes, which by the simultaneous demand which they make upon several industries, in some proportion determined by the harmonious satisfaction of their desires, throw these industries into sympathetic groups.[1] These four bonds mark an identity of interest between different industries.

The relationship is sometimes one of divergency or competition of trades. Where the same service may be supplied by two or more different commodities the trades are related by direct competition. Oil, gas, electricity, as illuminants, are a familiar example of this relationship. Many trades which

---

[1] For a full and valuable treatment of these harmonious relations, from the point of view of consumption and production, see Patten's *Economics of a Dynamic Society*.

produce commodities that are similar, but far from identical in character, feel this relationship very closely. The competition between various kinds of food, which with different kinds and degrees of satisfaction may produce the same substantial effects, between fish and meat, between various kinds of vegetables and drinks, enables us to realise something of the intricacy of the relations of this kind. In clothing we have antagonism of interests between the various fabrics which has led to great industrial changes. The most signal example is the rise of cotton, its triumph over woollen clothes by the earlier application of the new machinery, and over silk by the early superiority of its dyeing and printing processes.[1] So in recent years in the conflict among beverages, tea, and in a less measure cocoa, have materially damaged the growth of the coffee industry so far as English consumption is concerned. Where such rivalry exists, an industry may be as powerfully and immediately affected by a force which raises or depresses its competitor as by a force which directly affects itself.

§ 9. The growth of numerous and strongly-built structural attachments between different trades and markets related to different localities implies the existence of a large system of channels of communication throughout our industrial society. By the increased number and complexity of these channels connecting different markets and businesses, and relating the most distant classes of consumers, we can measure the evolution of the industrial organism. Through these channels flow the currents of modern industrial life, whose pace, length, and regularity contrast with the feeble, short, and spasmodic flow of commerce in earlier times. This advance in functional activity of distribution is thus expressed by Mr. Spencer:—"In early English times the great fairs, annual and other, formed the chief means of distribution, and remained important down to the seventeenth century, when not only villages, but even small towns, devoid of shops, were irregularly supplied by hawkers who had obtained their stocks at these gatherings. Along with increased population, larger industrial centres, and improved channels of communication, local supply became easier;

---

[1] Cf. Porter, *Progress of the Nation*, pp. 177-206.

and so frequent markets more and more fulfilled the purpose of infrequent fairs. Afterwards, in chief places and for chief commodities, markets themselves multiplied, becoming in some cases daily. Finally came a constant distribution, such that of some foods there is to each town an influx every morning; and of milk even more than once in the day. The transition from times when the movements of people and goods between places were private, slow, and infrequent, to times when there began to run at intervals of several days public vehicles moving at four miles an hour, and then to times when these shortened their intervals and increased their speed, while their lines of movement multiplied, ending in our own times, when along each line of rails there go at full speed a dozen waves daily that are relatively vast, sufficiently show us how the social circulation progresses from feeble, slow, irregular movements to a rapid, regular, and powerful pulse."[1]

The differentiation of function in the several parts of the industrial organism finds a partial expression in the localisation of certain industries. As there is growing division of labour among individuals and groups of individuals, so the expansion of the area of competition has brought about a larger and larger amount of local specialisation.

Roughly speaking, the West of Europe and of America has specialised in manufacture, drawing an ever larger proportion of their food supplies from the North-West States of America, from Russia, the Baltic Provinces, Australia, Egypt, India, etc., and their raw materials of manufacture from the southern United States, South America, India, etc., while these latter countries are subjected to a correspondent specialisation in agriculture and other extractive arts. If we take Europe alone, we find certain large characteristics which mark out the Baltic trade, the Black Sea trade, the Danube trade, the Norwegian and White Sea trade. So the Asiatic trade falls into certain tolerably defined divisions of area, as the Levant trade, the Red Sea trade, the Indian, the Straits, and East Indian, the China trade, etc. The whole trade of the world is thus divided for commercial purposes.[2] Though these trade divisions are primarily suggested by

---

[1] *Principles of Sociology*, vol. i. p. 500 (3rd edit.).
[2] For a detailed account of the national trade divisions, cf. Dr. Yeats, *The Golden Gates of Trade.*

considerations of transport rather than of the character of production, the geographical, climatic, and other natural factors which determine convenient lines of transport are found to have an important bearing on the character of the production, and convenience of transport itself assists largely to determine the kind of work which each part of the world sets itself to do.

The establishment of a world-market for a larger and larger number of commodities is transforming with marvellous rapidity the industrial face of the globe. This does not now appear so plainly in the more highly-developed countries of Europe, which, under the influence of half a century's moderately free competition for a European market, have already established themselves in tolerably settled conditions of specialised industry. But in the new world, and in those older countries which are now fast yielding to the incursions of manufacturing and transport machinery, the specialising process is making rapid strides.

Improved knowledge of the world, facile communication, an immense increase in the fluidity of capital, and a considerable increase in that of labour, are busily engaged in distributing the production of the world in accordance with certain dominant natural conditions. Those industrial forces which have during the last century and a half been operative in England, draining the population and industry from the Southern and Eastern counties, and concentrating it in larger proportions in Lancashire, the West Riding, Staffordshire, and round the Northumbrian and South Wales coal-fields, specialising each town or locality upon some single branch of the textile, metal, or other industries for which its soil, position, or other natural advantages made it suitable, are now beginning to extend the area of their control over the whole surface of the known and inhabited globe.

As large areas of Asia, South and Central Africa, Australia, and South America fall under the control of European commercial nations, are opened up by steamships, railways, telegraphs, and are made free receptacles for the increased quantity of capital which is unable to find a safe remunerative investment nearer home, we are brought nearer to a condition in which the whole surface of the world will be disposed for industrial purposes by these same forces which have long been confined in their direct and potent influence to a small portion of Western Europe and America. This vast expansion of the area of effective competition is beginning to specialise industry on the basis of a world-market, which was formerly specialised on the more confined basis of a national or provincial market. So in England, where the early specialisation of machine-industry was but slightly affected by outside competition, great changes are taking place. Portions of our textile and metal industries, which naturally settled in districts of Lancashire, Yorkshire, and Staffordshire, while the area of competition was a national one,[1] seem likely to pass to India, to Germany, or elsewhere, now that a tolerably free competition on the basis of world-industry has set in. It is inevitable that with every expansion of the area of competition under which a locality falls the character of its specialisation will change. A piece of English ground which was devoted to corn-growing when the market was a district one centred in the county town, becomes the little factory town when competition is established on a national basis; it may become the pleasure-ground of a retired millionaire speculator if under the pressure of world-competition it has been found that the manufacture which now thrives there can be carried on more economically in Bombay or Nankin, where each unit of labour power can be bought at the cheapest rate, or where some slight saving in the transport of raw material may be effected.

§ 10. The question how industry would be located, assuming the whole surface of the globe was brought into a single market or area of competition, with an equal development of transport facilities in all its parts; or in other words, " What is the ideal disposition of industry in a world-society making its chief end the attainment of industrial wealth estimated at present values?" is one to which of course no very exact answer can be given. But since this ideal represents the goal of modern industrial pro-

---

[1] Foreign competition with English textiles, though comparatively modern so far as the more highly developed machine-made fabrics are concerned, was keenly felt early in the century in hand-made goods. Schulze-Gaevernitz points out that the depression in work and wages of the hand-loom workers in 1820 was due more to foreign competition than to the new machinery. !Der Grossbetrieb, p. 41.)

gress, it is worth while to call attention to the chief determinants of the localisation of industries under free world-
competition. The influences may be placed in three
groups, which are, however, interrelated at many points.

(1) The first group may be called Climatic, the chief
influences of which are astronomical position, surface con-
tour, prevalent winds, ocean currents, etc. Climatic zones
have their own flora and fauna, and so far as these enter
into industry as agricultural and pastoral produce, as raw
materials of manufacture, as sustenance of labour, they are
natural determinants of the localisation of industry. In
vegetable products the climatic zones are very clearly
marked. "The boreal zone has its special vegetation of
mosses, lichens, saxifrages, berries, oats, barley, and rye;
the temperate zone its peas, beans, roots, hops, oats, barley,
rye, and wheat; this zone, characterised by its extent of
pastures, hop gardens, and barley fields, has also a distinctive title in the 'beer and butter region.' The warm
temperate zone, or region of 'wine and oil,' is characterised
by the growth of the vine, olive, orange, lemon, citron,
pomegranate, tea, wheat, maize, and rice; the sub-tropical
zone, by dates, figs, the vine, sugar-cane, wheat, and maize;
the tropical zone is characterised by coffee, cocoa-nut,
cocoa, sago, palm, figs, arrowroot, and spices; and the
equatorial by bananas, plantains, cocoa-nut, etc."[1]

(2) The second group is geographical and geological.
The shape and position of a country, its relation in space
to other countries, the character of the soil and sub-soil, its
water-supply, though closely related to climatic influences,
have independent bearings. The character of the soil, which
provides for crops their mineral food, has an important bearing upon the raw materials of industry. The shape and
position of the land, especially the configuration of its coast,
have a social as well as climatic significance, directing the
intercourse with other lands and the migrations of people and
civilisations which play so large a part in industrial history.

(3) Largely determined by the two groups of influences
named above are the forces which represent the national
character at any given time, the outcome of primitive race
characteristics, food supply, speed and direction of industrial

---

[1] Yeats, *The Golden Gates of Trade*, p. 12.   (Philip & Son.)

development, density of population, and the various other causes which enter in to determine efficiency of labour. The play of these natural and human forces in world-competition leads to such a settlement of different industries in different localities as yields the greatest net productiveness of labour in each part.

§ 11. But this world-competition, however free it may become, can lead to no finality, no settled appointment of industrial activity to the several parts of the earth. Setting aside all political and other non-economic motives, there are three reasons which render such local stability of industry impossible.

There is first the disturbance and actual loss sustained by nature in working up the mineral wealth of the soil, and the flora and fauna sustained by it, into commodities which are consumed, and an exact equivalent of which cannot be replaced. The working out of a coal-field, the destruction of forests which reacts upon the elementary climatic influences, are examples of this disturbance.

Secondly, there is the progress of industrial arts, new scientific discoveries applicable to industry. There is no reason to believe that human knowledge can reach any final goal: there is infinity alike in the resources of nature and in the capacity of the development of human skill.

Lastly, as human life continues, the art of living must continually change, and each change alters the value attached to the several forms of consumption, and so to the industrial processes engaged in the supply of different utilities. New wants stimulate new arts, new arts alter the disposition of productive industry, giving value to new portions of the earth. Ignoring those new material wants which require new kinds of raw material to be worked up for their satisfaction, the growing appreciation of certain kinds of sport, the love of fine scenery, a rising value set upon healthy atmosphere, are beginning to exercise a more and more perceptible influence upon the localisation of certain classes of population and industry in the more progressive nations of the world.

§ 12. The same laws and the same limitations which are operative in determining the character and degree of specialisation of countries or large areas are also seen to apply to smaller districts, towns, and streets. Industries engaged in producing valuable, durable material objects in wide demand are locally specialised; those engaged in providing bulky perishable non-material goods, or goods in narrow demand, are unspecialised. England, where internal intercourse has been most highly developed, and where internal competition has been freest and keenest, shows the most advanced specialisation in several of its staple industries. The concentration of cotton spinning in South Lancashire is an example, the full significance of which often escapes notice. From the beginning South Lancashire was the chief seat of the industry, but it is now far more concentrated than was the case a century ago. Several of the most valuable inventions in spinning were first applied in Derbyshire, in Nottingham, at Birmingham, and in Scotland. Scotland then competed closely in weaving with Lancashire. Now the Scotch industry is confined to certain specialities. In spite of the enormous growth of the manufacture, the local area it covers is even narrower than in last century. Within Lancashire itself the actual area of production has shrunk to some 25 square miles in the extreme south, while the two great cities are further specialised—Liverpool as the market for cotton, Manchester for yarn and cotton cloths.

Moreover, the localisation of various departments of the trade within Lancashire is still more remarkable. Not only have the old mills in which spinning and weaving were carried on together given way before division of labour, but the two processes are mostly conducted in different districts, the former in the towns immediately around Manchester, the latter in the more distant northern circuit. Nor is the specialisation confined to this. Spinning is again divided according to the coarser and finer qualities of yarn. The Oldham district, with Ashton, Middleton, and other towns south of Manchester, is chiefly confined to the medium numbers. Bolton, Chorley, Preston, and other northern towns undertake the finer numbers. In weaving there is even more intricate division of labour, each town or district specialising upon some particular line of goods.[1] Moreover, it must be borne in mind that the substitution of the factory for the domestic system and the

---

[1] Cf. Schulze-Gaevernitz's minute investigation of this whole subject, *Der Grossbetrieb*, pp. 98, 99, etc. Also cf. Holm in *British Industries*, edited by Professor W. J. Ashley.

continual enlargement of the average factory indicates an important progressive concentration. So the cotton industry does not in fact cover nearly so large a local area as when it was one-hundredth the size. The same is true of the other chief branches of the textile and metal industries. Nor is it only in the manufactures that towns and districts are closely specialised. The enormous increase of commerce due to machinery of manufacture and of transport requires the specialisation of certain towns for purely commercial purposes. London, Liverpool, Glasgow, and Hull are more and more devoted to the functions of storage and conveyance. Manchester itself is rapidly losing its manufacturing character and devoting itself almost exclusively to import and export trade. The railway service has made for itself large towns, such as Crewe, Derby, Normanton, and Swindon. Cardiff is a portentous example of a new mining centre created when the machine development of England was already ripe.

The specialisation of function in a large town is, however, qualified in two ways. The strong local organisation of a staple trade requires the grouping round it of a number of secondary or auxiliary trades. In large textile towns the manufactures of textile machinery, and of subsidiary materials, are found. The machine-making of Manchester is one of its most important industries, furnishing the neighbouring textile towns. Leeds is similarly equipped for the woollen trade. This is one of the respects in which the superior development of the English cotton industry over the continental ones is indicated. In Alsace alone of the continental centres has the concentration of industry advanced so far as to furnish a local machine industry specially devoted to cotton machinery. Germany is still largely dependent upon England for her machines.[1] So likewise with regard to co-ordinate trades, there is an advantage in the leading processes being grouped in local proximity, though they are not united in the same business. Thus we find dye-works and the various branches of the clothing trade largely settled in the large textile towns, such as Leeds, Bradford, Manchester, Bolton. The unit of local specialisation is thus seen to be not a single

[1] Schulze-Gaevernitz, p. 110.

trade, but a group of closely allied trades, co-ordinate, dependent, and derivative.

Round some large industries in which men find employment minor parasitic industries spring up stimulated by the supply of cheap abundant labour of women and children. In metal and machine towns such as Birmingham, Dudley, Walsall, in Newcastle-on-Tyne, and other shipbuilding towns, where the staple industries are a masculine monopoly, textile factories have been planted. The same holds of various mining villages and of agricultural villages in the neighbourhood of large textile centres. There is in the midland counties a growing disposition to place textile factories in rural villages where cheap female labour can be got, and where the independence of workers is qualified by stronger local attachments and inferior capacity of effective trade union organisation. As textile work passes more and more into the hands of women,[1] this tendency to make it a parasitic trade thriving upon the low wages for which women's labour can be got where strong and well-paid male work is established, will probably be more strongly operative.

§ 13. The specialisation of certain districts within the town, though far less rigid than in the mediæval town, is very noticeable in the larger centres of industry. Natural causes often determine this division of localities, as in the case of the riverside industries, brick-making and market-gardening in the outer suburbs. Round the central station in every

---

[1] The following table* shows the proportions of females in 1000 occupied persons in the chief textile industries of England and Wales.

	1861.	1871.	1881.	1891.	1901.
Cotton	567	598	620	609	628
Wool and Worsted .	461	513	561	557	582
Silk	642	676	691	667	702
Hemp, Jute, etc. .	265	304	374	393	492
Hosiery . . .	468	468	533	629	713
Lace	829	826	743	625	653
Carpets, etc. . .	183	312	362	440	517

* *General Report of Census*, p. 86.

large town, for convenience of work and life, settle a
number of industries related to the carrying trade. Every
trade, market, or exchange is a centre of attraction. So
the broking, banking, and the general financing businesses
are grouped closely round the Royal Exchange. Mark Lane
and Mincing Lane are centres of the corn and tea trades.
In all town industries not directly engaged in retail distribution there are certain obvious economies and conveniences
in this gregariousness. Agents, travellers, collectors, and
others who have relations of sale or purchase with a number
of businesses in a trade find a variety of disadvantages in
dealing with a firm locally detached from the main body, so
that when a district is once recognised as a trade centre, it
becomes increasingly important to each new competitor to
settle there. The larger the city the stronger this force of
trade centralisation. Hence in London, untrammelled by
guild or city regulations, we find a strong localisation of
most wholesale and some retail businesses. In retail trade,
however, the economic gain is less universal. Since retail
commodities are chiefly for use in the home, and homes
are widely distributed, the convenience of being near one's
customers and away from trade competitors is often a pre-
dominating motive. Shops which sell bread, meat, fish,
fruit, groceries, articles which are bought frequently and
mostly in small quantities, shops selling cheaper articles of
ordinary consumption, such as tobacco, millinery, stationery,
and generally shops selling articles for domestic use, the
purchase of which falls to women, are widely dispersed. On
the other hand, where the articles are of a rarer and more
expensive order, when it is likely that the purchaser will
seek to compare price and character of wares, and will pre-
sumably be willing to make a special journey for the purpose,
the centralising tendency prevails in retail trade. So we
find the vendors of carriages, pianos, bicycles, the heavier
articles of furniture, jewellery, second-hand books, furs, and
the more expensive tailors and milliners clustering together
in a special street or neighbourhood.

Effective competition in retail trade sometimes requires
concentration, sometimes dispersion of business. But the
most characteristic modern movement in retail trade is a
combination of the centralising and dispersive tendencies,
and is related to the enlargement of the business-unit

which we found proceeding everywhere in industry. The large distributing company, with a number of local branch agents who call regularly at the house of the consumer for orders, is the most highly organised form of retail trade. In all the departments of regular and general consumption the movement is towards this constant house-to-house supply. The wealthier classes in towns have already learned to purchase all the more perishable forms of food and many other articles of house consumption in this way, while the growing facilities of postage and conveyance of goods enable them to purchase from a large central store by means of a price-list all other consumables into which the element of individual taste or caprice does not largely enter. This habit is spreading in the smaller towns among the middle classes, so that the small dispersed retail businesses are becoming more and more dependent upon the supply of the needs of the working classes, and of such articles of comfort and luxury as may appeal to the less regular and calculable tastes of the moneyed classes. Just as in towns we have a constant automatic supply of water and gas instead of an intermittent supply dependent on a number of individual acts of purchase, so it seems likely that all the routine wants of the consumer will be supplied.

How far mechanical inventions may be applied to increase the facility and cheapen the cost of this distribution it is difficult to say. The automatic machine for distributing matches and sweetmeats is adaptable to many forms of routine consumption. In the larger stores many kinds of labour-saving machinery are already applied. As steam or electric power is adopted more widely in the local transport services the retail distribution of goods from a large single centre is likely to proceed apace, and a displacement of human labour by machinery similar to that which is taking place in manufacture will take place in distribution. So far as the wants of large classes of the public become regular and their consumption measurable in quantity, machinery will unquestionably take over the labour of distribution, especially in the large towns which are absorbing in a way convenient for mechanical distribution a larger proportion of the consuming public. With each new encroachment of machinery into the domain of the distributing trades the characteristics of machine-industry, enlarged mass of the business, increased area of the market, increased complexity of relations to other trades, increased specialisation of local activity will be clearly discernible.

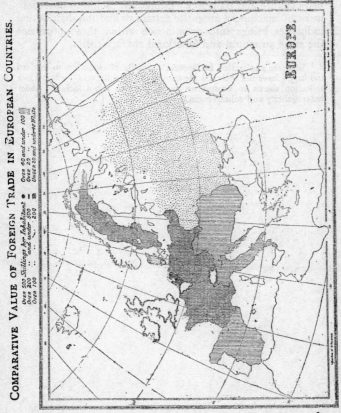

We thus see in the several departments of industry, under the pressure of the same economic forces, an expansion of size, a growing complexity of structure and functional activity, and an increased cohesion of highly differentiated parts in the business, the market, and in that aggregation of related trades and markets which forms the world-industry. The physical instrument by which these economic forces, making for increased size, heterogeneity, and cohesiveness,[1] have been able to operate is machinery applied to manufacture and transport. Moreover, each new encroachment of machinery upon the extractive and the distributing industries brings into prominence within these processes the same structural and functional characteristics.

[1] In a free application of Spencer's formula of evolution to modern industry I have not included the quality of " definiteness," which close reflection shows to possess no property which is not included under heterogeneity and cohesiveness.

CHAPTER VII.

COMBINATIONS OF CAPITAL.

§ 1. *Competition intensifies with Modern Capitalism.*
§ 2. *Experiments in Combination. The Birmingham Alliance.*
§ 3. *"Pools" in American Metal Trades.*
§ 4. *Conferences in Railroads and Shipping. Insurance Pools.*
§ 5. *"Corners" in Markets.*

§ 1. The increased size and complexity of the business-unit in those industries where the concentrative force of capitalism has operated cause changes in the relations between businesses contributing to the same market. When the growth in the normal size of the business is attended by a corresponding expansion of the market, the total number of competitors may remain as large as before, and the terms of their competition may remain unchanged. But in most branches of capitalist industry the market does not continue to expand as fast as the size of an effective business, so that the number of effective competitors in a market tends to be smaller. So long as the competition among the smaller number of large competitors remains as "free" as formerly among a larger number of small competitors, no radical alteration in the structure of the market takes place. All the productive economies tend as before to pass into the hands of the consumer in reduced prices of commodities. Nay, more than this, a competing firm cannot even keep to itself the advantages of some private individual economy if its competitor possesses some other private economy of equal importance. If A and B are two closely competing firms, A owing a special machine capable of earning for him 2 per cent. above the normal trade profit, and B possessing an equal advantage in a supply of cheaper labour, these private advantages are cancelled by competition, and pass into the pocket of the consuming public through reduced prices.

There is every reason to believe that with a diminution in the number of competitors and an increase of their size, competition grows keener and keener. Under old business conditions custom held considerable sway; the personal element played a larger part alike in determining quality of goods and good faith; purchasers did not so closely compare prices; they were not guided exclusively by figures, they did not systematically beat down prices, nor did they devote so large a proportion of their time, thought, and money to devices for taking away one another's customers.[1] From the new business this personal element and these customary scruples have almost entirely vanished, and as the net advantages of large-scale production grow, more and more attention is devoted to the direct work of competition. Hence we find that it is precisely in those trades which are most highly organised, provided with the most advanced machinery, and composed of the largest units of capital, that the fiercest and most unscrupulous competition has shown itself. The exact part which machinery, with its incalculable tendency to over-production, has played in this competition remains for later consideration. Here it is enough to place in evidence the acknowledged fact that the growing scale of the business has intensified and not diminished competition. In the great machine industries trade fluctuations are most severely felt; the smaller businesses are unable to stand before the tide of depression and collapse, or are driven in self-defence to coalesce. The borrowing of capital, the formation of joint-stock enterprise and every form of co-operation in capital have proceeded most rapidly in the textile, metal, transport, shipping, and machine-making industries, and in those minor manufactures, such as brewing and chemicals, which require large quantities of expensive plant. This joining together of small capitals to make a single large capital, this swallowing up of small by

---

[1] There still survive in certain old-fashioned trades firms which do business without formal written contracts, and which would be ashamed to take a lower price than they had at first asked, or to seek to beat down another's price.

large businesses, mean first and foremost an endeavour to escape the risks and dangers attending small-scale production in the tide of modern industrial changes. But since all are moving in the same direction, no one gains upon the other. Certain common economies are shared by the monster competitors, but more and more energy must be given to the work of competition, and the productive economies are partly squandered in the friction of fierce competition, and partly pass over to the body of consumers in lowered prices. Thus the endeavour to secure safety and high profits by the economies of large-scale production is rendered futile by the growing severity of the competitive process. Each big firm finds itself competent to undertake more business than it already possesses, and underbids its neighbour until the cutting of prices has sunk the weaker and driven profits to a bare subsistence point for the stronger competitors.

§ 2. The intensity of competition thus generated under developed capitalism, when a few large businesses find an increasing difficulty in disposing of their full output regularly and at a profitable price, drives the competitors to seek some arrangement with one another which shall mitigate the severity of the struggle.

These arrangements are primarily directed to restrain underselling by fixing price-lists, and when necessary and feasible, by regulating output: firms do not cease to compete, but endeavour to limit the terms of their competition. There is of course nothing new in this: in local industries, especially where goods are sold directly to consumers, prices never have been fixed by "free" competition; the regulations of Guilds and of Assizes have always been succeeded by conspiracies among local vendors to hold up prices. In the case of large capitalist industries the necessary mechanism of the market for buying raw material and for selling their product, the Corn or Cotton Exchange, the Clearing House for Railroads or Banks, the necessary organisation of the trade for obtaining quick and sure intelligence on matters of common trade interest, the growth of Wage Boards and other machinery for dealing with labour,—all these form a basis of association which can be utilised for regulating competition.

The earliest stage is one of informal agreement, starting

first among competing firms of a particular locality, and gradually extending so as to cover the entire trade, or a sufficient proportion to give the required control of price. This has been the typical movement in the British iron, steel, and engineering trades during recent years.

The statement of a representative trade journal in 1898 accurately conveys the state of those trades. "We have now in operation agreements or understandings as to prices in the rail, ship-plate, boiler-plate, bar iron, and other branches of the iron and steel trades of this country by means of which prices are fairly well maintained and cutting is largely prevented."[1]

Amid other schemes of combination or amalgamation which are in progress in the metal, textile, and other staple manufacturing and commercial industries in Britain these experiments for regulating prices by informal agreements are everywhere rife. Their success or failure depends in the main upon two conditions—first, the proportion of the total trade commanded by a few great competing firms; second, the state of the market as regards supply. When, as in most departments of the British metal and engineering trades, a few gigantic businesses dominate the market, the existence of a large number of small firms doing for the most part a purely local business, need not prevent the maintenance of a successful price list. On the other hand, an overstocking of the market, due to a large improvement of productive plant or a collapse in demand, may easily knock the bottom out of such an "agreement" and lead to secret or even open underselling.

The rapid changes, alike in capacity of production and in volume of demand, which are characteristic of modern markets, afford little security to "agreements" of competing firms unless accompanied by some effective guarantees or penalties for infringement of the conditions of the agreement. In order that agreements to maintain profitable prices may have any chance of enduring success it is perceived that they must be accompanied by provisions for the regulation of output, or for the proportionate distribution of "orders." In mining and manufacturing businesses limitation of "output" is in some countries the basis of an effective

---

[1] *Iron and Coal Trades Review* (quoted Macrosty, p. 184).

agreement. In England, however, little recourse has yet been had to this method of maintaining prices. When, as recently in the Lancashire cotton industry, competing firms have agreed to work short time, the policy has been adopted not in order to hold up prices, but to deal with a passing emergency due to a short supply of material. Although more than once in the South Wales coal trade the proposal has been made to limit the output and to distribute the orders among the various collieries, no experiment upon these lines has been tried.

But while most of the important British manufacturing industries are experimenting upon "informal agreements," a number of smaller trades, especially in metal industries have been seeking a firmer basis of association. "The Birmingham Alliance" is the name given to a species of combination, which, starting in the iron bedstead trade in 1890, was adopted by various minor branches of metal manufacture in the Midlands, and later by the dyeing trade of the West Riding and a few other industries of the second rank. Its prime basis was a formal agreement among the members of the Employers' Association to adopt a scientific system of "cost-taking," to add an agreed portion of profit to the true cost, and thus to reach a price-list to which every member should bind himself to adhere. The novel portion of the scheme lay in the extension of the combination so as to include labour. The Employers' Association entered into an alliance with the Trade Unions, signing a formal agreement whereby each employer bound himself to employ union members only, while the Trade Union bound itself only to supply men to employers who were members of the Association. On the basis of a certain permanent addition to existing wages a sliding scale was fixed, whereby future wages rose and fell in direct proportion to profits. The whole scheme was clinched by a Conciliation Board upon which employers and workers were equally represented, with provision, when necessary, for impartial arbitration. If an employer broke away from the Alliance or violated his pledges, the Board "called out" his workmen. The outside competitor was to be met "by well-arranged, careful, judicious, and systematic underselling, until he is compelled either to retire or to come to terms." A fighting fund was raised to deal with such cases, and a system of "rebates" was added in order to detach customers from foreign makers.

For several years the plan was successful in the bedstead and several other trades: prices were raised, profits were high, and large bonuses were added to wages. But the high profits were found in time to overstrain the economic strength of the Alliance, disloyal members of the Association began to practise under-selling by false invoices or secret commissions, while outside competition began to assume too formidable dimensions. As a result of this demoralisation, in 1900 the Bedstead Alliance broke down, followed or preceded in its fall by most of its imitators.

§ 3. This experiment serves to show that not even a formal agreement among firms as to selling prices is capable of being maintained unless the Association possesses some direct control over the output of the several firms, and can easily detect and adequately punish infractions of the agreement. A number of interesting experiments in Industrial Pooling in the United States are expressly directed to discover and test the best methods of maintaining such agreements.

"Manufacturers desiring to form a pool usually create an unincorporated organisation, such as the Bessemer Steel Association, the Merchants' Ore Association, or the Steel Rail Association. All agree to maintain a schedule of prices fixed by the Association and to limit their production accordingly. Each manufacturer is allowed to produce (or sell) only a certain percentage of the whole output, depending upon the capacity and advantages of his plant. To prevent violation of the agreement, a money deposit is often required from each, forfeitable to the Association."[1]

Expert accountants are employed: fines are imposed upon firms producing more than the allowed percentage, a corresponding bonus being paid to those producing less. Prices and allotments of output are arranged each November or December for the following year. A territorial division of the market is frequently practised. As a rule, local prices are arranged, by first fixing a uniform factory price,

[1] W. E. Belcher in an article on "Industrial Pooling" (*Quarterly Journal of Economics*, Nov. 1904), from which the following particulars are also taken.

and then adding a freightage from factory to the place of sale.

Several variations from this general type are extant. "Several pools have omitted the feature of percentage allotments, and have placed a tax upon all manufacturing." Another device is the joint sales agent. The combining firms agree to use a single party for their sole sales agent, he contracting with each of them separately, but fixing a uniform selling price. "Another form of pool is based on patents essential to the manufacture of the article. The patentee sells the rights of use, for a uniform royalty, to all who apply. He also limits the quota to be produced by each firm, above which amount the royalty increases rapidly.[1]

The steel and iron trades in the United States are honeycombed by such pools. The ore when dug is handled by an Association, claiming to fix prices and regulate output. In the manufacture of pig-iron an Association arranges prices among furnace men. Steel billets were pooled in 1896, and again since 1900; so also with heavy materials such as steel rails, beams, angles, bars, etc., and light materials such as chains, bolts, pipes, and tubing.

Few, if any, of these pools can be regarded as stable organisations. Their frequent collapse is regarded by Mr. Belcher as the natural result of early attempts at overgrasping by rises of prices. The chief interest which attaches to them is due to the fact that, like the English "Alliances," they represent endeavours of manufacturers engaged in capitalist industry to secure an element of monopoly profits without abandoning the independent ownership and control of their several businesses.

§ 4. The largely developed capitalism of the transport trades by rail and water has led to the adoption of methods of agreement in regulation or restraint of competition more enduring and successful than those agreements of manufacturers just described. In Great Britain and the United States, the two chief nations where railroads have been left to "private enterprise," railroad companies exposed to keen competition have organised common systems of rates for

---

[1] The Consolidated Seedless Raisin Co. and the National Harrow Co. are named as of this order of "pool."

freight and also for passenger traffic. In Great Britain these agreements to regulate "competition" are openly recognised; in America they are illicit, but operative all the same. The English method is by Conferences, of which there are two principal ones—"The English and Scotch Traffic Rates Conference" and "The Normanton Conference." "The English and Scotch Conference is composed of representatives (who are usually the chief goods managers) of all the companies, both English and Scotch, who are interested in the carriage of goods between places in England and places in Scotland by the various routes. These representatives meet once a month, and deal with all questions arising in connection with the making of new rates or the alteration of existing rates for competitive places between which more than one company can carry. The Normanton Conference, which was originally established to control the rate for a certain district of which Normanton, where its meetings were formerly held, was a convenient centre, has gradually so much extended its scope that it is now composed of representatives of nearly every company of any importance in England, and governs almost the whole of the competitive rates which are not dealt with by the English and Scotch Conference."[1]

The fixing of rates is sometimes supplemented by a further plan, which brings the agreement into closer resemblance to the industrial pool above described. This is known as the "Percentage Division of Traffic." "Supposing that there is a certain traffic to be conveyed between two towns or districts, and that there are two or more railway companies, each having a route of its own by which it is enabled to compete for the traffic. An agreement is come to that the receipts derived from the whole of the traffic carried by all routes shall be thrown into a common fund, and that each company shall be entitled to a certain percentage of the whole. . . . The percentages are usually adjusted on the basis of past actual earnings, but in settling the terms of the agreement due weight is accorded to any prospective advantage which may entitle one company to claim a larger proportion than it has carried in the past."[2]

[1] Sir G. Findlay, *The Working and Management of an English Railway*, p. 265.
[2] Findlay, p. 267.

In America, where all positive rate-agreements between competing railroad corporations are illegal, the machinery for such regulation is more informal and hidden from the public eye, but there can be no doubt that recourse is continually had to rate-fixing, and even to the pooling of business among competing roads.

"It is idle to say that where such a condition exists, where, for example, every one of the numerous lines transporting grain from Chicago, St. Louis, and kindred points to the Atlantic seaboard advance their rates upon the same day and by precisely the same amount, there has been no understanding between those companies. Nor do the carriers, as a rule, deny such concert of action, but they insist that it does not proceed to the point of an unlawful agreement."[1]

The term Conference is also used to describe the organisation by which competing shipping companies maintain fixed rates, and preclude outsiders from entering their trade. A Conference is an arrangement among the leading lines of steamships, plying on a particular sea route, to charge a fixed "fair" rate for freight and passenger traffic. Such an arrangement can only be effective on condition that all or nearly all the regular lines come into the Conference. For the power of a Conference is exercised directly on the shippers by means of a "rebate" system, which operates partly as a bribe, partly as a menace, inducing shippers to do business exclusively with members of the Conference. The system appears to have begun in the China trade, and the following circulars illustrate its working as early as 1884:—

"To those exporters who confine their shipments of tea and general cargo from China to Europe (not including the Mediterranean and Black Sea ports) to the Peninsular and Oriental Steam Navigation Company's, Messageries Maritime Company's, Ocean Steamship Company's, Glen, Castle, Shire, and Ben lines, and to the Steamships Oopack and Ningchow, we shall be happy to allow a rebate of 5 per cent. on the freight charged." Another circular issued by the same Conference in 1885 states that "shipments for London by non-Conference steamers, at any of the ports in China or

Hong-Kong, will exclude the firm making such shipment from participation in the return during the whole six-monthly period within which they have been made, even although the firm elsewhere may have given exclusive support to the Conference lines."[1] The object and effect of this method is to confine traffic to Conference lines with agreed rates, and to preclude "tramp" steamers or sailing vessels from calling in and taking business either at the Conference rates or at reduced rates.

The usual method has been for the steamship lines to charge, in addition to the freight rate, a "primage" of 10 per cent., with the understanding that after a stated time (say six months) they would refund the "primage" to shippers who had not shipped by "outside" steamers.

Since ocean routes are international highroads, such Conferences have naturally expanded beyond the limits of a single nation, and English, French, German, Dutch, and American companies have been drawn into the system, which has been extended from the Far East trade to the Cape, West Indian, Australian, North American, and South American trades. In the case of the stronger Conferences the "monopolies" thus established rest, not merely upon the system of rebates, but upon Post Office and other public subsidies, and upon port facilities which give them an advantage over outside companies.

The substantial identity of this method of limiting competition with that employed by railroads is admitted by the Chairman of the P. and O. Company in the following terms :—"It was not possible profitably to carry on shipping business unless there was uniformity of tariffs settled by a 'conference' of the shipping companies. These conferences might be compared to the agreements which existed between the various railway companies of the United Kingdom. Railways charged identical rates when running between the same points, although they competed in speed, train accommodation, and general facilities. This was exactly what the steamship companies did."[2]

The form of combination in which competition is most rigorously limited, and business independence reduced to

---

[1] Quoted Macrosty, p. 157.
[2] Annual meeting (quoted Macrosty, p. 158).

its lowest terms, is found in certain branches of the insurance business, notably in British Fire Insurance. The entire trade is in the hands of a very small number of companies, who organise a strict set of rates with heavy penalties for proved infractions, and agree to share the business which comes into each company, distributing it in a fixed proportion among the various companies. This system of re-investment, designed primarily to equalise risks, serves likewise to equalise business, leaving to the several companies a competition virtually confined to economies of collection and office administration. There is only one price offered to the insurer, though slight variations in the form of policy and mode of payment are doubtless utilised by the agents of the several companies to secure for their firm the initial handling of business.

§ 5. All the forms of combination in restraint of competition hitherto examined fall short in some measure or respect of an entire amalgamation or identification of interest among the combining businesses.

We must now proceed to consider cases where restraint of competition is pushed to an amalgamation which either merges the hitherto independent businesses or identifies their profitable interests. Such amalgamation or identification may be temporary, for the purposes of a single business *coup* or a series of *coups*, in which case no merger of economic or legal structure takes places; or it may be permanent, involving a disappearance of the economic and sometimes of the legal entity of the several businesses.

A temporary "combine" of normally competing businesses in order to "rig the market," "corner" the supply, hold up prices and take monopoly profits, though a frequent phenomenon in modern business enterprise, need not detain us long. Such "corners" are commonly contrived by securing in the transport or mercantile stages through which some commodity passes from the farm, mine, or mill, to the wholesale or retail market, a control of the whole supply, or a sufficiently large proportion of the supply, to give a mastery over selling prices.

The typical corner is a financial movement on one of the produce markets by which the wheat or cotton crops, or some other important supply of food or raw material, is held up for a time by speculators who hope by monopolising the supply to compel merchants or other speculators, who have bound themselves to deliver quantities of this commodity at a given date, to buy it from them at a greatly enhanced price.

The following description of a corner in wheat will serve for an example :—

"The man who forms a corner in wheat, first purchases or secures the control of the whole available supply of wheat, or as near the whole supply as he can. In addition to this he purchases more than is really within reach of the market by buying 'futures,' or making contracts with others who agree to deliver him wheat at some future time. Of course he aims to secure the greater part of his wheat quietly, at low figures; but after he deems that the whole supply is nearly in his control, he spreads the news that there is a 'corner' in the market, and buys openly all the wheat he can, offering higher and higher prices, until he raises the price sufficiently high to suit him. Now the men who have contracted to deliver wheat to him at this date are at his mercy. They must buy their wheat of him at whatever price he chooses to ask, and deliver it as soon as purchased, in order to fulfil their contracts. Meanwhile mills must be kept in operation, and the millers have to pay an increased price for wheat; they charge the bakers higher prices for flour, and the bakers raise the price of bread. Thus is told by the hungry mouths in the poor man's home the last act in the tragedy of the corner."[1]

While most of these corners organised by financiers are short-lived deals, it sometimes happens that a more durable "combine" is attempted, more nearly resembling the "industrial pools" already described. A single illustration of this method will suffice from the "Copper Syndicate," which for some time traded as "La Société Industrielle Commerciale de Métaux." Its history in brief was this: A body of French capitalists, for the most part not owners of mines or metals, but speculators pure and simple, placed in a common fund a sum of money with the intention of cornering the supply of tin. Before completing this design they were diverted into a larger speculation in the copper

[1] There need, of course, be no actual diversion of goods into the possession of the Ring: the essence of the monopoly consists in the control, not in the possession of goods.

market. In 1887 they entered into contracts with the largest copper-producing companies in various countries, agreeing to buy all the copper produced for the next three years at an agreed price, with an added bonus equivalent to half the profit from the sale of the same. In 1888 the Syndicate sought to extend its contracts with the chief mining companies to cover a period of twelve years, arranging with them also to limit the output of copper. For some time they held the market in their grip, and prices advanced considerably. But, partly owing to a failure to complete their contracts securing a reduction in output, and partly from inability to meet current liabilities, the corner was broken down in 1889, and the artificially inflated prices fell.

Other more durable "corners" or "combines" formed not by outside speculators but by merchants and manufacturers, resemble more nearly the Industrial Pools already described. Such, for example, was the famous "Big Four Cattle Combine" in Chicago, by which Messrs. Armour, Swift, Morris, and Hammond controlled the cattle and meat trade over a large part of the United States, fixing alike the prices paid to farmers for cattle and the retail prices for beef paid by consumers.

These early experiments in temporary or partial combination among firms independent in ownership and profitable interests, though they are disturbing elements of considerable magnitude at the present time, have no great or enduring importance as forms of capitalist association.

CHAPTER VIII.

CARTELS AND TRUSTS.

§ 1. The economic object of all the "agreements," "alliances," "combines," "pools," and "corners" described in the last chapter, is to establish some form or degree of "monopoly," the owners of the supply agreeing upon a selling price, and refusing to compete by underselling one another. In most cases, where a lasting control of the market is sought, the agreement between the businesses seeks to impose some regulations upon output, implying a certain amount of control over the conduct of the several businesses by the "combine."

From the standpoint of economic structure and function the difference between these "combines" and the complete amalgamation of a Trust is only one of degree, alike as regards (α) control of selling price, and (β) loss of independence in business control. Legally the difference no doubt is large, for whereas the Trust generally assumes the form of a publicly authorised corporate body (though the legality of particular forms may be contested), the partial or temporal combinations are in almost every instance extralegal or actually illegal.

A half-way house between the informal combinations we have been considering and the "Trust," or other complete amalgamation, is the "Cartel," as found in Germany, Austria, Belgium, and other Continental European countries. Though their progeners may be traced far back in Dutch and German industrial history, their present shape and importance are quite modern. Extending the idea of the Industrial Pool, the businesses adopting the Cartel have formed themselves into public corporations for the purpose of fixing uniform selling prices and regulating output, but without assuming a direct control management over the syndicated businesses or a uniform rate of profit.

§ 2. The best organised of these Cartels are in the coal and coke industries, and in the pig-iron, steel, and manufactured metal trades of Germany and Austria. The structure of the Cartel and its mode of operation is best illustrated in the important Coal Cartel of the Ruhr in Rhenish Westphalia.

The mineowners of the district form a selling company (with a nominal capital, the shares of which they hold), designed to act as their sole agent for the sale of their coal. This company, or syndicate, is organised in statutory form, as a corporation (*Actiengesellschaft*). Its duly appointed executive committee (*Vorstand*) is empowered to make contracts with the mineowners severally, binding itself to take from them and sell the output of the mines under certain arrangements as to price and payment, they in their turn undertaking to sell all their coal, coke, etc., to the syndicate, with the exception of certain portions allotted to their own use in their mining works, to their private use, and for certain purposes of purely local supply.

The mineowners also agree with the Syndicate and with one another to form an organisation or Association (*Versammlung*) in order to appoint a representative Council to fix the general price norms. assessments towards the upkeep of the Selling Syndicate, penalties for breaches of agreement, etc., and to make other arrangements for enforcing the common policy. The most important function of the association, however, is the appointment of a commission to determine the "participation"—*i.e.* the proportion of output to be allowed to each mine.

The committee of the Selling Syndicate, thus receiving from the Association its general regulations as to (*a*) proportionate output of the several mines, (*β*) general price norms, proceeds to apply and enforce the common policy —(1) buying and selling the coal, coke, and brickets produced by the syndicate mines; (2) fixing the actual selling price or prices in the competitive and non-competitive markets; (3) proposing to the association the assessments for the expenses of the syndicate; (4) examining the books of the individual mines; (5) proposing fines for breaches of agreement.

The effect of this somewhat complicated machinery is to establish a common selling agent and a single minimum price, and to regulate the general and the several outputs. The minimum selling price is that at which the syndicate takes the coal from the mineowners. Where the syndicate sells in competitive districts, it may sell as low as at this minimum. In non-competitive regions it often sells at a premium, in which case the surplus price is commonly, though not always, paid over to the mine which supplies it.

The syndicate itself is not worked as a profit-making company, all its expenses are covered by assessments on the mineowners; it is merely the selling instrument of a number of profit-seeking mineowners who seek to maintain high prices and to regulate output. There is no pooling of capital interests, no guarantee of a uniform rate of profit, or even of a uniform price paid to the several mineowners.[1]

The weak points of the Cartel appear to be two. First, the refusal of certain producers to enter the syndicate, preferring to keep their liberty and to pursue an alternative policy of selling at the higher prices secured by the syndicate where it is strong, or underselling it where it is weak. Second, the complaints of smaller and weaker mine-

---

[1] This description of the Ruhr Cartel is condensed from the valuable monograph on "Monopolistic" Combinations in the German Coal Industry, by Francis Walker (American Economic Association, 1904).

owners or manufacturers that the rate of participation (output) is fixed to their disadvantage as compared with the larger and stronger producers.

The fundamental defect appears, however, to lie in the fact that continuous employment cannot be guaranteed to the members of the Cartel. In order to meet or abate this defect a careful export policy forms a part of the working of the Cartel.

"We find that the Iron Kartell agreement fixes the quantity of manufactured iron which each establishment is allowed to produce, but 'in the contract are not reckoned products which are exported, either by being sent directly into the foreign country, or through being sold to manufacturing establishments (for example manufacturers of wagons or of locomotives), and by them used for export.' The result of arrangements of this nature would seem to be that a certain impulse is given to the export trade, more or less irrespective of the prices at which the goods can be sold in foreign countries. But 'the Kartell endeavours to avoid a volume of production exceeding the requirements of the home market; and its practice accordingly is not to encourage the export trade—a trade carried on at a lower rate of profit than the home trade, or even at a loss.'"[1] Most Cartels, however reluctant to encourage export trade at unprofitable rates, appear from time to time to be driven to this method of keeping their mines and works running. Not merely do they sanction and organise export trade at lower prices, but in many cases they encourage it by means of bounties. Indeed the development of the export trade was one of the earliest reasons for association among the mining interests,[2] and the modern development of export trade in German manufactured and semi-manufactured goods is largely the direct result of a Cartel policy. While the Cartels would like to regulate output and prices without encouraging a less profitable export trade, the tendency to over-production in modern manufactures is so strong that an absolute limitation of output to the needs of a regulated home market is often found impracticable, and some foreign outlet is allowed or encouraged as a concession to the urgency of the case.

[1] Grünzel, *Ueber Kartelle*, p. 217, quoted Cd. 1761, p. 328.
[2] Walker, p. 209.

The Coal and Iron Syndicates have during recent years adopted a general system of bounties or premiums paid, not to exporters of these raw materials, but to exporters of metal goods into which coal enters as a chief cost of production. As early as 1882 the iron interests of Westphalia and Siegenland appear to have given price rebates to certain groups of rolling-mills,[1] but the regular system of bounties in the mining and metallurgical industries seems to have begun about 1891.[2] As time went on this export policy of Cartels assumed a more highly organised shape, and in 1902 the coal, coke, pig-iron and "half-finished" iron, and steel industries of Rhenish Westphalia established at Düsseldorf a "Clearing-house for Export" in order to deal with premiums on export trade.[3] This clearing-house was empowered to fix bounties on the various goods, and the following were the figures fixed for the last quarter of 1902:—

1.50 m. per ton for coal.
2.50 m. ,, ,, raw iron (excl. coal bounty).
10.00 m. ,, ,, Halbzeug (incl. coal and iron bounty).

While this Cartel system appears most prominent in the coal, iron, and metal industries, German and Austrian Cartels have handled sugar, petroleum, twine, cotton, worsted and woollen yarn, a large variety of chemicals, besides a number of miscellaneous articles such as pencils, paper, cement, porcelain, glass, leather, rubber goods, electrical apparatus.[4]

The spread of Cartels in Germany has indeed advanced with great rapidity since the beginning of her modern era of industry. Whereas in 1870 there existed only five syndicates, the number in 1897 was placed at 345, covering virtually the entire field of manufacture and commerce. During the last few years combination among syndicates has reduced their number and increased their effective power.

§ 3. Though Cartels are often classed with Trusts, there is a tolerably wide difference between them in economic structure and in function. The American term "Trust" is here adopted as the most convenient term to describe a con-

---

[1] Walker, p. 220.
[2] Raffalovich, p. 23.
[3] Cd. 1761, p. 313.
[4] Cd. 1761, p. 358.

solidation of capital within a trade that is large enough and strong enough to control to an appreciable extent the supply and the selling price of the articles with which it deals.

The Cartel and the Industrial Pool, in which a number of separately-owned businesses participate, fall short, alike in control of production and of price, of the organic consolidation of interests comprised in a Trust. Unity in the organisation of an industry commanding a market is the essential feature of the Trust, which is thus identified with a Monopoly in that the real ownership of the whole or the bulk of a supply is vested in it.

This definition is at once narrower and wider than certain common uses of "Trust." For instance, in the United States the word is often applied to any large corporation, especially if it is formed by the amalgamation of a number of formerly independent businesses. Now in almost every field of capitalist enterprise, especially in banking, railroads and other transport, mining and metal-working industries, amalgamation and the absorption of weaker by stronger businesses has been rapidly proceeding in every advanced industrial community. But there is no reason to distinguish these amalgamations or combines from other large companies or private businesses for present purposes unless their construction has the object and the result of giving them a substantial power of monopoly.

If a business possesses this power, it matters not whether it has come into being by amalgamation of a number of competing equals, by the forcible absorption of weaker firms by a stronger, or by the creation of a single new corporation or private business in a new department of industry.

Still less are we concerned with the special legal origin and meaning of the term "Trust" in our economic treatment of monopolies, except in so far as it bears important testimony to the instability and weakness of the "industrial pool" or other formal or informal agreement among competing businesses. The inability of competitors in the oil, sugar, whisky, and other industries to secure faithful and effective co-operation, as regards output and prices, by any method short of a surrender of their separate stock to a body of Trustees empowered to exercise an absolute control over the conduct of their businesses, may possibly indicate that Cartels, Pools, and other "agreements" are merely transitory phases in the development of capitalist enterprise towards a higher and more perfect structure.[1]

§ 4. The Trusts with which we are concerned comprise all combinations of capital which are operated as business units and which exercise a substantial control of a market. The forms of combination may be classed as follows:—

α. "Trusts proper," where the whole or the majority of the stock of the different combining businesses is transferred to trustees who exercise full control, and issue certificates to the several owners, the latter retaining in some cases mortgages to the extent of the valuation of their factories.

The Standard Oil Trust in its original form was the leading case of absolute surrender to trustees, the Whisky Trust of conditional surrender.

β. Consolidations other than "Trusts proper," where practical unity of operation is secured with the retention of formal independence.

This may be a temporary arrangement, as when a railroad leases or rents another road, a policy sometimes adopted in other lines of business.

Or it may be a permanent arrangement, as when a railroad or other corporation purchases a controlling share of other corporations, operating them as parts of its single system.

When a separate corporation is formed for the purpose of securing a controlling share of a corporation or a number of competing companies in order to operate them as a single system, we have the so-called "holding Trust" or a "voting Trust" whose economic form nearly resembles the "Trust proper," though its legal or illegal status is somewhat different.

The holders of a majority of the stock in a company or a number of companies put the voting power of their stock

---

[1] The Whisky Trust best exemplifies the development from a weaker form of pool. For many years agreements had been made among the competing distillers, sometimes fixing an output, sometimes levying an assessment upon the quantity of corn mashed, in order to subsidise the export trade, so as, by relieving the pressure on the home market, to keep up remunerative prices. These pools were continually being broken, and the failure to maintain such agreements led to the formation of the Trust. Cf. Jenks, *The Trust Problem*, p. 108.

into the hands of a body of trustees or a Trust company, empowering the latter to carry on the affairs of the company or companies in accordance with some general line of policy previously determined.

"The individual shareholders may then pledge or sell or dispose of their stock in whatever way seems to them best, but the voting power remains in the hands of the trustees. The purpose of such a voting Trust is, of course, to preserve continuity of the policy which, for whatever reason, the shareholders prefer. In some cases it may be that the majority of the stockholders of the original corporation think it desirable to devote all the earnings for a specific period to the improvement of the property instead of to the payment of dividends. It might be impossible to continue such a policy with a shifting body of shareholders, many of whom might wish to receive annual dividends. If, however, the stock can be transferred, but the voting power remains in a few hands, the policy can be carried out consistently for a fixed period of years."[1]

The most notorious example of a holding trust was that known as the Northern Securities Company, formed for the purpose of placing in common hands a controlling share of the stock of four great railroads in order to restrain competition and to operate them as a single system. The legality of this form of trust in railroads has been successfully called in question, but modern financial development gives increasing prominence to this method of uniting multiform ownership of stock with concentrated control.

γ. Amalgamation, in which a complete "merger" of competing businesses is effected, as in the fusion of the New York Central and Hudson Railroad, or the fusion of the Union and the Castle Steamship lines in England.

This process of complete amalgamation, either by agreement of equals or by coercion and forcible absorption on the part of a stronger competitor, is of course the most general process of concentration of capital in every large iine of big industry. Where such amalgamation yields a basis of monopoly, it is entitled to rank as a "Trust" within the meaning of the word here taken, and probably

[1] Jenks, *The Trust Problem*, pp. 115, 116.

the majority of effective "monopolies" in manufacture, transport, and finance are built up in this way.

δ. Absorption of a number of competing businesses by a new company established for this purpose. The United States Steel Corporation and the Atlantic Shipping Combine are two conspicuous examples of this mode of establishing a Trust.[1]

§ 5. Many of these methods of combination have been followed for the purpose of securing economies of operation or of restraining a cut-throat competition, and not with a view to exercising any substantial powers of monopoly. Although such combinations are frequently classed as Trusts, they do not differ essentially as economic entities from other large companies which are not the products of combination, and they do not concern us in our study of Trusts as here identified with monopolies.

The monopoly power of Trusts is of course entirely a question of degree. No Trust is the sole source of supply throughout the whole of its market; no Trust is without actual or potential competition which limits its control of prices.

The lists of trusts and combinations which purport to show how large a proportion of the aggregate industry of the United States or other nations has definitely passed out of the competition stage into a stage of private monopoly are not reliable as sources of accurate measurement, though they are serviceable as indicating the extent of progress in concentrated capitalism in the several industrial departments. From this standpoint it is significant to find that in 1899 the *New York Journal of Commerce* published a list of 350 trusts and combinations in existence that year.

Large American corporations (mostly formed by combination) practically control the entire industry of land and water transport by steam and electricity, banking, insurance, and finance in general, the local services of water, gas, etc., besides the local and national telegraph and telephone systems, the industries of mining and of irrigation, the publication of books and newspapers, the great bulk of the wholesale and retail distribution in the cities, a large, prob-

---

[1] This classification follows closely the analysis of Von Halle in his *Trusts*, chap. iii.

ably increasing, ownership of lands and agriculture, a complete control over theatres and many other recreative industries, besides the control of almost all the large manufactures engaged in supplying the prime necessaries and conveniences of the people.

The summary of Industrial Combinations presented by the Census Report of the United States for 1900 gives an interesting indication of the classes of manufacture which have been most exposed to the growth of combination.

Industry Group.	No. of Combinations.	No. of Plants.	Capital.	Wage-earners.
			$	
1. Iron, steel, and products	40	447	341,779,954	145,609
2. Food and kindred products	22	282	247,944,675	33,165
3. Chemicals and allied products	15	250	176,512,835	28,401
4. Metals other than iron and steel ...	11	89	118,519,401	20,522
5. Liquors	28	219	118,459,158	7,624
6. Vehicles	6	65	85,965,683	34,422
7. Tobacco	4	41	16,191,818	17,661
8. Textiles	8	72	92,468,606	37,723
9. Leather, etc. ...	5	100	62,737,011	9,898
10. Paper and printing	7	116	59,271,691	16,706
11. Clay, glass, etc. ...	15	180	46,878,928	20,294
12. Lumber, etc. ...	8	61	24,470,281	10,778
13. Miscellaneous ...	16	118	45,408,869	17,243
Total	185	2,040	$1,436,625,910	400,046

The following[1] is a list of the articles manufactured or sold in 1900 by large corporations—*i.e.* with a nominal capital of over 10,000,000 dols:—Fertilisers, alkali, beet sugar, brick, brass, bicycles, railroad cars, cotton oil, electric-heating apparatus, fish (packed), window-glass, gas and electric-lighting fixtures, hides and leather, ice, linseed oil, lithograph productions, sewing machines, malt, school furniture, ships, silk thread, whisky, wire, steel-hoops, sugar (cane sugar), thread, tinplate, tobacco, woollen goods, writing paper, copper, snuff, bolts and nuts, borax, steel, lumber, pharmaceutical products, beer and ale (there

[1] Cf. W. M. Collier, *The Trusts*, p. 15.

being combinations of breweries in the following cities:
Chicago, San Francisco, Pittsburg, Boston, Cleveland and
Sandusky, Baltimore; also Milwaukee and Chicago); coal
and iron (industries of Colorado, also of Tennessee),
electric-car lighting apparatus, steel cars, cement, plug
tobacco, cotton yarn, matches, electric boats, electric
storage batteries, sewer pipe, chemicals, general electrical
apparatus, glucose sugar, granite ware, Cuban tobacco,
paper (news and printing), silver-plate, smokeless powder
and dynamite, steam pumps, "Bourbon" whisky (Ken-
tucky distilleries), iron (Lake Superior mines), cellulose,
biscuits, crackers and bread-stuffs, carbon, carpets, enamel-
ling and stamping, white lead, salt, screws, starch, tubes,
wall-paper, pine timber, passenger elevators, plate-glass,
print cloth, iron and steel, baking powder, rubber goods,
coal, window-sashes and doors, flour, petroleum and its by-
products, whisky, rope and twine, steel beams, steel rails,
beef, coal and iron, paper bags, typewriters, fruit, shoe
machinery, cast-iron pipe, dye-wood, flour, glue, leather,
rubber boots and shoes, varnish, writing paper, etc.

In what degree, over what market-area, and for how long,
these various corporations have been able to exercise a
power of "monopoly" is incapable of approximate
determination. Most of them have probably held some
measure of monopoly, but few have attained the large and
durable control of a market possessed for long periods of
time by the Standard Oil Trust or the Sugar Trust. If in
all these markets a single corporation controlled (say) 80
per cent. of the output, the security which competition
affords to the consuming public would have virtually disappeared. The percentage required to give a large limit of
effective control over prices will of course vary with the
class of commodity handled and with various conditions of
the market, but it may be safely asserted that the degree
and extent of monopoly-power exercised by most of the
above-named corporations falls far short of that exercised
by the classical examples just named.

Regarding the single large corporation as the instrument
of monopoly, there is no evidence to show that these
industrial corporations have yet developed sufficient strength
even in America to limit output or to hold up prices for any
considerable time except in the case of a small number of

commodities.[1] If we add to these Trusts the industrial pools and other combines, the durable monopoly exercised through industrial combination does not affect any large number of commodities. Regarded as a solid instrument of capitalist control the industrial trust is as yet feebly developed. Local combinations in retail trade in all probability exercise a larger and a more widespread influence upon the prices paid by consumers.

With a few exceptions the proved power of capitalist "monopoly" in America is vested, not in the industrial trusts, but, as we shall see, in transport and financial corporations and in corporations handling local services under charters or other privileges. The aggregate influence of the disturbances of price exercised by industrial trusts is doubtless considerable, but their power to hold up prices has hitherto been weak, irregular, and short-lived, so far as the great majority of the commodities they handle are concerned. It is very doubtful where a combination of mere manufacturers can maintain an effective monopoly even in a national market for which they obtain tariff protection. The real strength of a manufacturing or industrial trust is commonly, if not universally, derived from non-manufacturing processes with which it is connected.

While, therefore, there is ample evidence to show that industrial corporations, largely the result of combination of formerly competing firms, are everywhere engaged in trying to regulate output and to raise prices so as to earn

---

[1] "In many of the most important lines of industry combinations have secured control of a large percentage of the country's production. In other industries, although the percentage of the entire output controlled by combinations is not so large, still there are organisations with very large capital. In the raising or distributing of agricultural products, such combinations, though not unknown—*e.g.* the United Fruits Company—are still rare. While a beginning has been made towards the combination of mercantile industries, not merely in department stores, but also in the union of several large establishments along several lines, such as the combination organised by H. B. Claplin, yet by far the largest proportion of our mercantile business is owned and managed by relatively small concerns. Many manufacturing industries, such as clothing, dressmaking, millinery, small tools, electrical specialities, house-furnishing materials, the textiles, and numerous other articles are substantially free from combinations. The manufacture of cotton is perhaps the most important in which no combination of great size exists."—*Report of the Industrial Commission*, vol. xix. p. 604.

high profits, only a small minority have been able to maintain a successful career upon these lines.

The present stage, even in America where the movement
has gone fastest, is rather one of multiform experiment than
of achievement. A certain amount of regulation of prices
is doubtless operative in most large staple industries, but it
is mainly the result of temporary agreements among competing firms rather than the dictation of any single corporation that can be called a trust.

The fields of economic energy in America, where "corporations," "combinations," or trusts are strongly operative,
lie outside the manufacturing processes, and where a manufacturing trust is powerful its power is usually derived from
these non-manufacturing sources.

§ 6. Investigation of the origins and supports of successful "trusts" in America and elsewhere fails to show any
cases where the economy of the concentration of capital
establishes a monopoly in manufacture, at any rate over a
national or international market.

The point is one of great theoretical and practical importance. The economy of large-scale production is, as we
have seen, operative in most fields of machine production,
and experience seems to attest the fact that this economy
proceeds in different industries up to a different point,
establishing in each industry a maximum type of business:
if this maximum were exceeded certain wastes of business
management and other disadvantages would outweigh the
technical economies of larger-scale production. Now, if in
any industry the net economy of large-scale production continues up to or beyond the point in which the large business
can supply the entire market, a monopoly can clearly be
established upon this economy alone. A simple and widely
prevalent doctrine of economic evolution of industrial
society is based upon the assumption of the wide or general
operation of this tendency. This general operation is, indeed, rendered highly improbable by the wide expansion
of markets which comes with improved transport and
mechanism of selling. But there is no *à priori* reason why
a monopoly of a local, national, or even a world-market
should not be reached before the progressive economy of
large-scale production in a particular manufacturing industry has run out. In local markets it is indeed often the

case that a big man, possessing no other superiority than size, can crush a smaller competitor and establish a monopoly absolute within its limits, though even in such cases it is always open to argue that personal ability or energy is a factor in success.

When, however, we consider national or world-markets, it is more likely to be the case that the economy of large-scale production will be exhausted before a size of business adequate to monopoly is reached. While it is impossible to prove that a strong national Trust could not be formed out of the mere economy of large-scale production as operated by a man of normal business ability, there is no instance of any large industrial Trust seen to stand on this economy alone.

If any instances of effective Trusts standing upon the economy of concentrated capital alone exist, they must be sought in the region of finance rather than of ordinary industry, for it is in banking, insurance, and general finance that the essential force of modern capitalism is found; in finance mere size of credit appears to assign a progressive advantage without limit to the competitor for profitable business, or the manipulator of profitable *coups*.

§ 7. If we examine the actual rise and structure of trusts we shall always find the economy of large-scale production supported by some more certain basis of monopoly.

These supports may be provisionally classified[1] as follows :—

1. Superior access to raw materials.
2. Superior control of means of transport and distribution.
3. Differential advantages in production or marketing due to patents, trade marks, special processes.
4. Public franchises, licences, or other privileges bestowing monopoly or restricting competition.
5. Tariff legislation.

Reflection will show that these supports are not in every case mutually exclusive. Superiority of access to raw materials and to railroad transport, for example, are in part attributable to public franchises, while tariff legislation confers a differential advantage in markets.

[1] A fuller and more scientific classification of Monopolies is to be found in Ely's *Monopolies and Trusts*, chap. ii.

But for our purpose this classification will suffice. No American trust, industrial or other, seems destitute of one or more of these supports. So intricately interwoven are the conditions of industrial life that it is difficult to assign the relative importance which attaches to these various supports.

Many monopolies evidently draw their strength from advantages comprised in classes 3 and 4. Special inventions, secured by patents or secrecy, may be a single and sufficient basis of monopoly for a manufacturing firm of type-setters or electrical machinery or chemicals.

In the growth of the Sugar Trust, the Havemeyer and Spreckel's refineries gained their early predominance largely by the possession of patents securing to them economies of production. The same has been true of the Carnegie Steel Company and of other businesses which have acquired in their trade a position of sufficient eminence to enable them to force a combine upon businesses of inferior equipment.

Copyrights may furnish a similar power of monopoly to a newspaper or other publishing business. Largely based on these differential advantages of production are the uses of trade marks attesting reputation. In certain lines of manufacture—e.g. engineering, chemicals, scientific instruments, agricultural machines—all the most prominent firms have embedded in the capital value of the business some patents or other private methods of production, and not a few of the most successful trusts enjoy advantages of this class.

Other corporations possess powers of monopoly derived from legal grants of franchises or charters, conferring on them exclusive rights over profitable markets. The local service franchises, assigned to water, lighting, street railways, and other companies belong to this order. The amalgamation of these companies, formed upon purely local monopolies, into national or even international corporations, handling electric traction or telephone services, is an important development of recent capitalism. In the United States the railroads and telegraph companies, in Great Britain the railroads, derive a large part of the power of monopoly which they exercise over large areas of noncompetitive traffic from public charters, the rest being due to natural advantages of route, which drive down to private ownership of land. In the United States the growing amalgamation of competing railroads into a few large systems pooling rates is by far the most formidable aspect of the Trust question. The enormous grants of land conferred upon railroad corporations by charters emphasises the public character of the monopoly-power they wield.

Among monopolies affected or supported by public policy must be included restraints upon effective competition due to a public limitation upon licences to sell certain commodities. The brewing industry in England, and to a less extent in other countries, presents the most conspicuous instance of a growth of strong corporations enjoying monopoly profits derived from the limitation or practical extinction of local competition, based upon restrictions in the number of liquor-sellers imposed by public authority.

The banking system in many countries contains elements of publicly-bestowed monopoly in the sense of special rights to issue notes, or the enjoyment of special governmental aids, conferred upon a restricted number of banks.

§ 8. The most general support offered to Trusts by public policy is derived from the protective system of the Tariff. To what extent the Tariff is in reality "the mother of Trusts" is difficult to determine. There have been cases of trusts arising directly behind tariff walls erected in order to support them. The organ of the New York Reform Club a few years ago named a hundred instances of manufacturing trusts which it imputed to protection.[1] The list, however, contained many articles, such as electric supply, steel rails, anthracite coal, school books, cotton-seed oil, which enjoy other economic or public aids besides the tariff.

It must, however, be borne in mind that the concentration of industry must have gone already very far in a trade before the Tariff can be operative in creating a trust. The United States is itself a huge free-trade area, and unless, owing to the operation of other forces, the number of effective competitors in that market is already very small, the idea of amalgamation in a single corporation, so as to raise prices within the limits of the protective area, would not be feasible. The existence of a protective duty, or the probability of procuring one, is certainly a strong inducement for a business or a group of businesses already commanding a large

[1] See Von Halle, p. 50.

share of the home market to complete its combination with, or absorption of, its rivals.[1]

But a protective tariff can only create or facilitate a trust in cases where the conditions for an effective combination on a national scale have already been ripened by other forces making for monopoly. Upon the whole it would be safer to describe the Tariff as the foster-mother than the mother of Trusts. By feeding them at the expense of the body of consumers, and protecting them against invasion of the home market by foreign competition, it enables them to maintain their monopoly and to render it more profitable.[2] The same sort of assistance is also rendered the industrial pools and other combinations which in structure fall short of the completed Trust. It is probable that the net economy of large-scale production, apart from the supports of patents, railroad aid, and superior access to materials, may suffice in certain cases to raise the size and restrict the number of effective businesses so as to make tariff support the final determinant of a trust.

§ 9. But the actual history of the great representative American trusts seems to indicate that superior access to transport accommodation, and to supplies of raw materials, are the most important supports for an enduring trust. Among the "monopolies" or trusts of the first rank in size and in control of markets, the Standard Oil Trust, the Anthracite Coal Trust, and the United States Steel Cor-

[1] An illustration of this is given by Von Halle in the extension of the great Cordage Combination prepared in 1890 in anticipation of the McKinley Act. (*Trusts*, p. 51.)

[2] Professor J. W. Jenks (*The Trust Problem*, 40-41) does not think that in many instances the removal of the tariff would restore competition.

"The removal of the tariff, whether the industry were dependent upon it or not, would certainly destroy the rivals of the Trust before the Trust itself would go out of existence. In either case, however, the consumers would, beyond question, for the time being enjoy lower prices.

"It is also true that the removal of the tariff in many instances, by strengthening the competition from foreigners, would simply bring about an international combination."

The formation and maintenance of an international trust are, however, not "simple" processes, as even the history of the Standard Oil Trust testifies: the successful experiments are extremely few, and are confined to small trades or trades where the best sources of raw materials are so few as to be capable of being cornered.

poration stand out as the most representative. In each case the origin of the combination is traceable to special facilities of transport, and to a command over the best sources of supply of raw materials.

The early formation of the Standard Oil Company upon a basis of illicit rebates obtained by arrangement with the railroads passing through the oil district is a matter of ordinary knowledge. The rise of the Carnegie Steel Company (the nucleus of the present Steel Trust) upon a similar arrangement of preferential rates with the Pennsylvania Railroad is equally significant, though less notorious. The absolute control of the anthracite coal industry by a pooling of the interests of the seven railroads which traverse the coal district belongs to the same order of industrial facts. In each of these cases the control exercised through railway transport was flanked by a superior access to supplies of material. If the early oil wells had been scattered over various parts of the country instead of being concentrated in a limited region of Ohio, effective monopoly through transport could not have been organised. The narrow limitation of anthracite supply is essential to the compact organisation which operates these mines. The fundamental strength of the Steel Trust, the condition of its permanence, resides in its control of the Lake Superior ores and the facilities of handling and carrying them.

It is not, of course, necessary for a powerful manufacturing trust always to own and work the best supplies of raw materials, though, as we shall see, it is commonly a sound trust policy to acquire a direct control of these sources. A strong enough control over the means of transport by rail, steamship, or pipe line commonly yields sufficient command over the domestic or imported supplies to control the market. The Standard Oil Trust did not begin to acquire any amount of direct ownership of oil wells until well advanced in its career: it was able to buy the crude oil from producers upon its own terms, and still in large measure maintains this policy. So, too, the Steel Trust was already in existence before it acquired direct possession of the richest sources of iron ore.

In America the central factor in the organised control of industry by Trusts is the power of the railroads, dominating the rich natural sources of supply in mining and agriculture, and carrying raw material to the manufacturing centres and finished products to the great markets of the country.

In America the railroads have been the only effective high roads over the chief part of the country, the sole means of communication between East and West. So far as internal trade is concerned, the Mississippi, and during a portion of the year the northern chain of lakes, afford the only check upon the control of the railroads over the grain and meat traffic from the West and Middle States to the crowded East, the distribution of manufactured goods from the North-Eastern States over the whole continent, and the carriage of coal, iron, and other minerals from the mining districts to the manufacturing centres.

In the early days of railroad development a great number of small independent lines competed with one another for the work of transport. "As the systems grew agreements of various kinds were resorted to, beginning with rate agreements, continuing through pools, 1870 to 1887, transformed into traffic associations, 1887 to 1897 and 1898, and culminating in the community of interest principle, of which the Northern Securities Company is the most conspicuous example."[1]

So far as the most important traffic is concerned, that between the middle-west and the eastern states, this concentration has gone so far already that these groups, fairly stable in their composition, control nearly all the roads between Chicago and the coast, and stretch out their tentacles from Chicago through those great mining and agricultural states which are destined in the near future to become the chief homes of industry and population in the United States.

The actual nature of the bonds which associate the railroads with other business enterprise will appear when we discuss the financial aspect of modern capitalism. At present it suffices to point out that many of these railways own, control, and sometimes operate, mines, ironworks, irrigation works, canals, grain elevators, stockyards, and a great variety of businesses which have no essential connection with the railroad business, and from participation in

[1] Professor Meyer, *American Economic Association Report*, 1904, p. 112.

which they are often prohibited by the terms of their charters. But still more important are the indirect and often secret arrangements by which they bind themselves to favour trusts and combinations with which they are not organically connected. Special facilities of transport are the chief instrument of favour, and these facilities are classed as follows, by Professor Ely:

"(α) General facilities, as supplying cars to one competitor more promptly than to another; (β) rushing through the freight of the favoured shipper, while that of another is side tracked; (γ) furnishing better terminal facilities to one person than to another; (δ) maintenance of such relations between various modes of shipment—as, for example, between tank-cars and barrels, and between rail, water, and pipe line transportation—that advantages come to some which others do not enjoy; (ϵ) classifications of freight made and changed to the advantage of favoured classes; (ζ) making discriminations in favour of geographical sections in the interest of classes of shippers."[1]

A common business interest embodied in an agreement, or a mutually profitable understanding, between a trust and a railroad enables the trust to safeguard and utilise any other advantages it may possess from size, superior command of materials or of market, by inducing the railroad to afford assistance by all these various forms of differential treatment.

§ 10. The importance which railroad transport assumes in the working of industrial monopolies, especially in the United States, is easily intelligible. If we follow the flow of raw materials of industry from the primary extractive industries through the various manufacturing and mercantile processes which shape and place them at the disposal of consumers, we shall find that in most instances this stream of production is narrowest in the transport stage: the producers of the raw material are numerous and widespread, their product, left to competition, would tend to pass into the hands of a number of competing manufacturers who, in their turn, would pass on the finished goods to many wholesale merchants and retailers. But the collection and conveyance of raw materials, coal, grain, cotton, cattle,

---

[1] Ely, *Evolution of Industrial Society*, p. 210.

from the prime producers to the manufacturers or to the wholesale market forces the current into a narrow channel of transport, where competition, normally and necessarily checked, can easily be eliminated : hence it arises that a group of manufacturers or merchants, or of produce gamblers, can most effectively organise a monopoly or control of output and of market through the instrumentality of the railroad system. Where the railroads do not choose, or are unable, themselves to organise the monopoly, as they have done in the case of anthracite coal, they are open to enter a profitable compact with an independent corporation or pool, placing at the disposal of the latter the monopolistic power attaching to the transport stage.

Armed with such powers, the cattle trust organised by Armour, Swift, Morris, and Hammond, was able to fix the price which they would pay for cattle to the farmers who could find no other buyer than the trust, and to fix the price which consumers should pay for meat. Discrimination of freight rates, and other transport and terminal facilities, procured by the favour of railroads, were the actual economic force they exercised.

In other countries where the railroad factor is less dominant, as in Germany or England, special rates or facilities, procured either by political influence (where state railroads are involved) or by private arrangements, form a leading economy of trusts or other large organisations of capital. Where lower rates are accorded by railroads for long haulage in bulk, such discrimination, though sometimes illegal, cannot be regarded as unreasonable, for the lower rates correspond to the lower costs of carriage: there is no more reason why short haulage of small quantities should command the same rates as long haulage of bulk, than that any other retail prices should be as low as wholesale prices.

But where, as is common, rebates or other special facilities are accorded to shippers, irrespective of or in excess of these considerations of economy of haulage, the railroads are definitely makers of monopoly.

The transport factor in monopoly cannot, however, be worked with full effect unless in connection with some natural limitation of the supply of some raw material, or of the market for commodities.

If the raw material is procurable in many quarters, and of equal quality, its manufacture is less likely to be concentrated, and its flow will be less narrowed in the transport stage. A lasting corner of wheat, or even of cotton, is far more difficult than a corner of anthracite coal or even oil. On the other hand, where the best or most accessible supply of material is narrowly confined in locality, an effective monopoly may be established without railroad support.

For example, the paper trust which for a time controlled prices in the United States lived upon the monopoly which it possessed of the water power and lumber tracts so situated as to be available for the cheap production of paper.

The actual supports of the American trusts may be thus summarised: Control of railroad rates, control of limited sources of coal, iron, and other natural supplies, control of patents, protection against world competition by the tariff, and finally, the escape from such a ratio of taxation to the market value of their property as is borne by the smaller business man.[1]

§ 11. One other possible origin and support of a Trust requires recognition. We have seen that the economy of capitalist production makes for the establishment in every industry of a business whose size represents a maximum economy. Now in determining the *normal* limit of this business we recognised that economy of administration was a factor of prime importance. After a certain size and complexity is reached waste ensues from lack of central business control. But here and there a business man of abnormal energy and capacity may emerge, whose mind may carry the economy of large-scale administration far beyond the ordinary, introducing qualities of insight or of organisation that postpone the application of the law of diminishing returns, which otherwise prohibits an increase of the business beyond the normal limit.

Where the normal economies of large-scale production are exhausted before the business has grown to the size required to establish a national trust or monopoly, this rare business ability may suffice to lift it to the required level. Where comparatively few men get the opportunity to discover, train, and exercise a natural genius for business

[1] E. W. Bemis, *American Econ. Association Report*, 1904, p. 121.

organisation in a sufficiently large field of activity, it seems possible that here and there a business mind may be found so superior to his competitors that he crushes them and builds a monopoly upon their ruins.

Professor H. C. Adams thus propounds this view that a trust may arise from a monopoly of natural ability, as well as from a monopoly of raw materials, or of some other requisite:—

"A survey of the past hundred years of industrial change makes evident the fact that industry on its mechanical side has developed more rapidly than on the side of management and administration, and in any final explanation of congested competition, a phrase which appears to me to suggest a fairly accurate diagnosis of the industrial ills of our time, the scarcity of business talent holds an important place. . . . In as far as the centralisation of industrial power is traceable to failure in the supply of business ability, no permanent relief from the evils of Trusts may be expected until the highest grade of business intelligence becomes the common possession of the business world. The Trust may be regarded as a corner in business insight, business talent, and business courage."[1]

That rare business ability imparts great elasticity to the conception of a normal maximum size of business, and that in point of fact a successful Trust owes its success largely to the administrative and strategic genius of its chief organiser, must assuredly be admitted. There is, however, no evidence of the formation of a Trust resting upon business capacity alone: one or more of the other supports is present in every case.[2]

§ 12. Turning now to the structure of the Trust, we shall be prepared by the foregoing analysis to expect an extension of functions. In our general examination of the large modern business we saw that it extended both

[1] *American Econ. Ass.*, 1904, p. 104.

[2] So far as business genius is a factor in a successful Trust, it imparts an element of instability. For though "hereditary control" is far less usual in the United States than in England, the capacity to select and train a competent successor cannot be considered a normal part of the equipment of a great Trust-maker.

On this personal factor in business success see some interesting remarks by Professor S. J. Chapman, *Lancashire Cotton Industry*, p. 170.

longitudinally, to take in earlier and later processes, and latitudinally, adding new classes of products and by-products to its original line of production.

A Trust seeking to secure and strengthen its monopoly is impelled by considerations of more than ordinary force to a similar enlargement of its structure. Beginning by organising a particular process of manufacture, it is naturally driven to seek control or possession of the market of its chief raw materials, on the one hand, and of the markets for disposal of its manufactured goods upon the other. To secure not merely superior facilities of transport, but actual possession of the best sources of supply; to supply its goods directly to retail stores under its control and bound by agreement to sell only its goods and at prescribed prices, belong to the ordinary methods of Trust economy. Organising transport of raw materials and of finished goods in its own cars, tanks, or pipe lines, ships or barges, it proceeds to own and control the entire chain of productive and distributive processes. To this is commonly added the control of manufacturing and other processes subsidiary to the main operations, the possession of coal or electric supplies, the manufacture of machinery and other plant required to give self-sufficiency to a Trust. The latitudinal expansion takes the shape partly of new products and by-products, partly of the acquisition of interests in other kinds of products which, otherwise, competing with the product of the Trust, would limit its monopoly. This last extension is illustrated by the acquisition of gas companies by the Standard Oil Trust and of canals by the various Railroads.

The typical form taken by a Trust whose nucleus is a single manufacturing process is one which makes it co-terminous with a complete section of industry comprising all the processes which directly or indirectly contribute to the supply of a consumer's need for a given class of commodities.

This is best illustrated by the objects named in a clause of the charter of The United States Steel Corporation, which read as follows :—"To construct bridges, ships, boats, engines, cars and other equipment, railroads, docks, slips, elevators, waterworks, gasworks, and electric works, viaducts, canals and other waterways, and any other means of transportation, and to sell the same and otherwise to dispose of, or to maintain and operate the same."

Most of the industries above named are subsidiary or instrumental to the final objects of the Corporation, viz., the production and sale of various commodities of which steel is the chief material.

The double process of this Trust expansion may be thus illustrated :—

UNITED STATES STEEL CORPORATION.

Iron Ore, Coal Mines, Coke, Natural Gas.	Railroads, Ships, Docks, etc.	Blast Furnaces.	Rolling Mills, Furnaces, etc.	Steel { Hoops, Rails, Wire, Tube, Tin Plate, Bridges, Cars, Elevators, Engines, Electric Works, etc.

The properties owned are described officially in a general way as follows:—"78 blast furnaces, with a capacity of upwards of 6,500,000 tons of pig iron yearly, or half that of the United States in 1900; 149 steel works and six finishing plants, including bar mills, standard steel and plate mills, with an annual capacity of about 9,000,000 tons of finished material; 18,300 coke ovens; about 70 per cent. of the ore mines of the Lake Superior region, producing in 1900 12,724,900 tons; 70,830 acres of coal lands, about 30,000 acres of surface lands in the coke region, and 125 lake vessels, etc."

§ 13. There are four principal reasons why the Trust or close combination, with monopoly, assumes greater prominence in the United States than in England and elsewhere. First: the railroad as an economic factor is more important than elsewhere, and is able to render more assistance to mining, manufacturing, or commercial combinations. Secondly : the tariff, by securing to American producers the home market, renders profitable combinations more feasible than in a country of free imports. Moreover, in none of the protective countries of Europe have the great manufacturing interests obtained so exclusive a control over the tariff policy as in the United States. Thirdly: the corrupt domination of politics by business interests, stronger in the United States than in any great industrial nation of Europe, enables the great railroad and business corporations to procure municipal and state charters and other profitable privileges, to override many laws with impunity, and to avoid their fair share of contribution to the public purse. Fourthly: the greater absorption of the national energy in business operations, the greater field of selection for ability, the greater equality of opportunity to rise, the sanguine and audacious temperament of the American business man, coupled with freedom from many of the legal or customary restraints which hamper the "logical" evolution of capitalistic enterprise in Europe, have evolved a type of industrial and financial "hustler" with bigger ideas and more rapid and unscrupulous modes of realising them than is found in Europe.

§ 14. But while in this favouring atmosphere Trusts have grown bigger and more numerous, none of the conditions thus peculiar to America is essential to the formation of a Trust.

Without any assistance from a Tariff or from railroads we saw that in many branches of the metal and other manufacturing industries of Great Britain combinations, of a less rigorous order than a Trust, existed and were able to exercise a certain considerable control of prices.

There exist, indeed, in Britain many instances of mammoth businesses, formed by amalgamation, occupying so large and firm a place in domestic and foreign markets for particular classes or grades of goods, that in America they would assuredly rank as Trusts. The "monopoly" or superior competing power enjoyed is due in most cases largely to "good-will" or reputation, based partly upon patents and secret processes, upon long skill of management and workmanship, or in other words upon the "character of the work." In many of these cases the scale of the operations required for a successful undertaking implies enormous capital, inducing amalgamation and precluding any easy setting up of new competition. Recent amalgamations in the iron, steel, and engineering industries furnish a number of instances of firms which, though by no means outside competition, enjoy a degree of practical monopoly over certain market-areas and for certain sorts of governmental or private contracts.

To such an order would belong Platts of Oldham in cotton machinery, the Elswick Works (including Armstrong's and Whitworth's, etc.) in engineering and shipbuilding, Nettlefolds (amalgamating with Guest, Keen & Co. and other amalgamations) in the screw trade, Vickers and Co. (absorbing Maxim, Nordenfeldt, the Naval Construction and Armament Co., etc.) in the armour-plate trade.

As in the case of the American trust there is a growing tendency for these English companies to fortify themselves by securing the best available sources of raw material, and by extending their operations from the manufacture of saleable goods to the preparatory processes.

So, for example, we find Nettlefolds' absorbing the Patent Nut and Bolt Company which had previously absorbed the Dowlais Iron Company, comprising collieries, iron mines in Spain, blastfurnaces, steelworks, rolling mills, etc.[1] So likewise the great firm of John Brown & Co., manufacturers of armour plates and other shipping equipment, acquire collieries and iron-mines.[2]

In certain cases, where patents or command of raw materials are determinant factors in control of "cost" or of market, consolidation approaches so strong a form of monopoly as to rank as a real Trust. This is the case with Brunner, Mond & Co. in the chemical trade, where special inventions and scientific skill furnish the chief element of success; and with Borax Consolidated, which rests primarily upon the possession of all the important mines and sources of raw material.

In most British instances where a company possesses so

---

[1] Macrosty, p. 186.

[2] "Present appearances would lead us to expect that the steel industry will soon be confined to a comparatively small group of large units—Armstrong, Cammell, John Brown & Co., Vickers, Guest, Keen, the Weardale Co., the South Durham Co. (which alone aggregate some £21,000,000 capital), and some others. Under such an organisation competition may be as completely eliminated as under a trust of the most regular description."—Macrosty, *Econ. Journal*, Sept. 1902.

strong a position in the market as to earn abnormally high profits, not by cheapness of production alone but also by control of prices, this position rests upon patents, trademarks, superior access to raw material, upon means of carriage, or upon special contracts with government, or with some other monopoly. Unusual business capacity is commonly a requisite for the full utilisation of these bases of monopoly. Amalgamation of competing businesses and great size of capital may be conditions of success, but are not in all cases essential: the characteristic of such monopolies is rather the creation of a special market resting upon a unique sort of commodity, unique in form or in quality.

The Dunlop Pneumatic Tyre Company, Huntley & Palmer's Biscuit Company, Macmillan's Publishing Company (recently absorbing Bentley's), Cadbury's Cocoa, the *Times*, are instances of companies which enjoy such special markets, the commodities they sell competing rather with different classes or grades of commodities than with the same commodities produced by competing firms. The high differentiation of markets is the chief cause of the differential profits of these monopolies. The "monopoly" of Messrs. W. H. Smith & Sons in railway bookstalls, of the Union-Castle Line in South African trade, or of Messrs. Kynoch in small-arms contracts, rests upon special business arrangements which render outside competition inoperative.

In all such cases tolerably rigid limits exist for the monopoly. Other sorts of tyre continually compete with Dunlops, books and papers may be purchased outside the railway stations instead of at Smith's stalls, no government could give preference to Kynoch's if the tenders of this firm were exorbitantly high, and so forth.

§ 15. Though many of these businesses are virtually "trusts," the term in Great Britain has been usually reserved for certain amalgamations which have been formed with the avowed object of putting an end to competition and of controlling a market.

The earliest instances were the Salt Union, formed in 1888 with a capital of three millions in shares and one million in debentures, and the United Alkali Company in 1891 with six millions of shares and two and a half millions of debentures. Both sought to establish a monopoly by controlling sources of supply and by superior modes of production. Foreign competition broke these down.[1]

Textile manufactures have been a favourite field for British experiments, but history thus far attests more failures than successes. The strongest and most continuously successful of these trusts is that of Messrs. Coats in the thread trade.

Messrs. J. & P. Coats, after entering into a pool or selling union with their chief competitors, Clarke & Co., Chadwick & Co., and James Brook & Co., amalgamated with these firms in 1890. Shortly afterwards they made large investments in the English Sewing Cotton Co. and the American Thread Co., and in 1899 bought a Belgian firm. This series of amalgamations made them masters of the thread trade not only in Great Britain and America, but throughout the world.

The Bradford Dyers' Association, formed in 1898, united about 90 per cent. of the Bradford piece-dyeing trade, and has been fairly successful.

The Yorkshire Woolcombers' Association (formed in 1899), the Fine Cotton Spinners' and Doublers' Association (1898), the Calico Printers' Association (1899), the British Cotton and Wool Dyers' Association (1900), the United Velvet Cutters' Association (1900) appear to have been entirely unsuccessful, while several other textile experiments have not yet been sufficiently tested.

The careful analysis of British trusts presented by Mr. Macrosty (*Econ. Jour.*, Sept. 1902)[2] indicates that only a small number of experiments in this form of combination have been successful. Among the few successful ones we observe that almost all are in articles not exposed to the brunt of effective foreign competition: Messrs. Coats & Clarke are international, and control the world market; three are in the coal trade, where foreign competition is not practicable; one or two others, like the Wall Paper Manufacturers, cater for national tastes and requirements.

To this list of British industrial trusts a large number of brewing companies ought to be added. In fact, brewing is the most "trusted" British trade: an overwhelming pro-

---

[1] Cf. Hubbard, *Econ. Journal*, Ap. 1902.
[2] See opposite page.

Name.	Share and Loan Capital.		Vendors' share of Ordinary Stock.	Firms Combining.	Percentage of Trade.	Ordinary Dividend.					
	Original. £	Present (1902). £		No.		1897.	1898.	1899.	1900.	1901.	1902.
The Salt Union	4,200,000	2,400,000	9/20	64	—	Nil	Nil	Nil	Nil	Nil	10
United Alkali	8,420,550	8,420,000	—	51	—	Nil	Nil	Nil	Nil	Nil	Nil
J. & P. Coats	5,500,000	10,000,000	—	5	60	20	30	40	50	20	8
W. Cory & Son (coal)	2,500,000	2,650,000	All	8	—	7	7	7½	11	15	
English Sewing Cotton	2,250,000	3,000,000	1/4	15	—		Nil	8¾	7½	3¾	
Fine Cotton Spinners, etc.	4,000,000	6,650,000	1/8	31	—			8	8	9	
British Dyewoods and Chemicals	570,000	570,000	—	4	—					Nil	
Bradford Dyers	3,000,000	4,225,000	3/8 & def.	22	90			2	3	7	
Aberdeen Comb	300,000	300,000	3/8	3	90				9	4	
Rickett, Cockerell & Co. (coal)	900,000	900,000	All	2	—			8-13-11	4	6	
Yorkshire Indigo Dyers	450,000	468,000	1/2	11	—			6	12	8	8
Bradford Coal Association	199,000	249,000	All	8	90				8	8	5
British Oil and Cakes Mills	1,750,000	1,750,000	1/2	17	60				8	Nil	6
Yorkshire Wool Combers	1,931,800	1,965,800	All	38	—				7	Nil	
Barry, Ostlere & Shepherd	984,000	984,000	All	3	—				Nil	4	
United Indigo and Chemicals	240,000	240,000	1/3	8	—				7½	Nil	2½
Textile Machinery Association	290,000	299,000	All	7	—				6	Nil	
Calico Printers' Association	8,200,000	8,226,000	8/25	47	90				Nil	8	
Wall Paper Manufacturers	4,141,000	4,141,000	All	31	85				Nil	Nil	
British Cotton and Wool Dyers	1,820,000	1,492,480	1 7/20	46	98				8	Nil	Nil
Yorkshire Dyeware, etc.	226,000	294,000	All	5	85					Nil	
Bleachers' Association	6,750,000	6,791,000	All	53	75					6	3
Portland Cement Manufacturers	6,349,000	6,349,000	All	30	—						
Rivet, Bolt, and Nut Co.	550,000	550,000	All	15	—						
United Velvet Cutters	140,000	140,000	All	5	—						
Extract Wool and Merino	270,000	270,000	—	7	—					6	
J. & J. Baldwin	752,000	752,000	1/10	5	—					7	
Leeds Worsted Dyers	226,000	226,000	9/13	10	—					6	6
Imperial Tobacco Co.	14,518,000	14,510,000	All	13	—						

portion of the trade is controlled by great companies, largely formed by combination and absorption of competitors, enjoying virtual monopolies over local areas. These drink "trusts" stand on a different footing from other industrial combinations, deriving their strength from local monopolies of licences vested in public-houses which they own, and to which they furnish liquor.

The transport trade, especially the application of electric and other new means of carriage and communication, exhibits some of the strongest forms of monopoly. Partly a "pool" based upon mutual arrangements of rates, etc., our railroad system exhibits in England and Scotland several instances of amalgamation in order to repress competition, while over large tracts of country certain roads possess a control of rates which is liable to gross abuses. In other departments the National Telephone Company and the Electric Traction Company are instances of powerful businesses wielding for some years many of the distinctive powers of a full-fledged Trust.

§ 16. In different branches of transport, manufacture, mining, distribution, and finance we have traced the growth of organised restraints on competition, issuing in corners, pools, trusts, or other forms of monopoly. In the supply of wants which lie outside the ordinary region of industrial and commercial activity, belonging rather to the world of intellect and art, the same tendency is sometimes operative. The theatre in the United States, and to an increasing extent in England, presents the most striking example of the dominion of a trust. The ordinary "consumer" of the drama is in most American and many English cities compelled to buy whatever theatrical performances Mr. Frohman chooses to sell, at prices and on other conditions imposed by a monopolist: the actor can only place his services before the public through the instrumentality of Mr. Frohman.

The newspaper press, in many instances a local monopoly by the nature of the case, now exhibits distinct tendencies towards the formation of "Trusts" which shall control over wide areas the sale of news and the manipulation of public opinion. In Great Britain the two firms of Messrs. Harmsworth and Messrs. Pearson have already acquired newspapers in a considerable number of large cities, and are extending the number of their properties with a view to economy of production and monopoly of market, through the publication of a "simultaneous newspaper" appearing in all the great centres of population, comprised in part of common news and "editorial policy" provided from a single centre, in part of local news and policy superimposed upon the former.[1]

In another department of literature—the supply of school books, the American Book Company deserves to rank as an example of a powerful trust whose main strength is derived from controlling the State school system through methods familiar to American politics.

How far a Church organising the sole supply of a special sort of religious service, supported by the monetary payments of its adherents, can be regarded as a business corporation is doubtless open to dispute. But in the highly centralised system and careful business arrangements of the Christian Science Church, furnishing literature and other services at distinctly "monopoly" prices, we have a modern example of a spiritual "trust," operating by methods which, though doubtless analogous to those always employed by the Roman Catholic and other powerful churches, are more crudely "monopolistic" in their form.

§ 17. One other point of great significance in the "trust" movement deserves attention here. Though tariffs and other national laws and customs tend to keep the structure of capitalism within national limits, powerful forces make for business internationalism, and the international trust is already in the field.

This internationalism takes various shapes. Sometimes it implies the control of a foreign market by a trust whose productive operations are conducted in the single country of its origin; though subordinate companies may be registered in the foreign country, as in the case of the Standard Oil Company with its Anglo-American attachment, or Burroughs & Wellcome in the drugs trade. In other cases there is an amalgamation of firms in different countries for the formation of an international trust, though here also the forms of national companies are frequently preserved. The Coats &

---

[1] An interesting article by Mr. Alfred Harmsworth in the *North American Review* for January 1901, describes the economy of this form of "Trust."

Clarke Thread Trust, already named, the Nobel Dynamite
Trust (with its subsidiary companies in Scotland, Germany,
and elsewhere), and the Atlantic Shipping Trust are among
the largest examples of this class.   The absorption of the
American firm of Brooke & Co. ("Monkey Brand") by Lever
Brothers ("Sunlight" Soap), the new company establishing
factories also in Germany and Switzerland; the absorption
of Bryant & May's Match Company by the American Star
Company, are instances of more limited monopolies standing
on an international basis.

The Atlantic Shipping Trust and the combination of
financial interests in the electric traction business of
America and Great Britain are the largest examples of the
trend towards internationalism in the Trust movement.

The largest proposal for an extension of the trust
principle to international competition was that projected
by the steel trade in 1904, when a provisional agreement
was reached between the American Steel Trust and the
leading groups of British, German, Belgian, and French
producers for a regulation of the output of steel rails.[1]   The
basis of the agreement as between the chief European
countries was the allotment to each nation of a fixed percentage of output; British works producing 53.50%, German
28.83%, and Belgian 17.67%.   France was to come in on a
somewhat different basis, adding to the British-German-
Belgian total of 100 units 4.8 for the first year, 5.8 for the
second, and 6.4 for the third year of the agreement.   Each
country was then to apportion its share of the output to its
constituent companies.   All the large British firms were
involved in the arrangement which, if successfully executed,
seemed likely to control well-nigh the entire world output.

§ 18. The wide prevalence of concentration of capital in
pools, trusts, and various local, national, or international
combinations, discovered to exist in the various fields of
industry, may seem inconsistent with the large volume of
evidence as to the survival of small businesses.   The in-
consistency is, however, only apparent.   Over the whole
field of industry, if every form of occupation be included,
neither the aggregate number of small businesses nor the
proportion of the workers employed in them is declining;

---

[1] Carried into effect in the summer of 1905.

but the economic independence of many sorts of small
businesses is encroached upon by organised capitalism,
which in almost every current of production plants itself at
the narrowing of the stream, to impose tolls upon the traffic
as it passes to the consumer.

The small producer still survives in large numbers in
agriculture; but as successful modern agriculture requires
use of considerable capital and large opportunities of market,
the small farmer becomes more and more dependent on the
moneylending company and the railroads.   In manufacture, the small artisan, the jobbing plumber or other
"builder," the Sheffield grinder or the little brassfounder in
Birmingham, the home-working tailor or cabinetmaker,
though surviving in great numbers, are more closely attached
to big firms of manufacturers or contractors who take their
work, and often stand behind them with "credit."   The
independence of the small "sweating" business in so
many of the clothing and other trades is of course merely
nominal.   Much the same holds of the commercial businesses : most of it is "agency" business which, alike in
wholesale trade and in retail, binds the merchant or shopkeeper to some big manufacturing, shipping, mining, or
commercial company for which he does business.   The
immense growth of "packet" goods in retail trade and
the general extension of the "tied" store system illustrate
this growth of dependency.

The same influences penetrate the world of art and
literature, and even the professions : multitudes of jobbing
journalists attached to one or two newspaper offices, of
authors working for publishers or syndicates, artists whose
only chance of selling is the art-shop : actors, musicians,
doctors, teachers, even clergymen, earning their hazardous
livelihood through the instrumentality of a company of
middlemen.

The measure of the power of concentrated capitalism
is therefore by no means confined to the immediate area of
capitalistic operations.   In the long series of productive
and distributive processes by which raw materials of material
or immaterial wealth are created and passed on for sale to
the consumer there will commonly be some process which
involves a high capitalist organisation.   In this case, though
every other process lay in the region of small competitive

business, the monopolist control may lay a heavy hand upon all the other processes and impose on the ultimate consumer a tax as great as if the whole chain of processes were conducted in the sphere of monopoly. Such a power may be and often is exercised over small farmers or fishermen, and over the consuming public, by the carrying companies, or by the ring that controls the wholesale market: it may emerge in a manufacturing process where a few great businesses are able to combine, a corner in the produce market may from time to time usurp this power, or, after free competition in all earlier stages of production and of trade, rings of retail dealers may hold up local prices so as to take the profits of monopoly. Everywhere the "competitive system" is honeycombed by combinations exercising some form or degree of "monopoly"—*i.e.* presenting in some market the attitude of a single seller able within limits to impose his price. It matters comparatively little to the consumer whether "free competition" is "held up" by monopoly in several of the processes of production and of commerce or in only one: one strong "combine," fastening on a single necessary process, can exercise the same amount of control over the output and the selling price of a commodity as half-a-dozen different combines handling earlier and later processes in the same productive series.

In point of fact the existence of one strong pool or trust arising in a single stage of production, as for instance in the carrying of oil or the refining of sugar, prevents the independent combination of producers or distributors at any other process in the trade, absorbing the entire profits of monopoly by suckage at the narrowest point. Though, as we have seen, the "organisation" of a trade at a particular point tends to spread to the organisation of the earlier and later processes and to the control of subsidiary and competing processes, this effective stoppage of competition cannot yet be said to have spread over any large proportion of the general field of industry. The survival of keen competition in so many markets attests, in part, the rudimentary condition of the new arts of capitalistic "organisation." But in part it is attributable to the control exercised by a "ring," "pool," or other combine which, instead of directly controlling the earlier processes, forces them to cut-throat competition, in order that it may buy cheap and sell dear. While therefore the greater part of our industrial system still continues to be competitive, the area of the power of capitalist combination is growing and the effective protection furnished by competition to the consumer is diminishing.

CHAPTER IX.

ECONOMIC POWERS OF THE TRUST.

§ 1. It remains to investigate the actual economic power which a "monopoly" possesses over the several departments of an industrial society. Although the "trust" may be taken as the representative form of monopoly of capital, the economic powers it possesses are common in different degrees to all the other weaker or more temporary forms of combination, and to the private business which, by the possession of some patent, trade secret, or other economic advantage, is in control of a market. These powers of monopoly may be placed under four heads in relation to the classes upon whose interests they operate—(*a*) business firms engaged in an earlier or later process of production; (*b*) actual and potential competitors or business rivals; (*c*) employees of the trust or other monopoly; (*d*) the consuming public.

(*a*) The power possessed by a monopoly placed in the transport stage, or in one of the manufacturing or merchant stages, to "squeeze" the earlier or less organised producers, has been illustrated by the treatment of farmers by the railways and by the Elevator Companies and the Cattle Trust of the United States. The Standard Oil Trust, as we saw, preferred, until quite recently, to leave the oil lands and the machinery for extracting crude oil in the hands of unattached individuals or companies, trusting to their position as the largest purchasers of crude oil to enable them to dictate prices. The fall in the price paid by the company for crude oil from 9.19 cents in 1870 to 2.30 in 1881, when the Trust was formed, and the maintenance of an almost uniform lower level from 1881 to 1890, testifies to the closeness of the grip in which the company held the oil producers; for although improvements in the machinery for sinking wells and for extracting oil took place during the period, these economies in production do not at all suffice to explain the fall. Indeed, the method of the company's transactions with the oil producers, as described by their own solicitor in his defence of the Trust, is convincing testimony of their control of the situation:—"When the producer of oil puts down a well, he notifies the pipe line company (a branch of the Trust), and immediately a pipe line is laid to connect with his well. The oil is taken from the tank at the well, whenever requested, into the large storage tanks of the company, and is held for the owner as long as he desires it. A certificate is given for it, which can be turned into cash at any time; and when sold it is delivered to the purchaser at any station on the delivery lines."[1] In similar fashion the Sugar Trust controlled the market for raw sugar. Nor was this power exercised alone over the producers of raw sugar. It extended to dictating the price at which the wholesale grocers who took from them the refined sugar should sell to their customers.[2]

The Wall Paper Manufacturers' Trust made an arrangement with the dealers binding them to abstain from buying foreign papers for ten years.

In the petroleum business the Standard Oil Company adopted the most rigorous means of enforcing its monopoly on retailers. An oil-dealer who attempted to trade with its competitors was approached by an agent of the Trust, who informed him that, unless he ceased his "free" buying, a local store would be opened to undersell him.[3] In other cases a rebate system, not dissimilar from that prevailing in the Shipping Conferences is practised. For instance, in America,

---

[1] S. C. T. Dodd, *The Forum*, May 1892.

[2] "Trusts in the United States," *Economic Journal*, p. 86.

[3] Cf. Lloyd, *Wealth against Commonwealth*, p. 250; and Tarbell, *History of the Standard Oil Trust.*

in the cigarette and alcohol trades, the trust gives a rebate
of 5 per cent. or 7 per cent. to customers who can prove
that within a given time they have bought their supplies
exclusively from the Trust.[1]

This power of a monopoly is not merely extended to the
control of prices in the earlier and later processes of production and distribution of the commodity. One of the
most potent forms it assumes in manufactures where
machinery is much used is a control over the patentees
and even the manufacturers of machinery. Where a strong
Trust exists, the patentee of a new invention can only sell
to the Trust and at the Trust's price. Charges are even
made against the Standard Oil Trust and other powerful
monopolies to the effect that they are in the habit of
appropriating any new invention, whether patented or not,
without paying for it, trusting to their influence to avoid the
legal consequences of such conduct. There is indeed
strong reason to believe that the irresponsible position in
which some of these corporations are placed induces them
to an unscrupulous use of their great wealth for such
purposes.

§ 2. (b) Since the prime object of a Trust is to effect
sales at profitable prices, and prices are directly determined
by the quantitative relation between supply and demand, it
is clearly advantageous for a Trust to obtain as full a power
in the regulation of the quantity of supply as is possible.
To control a predominant share of the output is indeed an
essential to the real existence of a Trust. In England it is
a common maxim of business that a minimum of 70 per
cent. of the trade is indispensable to the success of consolidation, and in almost every instance of a strong trust the
proportion is considerably larger than this, the Wall Paper
Manufacturers, for example, claiming to control 98 per cent.
of the trade. Though the Standard Oil Company on reconstruction in 1899 claimed only to produce about 65 per
cent. of the country's total output of refined oil, its proportionate control over the eastern and middle western
market was far larger than this figure, while Mr. Havemeyer
testified in 1897 that the American Sugar Refining Company was supplying 90 per cent. of the total national

[1] Von Halle, p. 77.

consumption. In many articles of steel a single combination controls 75 to 80 per cent. of the output, and in some
lines even more.[1]

In order to effect this control the Trust will pursue a double
policy. It will buy up such rival businesses as it deems can
be worked advantageously for the purposes of the Trust.
The price at which it will compel the owners of such
businesses to sell will have no precise relation to the value
of the business, but will depend upon the amount of trouble
which such a business can cause by refusing to come into
the Trust. If the outstanding firm is in a strong position
the Trust can only compel it to sell by a prolonged process
of cutting prices, which involves considerable loss. For
such a business a high price will be paid. By this
means a strongly-established Trust or Syndicate will bring
under its control the whole of the larger and better-
equipped businesses which would otherwise by their competition weaken the Trust's control of the market. A smaller
business, or an important rival who persistently stands out
of the Trust, is assailed by the various weapons in the hands
of the Trust, and is crushed by the brute force of its stronger
rival. The most common method of crushing a smaller
business is by driving down prices below the margin of
profit, and by the use of the superior staying power which
belongs to a larger capital starving out a competitor. This
mode of exterminating warfare is used not merely against
actually existing rivals, as where a railway company is known
to bring down rates for traffic below cost price in order to
take the traffic of a rival line, but is equally effective against
the potential competition of outside capital. After two or
three attempts to compete with Jay Gould's telegraph line
from New York to Philadelphia had been frustrated by a
lowering of rates to a merely nominal price, the notoriety of
this terrible weapon sufficed to check further attempts at
competition. In this way each strongly-formed Trust is
able to fence off securely a certain field of investment, thus
narrowing the scope of use for any outside capital. This
employment of brute force is sometimes spoken of as
"unfair" competition, and treated as something distinct
from ordinary trade competition. But the difference drawn

[1] *Report of Industrial Commission*, vol. xix. p. 604.

is a purely fallacious one. In thus breaking down a competitor the Trust simply makes use of those economies which we have found to attach to large-scale businesses as compared with small. Its action, however oppressive it may seem from the point of view of a weaker rival, is merely an application of those same forces which are always operating in the evolution of modern capital. In a competitive industrial society there is nothing to distinguish this conduct of a Trust in the use of its size and staying power from the conduct of any ordinary manufacturer or shopkeeper who tries to do a bigger and more paying business than his rivals. Each uses to the full, and without scruple, all the economic advantages of size, skill in production, knowledge of markets, attractive price-lists, and methods of advertisement which he possesses. It is quite true that so long as there is competition among a number of fairly equal businesses the consuming public may gain to some extent by this competition, whereas the normal result of the successful establishment of a Trust is simply to enable its owners to take higher profits by raising prices to the consumer. But this does not constitute a difference in the mode of competition, so that in this case it deserves to be called "fair," in the other "unfair."

It is even doubtful whether such bargains as that above described between the Standard Oil Company and the Railways, whereby a discriminative rate was maintained in favour of the Company, is "unfair," though it was underhand and illegal. In the ordinary sense of the term it was a "free" contract between the Railways and the Oil Company, and in spite of its discriminative character might have been publicly maintained had the law not interfered on a technical point. The same is even true of the flagrant act of discrimination described by Mr. Baker:—"A combination among manufacturers of railway car-springs, which wished to ruin an independent competitor, not only agreed with the American Steel Association that the independent company should be charged $10 per ton more for steel than the members of the combine, but raised a fund to be used as follows : when the independent company made a bid on a contract for springs, one of the members of the Trust was authorised to under-bid at a price which would incur a loss, which was to be paid out of the fund. In this way the competing company was to be driven out of business."[1] These cases differ only in their complexity from the simpler modes of underselling a business rival. Mean, underhand, and perhaps illegal many of these tactics are, but after all they differ rather in degree than in kind from the tactics commonly practised by most businesses engaged in close commercial warfare. If they are "unfair," it is only in the sense that all coercion of the weak by the strong is "unfair," a verdict which doubtless condemns from any moral standpoint the whole of trade competition, so far as it is not confined to competing excellence of production.

The only exercise of power by a Trust or Monopoly in its dealings with competing capital which deserves to be placed in a separate category of infamy, is the use of money to debauch the Legislature into the granting of protective tariffs, special charters or concessions, or other privileges which enable a monopoly company to get the better of their rivals, to secure contracts, to check outside competition, and to tax the consuming public for the benefit of the trust-maker's pocket. Under this head we may also reckon the tampering with the administration of justice which is attributed, apparently not without good reason, to certain of the Trusts, the use of the Trust's money to purchase immunity from legal interference, or, in the last resort, to buy a judgment in the Courts.

How far the more or less definite allegations upon this subject are capable of substantiation it is beyond our scope to inquire, but certain disclosures in connection with the Tweed Ring, the Standard Oil Company, the Anthracite Coal Trust, and other syndicates induce the belief that the more unscrupulous capitalists seek to influence the Courts of Justice as well as the Legislature in pursuance of their business interests. Contributions to party funds for the purpose and with the result of influencing tariff and other legislation in their interest are methods of Trusts which, though matter of common belief, are difficult of proof. We have, however, the admission of Mr. Havemeyer before a Committee of Congress that the Sugar Trust contributed in Republican States to the fund of the Republican party, in Democratic States to that of the Democratic party,

[1] Baker, *Monopolies and the People*, p. 85.

in order to stand well with the dominant political power in each State.[1]

§ 3. (c) The more or less complete control of the capital engaged in an industry, and of the market, involves an enormous power over the labour engaged in that industry. So long as competition survives, the employee or group of employees are able to obtain wages and other terms of employment determined in some measure by the conflicting interests of different employers. But when there is only one employer, the Trust, the workman who seeks employment has no option but to accept the terms offered by his employer. His only alternative is to abandon the use of the special skill of his trade and to enter the ever-swollen unskilled labour market. This applies with special force to factory employees who have acquired great skill by incessant practice in some narrow routine of machine-tending. The average employee in a highly elaborated modern factory is on the whole less competent than any other worker to transfer his labour-power without loss to another kind of work.[2] Now, as we have seen, it is precisely in these manufactures that many of the strongest Trusts spring up. The Standard Oil Company or the Steel Trust are the owners of their employees almost to the same extent as they are owners of their mills and machinery, so subservient has modern labour become to the fixed capital under which it works. It has been claimed as one of the advantages of a Trust that the economies attending its working enable it to pay wages higher than the market rate. There can be no question as to the ability of the stronger Trusts to pay high wages. But there is no power to compel them to do so, and it would be pure hypocrisy to pretend that the interests of the labourers formed any part of the motive which led a body of keen business men to acquire a monopoly. One of the special economies which a large capital possesses over a small, and which a Trust possesses *par excellence*, is the power of making advantageous bargains with its employees.

A few of the stronger Trusts have recognised the advantage of detaching their employees from the general "labour movement," by introducing a small element of

---

[1] Cf. Jenks, *The Trust Problem*, p. 192.   [2] Cf. Chapter XV.

"profit-sharing," or by offering an inducement to them to invest their small savings in shares of the corporation. A small fraction of monopoly profits, thus laid out, purchases industrial peace, and helps to induce in the general public a belief that the profits of a Trust enrich many instead of a few. It is claimed with some reason that the Standard Oil, Steel, and a few other Trusts are administered with sufficient intelligence to recognise "the economy of high wages" for responsible and high-skilled employees. But the wages and other conditions of labour prevalent among the less skilled workers in the Anthracite Coal Mines[1] and in other strongly "trusted" industries prove that the working classes in general have nothing to gain from the economy of industrial monopoly.

But the practical ownership of its employees involved in the position of a monopoly is by no means the full measure of the oppressive power exercised by the Trust over labour. Since the means by which Trust prices are maintained is the regulation of production, the interests of the Trust often require that a large part of the fixed capital of the companies entering the Trust shall stand idle. "When competition has become so fierce that there is frequently in the market a supply of goods so great that all cannot be sold at remunerative prices, it is necessary that the competing establishments, in order to continue business at all (of course, under perfectly free competition many will fail), check their production. Now an ordinary pool makes provision for each establishment to run in one of the two ways suggested. Manifestly a stronger organisation like the Trust, by selecting the best establishments, and running them continuously at their full capacity, while closing the others, or selling them, and making other use of the capital thus set free, will make a great saving."[2] The Whisky Trust presents a notable instance of this economy. When the whisky trade was worked under the looser organisation of an industrial pool, each of the constituent distilleries worked below its full capacity, one year at 40 per cent., another even at 28 per cent. of its former output. But when the 80 distilleries had entered the closer form of a

---

[1] Roberts, *Anthracite Coal Industry*.
[2] J. W. Jenks, "Trusts in the United States," *Economic Journal*, vol. ii. p. 80.

Trust, in the following year all were closed with the exception of the 12 best situated and best equipped: these ran at full capacity, and their aggregate output was as large as that of the 80 which had been running before.[1] When at the beginning of 1894, Mr. Carnegie combined with six other steel manufacturers, so as to bring 65 per cent. of the output under his control, outsiders were paid large sums to close their establishments.[2]   The same policy has been adopted among others by the Cotton Oil Trust, the Sugar Trust, and the Rubber Trust.[3]   All the greater Trusts, in fact, have followed this plan of closing entirely the weaker establishments and running only the stronger, thereby effecting a saving in capital and labour.[4]

Here we see a Trust exercising its economic power of regulating production.   That power, as we shall see below, is not merely confined to closing the inferior mills in order that the same aggregate output may be obtained by a full working of the more efficient plant.   Where over-production has occurred it is to the interest of the Trust to lessen production.   With this end in view it will suddenly close half the mills, or works, or elevators in a district.   The owners of these closed plants get their interest from the Trust just as if they were working.   But the labour of these works suddenly, and without any compensation for disturbance, is "saved"—that is to say, the employees are deprived of the services of the only kind of plant and material to which their skilled efforts are applicable.   It is probable that one result of the formation of each of these larger trusts has been to throw out of employment several thousands of workers, and to place them either in the ranks of the unemployed or in some other branch of industry where their previously acquired skill is of little service, and where their wages are correspondingly depressed.   This saving of labour is not confined to the productive processes.   When the American Steel and Wire Company (now a branch of the great Steel Trust) was formed, the services of 200 salesmen were dispensed with : one of the early economies of the Whisky combine was the dismissal of 300 "travellers."   From the account given above of the

---

[1] Jenks, *The Trust Problem*, p. 34.
[2] Von Halle, p. 62.   [3] Von Halle, pp. 66, 108.
[4] J. W. Jenks, *The Trust Problem*, p. 33.

changes in organisation of production under the Trust it might appear that the effect upon labour was not to reduce the net employment, but to give full, regular employment to a smaller number instead of partial and irregular employment to many, and that thus labour, considered as a whole, might be the gainer. An industrial movement which substitutes the regular employment of a few for the irregular employment of many is so far a progressive movement. But it must be borne in mind first that there is usually a net reduction of employment, a substitution not of 50 workers at full-time for 100 at half-time, but of 30 only. For not only will there be a net saving of labour in relation to the same output, the result of using exclusively the best equipped and best situated factories, but since the Trust came into existence in order to restrict production and so raise prices, the aggregate output of the business will be either reduced or its rate of increase will be less than under open competition. The chief economy of the Trust will in fact arise from the net diminution of employment of labour. As the Trust grows stronger and absorbs a larger and larger proportion of the total supply for the market, the reduction of employment will as a rule continue. Of course, if the scale of prices which the Trust finds most profitable happens to be such as induce a large increase of consumption, and therefore to permit an expansion of the machinery of production, the aggregate of employment may be maintained or even increased. But, as we shall see below, there is nothing in the nature of a Trust to guarantee such a result. The normal result of placing the ordering of an industry in the hands of a monopoly company is to give them a power which it is their interest to exercise, to narrow the scope of industry, to change its *locale*, to abandon certain branches and take up others, to substitute machinery for hand labour, without any regard to the welfare of the employees who have been associated with the fixed capital formerly in use. When to this we add the reflection that the ability to choose its workmen out of an artificially made over-supply of labour, rid of the competition of other employers, gives the Trust a well-nigh absolute power to fix wages, hours of work, to pay in truck, and generally to dictate terms of employment and conditions of life, we understand the feeling of distrust and antagonism with which the working classes regard the growth of these great monopolies on both sides of the Atlantic.

§ 4. Those who admit that a Trust is in its essence a monopoly, and that it is able, by virtue of its position, to sell commodities at high prices, sometimes affirm that it is not to the interest of a Trust to maintain high prices, and that in fact Trusts have generally lowered prices.

Since the direct test of the strength of a monopoly consists in its control over prices, great interest attaches to these questions. Difficulties, however, present themselves directly we seek to ascertain the facts. It is true that we can easily learn the fluctuations in prices alike of the "trusted" commodities and of their chief raw materials before and after the formation of the trust. Thus we can ascertain whether as a matter of fact trusts have reduced prices, or to what extent they have raised them. By comparing the curves for raw materials and for finished commodities we can ascertain, though with less exactitude, whether the margin has increased or diminished: if it has increased we may generally conclude that the Trust is earning monopoly profits by holding up prices to consumers, not necessarily above the earlier level, but above the level to which they would have sunk if the trust were forced to be content with a normal rate of profit. A most careful investigation of the subject from this point of view was made by Professor Jenks for the "Industrial Commission." Dealing with the Sugar Trust he reaches the conclusion that "The sugar combination has, beyond question, had the power of determining for itself, within considerable limits, what the price of sugar should be, low or high, with or without competitors, although, when there has been competition, it has chosen to cut prices to drive out its rivals rather than to run the risk of letting them gradually take its market on account of its high prices. During about nine of the twelve years which have passed since the organisation of the Trust, the margin between raw and refined sugars has been considerably higher[1] than it was for three years before

---

[1] We cannot however conclude from this that the margin of profit rises *correspondingly*, for "in order that the profits may be the same the margin between the price of the raw material and that of the finished product should generally increase slightly with the increase in price of the raw material" (p. 133).

the Trust was organised and than it has been during the three years when there has been vigorous competition."[1] The Whisky Trust has been less successful in manipulating prices, for "whisky combinations have been able to hold prices and profits high only for short periods, inasmuch as they have almost invariably attempted to overreach and secure too high profits."[2]

The effort of the Standard Oil Trust is thus summarised: "The Standard Oil Trust was formed in 1882. From that time on, for a period of eight or nine years, it is noticeable that there is only a slight decrease in the margin. From 1891 until 1898 the margin seems to have been steadily nearly or just a cent. lower than for the period preceding. But the period of the smallest margin seems to have been in the years 1893 and 1894. During the last two years[3] there has been a decided increase, not merely in the price of refined petroleum, but also in the margin between crude and refined."[4] This larger margin does not imply a corresponding rise of profit, since there is an added cost of refining to be taken into consideration.

The chart of prices in the Tin Plate trade showed that the immediate effect of the combination was to raise the margin, and the rise of profit thus obtained was afterwards increased by a reduction in the cost of manufacture.[5] The same general results followed the formation of the Steel and Wire Company (now absorbed in the Steel Trust). "Margins as well as prices of production increased rapidly from the date of combination."

§ 5. But while such investigations may serve to illustrate the control over prices which it is the main object of a Trust to secure, they do not enable us to measure the "monopoly" element in consumers' prices, or the net profit beyond the normal business rate, which accrues to a Trust.

It may pay a Trust not only to lower prices to consumers, but even to reduce the margin between the price of its materials and of its finished articles; nay, it may pay a Trust in absolute control of its market to reduce the margin between cost of production and selling prices per unit of its aggregate output. This reduced margin of profit may still contain a monopoly element which, when the

---

[1] Jenks, p. 139.　　[2] *Idem*, p. 149.　　[3] *I.e.* 1898-1900.
　　[4] Jenks, pp. 153-4.　　[5] Jenks, p. 163.

whole output is taken into consideration, represents the largest aggregate profit which the monopoly is capable of yielding.

It is only from a deductive treatment of the subject that it is possible clearly to prove that Trusts possess a power over prices antagonistic to the interests of the consuming public.

A trust or any other business with a complete monopoly of any class of goods for which there is a market will strive to fix that price which will yield the largest net return from the business. The prime question will be, "How many articles shall I produce and offer for sale?" The answer to this question will depend upon the relations between two sets of calculations, the one set having reference to expenses of production, the other to elasticity of demand on the part of consumers.

On the side of expenses of production, the tendency to restrict or enlarge his output depends of course upon how far his business conforms to the laws respectively of diminishing, of constant, or of increasing returns—in other words, upon the limit of maximum efficiency in the size of his business. So long as a further enlargement of output can be made with a reduction of expense per unit of the whole output, our monopolist will tend to enlarge his output. But he will check this tendency by regard to the demand side of the problem. If he produces a small amount he can sell it at a high price, to dispose of a larger supply involves a lowering of price. If the article supplies a keen, widely-felt need, or strongly stimulates a craving for increased consumption among those who take off the earlier increments of supply, a large increase of supply may be attended by a comparatively small fall in prices. On the other hand, if the article has a weak hold upon the consuming public, satisfying the shallow taste of a small special group, dependent upon "rarity" for its appreciation, or easily displaced in the public favour by some other commodity, a larger output can only be disposed of at a great reduction of price. It is the relation between these two technically unconnected considerations that determines the practical power of a monopolist over prices. As expenses of production fall, urging the monopolist to increase his output, so the selling prices for his output likewise falls, urging him to restrict his output. The actual maximum output, the production and sale of which will yield him the largest aggregate profit, must obviously depend upon the relative pace of those two price movements.

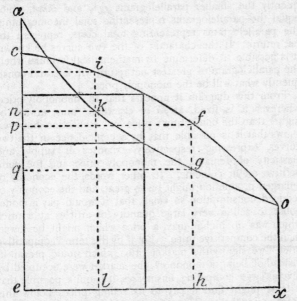

The above diagram[1] furnishes a geometrical expression of this play of forces, and indicates the difference between the determination of a competitive and a monopoly price for a business conforming in the main to a law of increasing returns.

"In the diagram the curved line *ao* is taken to represent the varying cost of production, and is hence called the supply curve : the line *co*, representing the *state of demand*, is similarly called the demand curve. The line *ox* would represent the price under competitive conditions. The perpendiculars *fh* and *il* represent the prices that would be fixed by the demand if the monopolist were to limit the

[1] Adapted with a slight alteration from Ely and Wicker's *Elementary Principles of Economics*, p. 184.

supply to *eh* or *el* respectively. The lines *gh* and *kl* would represent the total cost per unit of producing these various quantities. The parallelograms *ghqe* and *klne* represent the total costs of the different quantities, and the parallelograms *fhpe* and *ilme* represent the total returns from sales. Consequently the smaller parallelograms *fgpq* and *ikmn*, which equal the parallelograms representing total income, minus the parallelograms representing total costs, represent the net return. If the character of the two curves be known, it is possible to determine by mathematical formulæ where the parallelogram of greatest net return will fall, and consequently what will be the monopoly price."

From this diagram it appears that the monopoly price, wherever it is fixed, at *fh* or elsewhere, must always be higher than the competitor's price *ox*. Reflection, however, shows that it is possible that by a coincidence in the two curves, expressing respectively expenses of supply and elasticity of demand, the monopoly price and the competitive might coincide. In other words, the economy of enlarged production might be so great, and the economy of reduced consumption so small, that it would pay a monopolist to sell a very large quantity of articles at a price which was no higher, nay, a price which might be lower, than the competitive price. For if by this term "competitive price" we signify the market price which would prevail if, instead of being a monopoly, the market were occupied by several large competing businesses, it is quite possible that a trust might find it pay to fix selling prices below this point. For the expenses of competition, which a monopoly *ex hypothesi* saves, must be taken into consideration in determining a competitive price : a trust might find it profitable to fix a price which would represent some positive gain to the consuming public from the establishment of its monopoly. It is probable that under the pressure of those forces actual cases have arisen where the public has enjoyed under a monopoly lower prices than would have prevailed under competition or some looser form of combination.

§ 6. The real danger of Trusts in their control of prices appears when we consider this control in relation to the various classes of commodities which form the subjects of monopoly.

(a) The urgency of the need which a commodity satisfies enables the monopolist to charge high prices. Where a community is dependent for life upon some single commodity, as the Chinese on rice, the monopolist is able to obtain a high price for the whole of a supply which does not exceed what is necessary to keep alive the whole population. Thus a monopolist of corn or rice in a famine can get an exorbitant price for a considerable supply. But after the supply is large enough to enable every one to satisfy the most urgent need for sustenance, the urgency of the need satisfied by any further supply falls rapidly, for there is no comparison between the demand of famine and the demand induced by the pleasures of eating.

A monopoly of a necessity of life is therefore more dangerous than any other monopoly, because it not merely places the lives of the people at the mercy of private traders, but because it will often be the interest of such monopolists to limit supply to the satisfaction of the barest necessaries of life.

Next to a necessary in this respect will come what is termed a "conventional necessary," something which by custom has been firmly implanted as an integral portion of the standard of comfort. This differs, of course, in different classes of a community. Boots may now be regarded as a "conventional necessary" of almost all grades of English society, and a monopolist could probably raise the price of boots considerably without greatly diminishing the consumption. Half a century ago, however, when boots were not firmly established as part of the standard of comfort of the great mass of the working classes, the power of a monopolist to raise prices would have been far smaller.

As we descend in the urgency of wants supplied we find that the comforts and luxuries form a part of the standard of life of a smaller and smaller number of persons, and satisfying intrinsically weaker needs, are more liable to be affected by a rise of price.

(b) Closely related to this consideration, and working in with it at every point, is the question of the possibility of substituting another commodity for the one monopolised. This everywhere tempers the urgency of the need attaching to a commodity. There are few, if any, even among the commodities on which we habitually rely for food, shelter, clothing, that we could not and would not dispense with if prices rose very high. The incessant competition that is going on between different commodities which claim to satisfy some particular class of need cannot be got rid of by the monopoly of one of them. This is probably the chief explanation of the low prices of the Standard Oil. As an illuminant, oil is competing with gas, candles, and electricity, and unless the monopoly were extended laterally so as to include these and any other possible illuminants, the Trust's prices cannot be determined merely by the pressure of the need for artificial light. Though to a modern society artificial light is probably even more important than cane sugar, a Sugar Trust may have a stronger monopoly and be able to raise prices higher than an Oil Trust, because the substitutes for cane sugar, such as molasses and beetroot, are less effective competitors than gas, candles, and electricity with oil.

The power of railway monopolies largely depends upon the degree in which their services are indispensable, and no alternative mode of transport is open. Sometimes, however, they miscalculate the extent of their power. The high railway rates in England have recently led in several quarters to a substitution of road and canal traffic in the case of goods where rapidity of conveyance was not essential. So also in other cases sea-transport has been substituted.

The stronger monopoly of American railways consists partly in the fact that distances are so great, and the sea-board or other water conveyance so remote, that over a large part of the Continent the monopoly is untempered by alternative possibilities of transport.

The reverse consideration, the possibility of substituting the article of monopoly for other articles of consumption, and so securing a wider market, has quite as important an influence on prices. The possibility of substituting oil for coal in cooking and certain other operations has probably a good deal to do with the low price of oil. A Trust will often keep prices low for a season in order to enable their article to undersell and drive out a rival article, a competition closely akin to the competition with a rival producer of the same article. When natural gas was discovered in the neighbourhood of Pittsburg, the price was lowered sufficiently to induce a large number of factories and private houses to give up coal and to burn gas. After expensive fittings had been put in, and the habit of using gas established, the Gas Company, without any warning, proceeded to raise the rates to the tune of 100 per cent. When we ascend to the higher luxuries, the competition between different commodities to satisfy the same generic taste, or even to divert taste or fashion from one class of consumption to another class, is highly complicated, and tempers considerably the control of a Trust over prices.

The power of a company which holds the patent for a particular kind of corkscrew is qualified very largely not only by competition of other corkscrews, but by screw-stoppers and various other devices for securing the contents of bottles. The ability to dispense with the object of a monopoly, though it does not prevent the monopolist from charging prices so much higher than competition prices as to extract all the "consumer's rent," of the marginal consumer, forms a practical limit to monopoly prices.

(c) Lastly, there is the influence of existing or potential competition of other producers upon monopoly prices. Where prices and profits are very high a Trust is liable to more effective competition on the part of any surviving independent firms, and likewise to the establishment of new competitors. This ability of outside capital to enter into competition will of course differ in different trades. Where the monopoly is protected by a tariff the possibility of new competition from outside is lessened. When the monopoly is connected with some natural advantage or the exclusive possession of some special convenience, as in mining or railways, direct competition of outsiders on equal terms is prohibited. Where the combination of large capital and capable administration is indispensable to the possibility of success in a rival producer, the power of a monopoly is stronger than where a small capital can produce upon fairly equal terms and compete. If the monopoly is linked closely with personal qualities and with special opportunities of knowledge, as in banking, it is most difficult for outside capital to compete effectively.

§ 7. These considerations show that the power of a Trust or other monopoly over prices is determined by a number of intricate forces which react upon one another with varying degrees of pressure, according as the quantity of supply is increased or diminished. But a Trust is always able to charge prices in excess of competitive prices, and it is generally its interest to do so. It will commonly be to the interest of a Trust or other monopoly to maintain a lower scale of prices in those commodities which are luxuries or satisfy some less urgent and more capricious taste, and to maintain high prices where the article of monopoly is a common comfort or a prime necessary of life for which there is no easily available substitute.

CHAPTER X.

THE FINANCIER.

§ 1. The structure of modern Capitalism tends to throw an ever-increasing power into the hands of the men who operate the monetary machinery of industrial communities, the financial class. For large enterprises the financier has always been a necessary man: in the ancient and the mediæval world he found large sums of money to meet the emergencies of kings and great nobles, ecclesiastical or civil, to furnish military or naval expeditions, and to facilitate the larger forms of commercial enterprises which needed capital. Small financiers, as usurers or money-lenders, have at all times lived upon the irregularities and misfortunes of the farming, artisan, and small trading classes. But not until the development of modern industrial methods required a large, free, various flow of capital into many channels of productive employment did the financier show signs of assuming the seat of authority he now occupies in our economic system. Every important step which we have traced in the growth of industrial structure has favoured the segregation of a financial from a more general capitalist class, and has given it a larger and a more profitable control over the course of industry.

The elaborate differentiation of industrial processes into separate businesses, the concatenation of a long series of different businesses contributing directly to the production of each class of commodities, the relation of each member of this series to dependent or subsidiary businesses, each of which is itself a member of another series of separately ordered processes, the interdependence of the most widely divergent manufacturing or commercial processes through the use of some common source of mechanical power, or some instrument of transport, the expansion of local into national and world-markets which bring what were formerly separate self-sufficing industrial systems into unity—the working of such an industrial organisation implies a delicate and intricate mechanism of adjustments. In order that such a system may work properly and economically there must be an automatic apparatus for the application of economic stimuli and the generation of productive power at points of industrial deficiency, and a corresponding application of repressive checks at points of industrial excess: industrial power must be distributed in some general form throughout the entire organism to be transmuted into special kinds of productive energy where there is need.

This growing necessity of modern industry has reacted in two important ways upon the economic structure—first by producing a radical change in the structure of the business-unit, and secondly in giving rise to "a class of pecuniary experts whose business is the strategic management of the interstitial relations of the system."[1]

The quick rise of new manufacturing and commercial business demanded a freer movement of capital than the older business structure could easily procure: old-established, private businesses sought to expand: men with keen wits capable of seizing opportunities rose "from the ranks" and needed the use of capital; vast new forms of enterprise in railroads, mining, etc., demanded larger capital than private finance could furnish. Hence the need of a reformation of business structure upon a basis of co-operative capital, drawn from innumerable private sources, welded into large masses

---

[1] Veblen, *The Theory of Business Enterprise*, p. 29.

and utilised for profitable industry by able directors of large
business enterprises. The wider spread increase of wealth
from new industrial methods enabled far more people than
before to effect private savings: the economy of large-scale
production precluded them from setting up in business for
themselves upon the small capital they thus commanded,
while improved methods of commercial intelligence greatly
widened the area of secure investment, tending more and
more to separate capital from the presence and direct
control of its owners, and to place it at the disposal
of big business men who paid interest to its owners for
its use.

Thus it has come to pass that in every field of capitalist
industry joint-stock enterprise has been rapidly displacing
privately-owned businesses. So long as the new class of
small investors had only the alternative of effecting loans or
mortgages at small fixed rates of interest, or of incurring
"unlimited liability" by investments which they could
neither watch effectively nor easily withdraw, the growth of
co-operative capital was comparatively slow. But after
"limited liability" was set on a solid legal footing[1] the
movement became very rapid and widespread. The application of this new capitalist structure, first to public loans,
then to railroad, shipping, mining, and banking enterprises,
the enormous expansion of public or "company" development in the supply of municipal services, and finally the
extension to industrial companies of every sort and size,
have revolutionised the character of modern economics and
politics. Countless thousands of citizens in America or
Great Britain are part-owners of lands, railroads, minerals,
factories, municipal plants, and public revenues in all parts
of the civilised or semi-civilised world. Primarily this
signifies a divorcement of political from economic interests
for large sections of these nations: politically they are
members of a single nation with an area of influence and
interest thus circumscribed, economically they are to an
ever-growing extent cosmopolitans. In what important
ways this economic internationalism is moulding world-
politics is obvious, the cross-ownership among nations is by
far the most substantial guarantee of the development of a

[1] In Great Britain by Acts 18 and 19 Vict., c. 133 (1855), consolidated by 25 and 26 Vict., c. 89 (1862).

general policy of **peace.** Economic internationalism is the precursor and the moulder of political international-ism, the beginnings of which are laid in a common postal system, a public or semi-public organisation of railroads, shipping routes, banking and telegraphs, and the increasing exercise of public protection for foreign investments. The early beginnings of this cross-ownership among different nations are, indeed, often sources of national quarrels and even of wars, where the owners of foreign investments which are in peril of repudiation, or are otherwise injured by "bad government," are possessed of sufficient political influence in their own nation to utilise the public purse and the public force in order to safeguard or improve their stakes in foreign parts. But the wider normal tendency is towards a political solidarity which shall reflect the growing economic solidarity of nations.

§ 2. This obvious result of the community of economic in-terests is, however, gravely impeded by certain group-interests of financiers within the several nations which do not coin-cide with, and are often antagonistic to, the more stable interests of international investors.

A clear understanding of the place occupied by the financier in modern capitalism and of the harmony and divergence of interests between him and the investor is essential to the study of the industrial system of to-day.

The modern financier may be regarded as the product of the joint-stock company,[1] and can best be understood by studying the "natural history" of this form of modern busi-ness structure. The theory of a "company" is that a number of persons owning some capital which they cannot

---

[1] There is another tap-root of finance—namely, the development of national borrowing, which plays perhaps an even more important part than joint-stock enterprise in the business of some of the greatest European financial houses. The great family group of Rothschilds, and to a less extent such firms as Baring's, Hambro's, Stern's, and Goschen's, have devoted themselves to floating, dealing in, and mani-pulating those public debts which are the financial expression of modern political movements. This oldest field of profitable finance has expanded enormously with the development of public expenditure upon war, armaments, and productive enterprise in Europe, the Far East, and in South America. Immensely important as is this field, it lies, however, so far outside the area of our investigation that we can only bestow upon it a few passing glances indicative of its reactions upon private capitalism.

otherwise profitably employ agree to "pool" their capitals, so as to form a capital large enough for profitable use in some business which they select: they choose directors to represent their interests and to exercise a general control over the business, subject to their over-ruling in a general meeting of shareholders; the directors appoint managers, who are in command over the actual industrial processes; the supreme and ultimate control always rests with the body of shareholders, and the motive of the undertaking is to furnish them with the largest profit upon their capital.

The formal structure of a company as a legal entity reflects this theory. The actual origin and working of most companies, however, is very different. A practical business man gets hold of what may be called "a profitable notion." This "notion" may have a solid concrete basis in some actual business which he has been running on his own account, and which he thinks can be "put upon the market" in a form to attract investors and enable him either to escape from active business life with a large independent income or to remain in command with so much more capital at his disposal that he can greatly increase the net value of his property. Or the "profitable notion" may reside in some patent of a new process of manufacture, the utilisation of some new source of supply, the opening of some new market, or, finally, in some new business organisation which, by "pooling" or amalgamation, shall effect economies of cost or control of market.

Whatever be the basis of the "notion" the business man is concerned with its vendibility in the investment market. In order to make it into a marketable commodity he must have recourse to the assistance of general financiers who are dealers in "vendible notions," and are able to put them on the market in such a manner as to tempt the investing public into buying. Such a "promoter" will sometimes be himself a great capitalist, or will have intimate business associations with some great banking or finance company which is prepared to "back" the project by "underwriting" shares. If the project be "sound"—*i.e.*, either immediately vendible or industrially profitable as an interest yielding investment, the "promoters" will dispose of certain blocks of shares to other capitalists, and will participate themselves before putting it upon the open market.

The initial arrangements will be dominated by the desire of the " vendor " of the project and the " promoter " to procure for themselves the largest possible proportion of the profits which may accrue, either from the sale of shares to the investing public, or from the development of a steadily remunerative business in case the project is well fitted for a prolonged industrial career. If it is designed to work the Company as a profit-making concern, the vendors and their financial backers will commonly retain a sufficient proportion of the share-capital to enable them to keep control over business operations. In America it is common in the construction or reconstruction of Corporations formed for profitable working, for the promoting group to retain in their hands all or nearly all the ordinary shares, letting in the general public only as mortgagors. In England the usual policy has been to offer to the public a large holding of ordinary shares, as well as the bulk of preference shares and debentures, and to trust to the prestige of the directorate, backed by a sufficient support of personal holdings, to enforce the policy of the board. Such is the case in most British Railways, Banking or Brewing Companies—a widespread ownership of the stock accompanied by a sufficient control of voting power by the directorate to give them command.

In form, therefore, an economic democracy with an elective responsible government, the joint-stock company is in most instances a close oligarchy: the monetary support of the public is wanted but not their direction. Diffused ownership with concentrated control is the distinctive feature of the Company; so far from the investors choosing their board of directors, the board their chairman, and the directors executing the will of the investors, the actual process is the reverse. The chairman, probably the nominee of some big promoting capitalist, is given the post and one or two financial or ornamental supporters are put in as fellow-directors: this tiny group nominate the rest of the directorate and force their selection in the meeting of shareholders; having the initiation of the business in their hands they dictate the policy, retain despotic power in all vital matters, communicate to the shareholders what is convenient, conceal what is inconvenient, and resist—almost in every case successfully—attempts of a refractory minority, or even majority, to question their conduct, or alter the composition of the board.

High considerations of industrial expediency, if not of necessity, seem to require the maintenance of an effective oligarchy in the control of business, though at the same time requiring a wider distribution in the ownership of the capital engaged: this expediency of concentrated control forms the rational basis of a financial power which, as we shall see, is liable to great and dangerous abuses.

§ 3. This "Company" structure of modern business which is now virtually in possession of the entire field of capitalism in the mining, transport, banking, and large manufacturing industries has given rise to financial methods and interests requiring further study.

The first salient point in this study of the relation between modern finance and modern concrete industry is the figure of the ordinary investor. Now an investor is animated by one of two motives—either the desire to hold stocks or shares in order to get income from the profitable conduct of the business which they represent, or the desire to sell at a rise and so secure by a *coup* an addition to his capital. The two motives are frequently combined in the same person and in relation to the same class of shares: some buy to hold, others to sell, and a large number of men engaged in some special business or other avocation are continually engaged in shifting their investments, partly in order to earn higher interest, partly to make profitable *coups*. There are also classes of men who, quitting some special calling, virtually occupy themselves in these more or less speculative aspects of investment, never organising any financial operation but operating through brokers on the stock markets.

A very large proportion of the well-to-do classes who possess some property or have made some savings are occupied in investing them in businesses the nature of which they cannot really know, and the conduct of which they cannot as shareholders appreciably influence. The suckage of new capital demanded for the expansion of old industries and the establishment of new comes mainly from these classes of small and middling investors, who know little of the actual working of the financial system and cannot by their industrial action control it. What we have here is in fact a great capitalist proletariat, who bear to the operators of finance a relation closely analogous to that which the labouring proletariat bear to the employing class. The ordinary investor, the small capitalist, must sell the use of his capital, as the labourer must sell the use of his labours, to some organiser of a business enterprise if he is to get any advantage from possessing it. Now, since his capital is evidently wanted to co-operate with labour-power in actual operations of industry, it might seem natural that he should sell his use of capital direct to the same man who buys labour-power, the *entrepreneurs* or managers of a business concern. In a simpler state of business this is what happened—the owner-employer privately borrowed money or obtained advances for the conduct of his business. But in the more developed business-form the "financing" becomes a function separate from that of business management and passes to a separate class of promoters, bankers, brokers, and other financiers. These classes are "middlemen" between the investor and the *entrepreneur* or organiser of concrete industry, gathering up from countless sources the idle capital of the community, and directing it through the various channels of investment. Such men are the wholesale dealers in "money" or fluid capital, and the private owner of capital must place it in their hands if he wishes to employ it. The "terms" he can get for its use, and the economic nature of the use to which it is actually put, are largely imposed upon him by the regulations of the financial system, similarly as the terms of the employment of various sorts of labour are directly imposed by the rules or customs of employers and the technical exigencies of the trade. A large fraction of this garnered "capital" lies at any given time in the possession and at the disposition of bankers, stock and bill brokers, in a fluid form, supporting the general volume of credit by which the operations of buying and selling are conducted in business. The rest of it is invested in stocks and shares and mortgages, the owners receiving (or being entitled to receive) scrip representing a claim upon the capital value of certain concrete business forms and on a share of their earnings.

Even in the simplest form of conducting a small business on the safest basis the element of speculation exists. Opportunities of extending the business, or of adopting some new plant or machine, induce the business-man to borrow from neighbours their savings; or some unforeseen misfortune drives him to seek a temporary loan in order to tide him over the emergency: he borrows in order to make an additional profit or to spread over a longer period a loss which falling at a single blow might break him. In both cases there is a risk, in both cases he gives security to the lender by giving him a mortgage or other lien upon his property, in both cases he trades on "credit," buying and selling goods which in part belong not to himself but to his creditors.

The distinctive characteristic of modern large business is that this abnormal and occasional practice has become universal and perpetual, and that a large intricate financial machinery exists for operating it. Credit enters into the financial structure of the company business at its inception in the form of capitalisation: it enters into the functional activity of the business in the way of discounting bills, bank advances, and other temporary loans.

The whole system is one of betting: not indeed blind gambling, but speculation in which foresight and chance play parts of varying magnitude. In the borrowing of the simpler business man the latter backs his skill and luck to produce and sell within a given time a sufficient quantity of goods at a sufficient price to enable him to pay back his loan with interest, at the same time earning for himself a profit. Both borrower and lender here evidently look in this "speculation" to the probability of profitable sales.

What is true here, remains true of the more elaborated speculative system of modern "credit." The financial basis of the whole "credit" system is the estimate of "earning capacity," the ability of the actual business apparatus to market goods at such a rate and such a margin over cost as will enable a profit to be paid: the diseases or errors of the credit system are all attributable either to miscalculations or misrepresentations of this "earning capacity."

§ 4. In honest company business, although the form of the capitalisation is to attribute a separate value to the tangible assets—land, buildings, machinery, stock, etc., and the intangible assets such as patents and goodwill, the real valuation of the assets is upon earning capacity. If, as often happens, the tangible assets are valued at cost of production or of replacement, the intangible assets can only be valued by their net productivity, which in its turn can only be estimated by attributing to them all the capital value of the estimated future earnings beyond what is assigned as the cost or replacement of the tangible assets. Goodwill is indeed the elastic asset commonly used to stretch the capitalisation up to or beyond the limit of the capitalised earning capacity.

A sound estimate of earning capacity is thus the sheet-anchor of honest finance in formation of companies. Based partly upon a just actuarial account of normal earnings in the past, partly upon the probabilities of an expansion of profitable business in the future, it derives chiefly from the latter a large degree of uncertainty. In taking past earnings as a basis of calculation of future earnings, even where past earnings are fairly computed, a conservative financier would take into consideration the probability of new methods of production in the hands of energetic rivals as discounting the value of present goodwill and patents. On the other hand, where the object of the formation of a Company is to establish a Pool or Trust or other "monopoly," it is legitimate to take account of this power to control the market and to hold up prices as a factor in earning-capacity.

It is evident that, however carefully financed, a large Company, whether its putative earning capacity depends largely upon control of markets or upon the ordinary competitive weapons of organisation, patents, goodwill, etc., or even upon improved economies of production, is highly speculative in its present value. In the present stage of capitalist development, where new nations are rapidly entering the field of competitive production, where the industrial arts are shifting so quickly, and where new markets are constantly arising from an extension of communications and an expansion of wants, it is probable that this essential factor of speculation is growing larger, rendering it more difficult to forecast earning-capacity with any degree of accuracy. A well-established business, with an expensive equipment of the best plant and an excellent name, is liable at any time to be outclassed by a rival with some new machine, and to be obliged to "scrap" its valuable plant or see its earning capacity ooze out, leaving

its assets, tangible and intangible, quite valueless. A
famine in India may knock out the margin of his profit by
raising the price and restricting the supply of his cotton or
other raw material, a coal strike may stop his source of
power, a war in China or a revolution in Argentina may
destroy his market; with every expansion in number and
variety of markets in which he buys and sells comes an
increasing number of incalculable risks. Though some of
these may be cancelled on the theory of putting one's eggs
in several baskets, the net result is to render future earning-
capacity less calculable. Indeed, the growing variety and
magnitude of these risks has largely given rise to that great
department of modern finance known as Insurance, which,
by discounting and distributing certain specific risks, such
as loss by fire, loss at sea, dishonesty of employees, etc.,
counteracts to some extent this growing incalculability of
future earnings.

§ 5. The limits of the sound and useful service of the
promoters and financiers in constructing and in floating a
Company are now quite evident. They consist in a just
calculation on actuarial and other bases of the future
earning-capacity of the business, its capitalisation upon
these bases, and the distribution of the stocks and shares
and their marketing in forms most convenient to the
investing public, who are informed of the true nature of the
business into which they put their money. An agreed and
recognised rate of commission for such work of financial
construction and promotion, with a further commission for
underwriting, paid either by the vendors or by the Company
or both, would be the gain of the promoter and financier
most conformable to reasonable business methods. Placing
a business upon a basis where it can command more
working capital and more bank credit increases its competitive, and in some instances even its industrial, efficiency,
and is entitled to payment for this service.

But the actual operation of the promoter and financier in
construction of Companies and the nature of the gains
which accrue to them are not normally confined within
these limits. The vendors, promoters, and underwriters of
a Company are not unnaturally given to calculating in the
first place how much they individually and collectively can
get out of the business enterprise, or in other words how

little they can leave to the ordinary investing public whose capital they want to attract. It is their profit and not the interest upon the shares of investors that is the originating motive of most Companies, as we have seen.

Now, they may take these profits in three different ways. By over-valuation of the earning capacities of the various plants of amalgamating businesses, of the patents and especially of the goodwill[1] and other invisible assets, they may bloat out the capital value of the Company to the utmost, distributing among themselves in vendors' and promoters' shares and in other payments as much of the more vendible stocks as they can conceal, substituting in this capitalisation the consideration of immediate vendibility for future earning-capacity. So far as they can succeed in raising the immediate market value of the stocks they have allotted to themselves for services or obtained by the ordinary method of subscription, it will be to their interest to unload these stocks upon the market before the inflated capitalisation of the market is effectively exposed.

A great deal of "bogus" company promotion and even of more substantial promotion of family businesses and of combinations is primarily motived by the desire of the financial promoters to scoop out the whole value of the Company by this method of extraction, which shall leave the swollen carcase to shrivel to its meagre unprofitable dimensions in the hands of deluded investors. The arts of

---

[1] "This goodwill is chiefly a capitalisation of the differential advantages possessed by the several concerns as competitors in business, and is for the most part of no use for other than competitive business ends. It has for the most part no aggregate industrial effect. The differential advantages possessed by business concerns as competitors disappear when the competitors are merged in the degree in which they cease to compete with rival bidders for the same range of business. To this aggregate defunct goodwill of the consolidated concerns (which in the nature of things can make only an imaginary aggregate) is added something in the way of an increment of goodwill belonging to the new corporation as such."—Veblen, *Theory of Business Enterprise*, pp. 126-7.

(So far, however, as goodwill is expressed in terms of "credit," this consolidation may create a value of goodwill larger than the cancelled goodwill of the amalgamating units: the credit of the new corporation may be greater than the added credits of the old ones. This Veblen admi ts, p. 168 note.—J. A. H.)

drawing a prospectus and of "making a market" are devoted to the single end of producing a temporary boom. Improper accountancy misrepresents the value and the past profits of the business that is incorporated, expert engineers, chemists, etc., are paid to over-estimate the productive and profit-earning capacity of the mines, machinery, and other plant acquired by the Company; well-known business names, and in Great Britain politicians and titled personages, are procured for the directorate; the bright and solid prospects of the business are set out with consummate literary skill, every present defect or future risk carefully concealed; the whole glamour of the pro-position is suddenly flashed before the face of the confiding public by a parade of full-page advertisements. Any sluggishness or suspicion of the investing public is over-come by making a market, the promoters manipulating prices by collusive dealing on the market, until the outside investor is lured on to buy.

The motive and effect of these financial arts are to create a false confidence on the part of the ordinary capitalist or investing public which expresses itself in a temporary boom of watered stocks.

This of course does not exhaust the functions of the promoter, especially where an amalgamation or the forma-tion of a "trust" is the object of the Company. Here there is much scope for strategic work of a preparatory nature: rival interests must be fused upon terms advantageous to the trust-makers, with much use of bluff, intrigue, threats, bribes, and actual processes of "freezing out." When strong businesses "stand out" they can often obtain an exorbitant price for consenting to come in, and this exor-bitance is a large factor in the over-capitalisation of the Company.[1]

This formal over-capitalisation or statement of the earn-ing capacity of the Company in an excess of shares, would, however, be comparatively harmless (and useless to pro-moters) unless the processes of over-valuation were con-cealed. When this over-capitalisation, attended by a sale of inflated stock by the promoters, takes place, the business is of course one of organised deception, that of a profes-

---

[1] The Atlantic Shipping Combine well illustrates this point.

sional dealer palming off a shoddy or adulterated article on to an ignorant amateur public.[1]

While this fraudulent method of flotation is only too common a practice of professional promoters, profits of company formation are not confined to this origin. Even where the vendors dispose of the great majority of their shares it does not follow that the profit they extract involves a deception of, or a loss to, the investing public. Where the new form of the Company represents a real economy in production, marketing, and credit, as compared with the older business or businesses, the promotion creates an actual fund of gain which the vendors or promoters are able to take while selling to the public shares which are genuinely interest-bearing securities. Where for private reasons of convenience a family business is converted into a public company, the promotion has often been conducted without deception, the vendors realising in shares held or sold a substantial profit from the superiority of the new over the old business form. But where it is possible in modern business life to make a large additional gain within the limits of legality, it is generally made and a profession is founded in order to make this sort of gain. Hence a larger proportion of modern Company promotion is initiated by professional promoters who are not primarily concerned with the gains which represent technical improvements of the Company structure, but with the gains got from an artificially produced vendibility of shares.

§ 6. Most financiers or money-dealers, however, are not chiefly engaged in promoting Companies, but in getting profits from handling the stocks and shares upon the market. As in Company construction so here the business rests on a real foundation of utility or productivity. This utility consists in using skilled foresight, so as to direct the flow of industrial capital into

---

[1] For simplicity we have assumed that the "promoters" clear out of the Company after a first unloading of their shares upon an artificially inflated market. Often it is quite otherwise; they retain a sufficient control over the ordinary shares to enable them, after the Company has failed and gone into liquidation, to assume the task of reconstruction, during which they can freeze out the surviving interests of outsiders and either secure the real assets of the reconstructed company for profitable holding, or play anew the former game of unloading inflated shares upon a newly-made market.

the most serviceable industrial channels. For the rises and falls of stocks and shares, so far as they are naturally induced, and rest upon sound business information, are the financial machinery directing the creation of the various quantities of concrete capital required to co-operate with labour in the most efficient working of the various industries. The really useful skill of stockbrokers, billbrokers, bankers, and other financiers who handle stocks and shares, buying or selling them, discounting them or advancing money on their security, consists in intimate knowledge of the industrial and commercial facts that give value to the pieces of paper which they handle—in other words, a knowledge of the relative strength and weakness of the various trades and of the particular businesses which operate in them. It is their function to stimulate and direct the flow of credit, and through credit of actual industrial power, from failing to thriving trades, and from ill-ordered and unprofitable to well-ordered and profitable businesses. To assist in putting capital where it is most wanted is thus the social function of these orders of financiers. The performance of this work requires not only large and accurate knowledge of facts, but high qualities of combination and of constructive imagination in interpreting the probable course of future movements. Dealing in the most mobile, changeful, and divisible forms of vendible goods, the money-market is of all markets the most complex and at the same time the most unified in its structure, and it admits of a high order of specialisation. Groups of brokers or financiers attach themselves to particular classes of stocks, the classification being partly local—*e.g.*, South African mines or American railroads.

The "legitimate" business of this finance is to operate the machinery for the distribution of capital by accurate registration and calculation of price-movements. Since the limits of calculation are often very narrow, the element of chance or speculation must enter in as a necessary ingredient of the business so far as any individual operation is concerned. But while the ignorance of most amateur investors converts their investments into mere acts of gambling, the professional financier is not properly a gambler. When he departs from "legitimate" finance it is not primarily to gamble but to manipulate prices, so as to assist his calculations. Instead of merely predicting price-changes he endeavours to produce them. If he is able in any way to cause and to regulate fluctuations of prices in any class of securities, he can buy at the bottom and sell at the top, an obviously advantageous method: if he can sit for some time upon a class of stocks, rocking the values up and down at will, he may be able to extract from the ordinary investing public a larger quantity of money than could be got by any single *coup* of Company promotion. Any group of financiers furnished with large enough resources may fasten upon a stock, using it either to milk the innocent investing public by preconcerted price movements which deceive them into buying and selling at a loss, or to corner the stock and squeeze other financiers not "in the know" by forcing them to buy stock at monopoly prices in order to fulfil their engagements. But the financiers, who are themselves promoters or directors of a Company and have retained large blocks of shares, can play this profitable game at a great advantage. Instead of over-capitalising a Company at construction and clearing out by a single act of "unloading," they may retain their shares and use them for what is euphemistically termed "speculating" on the bourse, but what is in reality an alternate "rigging and depressing of prices." Superior or early access to information affecting the movement of prices gives them their first advantage; this they may supplement by manipulating public opinion through the press; finally, their financial position and control of movements enables them more effectively than outsiders to bull and bear the market. An intrinsically unsound business, with incalculable or fluctuating assets, best lends itself to such operations. A classical example in modern finance is the South African Chartered Company, a wildly speculative venture of such magnitude and superficial possibilities, so well adapted to political and sentimental appeals, as to enable its crafty organisers to plan and execute price movements of enormous range. The advantages enjoyed by financiers "in the know" are well illustrated by the record of the holding of Chartered Shares before and after the Jameson Raid by Messrs. Rhodes, Beit, Rudd, and their intimates in South African finance.

These operations of financiers in managing the play of

mobile stocks resembles the keeping of gaming tables: from their standpoint it is business, from that of their clients it is gambling; under normal circumstances and in the long run there is little risk for them—they must win, the amateurs who play with them must lose.

§ 7. The skilled financier, who makes large gains by "speculative" business in floating companies and planning *coups* upon the Stock Exchange, desires, if he retains any "conservative instinct," to possess some substantial, profitable stake in the world of finance, some considerable investment in real estate or in regularly remunerative businesses : such holding substantiates his credit, gives him social position and respectability, and so assists his speculative operations, besides furnishing a soft bed on which to fall in the event of some knock-down blow. The master of modern finance does not therefore use all his resources in speculative business, nor does he find it to his interest to impart mobility to every form of investment. In his career he enjoys exceptional opportunities of making or discovering genuinely profitable investments based upon the control of rich natural resources or other protective support. The directors of the Standard Oil Trust or of the East Rand Mines or De Beers do not "gamble" with such stocks, nor do they let out of their hands at any time the control of these profitable businesses: they only speculate with the surplus gains which spring from such "monopolies," and with the cumulative profits of their well-directed speculations.

The financial class, then, as distinguished from the main body of capitalists or amateur investors, grafts upon its legitimate and useful function of determining and directing the most productive flow of capital, three methods of private gain, each of which is a corruption and abuse of its true function.

Planning and promoting Companies based, not upon economy of industrial or financial working, but upon an artfully enhanced vendibility of shares, they cause a waste of general capital by obtaining an excessive subscription to the Company and diverting the excess into their own pockets, thus imparting insecurity to otherwise sound businesses, damaging their credit and impeding their productive operations. To this waste must, of course, be added the injury wrought by floating "bogus" Companies which have no actual foundation in the business world; the wide prevalence of these criminal adventures not only wastes capital, but, disturbing public confidence, further impedes the easy, natural flow of capital throughout the industrial organism.

Creating or stimulating fluctuations of prices in order to contrive corners or to practise concerted *coups* is an even more injurious dislocation of the social machinery of finance: it is a falsification of the automatic register of values expressly designed to determine the most productive application of capital.

Finally, the creation, absorption, and supreme control of the most profitable forms of natural monopoly and other abnormally prosperous businesses impart a strength and solidity to the new financial oligarchy which enable it to fasten its hold still more firmly on the necks of the proletariat of capital, who thus, cut off more and more from secure investments, are driven into the "gambling hells" of speculative stocks and shares kept by these masters of finance.

The multitude and magnitude of these interferences with the delicate adjustments of the financial machinery directing the flow of capital involve other indirect consequences of importance. They impart debility and irregularity to the actual processes of production and of commerce under the new order of capitalism. The business of a Company whose stock, over appreciated upon construction, is allowed afterwards to slide, or is made the sport of gamblers who toss it up and down for private financial purposes, is rendered insecure: the actual flow of capital into it, plundered at the source, is insufficient for its full expansion, attempts to "support the market" by earning good profits through economy of "costs" or other unsound business finance, drive the Company into difficulties, force it to call up more of its capital, weakening its general credit, while special emergencies impel it to seek advances from bankers and other accommodations.

§ 8. From the financial standpoint the whole of the economy of large-scale production, and in particular of joint-stock enterprise, may be summed up in the single phrase, enlarged credit. This credit, however, is not merely drawn from the investing public in the form of subscription to its stocks and bonds: the "capital" thus created is also a basis for a more elastic sort of credit required in the actual running of a modern business. In order that a business may make its maximum earnings it must secure the quickest turnover and the largest volume of business. This expansion of the rate and volume of actual business involves the use at certain times of a far larger amount of "money" than is actually owned by the Company: the Company must buy more than it can pay for in cash, and must obtain from elsewhere the purchasing power. It is driven constantly to increase its liabilities and to discount its bills. In other words, it must have recourse to bank credit, using its actual capital, visible and invisible, as collateral security upon which to obtain the use of a far larger amount of credit. Although interest or discount must be paid for this bank credit, it is obviously profitable to use it so far as the increased volume of business thus made possible yields a margin of profit in excess of the rate paid to the bank for "credit." Since any firm which employs this command of credit to the full has an advantage over another firm which does not so utilise it, the impulsion to its full employment in competitive trade becomes evident. "Under modern conditions," writes Professor Veblen,[1] "business cannot profitably be done by any one of the competitors without the customary recourse to credit. Without the customary recourse to credit a 'reasonable' return could not be obtained in the investment."

But where businesses are normally worked upon a basis in which credit is strained to its utmost, it is clear that any abnormal occurrence causes trouble. Where in addition to the risks to which all industries are more or less exposed, from natural accidents, political changes, labour conflicts, etc., operations of financiers upon the stock and produce markets are taken into account, we perceive that businesses using their maximum credit must come more and more to lean on "banks" and "finance companies." Even where businesses are not developed in the fullest form of capitalism, the frequent recourse to bank-credit plays an important part, and it is clearly seen that in all "capitalist" trades the private business, or the "unlisted" company whose stocks are not freely negotiable, stands at a great disadvantage for all purposes of expansive trade, through its inability to get bank-credit upon easy terms.

Looking at the matter from the other side we perceive that bill discounting and temporary advance to business firms form an ever-growing part of the banking business. Where, as in London, bill-brokers form a distinct class dealing with the better sorts of paper, they are chiefly financed by banks. The large profitable business of modern banking consists ever more largely in selling short pieces of " credit " to business firms. It is necessary to any competitive firm to buy this " credit," and the price it has to pay may not seem unreasonable.

The bank loan system is rightly regarded as a natural adjunct to the financial structure of the joint-stock company, part of a financial system for applying capital at places and at times where it may be most productively used. A sound working of bank loans extends the actual business operations of firms which can obtain such loans, and since *ceteris paribus* a competently conducted firm will more readily obtain such credit than an incompetently conducted one, the net result is to enhance the general efficiency of the industrial system.[1]

When full account is taken of the double part played by banks in financing companies, first as promoters and underwriters, often as large holders of blocks of shares undigested by the investing public, secondly as money-merchants discounting bills and advancing money, it becomes evident that the business of the modern banker is largely that of the general financier and that the financial dominance in capitalist industry is exercised in great measure by bankers.

[1] Professor Veblen appears to hold that no considerable net increase of industrial productivity accrues from this use of credits. " They are business capital only; they swell the volume of business as counted in price, etc., but they do not directly swell the volume of industry, since they do not add to the aggregate material apparatus of industry, or alter the character of the processes employed, or enhance the degree of efficiency with which industry is managed " (p. 99). But this is only true on the supposition which Professor Veblen appears to make (p. 98) that an incompetent manager has an equal access to such " credit " with a competent one. Surely this is not the case. Bank credit tends to put more actual industrial power in the hands of the more competent and thus to " enhance the degree of efficiency with which industry is managed."

The general spread of the use of banks in all business communities makes bankers the holders of all the margins of uninvested savings and other moneys not in immediate use. It is this fund of deposits that furnishes the "credit" which the banks supply in floating and financing companies. Not only do they participate in the legitimate and illegitimate profits of company promoting, but the intricate relations which subsist between industrial companies and particular banks enable the latter in many instances to squeeze the former in the price paid for credit, though there are other cases where a bank, having become deeply involved with a company by pawnings of the company's share or debenture capital, or through excessive advances, is itself squeezed by the company. Weaker companies, however, which, by over-capitalisation, incompetent management, or misfortune, are often in need of temporary assistance, become bond-slaves to a bank, which is not only able to extort exorbitant prices for its services, but can at any time by forcing the company into liquidation gain possession of what really valuable assets it contains. Reckless or dishonest construction of companies, weakening the financial structure at the outset of its career, obliges a large amount of modern business to pay heavy toll to bankers for "credit" which costs dearer in proportion to its urgency.

This brief study of the finance of capitalism makes it clear, first, that a complex financial machinery is essential to the delicate adjustment of modern industry; secondly, that this machinery operated for private profit can often earn the highest profits by causing industrial dislocation and maladjustments.

§ 9. As "credit" becomes more and more the vital force of modern business, the class that controls credit becomes more powerful and takes for itself as "earnings" a larger proportion of the product of industry. If, however, "credit" were left to the free competition of a large number of bankers and financiers, this control would not imply mastery. In order to comprehend the power of finance we must look a little closer at its structure. In no other business operation is the advantage of a large over a small capital so obvious: nowhere else is the force making for concentration of business so evident. If any limit exists to the "law of increasing returns" in banking, insurance, and finance, it is

not easily discernible. Great operations of public or
private finance, the floating of public loans or great
industrial combinations, the contrivance and execution of
great movements in the stock and share markets, can only
be conducted with the suddenness and secrecy which are
requisite to safety and success by financial businesses of
the first order of magnitude. Great businesses alone can
stand their ground against the larger shocks to the general
credit of a nation, or can rely upon their political influence
to secure governmental aid in cases of real emergency.
Thus it arises that a large proportion of the most profitable
business of financiers is never exposed to effective competition, and the prices they receive for their services are
"monopoly" prices: either it is business which they
initiate and organise and for which they charge "what the
business will bear," or it is business whose size and delicacy
forbid close bargaining, or finally it is money-lending in
which advantage can be taken of the urgent needs of the
applicant for loans.

Although no statistics are procurable, it is certain that
the profits of "finance" form a constantly increasing toll
on industry. It is also probable that this toll and the
control it represents are concentrated in a few hands.
Though the diffused ownership of capital makes a large
number of persons small participants in the profits of
finance, these gains of the small investor are kept at a
minimum by the application to banks and finance companies
of the methods of company construction above described.
The share of the proletariat of capitalists in the net gains of
financial business is very small as compared with that of the
magnates of finance.

In parts of the world where economic conditions are
most favourable to the rapid ripening of finance, we perceive
the actual wielding of great masses of concentrated "credit"
by little groups of financiers in ways which enable us to
appreciate the significance of this most important product
of modern capitalism. That the concerted action of a
small number of banks and financial companies in New
York could produce the panic and the depression which
swept over the United States in 1893 was an early mani-
festation of a power which is now stronger and more closely
organised.

A study of the origins and careers of the great American financiers discloses three chief sources of financial power; railroads, industrial trusts and banking, and the union in the same hands of the control of these three economic functions is an instructive testimony to the nature of the new power. The railroad kings and the great industrial trust makers are drawn by economic necessities into general finance. The control exercised by American railroads over agriculture, irrigation, mining, city development, has led railroad men into the promotion of all sorts of business enterprises more or less dependent upon railroads; while the tortuous financial history of most roads has necessitated a constant recourse to the general machinery of finance. Though the same is not equally true of the man who makes his pile by the successful operation of an industrial trust, another economic necessity drives him into general finance. The profitable management of a trust depends primarily upon regulation of output, which involves a limitation of the employment of capital. It is thus impossible *ex hypothesi* for a trust-maker to find full continuous employment for the high profits he makes by extending the plant and working capital of his own business: such a policy would be evidently suicidal. He must look outside his own business for fields of profitable investments for his profits. If he occupies himself, as sometimes he does, in organising other industrial trusts in businesses related to his own, his success yields new profits which must seek employment further afield. Thus the profits arising from specific monopolies in the transport or the manufacturing world are logically forced into the more general regions of finance. They form a large and a growing fund of free capital which naturally associates itself with the free funds held by bankers, and operates by the ways we have described in fastening a general control of finance upon business that enables the financial class to extract a larger share of the general wealth. So trust-makers such as Messrs. Rockefeller, Rogers, Havemeyer, and railway men such as Harriman, Gould, Depew, or Vanderbilt, become bankers or directors of insurance companies; while bankers like J. P. Morgan organise steel and shipping combines and sit on a number of railroad and industrial directorates.

The following table illustrating these transverse business

affiliations was drawn up by Professor Meyer.[1] "The names," he adds, "have been selected at random and the table could be extended through hundreds of names." It

	Bank	Trust	Insurance	Safe Deposit and Guarantee	Railway	Telegraph	Telephone	Cable	Express	Steamship	Real Estate	Manufactures	Unclassified	Total
Alexander, J. W.	3	2	1	1			1						1	8
Babcock, S. D.	2	4	3		3					1	6		1	21
Baker, Geo. F.	6	7	3	2	8						1	9		36
Belmont, August	6	5	3	1	10					1	1	7	2	35
Cannan, H. W.	1	2	1	2	7					1	1	1	2	17
Cox, C. F.	1			1	26									29
Depew, C. M.	1	4	1	3	53	1						2	2	67
Fish, Stuyvesant	3	1	2	1	3	1		1		1			2	13
Gary, E. H.	2				6	8	2	1		1		23	1	34
Gould, Geo. J.	1	1	1	2	23	1			1	1			2	42
Harriman, E. H.	3	2	1	1	25	1			1	3	1	2	2	37
Hyde, J. H.	5	4	5	4	6							11		27
Lamont, D. S.	1	2	2		21	2				2	1	3		30
Morgan, J. P.	1		1		22							2		33
Rockefeller, Wm.	6	1	1	2	9							22		28
Rossiter, E. V.	2			1	31	6	1	1		1		6		39
Sage, Russell	2				11									26
Schwab, C. M.		1	6	2	5	1						22	2	28
Stillman, J.	10	6	1		12		1				1	6	4	48
Twombly, H. McK.	1	2			28						2	1		35
Vanderbilt, W. K.	1				50							1	3	54

(From the Directory of Directors for New York, 1902.)

represents the number and kind of companies in which certain men act as directors or officials.

Or we may take the case of a single great trust, the

[1] American Econ. Assn. Report, 1904, p. 111.

Standard Oil Company, and watch the necessary affiliations that it forms. For five years past the Oil Trust has yielded dividends averaging forty-five million dollars a year, or nearly 50 per cent. on its capitalisation. Probably one-third of this goes into the hands of Mr. John D. Rockefeller and 90 per cent. into the little controlling group. "Consider," writes Miss Tarbell, "what must be done with the greater part of this $45,000,000. It must be invested. The oil business does not demand it. There is plenty of reserve for all of its ventures. It must go into other industries. Naturally, the interests sought will be allied to oil. They will be gas, and we have the Standard Oil crowd steadily acquiring the gas interests of the country. They will be railroads, for on transportation all industries depend, and besides, railroads are one of the great consumers of oil products and must be kept in line as buyers. And we have the directors of the Standard Oil Company acting as directors on nearly all of the great railways of the country—the New York Central, New York, New Haven, and Hartford, Chicago, Milwaukee & St. Paul, Union Pacific, Northern Pacific, Delaware, Lackawanna & Western, Missouri Pacific, Missouri, Kansas & Texas, Boston & Maine, and other lesser roads. They will go into copper, and we have the amalgamated scheme. They will go into steel, and we have Mr. Rockefeller's enormous holdings in the steel trust. They will go into banking, and we have the National City Bank and its allied institutions in New York City and Boston as well as a long chain running over the country."[1]

The central ganglion of the great financial system of which the Standard Oil Co., the United States Steel Corporation, and the "Big Four" Railroad Combine are the main industrial arteries, is the National City Bank and its connections. The National City Bank is the creation and the direct financial organ of the Standard Oil Company. Four National City Bank directors sat (1905) as president, vice-president and trustees on the board of the great insurance company the "New York Life"; its vice-president was a trustee of the "Mutual Life" of New York, while another directed the Equitable Trust Co. and the

[1] "History of the Standard Oil Trust," *Maclure*, Oct. 1904.

Mercantile Trust, which are in large part owned by the Equitable Life.

On the directorate of the United States Mortgage and Trust Co. were eight trustees of the Mutual Life and two of the Equitable Life, while on the Guaranty Trust directorate sat the President of the Mutual Life, Mr. Rogers of the Standard Oil and the Mutual Life, and Mr. E. H. Harriman of the Mercantile Trust and Equitable Trust. This cluster of life insurance companies, owning probably more than half the combined assets of insurance in America, and affiliated through their directorate and their investments with a number of trading banks and trust companies, represented a huge solidarity of "credit" controlled from a common centre by a tiny group, and directed now to the formation of a Steel or Shipping Combine, now to the enlargement of a railroad system, now to some huge deal in Amalgamated Copper. The triangle of forces in American capitalism, represented by railroad amalgamations, industrial trusts, and banking corporations, tends more and more to assume the shape of a purely financial power; a mass of credit directed to any point of the economic system where it is required to force an industrial combination, to finance a mining or railroad *coup*, or to crush some threatened invasion upon one of its "spheres of influence." The main stress of its recent application is towards a strengthening of its hold over the railroad system of the country, which it rightly regards as the best means of securing a permanent control over the natural resources and the industries of the country.

The solidarity of financial interests which has been described is of course far from complete:[1] at many points it represents an alliance, informal and temporary, not a fusion. Moreover, this credit-mass wielded for many common purposes by Messrs. Rockefeller & J. P. Morgan is often confronted by other alliances of credit which it must fight, in Wall Street in the Legislature and the Courts. In the railroad, the banking, and the industrial world; the spirit of combination bubbles up in many places into

[1] The American correspondent of the *Economist* (quoted Raffalovich, p. 143) in 1901 named five financiers—John D. Rockefeller, E. Harriman, J. P. Morgan, W. K. Vanderbilt, and George Gould as possessing amongst them a fortune of 800 million dollars, and representing with

financial shapes seeking expansion in alien enterprises where they meet opposition. Though the financial combination described above is all powerful over certain areas of industry, transport, and finance, in others it encounters stout resistance; even in its component companies there are many cross-currents of interest, and strong temporary unions of other credit forces can sometimes be formed for some concrete purpose of attack.

A supreme control over the financial machinery of a great industrial community is not practicable save by securing a firm control over one of the main arteries of the industrial body. Even the close monopoly of so important a commodity as oil is a quite inadequate basis: nor does steel admit of a sufficiently absolute dominion. Control of the main highroads, the railroad system, is the only practicable means of attaining full financial supremacy, and to that end the most powerful group of American financiers is evidently looking. The fight for the railroads is the most urgent issue in the economic evolution of America. But the main and ultimate object is not the power to levy tolls upon the transport industry, but to obtain a fulcrum sufficiently solid to enable them to work the lever of financial supremacy.

§ 10. One other aspect of the finance of capitalist concentration demands attention. A trust or other combine cannot,

their allies a control of 8000 million dollars invested in railroads, banks, and industrial businesses out of a total of 17,000 employed in these branches. He grouped them as follows:—

	Rails.	Banks.	Industrial Trusts.	Total.
Standard Oil, Gould, Harriman	1,997 ...	85 ...	746 ...	2,828
Morgan	1,691 ...	122 ...	1,677 ...	3,490
Vanderbilt	753 ...	12 ...	10 ...	775
Pennsylvania Railroad ...	870 ...	— ...	30 ...	900
	5,311	219	2,463	7,993

The chief interest attaching to this rough calculation consists in the relative importance of the several classes of undertaking in the Trust economy. Since 1901 these groups have drawn much closer, though not yet working in full harmony.

The *Summary of the Census, 1900*, p. 329, gives a considerably smaller figure for the capital of Industrial Trusts, the Steel Trust not then being formed.

it is pointed out, find room to invest its profits within the "trusted" industry: it must go outside. These profits pass, as we see, into general finance, and are thence directed into forming and financing other trusts and large businesses. Thus the process of concentration and consolidation proceeds apace over all those industrial fields where capitalist methods of production prevail. But if a single trust cannot usefully absorb its profits, neither can a group of trusts. The movement, therefore, seems to be attended by a growing restriction of the field of investment. Thus there is a growing natural pressure towards the acquisition of markets outside the present area of monopoly, in America, the national tariff-protected market. The fruits of this pressure are already visible in the economic policy of the American trusts, in the shape of a demand for larger external outlets for their goods and their investments. Without such outlets the "trust" movement is ultimately suicidal, larger and larger masses of "profits" will be annually earned which cannot be put into the trust-machine and cannot find any other profitable use. This "free" capital will either tend to pass into the hands of businesses which would attack the trusts, or it must find outside employment. The pressure is already felt in the large manufacturing corporations: some relief is found in a policy of subsidising export trade, and in seeking foreign investments in electric and other fields of enterprise where they can push most successfully without tariff aid. The ill-contrived and extravagantly financed Atlantic Shipping Combine was an early and crude attempt to reach after a new policy which is required by the logic of the evolution of trusts.

Another expression of the same economic need, fraught with even graver importance, is the new public policy of American political expansion. The economic tap-root, the chief directing motive of all the modern imperialistic expansion, is the pressure of capitalist industries for markets, primarily markets for investment, secondarily markets for surplus products of home industry. Where the concentration of capital has gone furthest, and where a rigorous protective system prevails, this pressure is necessarily strongest. Not merely do the trusts and other manufacturing trades that restrict their output for the home market more urgently require foreign markets, but they are also more anxious to secure protected markets, and this can only be achieved by extending the area of political rule. This is the essential significance of the recent change in American foreign policy as illustrated by the Spanish War, the Philippine annexation, the Panama policy, and the new application of the Munroe doctrine to the South American States. South America is needed as a preferential market for investment of trust "profits" and surplus trust products: if in time these states can be brought within a Zollverein under the suzerainty of the United States, the financial area of operations receives a notable accession. China as a field of railway enterprise and general industrial development already begins to loom large in the eyes of foresighted American business men; the growing trade in American cotton and other goods in that country will be a subordinate consideration to the expansion of the area for American investments. Diplomatic pressure, armed force, and where desirable, seizure of territory for political control, will be engineered by the financial magnates who control the political destiny of America. The strong and expensive American navy now beginning to be built incidentally serves the purpose of affording profitable contracts to the shipbuilding and metal industries: its real meaning and use is to forward the aggressive political policy imposed upon the nation by the economic needs of the financial capitalists.

It should be clearly understood that this constant pressure to extend the area of markets is not a necessary implication of all forms of organised industry. If competition was displaced by combinations of a genuinely co-operative character in which the whole gain of improved economies passed, either to the workers in wages, or to large bodies of investors in dividends, the expansion of demand in the home markets would be so great as to give full employment to the productive powers of concentrated capital, and there would be no self-accumulating masses of profit expressing themselves in new credit and demanding external employment. It is the "monopoly" profits of trusts and combines, taken either in construction, financial operation, or industrial working, that form a gathering fund of self-accumulating credit whose possession by the financial class implies a contracted demand for commodities and a correspondingly restricted employment for capital in American industries. Within certain limits relief can be found by stimulation of the export trade under cover of a high protective tariff which forbids all interference with monopoly of the home markets. But it is extremely difficult for trusts adapted to the requirements of a profitable tied market at home to adjust their methods of free competition in the world markets upon a profitable basis of steady trading. Moreover, such a mode of expansion is only appropriate to certain manufacturing trusts : the owners of railroad, financial, and other trusts must look always more to foreign investments for their surplus profits. This ever-growing need for fresh fields of investment for their profits is the great crux of the financial system and threatens to dominate the future economics and the politics of the great Republic.

The financial economy of American capitalism exhibits in more dramatic shape a tendency common to the finance of all developed industrial nations. The large, easy flow of capital from Great Britain, Germany, Austria, France, etc., into South African or Australian mines, into Egyptian bonds, or the precarious securities of South American republics, attests the same general pressure which increases with every development of financial machinery and the more profitable control of that machinery by the class of professional financiers. To a limited extent this cosmopolitanisation of finance is a natural and normal result of improved material and moral communication between the various nations of the earth. But in large measure it arises from a restriction of home markets which must be called artificial in the sense that industrial and financial trusts, pools, and other combinations, taking out of the aggregate product a larger quantity of "profit" than they can employ for further profit in these or other home investments, are impelled ever to look further afield and to use all their financial and political influence to develop foreign markets by such pacific or forcible means as will best serve their purpose. In every case the financier is the instrument or vehicle of this pressure: a swelling stream of investors' savings is constantly passing into the banking and financial system which he controls ; in order to keep it flowing with greatest gain to himself he must find or fashion fresh investments.

§ 11. The most compact exposition of capitalist finance is contained in the recent history of South Africa. A poor and sparsely peopled country, it disclosed within a few years two highly concentrated forms of natural treasure, the diamond mines of Kimberley and the Rand gold-reef. The most economical working of the diamond mines involved expensive plant and favoured large capitalists, while profitable sales involved limitation of output so as to realise high prices for a luxury whose value depended largely upon regulation of supply. By 1887 consolidation of interests had proceeded so far that Mr. Rhodes, financed by Messrs. Rothschild, was able to propose to Mr. Barnato an amalgamation which gave the De Beers' Company a complete ownership and control of the productive mines. This diamond mining trust, controlling by far the most important contribution to the world's supply, fortified itself by a complete organisation of the marketing process, so that the directors of De Beers virtually regulate the entire supply, limit output and fix prices on a calculation of maximum net profits[1] which in 1904 amounted to three million pounds sterling.

The profitable working of De Beers formed the financial nucleus of the early speculative gold-mining companies in the Potchefstroom and Witwater Rand districts, and when, early in the nineties, the full richness of the banket reef of the Rand was disclosed, the De Beers financiers were found in control of the greater part of the most valuable mines in the two associated groups of Wernher, Beit & Co., and the Consolidated Goldfields of South Africa (Messrs. Rhodes, Rudd & Rothschild). The conditions of the gold-mining, while favourable to large capitalist methods, did not render feasible a close amalgamation of interests on the De Beers pattern. In the first place there was no necessity to limit output, the interests of the financiers lay in encouraging every expansion of mining which could pay or form a basis of company promotion; secondly, the size of the new goldfield and the cropping up of the reef at so many points assisted the entrance of many groups of cosmo-

---

[1] Although the recently discovered Premier Mine in the Transvaal is independently organised for production and disavows all connection with De Beers, there can be no doubt that in the merchandising of the diamonds a thoroughly effective agreement is maintained.

politan financiers, who set up more or less conflicting interests. From these groups a few men, mostly Jews, forced their way into the inner circle of Transvaal finance; but upon the whole the De Beers group have throughout kept the lead: most of the profitable surface and deep level mines fell under their control, and the manipulation of the most tempting new propositions in the share-markets was in their hands. Moreover, the vast speculative exploit of the South African Chartered Company was the financial offspring of De Beers, and entered the investment market backed by all the financial prestige of the diamond and gold kings.

The most distinctive feature of South African finance, however, has been the skilled use which the financiers made of political machinery to assist them in improving and marketing investments. The actual lands which form the material basis of industrial and speculative exploitation, Kimberley, the Rand, Rhodesia, have in each case involved in their acquisition the application of a medley of non-economic forces, legal treachery in the case of Kimberley, the dupery of "concessions," riveted by armed force in Rhodesia, bribery and diplomatic coercion followed by war in the Transvaal. The financiers worked "politics" and the coercive machinery of the State at every turn in their career: to obtain special legislation for the diamond industry, to promote railroad facilities, and to secure immunity from taxation they required influence in the Cape Government: the flotation of the Chartered Company and the "protection" of its properties against native risings involved imperial influence; the management of Mr. Kruger's government in the Transvaal kept them incessantly dabbling in the internal politics of that country, seeking concessions and other privileges, planning raids and ultimately organising a catastrophe which was worked on their behalf and by their express machination at the prodigious expense of the British Government. In new, unsettled countries the financier is in constant need of political assistance; he needs political control in order to mature his financial operations, and he is able to obtain it. The power of the little group of men who wield the finance of De Beers and the Rand is virtually absolute in the politics of South Africa: their control over the finances of the country, public and private, enables them to wreck any political schemes antagonistic to their interests; all that money can do in a poor country to elect representatives, influence officials, and secure legislation, they can command. To realise the fulness of this power to paralyse effective opposition we must remember that not only are the mining industries under their control, the only solid sources of riches the whole country possesses, but that upon them depend the success or failure of the trading interests at the ports and in Kimberley and Johannesburg, of the public and private railroad and telegraphic companies, the banking and insurance businesses, the collieries and iron-mines, irrigation, and all other manufacturing and agricultural works demanding capital. Not merely are all these industries economically dependent on the mines, but the mineowners supply their capital and appoint their officers. Nowhere in the world has there ever existed so concentrated a form of capitalism as that represented by the financial power of the mining houses in South Africa, and nowhere else does that power so completely realise and enforce the need of controlling politics. The newness of the country and the absence of any earlier growth of strong vested interests have enabled these financiers, drawn from all the European countries, to develop the latent powers of pure finance more logically than elsewhere ; the immensely rapid possibilities of financial exploitation has attracted thither not a few financial intellects of the highest order, men who have known how to adapt finance to the particular environment and to operate at once upon the racial and economic antagonisms within their area of industrial operations, and upon the patriotic sentiments in Great Britain needed to secure for their investments the political and military assistance necessary to mature them. Their strategy has been large and masterful. Recognising that the success of their financial operations and of their political adjuncts was dependent upon the movement of public opinion and public sentiment in South Africa and Great Britain, they bought the leading organs of the South African press, subsidised political parties in Africa and Great Britain, and organised a moral propaganda among the churches and the philanthropic bodies. By thus creating a volume of public

interest and confidence in South African "development"
they secured an atmosphere favourable to investment;
by playing upon fears, suspicions, and sentimental aspirations they produced an agitation of the public mind
reflected in the share-market; by a concentrated exertion of all their moral and intellectual influence they
engineered a catastrophe, from the ruin of which they
have emerged with a firmer grip than ever upon the
substantial resources of the country and its government,
which implies a more profitable handling of the share-
market.

The exigencies of South African finance in relation to
local concrete circumstances involve a financial control in
which several elements or strains are distinguishable. In
the acquisition of the material bases of finance the services
of a class of adventurous explorers and concession-mongers
were essential; to this class men like Rudd, Jameson,
Maguire, and even Rhodes himself must be relegated,
though the political and financial ability of the last-named
gives him other claims. The main work of building the
structure of South African finance is, however, attributable
to the presence of a group of "pure financiers," many of
whom, in early origin diamond dealers at Kimberley, found
an illimitable opportunity in the construction and handling
of mining properties in the diamond and gold fields, and
later in Rhodesia. Of this class the Beits, Barnatos, Albus,
Neumanns, Ecksteins, may be taken as leading examples:
most of the abler and more successful members of this class
are Jews, originally from the European continent, though
assimilating with ease and fervour to the environment of
British sentiment, which is helpful to their financial designs.
The admission even to the inner financial circle of a few
members of the British aristocracy, attracted by the sheer
spirit of adventure, was valuable, not only for the vulgar
purpose of prospectuses, but for the slower and more
delicate work of constructing political and "social"
supports for the Rhodesian bubble. So we find men like
the Duke of Abercorn, Earl Grey, Lord Harris, taking an
active part in South African finance. These factors of
British influence are needed for the profitable working of
big "confidence tricks," and the great masters of the
financial machine can well afford to "let in" a certain

number of decorative personalities, few of whom, however, are allowed to touch the levers.

The co-operation of these three separate strains was for a time concealed by the dominating public part played by Mr. Rhodes, who, essentially a combination of the first two strains, adventurer and financier, was able, by his political genius, to give a temporary cloak of political significance to adventures which were *au fond* operations on the stock-markets. His disappearance has exposed to plainer view the actual mechanism of South African finance and its direction by the small group of "mineowners" and "merchants" in Johannesburg, Kimberley, and London. The profitable working of their "system" follows the lines which are more fully set forth in our main analysis. The masters of the system retain for themselves the ownership and dividends of the most solid and remunerative properties in the diamond and gold fields. The everyday investor cannot buy the ordinary shares of De Beers or of the best Deep Level Mines upon the Rand. Here is the first source of profit, the fruit of careful selection among the many propositions which pass through their hands. Other shares or debentures relating to poorer or more precarious propositions, the values of which being more sensitive are more amenable to skilled manipulation, are used to tempt the investing or the gambling public, the professional "croupiers" raking in the profits of the table. Last, not least, comes the periodic harvest of company flotation, where more highly-organised displays of financing enable the promoters to make a number of large "scoops" out of the public credulity, craftily stirred and stimulated at times when a period of industrial prosperity has furnished a swollen supply of savings. If it were possible to set forth the ownership of the shares in the chief companies, this concentration of financial power would be most convincing; all the great financial interests would be seen closely linked by transverse ownership. The following tables[1] dealing with the directorships held (1905) by a number of leading financiers illustrates, though less perfectly, the solidarity of financial control :—

---

[1] Constructed from the Directory of Directors and the Stock Exchange Year Book, 1905.

SOUTH AFRICAN COMPANY DIRECTORS.

	Diamonds.†	Gold.	Chartered Co.	Lands and Exploration.	Banks and Finance.	Railways.	Telegraphs.	Coal.	Miscellaneous.
Albu, S.	—	14	—	—	1	—	—	—	—
Albu, L.	—	10	—	—	—	—	—	1	—
*Beit, A.	1 (de B.)	2	1	—	2	2	—	—	—
*Eckstein, F. ...	—	2	—	—	—	—	—	—	—
English, R. ...	3 (de B.)	—	—	—	—	—	—	—	—
English, F. A. ...	1 (P.)	—	—	—	—	—	—	—	—
Farrar, Sir G. ...	—	8	—	1	1	—	—	1	—
Farrar, S. H. ...	—	11	—	2	1	—	—	1	—
Goldie, H. ...	—	20	—	3	1	—	—	—	—
Harris, Lord ...	—	1	—	—	1	—	—	—	—
Hamilton, J. J. ...	—	4	—	—	4	—	—	—	—
Jameson, L. S. ...	—	1	1	—	—	—	—	—	—
Joel, S. B. ...	1 (de B.)	7	—	1	1	—	—	1	2
Maguire, J. R. ...	—	1	1	2	2	3	1	—	—
Meyer, C. ...	1 (de B.)	1	—	—	—	—	—	—	—
Michell, Sir L. L.	1 (de B.)	—	1	—	—	—	—	—	—
Mosenthal, H. ...	2 (de B.)	1	—	1	—	—	—	—	—
*Neumann, S. ...	1 (P.)	13	—	1	1	—	1	—	—
*Phillips, L. ...	—	9	—	1	—	—	—	—	—
Reyersbach, L. ...	1 (P.)	3	—	—	—	—	—	—	—
Robinson, J. B. ...	1	15	—	1	—	—	—	—	—
*Rube, C.	—	37	—	1	1	—	—	—	1
Rudd, C. D. ...	—	3	—	—	1	—	—	—	—
*Wernher, J. C. ...	(1 de B.)	2	—	—	—	—	1	—	—

* Directors of Wernher Beit (merchants) or of Rand Mines.
† De B. = de Beers Consolidated; P. = Premier.

The following facts assist us to understand the nature of the consolidation which the table suggests. Messrs. Wernher, Beit, Eckstein, Phillips, and Rube are members of a "mercantile" firm in London and Johannesburg. Two of these, Messrs. Wernher and Beit, are life governors of De Beers: they are also directors of the Rand Mines, forming with Mr. S. Neumann the London Committee of that Company. Now, Mr. S. Neumann is also on the London Committee of the Premier (Transvaal) Diamond Company, sitting there with three other directors, one of whom is Mr. F. A. English. Mr. F. A. English is not a director of De Beers, but Mr. R. English is. Thus the relations between the two (independent?) diamond groups are tolerably clear. None of the Wernher Beit directors sits on the Consolidated Goldfields directorate, but Mr. Maguire, a director of this latter Company, sits on the directorate of the Chartered Company with Messrs. Beit and Sir L. L. Michell, both of De Beers. The connection with the Farrar group is equally plain: Sir G. Farrar sitting on the directorate of the important H. F. Company, while Mr. S. H. Farrar sits on the London Committee of that Company with Mr. Beit and Mr. S. Neumann. On the E. Rand Proprietary Mines Sir G. Farrar and Mr. S. H. Farrar sit with Mr. L. Phillips of Wernher Beit and Mr. F. Drake of the Rand Mines. On the directorate of the Albu group (W. Rand Consolidated Mines) Messrs. C. S. Goldmann and A. Reyersbach sit with the Albus; the former sitting with Mr. Phillips, S. Goldmann, and the Farrars on the E. Rand Proprietary Mines; the latter a director of the Premier Diamond Company. C. Meyer of De Beers is a director of Goltz & Co., while S. B. Joel of De Beers is a member of the firm of Barnato Brothers (merchants).

Following these illustrative lines of connection we can perceive the close union of management between all the chief gold groups, and between gold and diamonds and the speculative finance of the Chartered Company, while the railroads, banks, collieries, telegraphs, exploration companies, and newspapers are seen to be appendages of this central cluster.

The small inner ring of South African finance may be thus indicated from the directorate of the five most representative companies :—

	De Beers.	Premier.	Rand Mines.	Goldfields.	Chartered Company.
Beit, A.	I	—	I	—	I
Jameson, L. S. ...	I	—	—	—	I
Maguire, R. ...	—	—	—	I	I
Michell, Sir L. L.	I	—	—	—	I
Neumann, S. ...	—	I	I	—	—
Wernher	I	—	I	—	—

To these we may add the names of Mr. F. Eckstein, Lord Harris, and perhaps Sir G. Farrar, chairmen respectively of several of the most important companies.

It would be safe to say that this tiny group of men hold in their control the financial, the industrial, and the political destinies of South Africa. Every important interest is directly managed by these men and their close business associates. All, with the exception of Lord Harris and Mr. Maguire (of the Goldfields), and Sir G. Farrar, are De Beers and Wernher Beit men. It will be seen by reference to the earlier table that this same small group directly control banks, railways, telegraphs, coal mines, and through the finance or trust companies which they direct are able to control many other companies. Most of the strongest Press is also in their hands. The following rough diagram correctly delineates the situation :—

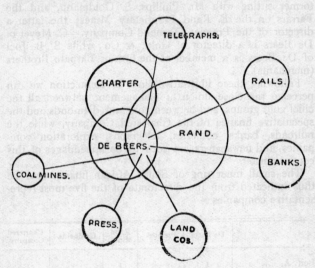

CHAPTER XI.

MACHINERY AND INDUSTRIAL DEPRESSION.

§ 1. The leading symptom of the disease called Depression of Trade is a general fall of wholesale prices, accompanied by a less than corresponding fall of retail prices. Whatever may be the ultimate causes of a trade depression, the direct and immediate cause of every fall of price must be a failure

18

of demand to keep pace with supply at the earlier price. So long as those who have goods to sell can sell all these goods at the price they have been getting, they will not lower the price. The direct efficient cause then of any fall of price is an actual condition of over-supply at earlier prices. A very small quantity of over-supply will bring down prices in a business, or in a whole market, provided the competition between the businesses is keen. Where such a fall of prices quickly stimulates demand so that the over-supply is carried off and the rate of demand is equated to the rate of supply at the lower price level, the condition is commonly described as a "tendency to over-supply." But it is important to bear in mind that in strictness it was not a "tendency" but an actually existing quantity of over-supply which brought down the price.

Where any fall of price thus brought about quickly stimulates a corresponding increase of demand, stability of prices follows, and there will be a full, healthy production at the lower prices.

The mere fact then that prices are generally lower than they were five or ten years ago is no evidence of depressed trade. Depressed trade signifies not merely low prices but relaxed production : more has been produced than can be sold at the lowest profitable prices, and markets are congested with stock, but less is being produced than could be produced with existing means of production. The fact which faces us in a period of depression is an apparent excess of productive power. If this excess were of labour alone it might be explained with some plausibility as due to the displacement of labour by machinery. For it has been admitted that the first and immediate effect of introducing labour-saving or labour-aiding machines may be a diminution in the demand for labour, even when the labour of making and repairing the machines and of distributing the increased product which finds a sale is taken into consideration. The simultaneous application of a number of new forms of machinery attended by other general economies in the organisation of industry might seem to explain why for a time there should be a general redundancy of labour in all or most of the chief industries of a country. Such an over-supply of labour would result from the accumulated action of "first effects."

When the cheapening influences of machinery had time to exercise their full natural influence in stimulating consumption the labour temporarily displaced would be again fully utilised ; for the moment, past labour saved and stored in forms of fixed capital would do a great deal of the work which would otherwise be done by present living labour. But such an explanation is wholly negatived by the fact that in a depressed condition of trade there is an excess of forms of capital as well as of labour. There exists simultaneously a redundancy of both factors in production. Labourers are out of work or are in irregular employment, mills and factories are closed or working short time, the output of coal and metals is reduced, and yet with this relaxed production the markets are glutted with unsold goods unable to find purchasers at a price which will yield a minimum profit to their owners. To this must be added, in the case of the extractive industries, agriculture, mining, etc., the exclusion from productive use of land which had formerly found a profitable employment.

§ 2. To this condition of industry the antithetical terms, over-production and under-production, may be both correctly applied, according as one regards production as a state or as a process. The state of trade in a depression is one of over-production—the industrial body is congested with goods which are not drawn out for consumption fast enough. This plethora debilitates the industrial body, its functional activities are weakened. The slackness of trade thus induced is rightly described as under-production.

It is commonly said by English writers upon economics that the state of over-production, the redundancy of capital and labour, though found in one or two or several trades at the same time, cannot be of general application. If too much capital and labour is engaged in one industry there is, they argue, too little in another, there cannot be at the same time a general state of over-production. Now if by general over-production is meant not that every single industry is supplied with an excess of capital, but that there exists a net over-supply, taking into account the plethora in some trades and the deficiency in others, this assertion of English economists is not in accordance with ascertained facts or with the authority of economists outside of England.

§ 3. If a depression of trade signified a misapplication of

capital and labour, so that too much was applied in some industries, too little in others, there would be a rise of prices in as many cases as there was a fall of prices, and the admitted symptom of depression, the simultaneous fall of price in all or nearly all the staple industries, would not occur. The most careful students of the phenomena of depressed trade agree in describing the condition as one of general or net excess of the forms of capital. They are also agreed in regarding the enormous growth of modern machinery as the embodiment of a general excess of producing power over that required to maintain current consumption.

Lord Playfair, writing on this subject in 1888, says, "It matters not whether the countries were devastated by war or remained in the enjoyment of peace ; whether they were isolated by barriers of Protection or conducted these industries under Free Trade ; whether they abounded in the raw materials of industry or had to import them from other lands ; under all these varying conditions the machine-using countries of the world have felt the fifteen years of depression in the same way, though with varying degrees of intensity." His conclusion is "that the improvements of machinery used in production have increased the supply of commodities beyond the immediate demands of the world."[1] In support of this position he adduces the authority of continental writers such as Dr. A. von Studnitz, Piermez, Jules Duckerts, Laveleye, Trasenster, Annecke, and Engel. In the United States, Carroll Wright, David Wells, and Atkinson are foremost in upholding this to be the explanation of depression of trade. Mr. Carroll D. Wright, Commissioner of Labour at Washington, is emphatic in his assertion of the fact. " So far as the factories and the operatives of the countries concerned are to be taken into consideration (England, the United States, France, Belgium, Germany), there does exist a positive and emphatic over-production, and this over-production could not exist without the introduction of power-machinery at a rate greater than the consuming power of the nations involved, and of those dependent upon them, demand ; in other words, the over-production of power-machinery logically results in the over-

----

[1] *Contemporary Review*, March 1888.

production of goods made with the aid of such machinery, and this represents the condition of those countries depending largely upon mechanical industries for their prosperity."[1] The Reports of the English "Commission on the Depression of Trade and Industry" make similar admissions of an excess of producing power as distinct from a mere miscalculation in the application of capital and labour. The Majority Report, defining "over-production" as "the production of commodities, or even the existence of a capacity for production at a time when the demand is not sufficiently brisk to maintain a remunerative price to the producer," affirms "that such an over-production has been one of the prominent features of the course of trade during recent years, and that the depression under which we are now suffering may be partially explained by this fact. . . ."[2] The Minority Report lays still stronger stress upon "systematic over-production," alleging "that the demand for commodities does not increase at the same rate as formerly, and that our capacity for production is consequently in excess of our home and export demand, and could, moreover, be considerably increased at short notice by the fuller employment of labour and appliances now partially idle."[3] Brentano speaks of German Kartels as "providing a parachute to enable the victims of over-production to get safely down to a solid basis."

The most abundant information regarding the excess of the machinery of production in the several branches of industry has been given by Mr. D. A. Wells, who regards machinery as the direct cause of depressed trade, operating in three ways—(1) increased capacity of production, (2) improved methods of distribution, (3) the opening up of new abundant supplies of raw material. Thus production grows faster than consumption. "In this way only is it possible to account for the circumstances that the supply of the great articles and instrumentalities of the world's use and commerce have increased during the last twelve or fifteen years in a far greater ratio than the contemporaneous increase of the world's population or of its immediate consuming capacity."[4]

The earlier inventions in the textile industries, and the general application of steam to manufacture and to the trans-

---

[1] *Report on Industrial Depressions*, Washington, 1886.
[2] Report, pars. 61-66.   [3] Report, par. 106.
[4] *Contemporary Review*, July 1887.

port services, have played the most dramatic part in the industrial revolution of the last hundred years. But it should be borne in mind that it is far from being true that the great forces of invention have spent themselves, and that we have come to an era of small increments in the growth of productive power. On the contrary, within this last generation a number of discoveries have taken place in almost all the chief industrial arts, in the opening up of new supplies of raw material, and in the improvement of industrial organisation, which have registered enormous advances of productive power. In the United States, where the advance has been most marked, it is estimated that in the fifteen or twenty years preceding 1886 the gain of machinery, as measured by "displacement of the muscular labour," amounts to more than one-third, taking the aggregate of manufactures into account. In many manufactures the introduction of steam-driven machinery and the factory system belongs to this generation. The substitution of machinery for hand labour in boot-making signifies a gain of 80 per cent. for some classes of goods, 50 per cent. for others. In the silk manufacture there has been a gain of 50 per cent., in furniture some 30 per cent., while in many minor processes, such as wood-planing, tin cans, wallpapers, soap, patent leather, etc., the improvement of mechanical productiveness per labourer is measured as a rise of from 50 to 300 per cent. or more. The gain is, however, by no means confined to an extension of "power" into processes formerly performed by human muscle and skill. Still more significant is the increased mechanical efficiency in the foundational industries. In the manufacture of agricultural implements the increase is put down at from 50 to 70 per cent., in the manufacture of machines and machinery from 25 to 40 per cent., while "in the production of metals and metallic goods long-established firms testify that machinery has decreased manual labour 33⅓ per cent." The increase in the productive power of cotton mills is far greater than this. From 1870 to 1884 the make of pig-iron rose 131 per cent. in Great Britain and 237 per cent. in the rest of the world.[1] "In building vessels an approximate idea of the relative labour

---

displacement is given as 4 or 5 to 1—that is, four or five times the amount of labour can be performed to-day by the use of machinery in a given time that could be done under old hand methods."[1]

In England the rise in productiveness of machinery is roughly estimated at 40 per cent. in the period 1850 to 1885, and there is no reason to suppose this is an excessive estimate. In the shipping industry, where more exact statistics are available, the advance is even greater. The diminution of manual labour required to do a given quantity of work in 1884 as compared with 1870 is put down at no less than 70 per cent., owing in large measure to the introduction and increased application of steam-hoisting machines and grain elevators, and the employment of steam power in steering, raising the sails and anchors, pumping, and discharging cargoes.[2] In the construction of ships enormous economies have taken place. A ship which in 1883 cost £24,000 can now be built for £14,000. In the working of vessels the economy of fuel, due to the introduction of compound-engines, has been very large. A ton of wheat can now be hauled by sea at less than a farthing per mile. Similarly with land haulage the economy of fuel has made immense reductions in cost. "In an experiment lately made on the London and North Western Railway, a compound locomotive dragged a ton of goods for one mile by the combustion of two ounces of coal."[3] The quickening of voyages by steam motor, and by the abandonment of the old Cape route in favour of the Suez Canal, enormously facilitated commerce. The last arrangement is calculated to have practically destroyed a tonnage of two millions. The still greater facilitation of intelligence by electricity did away with the vast system of warehousing required by the conditions of former commerce. These economies of the foundational transport industries have deeply affected the whole commerce and manufacture of the country, and have played no inconsiderable part in

[1] *Report of the Commissioner of Labour*, Washington, 1886, pp. 80 to 88.

[2] D. A. Wells, *Contemporary Review*, August 1887.

[3] Lord Playfair, in the *Contemporary Review*, March 1888, gives a number of interesting illustrations of recent economies in transport and manufacture.

bringing about the general fall of prices by lowering the expenses of production and stimulating an increased output.

Excessive production of transport-machinery, especially of railways, has played an important part as an immediate cause of modern trade depression. The depression beginning in 1873 and culminating in 1878 is described as having its origin "in the excessive lock-up of capital in the construction of railways, especially in America and Germany, many of which, when built, had neither population to use them nor traffic to carry; in the wild speculation that followed the German assertion of supremacy on the Continent; in the exaggerated armaments, which withdrew an inordinate amount of labour from productive industry, and over-weighed the taxpayers of the great European nations; and in over-production in the principal trades in all European countries."[1]

Mr. Bowley points out that "after each of the great railway booms of the century, for instance in England about 1847, in America before 1857 and 1873, in India in 1878, and on the Continent in 1873, the collapse has been very violent; for the materials are bought at exaggerated prices; the weekly wage during construction is enormous; no return is obtained till the whole scheme, whose carrying out probably lasts many years, is complete."

A great deal of this railway enterprise meant overproduction of forms of transport-capital and a corresponding withholding of current consumption. In other words, a large part of the "savings" of England, Germany, America, etc., invested in these new railways, were sterilised; they were not economically needed to assist in the work of transport, and many of them remain almost useless, as the quoted value of the shares testifies. It is not true, as is sometimes suggested, that after a great effort in setting on foot such gigantic enterprises, a collapse is economically necessary. If the large incomes and high wages earned in the period prior to 1873, when capital and labour found full employment in these great enterprises, had been fully applied in increased demand for commodities and an elevated standard of consumption, much of the new

---

[1] *Statist*, 1879, quoted Bowley, *England's Foreign Trade in the Nineteenth Century*, p. 80.

machinery of transport, which long stood useless, would have been required to assist in forwarding goods to maintain the raised standard of consumption. This argument, of course, assumes that ignorance or fraud have not caused a misdirection of investment. There is no evidence to indicate that the vast sums invested in 1869-72 in railway enterprise could have found any safer or more remunerative investment. It is the overflow of "savings," after all capital economically needed to carry on the work of production to supply steady current wants has been secured, that flows into the hands of speculative company-promoters. Such savings are not diverted from safe and useful forms of investment, they are "savings" which ought never to have been attempted, for they have no economic justification in the needs of commerce, as is proved by results.

§ 4. The direct causal connection between the increased productive power of modern machinery and trade depression clearly emerges from a comparison of the fluctuations in the several departments of industry in different industrial countries. As modern machinery and modern methods of commerce are more highly developed and are applied more generally, trade fluctuations are deeper and more lasting. A comparison between more backward countries largely engaged in raising food and raw materials of manufacture for the great manufacturing countries is sometimes adduced in support of the contention that highly-evolved industry is steadier. But though Mr. Giffen is undoubtedly correct in holding that depressions are often worse in countries producing raw materials than in manufacturing countries,[1] this is only true of raw-material producing countries which produce for export, and which are therefore dependent for their trade upon fluctuations in demand for commodities in distant markets whose movements they are least able to calculate or control. Irregularity of climate, disease, and other natural causes must be a constant source of fluctuation in the productivity of agriculture. But those non-manufacturing countries which are little dependent upon commerce with manufacturing nations, and which are chiefly self-supporting, will of necessity retain a larger variety of agriculture and of other primitive industries, and will there-

---

[1] *Essays in Finance*, vol. i. p. 137, etc.

fore be less at the mercy of some climatic or other injury than a country more specialised in some single crop or other industry The specialisation impressed upon a backward country by commerce with advanced industrial countries, confining it to growing cotton or wheat or sheep or wine, exaggerates the irregularity imposed by nature upon its productivity, by making it subservient to the fluctuating demands of distant and wholly incalculable markets. The fluctuations brought about by irregular consumption and uncontrolled production in highly-evolved industrial countries are thus reflected with terrible force upon the more primitively-ordered parts of the industrial world. Thus does the character of modern machine-industry impress itself on the countries which feed it with raw materials.

If we turn to investigate the several departments of industry in the more highly-evolved communities, where statistics yield more accurate information, we have most distinct evidence that so far as the world-market is concerned, the fluctuations are far more extreme in the industries to which machine-production and high organisation have been applied. An investigation of changes of wholesale prices indicates that the most rapid and extreme fluctuations are found in the prices of textile and mineral materials which form the foundation of our leading manufactures. A comparison of the price changes of food as a whole, and of corn prices with textiles and minerals, shows that especially during the last thirty years the fluctuations of the latter have been much more rapid and pronounced. (See following diagrams.)

§ 5. It ought to be clearly understood that the real congestion with which we are concerned, the over-supply, does not chiefly consist of goods in their raw or finished state passing through the machine on their way to the consumer. The economic diagnosis is sometimes confused upon this point, speaking of the increased productive power of machinery as if it continued to pour forth an unchecked flood of goods in excess of possible consumption. This shows a deep misunderstanding of the malady. Only in its early stages does it take this form. When in any trade the producing power of machinery is in excess of the demand at a remunerative price, the series of processes through

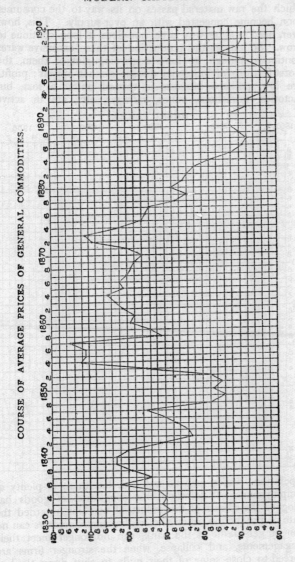

COURSE OF AVERAGE PRICES OF GENERAL COMMODITIES.

which the raw material passes on its way to the consumer
soon become congested with an over-supply. This, however, need not be very large, nor does it long continue to
grow. So long as the production of these excessive wares
continues, though we have a growing glut of them, the
worst features of industrial disease do not appear; profits
are low, perhaps business is carried on at a loss, but
factories, workshops, mines, railways, etc., are in active

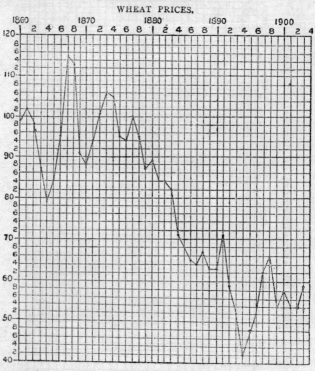

WHEAT PRICES.

operation; wages may be reduced, but there is plenty of
employment. It is when this congestion of goods has
clogged the wheels of the industrial machine, retarded the
rate of production, when the weaker manufacturers can no
longer get credit at the bank, can no longer meet their
engagements, and collapse, when the stronger firms are
forced to close some of their mills, to shut down the less
productive mines, to work short hours, to economise in
every form of labour, that depression of trade assumes its

more enduring and injurious shape. The condition now is
not that of an increasing glut of goods; the existing glut
continues to block the avenues of commerce and to check
further production, but it does not represent the real
burden of over-supply. The true excess now shows itself
in the shape of idle machinery, closed factories, unworked
mines, unused ships and railway trucks. It is the auxiliary
capital that represents the bulk of over-supply, and whose
idleness signifies the enforced unemployment of large
masses of labour. It is machinery, made and designed to
increase the flow of productive goods, that has multiplied
too fast for the growth of consumption. This machinery
does not continue in full use, a large proportion of it is not

GENERAL FOOD PRICES.

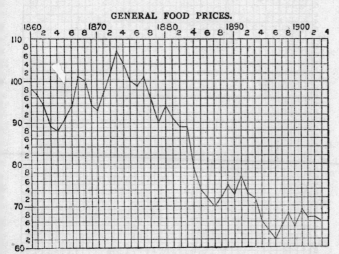

required to assist in producing the quantity of consumptive
goods which can find a market, and must of necessity stand
idle; it represents a quantity of useless forms of capital,
over-supply, and its unused productive power represents
an incomparably larger amount of potential over-supply of
goods. Economic forces are at work preventing the con-
tinuation of the use of this excessive machinery; if it were
used in defiance of these forces, if its owners could afford to
keep it working, there would be no market for the goods
it would turn out, and these too would swell the mass of
over-supply.

§ 6. The general relation of modern Machinery to Commercial Depression is found to be as follows:—Improved

machinery of manufacture and transport enables larger and larger quantities of raw material to pass more quickly and more cheaply through the several processes of production. Consumers do not, in fact, increase their consumption as quickly and to an equal extent. Hence the onward flow of productive goods is checked in one or more of the manu-

MINERAL PRICES.

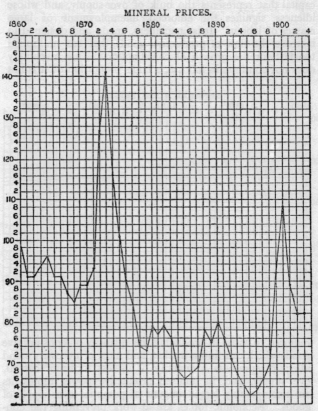

facturing stages, or in the hands of the merchant, or even in the retail shop. This congestion of the channels of production automatically checks production, depriving of all use a large quantity of the machinery, and a large quantity of labour. The general fall of money income which has necessarily followed from a fall of prices, uncompensated by a corresponding expansion of sales, induces a shrinkage of consumption. Under depressed trade, while the markets

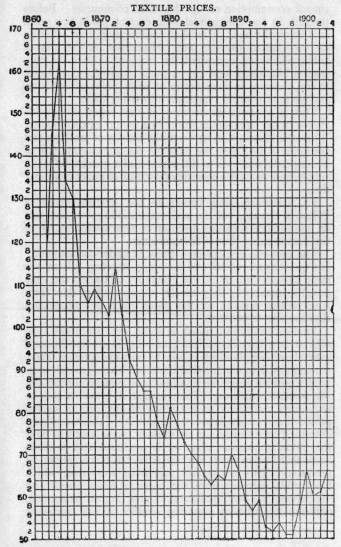

TEXTILE PRICES.

continue to be glutted with unsold goods, only so much current production is maintained as will correspond to the shrunk consumption of the depressed community. Before the turn in the commercial tide, current production even falls below the level of current consumption, thus allowing for the gradual passage into consumption of the glut of goods which had congested the machine. After the congestion which had kept prices low is removed, prices begin to rise, demand is more active at each point of industry, and we see the usual symptoms of reviving trade.

This is an accurate account of the larger phenomena visible in the commercial world in a period of disturbance. When the disease is at its worst, the activity of producer and consumer at its lowest, we have the functional condition of under-production due to the pressure of a quantity of over-supply, and we have a corresponding state of under-consumption.

§ 7. Machinery thus figures as the efficient cause of industrial disease, but the real responsibility does not rest on the shoulders of the inventor of new machinery, or of the manufacturer, but of the consumer.

The root-evil of depressed trade is under-consumption. If a quantity of capital and labour is standing idle at the same time, in all or in the generality of trades, the only possible reason why they remain unemployed is that there is no present demand for the goods which by co-operation they are able to produce.

English economists, most of whom, ever since the time of J. B. Say, have denied the possibility of the condition of general over-supply which is seen to exist in depressed trade, are contented to assume that there can be no general over-supply because every one who produces creates a corresponding power to consume. There cannot, it is maintained, be too much machinery or too much of any form of capital provided there exists labour to act with it; if this machinery, described as excessive, is set working, some one will have the power to consume whatever is produced, and since we know that human wants are insatiable, too much cannot be produced. This crude and superficial treatment, which found wide currency from the pages of Adam Smith and McCulloch, has been swallowed by later English economists, unfortunately without inquiring whether it was consistent with industrial facts. Since all commerce is ultimately resolvable into exchange of commodities for commodities, it is obvious that every increase of production signifies a corresponding increase of power to consume. Since there exists in every society a host of unsatisfied wants, it is equally certain that there exists a desire to consume everything that can be produced. But the fallacy involved in the supposition that over-supply is impossible consists in assuming that the power to consume and the desire to consume necessarily co-exist in the same persons.

In the case of a glut of cotton goods due to an increased application of machinery, the spinners and manufacturers have the power to consume what is produced, while a mass of starving, ill-clad beings in Russia, East London —even in Manchester—may have the desire to consume these goods. But since these latter are not owners of anything which the spinners and manufacturers wish to consume or to possess, the exchange of commodities for commodities cannot take place. But, it will be said, if the Lancashire producers desire to consume anything at all, those who produce such articles of desire will have the power, and possibly the desire, to consume more cotton goods, or at any rate the desire to consume something produced by other people who will have both power and desire to consume cotton goods. Thus, it will be said, the roundabout exchange of commodities for commodities must be brought about. And this answer is valid, on the assumption that the Lancashire producers desire to consume an equivalent of the goods they produce. But let us suppose they do not desire to do so. The reply that since human wants are insatiable every one with power to consume must have desire to consume, is inadequate. In order to be operative in the steady maintenance of industry the desire to consume must be a desire to consume *now*, to consume continuously, and to consume to an extent corresponding with the power to consume.

Let us take the Lancashire trade as a test case. Evidently, there could be no superfluous capital and labour in Lancashire trade if the cotton-spinners, manufacturers and their operatives, increased their own consumption of cotton goods to correspond with every increase of output.

But if they do not do this, they can only make good

and maintain their capital and labour in employment by persuading others to increase their consumption of cotton goods. How can they do this? If, instead of desiring to consume more cotton goods, the Lancashire employers and operatives desire to consume, and do actually consume, more hardware, houses, wine, etc., then the increased consumption of these things, raising their prices and so stimulating their production, and distributing a larger purchasing-power among the capitalists and operatives engaged in producing the said hardware, houses, wine, etc., will enable the latter to consume more cotton goods, and if these desire to do so, their effective demand will maintain the new capital and labour employed in Lancashire trade.

But if, instead of taking this course, the Lancashire capitalists and operatives want not to consume either cotton or anything else, but simply to *save* and put up more mills and prepare more yarn and cloth, they will soon find they are attempting the impossible. Their new capital, and the fresh labour conjoined with it, can only be employed on condition that they or others shall increase their consumption of cotton goods. They themselves *ex hypothesi* will not do so, and if the capitalists and operatives engaged in setting up the new cotton-mills, etc., will consent to do so, this only postpones the difficulty, unless we suppose a continuous erection of new mills, and a continuous application on the part of those who construct these mills of the whole of their profits and wages in demanding more cotton goods— a *reductio ad absurdum*. In short, cotton capitalists and operatives can only effect this saving and provide this increased employment of capital and labour on condition that either those engaged in erecting and working the new mills shall spend all their income in demanding cotton goods, or that other persons shall diminish the proportion of their incomes which hitherto they have saved, and shall apply this income in increased demand for cotton goods.

Now if the same motives which induce Lancashire capitalists and workers to refuse to increase their present consumption *pari passu* with the rate of production are generally operative, it will appear that capital and labour lie idle because those who are able to consume what they could produce are not willing to consume, but desire to postpone consumption—*i.e.*, to save.

§ 8. The process of "Saving" has received but scant attention from economic writers. Jevons appears to have held that superfluous food and other necessary consumptive goods, in whosoever hands they were, constituted the only true fund of capital in a community at any given time. Sidgwick also holds that all "Savings" are in the first instance "food." That this is not the case will appear from the following example:—A self-sufficing man produces daily for his daily consumption a quantity of food, etc., denoted by the figure 10. 5 of this is necessary and 5 superfluous consumption. This man, working with primitive tools, discovers an implement which will greatly facilitate his production, but will cost 4 days' labour to make. Three alternatives are open to him. He may spend half his working day in producing the strictly necessary part of his previous consumption, 5, and devote the other half to making the new implement, which will be finished in 8 days. Or he may increase the duration of his working day by one quarter, giving the extra time to the making of his new implement, which will be finished in 16 days. Or lastly, he may continue to produce consumptive goods as before, but only consume half of them, preserving the other half for 8 days, until he has a fund which will suffice to keep him for 4 continuous days, which he will devote to making the new implement. If he adopts the first alternative, he simply changes the character of his production, producing in part of his working day future goods instead of present consumptive goods. In the second he creates future goods by extra labour. In the third case only does the "saving" or new "capital" take as its first shape food. In the same way a community seeking to introduce a more "roundabout" method of production requiring new plant, or seeking to place in the field of industry a new series of productive processes to satisfy some new want, may achieve their object by "saving" food, etc., or by changing for awhile the character of their production, or by extra labour. Thus new capital, whether from the individual or the community point of view, may take either "food" or any other material form as its first shape.

Since "savings" need not take the shape of food or any article capable of immediate consumption, Adam Smith and J. S. Mill are clearly wrong when they urge in terms almost identical[1] that what is saved is necessarily consumed, and consumed as quickly as that which is spent. The antithesis of saving and spending shows these writers, and the bulk of English economists who follow them, are misled, because they regard " saving " as doing something with money, and do not sufficiently go behind the financial aspect of putting money into a bank.

A closer analysis of saving yields the result that, except in one of the simple cases taken in our example above, where " saving " implied withholding consumable goods from present consumption, every act of saving in a complex industrial society signifies making, or causing to be made, forms of capital which are essentially incapable of present consumption—*i.e.*, future or productive goods.

Each member of an industrial community receives his money income as the market equivalent of value created in goods or services by the requisites of production, land, capital, labour which he owns. For every £1 paid as income an equivalent quantity of material or non-material wealth has been already created.

Let A be the owner of a requisite of production, receiving £500 a year as income in weekly payments of £10. Before receiving each £10 he has caused to come into existence an amount of wealth which, if material goods, may or may not be still in existence ; if services, has already been consumed. It is evident that A may each week consume £10 worth of goods and services without affecting the general condition of public wealth. A, however, determines to consume only £5 worth of goods and services each week, and puts the other £5 into the bank. Now what becomes of the £5 worth of goods and services which A might have consumed, but refused to consume? Do they necessarily continue to exist so long as A is credited with the money which represents their " saving " ; if so, in what form ? In other words, what actually takes place in the world of commerce when money income is said to be saved, what other

---

" What is annually saved is as regularly consumed as what is annually spent, and nearly in the same time too ; but it is consumed by a different set of people." (*Wealth of Nations*, p. 149 *b*, McCulloch.) " Everything which is produced is consumed ; both what is saved and what is said to be spent, and the former quite as quickly as the latter." (*Principles of Political Economy*, Book I., chap. v., sec. 6.)

industrial facts stand behind the financial fact of A deposit
ing part of his income in the bank as "savings"?

To this question several answers are possible.

(1) B, a spendthrift owner of land or capital, wishing
to live beyond his income, may borrow from the bank
each £5 which A puts in, mortgaging his property.   In
this case B spends what A might have spent; B's property
(former savings perhaps?) falls into A's hands.   A has
individually effected a "saving" represented by tangible
property, but as regards the community there is no saving
at all, real or apparent.

(2) C, a fraudulent promoter of companies, may by
misrepresentation get hold of A's saved money, and may
spend it for his own enjoyment, consuming the goods and
services which A might have consumed, and giving to A
"paper" stock which figures as A's "savings."   Here A
has individually effected no saving.

From the point of view of the community there is no
real saving (C has consumed instead of A), but so long
as the "stock" has a market value there is an apparent
saving.   To this category belongs the "savings" effected if
A lends his money to a government to be spent on war.
From the standpoint of the community there is no saving
(unless the war be supposed to yield an asset of wealth or
security), but A's paper stock represents his individual
saving.   A's "saving" is exactly balanced by the spending
of the community in its corporate capacity, A receiving a
mortgage upon the property of the community.[1]

(3) D and E, manufacturers or traders, engaged in producing luxuries which A used to buy with his £5 before
he took to saving, finding their weekly "takings" diminished
and being reduced to financial straits, borrow A's "savings"
in order to continue their business operations, mortgaging their plant and stock to A.   So long as, with the
assistance of A's money, they are enabled to continue producing, what they produce is over-supply, not needed to
supply current consumption, assuming the relation between
spending and saving in the other members of the community remains unaltered.   This over-supply is the material

[1] An able analysis of the nature of " paper savings " is found in
Mr. J. M. Robertson's *Fallacy of Saving.*   (Sonnenschein.)

representative of A's " savings." So far as real capital is concerned there is no increase by A's act of saving, rather a decrease, for along with the net reduction in the consumption of luxuries on the part of the community due to A's action, there must be a fall in the " value" of the capital engaged in the various processes of producing luxuries, uncompensated by any other growth of values. But by A's " saving" new forms of capital exist which bear the appearance of capital, though in reality they are " over-supply." These empty forms represent A's saving. Of course A, with full knowledge of the facts, would only lend to D and E up to the real value of their mortgaged capital. When this point was reached D and E could get no further advances, and their stock and plant would pass into A's hands. From the point of view of the community A's action has resulted in the creation of a number of material forms of capital which, so long as the existing relations between the community's production and consumption continue, stand as over-supply.

(4) A may hand over his weekly £5 to F on security. F by purchase obtains the goods which A refused to consume, and may use them (or their equivalent in other material forms) as capital for further production. If F can with this capital help to produce articles for which there is an increasing consumption, or articles which evoke and satisfy some new want, then A's action will have resulted in "saving" from the point of view of the community—*i.e.*, there will be an increase of real capital; forms of capital which would otherwise have figured as over-supply have the breath of economic life put into them by an increase in general consumption. No real difficulty arises from a doubt whether the goods and services which A renounced were capable of becoming effective capital. The things he renounced were luxurious consumptive goods and services. But he could change them into effective capital in the following way:—Designing henceforth to consume only half his income, he would deliberately employ half the requisites of production which furnished his income in putting extra plant, machinery, etc., into some trade. Whether he does this himself, or incites F to do it, makes no difference; it will be done. In this way, by establishing new forms of useful capital, A can make good his saving, assuming an

increase of general consumption. These are the four
possible effects of A's saving from the point of view of the
community—

(1) Nil.
(2) Bogus or "paper" saving.
(3) Over-supply of forms of capital.
(4) Increase of real capital.

It appears then that every act which in a modern
industrial society is "saving," from the standpoint of the
community, and not a mere transfer of "spending" from
one person to another, consists in the production of a form
of goods in its nature or position incapable of present
consumption.

This analysis of "saving" convicts J. S. Mill of a double
error in saying, "Everything which is produced is consumed;
both what is saved and what is said to be spent; and the
former quite as rapidly as the latter." In the first place, by
showing that "saving," from the point of view of the community, generally means producing something incapable of
present consumption, it proves that even if what is "saved"
is consumed, it is not consumed as quickly as what is spent.
Mill seemed to think that what was "saved" was necessarily
food, clothing, and so-called finished goods, because "saving"
to him was not a process, but a single negative act of
refusing to buy. Because a man who has "saved" has
command of an extra stock of food, etc., which he may
hand over to labourers as real wages, he seems to think that
a community which saves will have its savings in this form.
We see this is not the case. Even where in a primitive
society extra food is the first form savings may take, it
belongs to the act of saving that this food shall not be
consumed so soon as it was available for consumption.
In short, Mill's notion was that savings must necessarily
mean a storing up of more food, clothing, etc., which,
after all, is not stored, but is handed over to others
to consume. He fails to perceive that a person who
saves from the social as opposed to the individual
point of view necessarily produces something which
neither he nor any one else consumes at once—*i.e.*,
steam engines, pieces of leather, shop goods. A "saving"
which is merely a transfer of spending from A to B is
obviously no saving from the point of view of the com-

munity to which both A and B belong. If A, who is said to save, pays wages to B, who makes a machine which would otherwise not have been made, when this machine is made something is saved, not before.

Though Mill does not seem, in Bk. I. chap. v., to regard increased plant, machinery, etc., as "savings," but rather as something for which "savings" may be exchanged,[1] the more usual economic view of "savings" embodies part of them in plant and raw material, etc., and considers the working up of these into finished goods as a "consumption." But though industrial usage speaks of cotton yarn, etc., being consumed when it is worked up, the same language is not held regarding machinery, nor would any business man admit that his "capital" was consumed by the wear and tear of machinery, and was periodically replaced by "saving." The wearing away of particular material embodiments of capital is automatically repaired by a process which is not saving in the industrial or the economic sense. No manufacturer regards the expenditure on maintenance of existing plant as "saving"; what he puts into additional plant alone does he reckon "savings." It would be well for economists to clearly recognise that this business aspect of capital and saving is also the consistent scientific aspect. "Saving" will then be seen to apply exclusively to such increased production of plant and productive goods as will afterwards yield an increased crop of consumptive goods, provided the community is willing to consume them. "Saving" is postponed consumption—*i.e.*, the production of "future goods," plant, machinery, raw materials in their several stages, instead of commodities suitable for immediate consumption.

§ 9. There are, in fact, two distinct motives which induce individuals to continue to produce, one is the desire to consume, the other the desire to save—*i.e.*, to postpone consumption. It is true that the latter may be said also to involve a desire to consume the results of the savings at some indefinitely future time, but the motive of their production at present is a desire to reduce the quantity of the present consumption of the community, and to increase the quantity of postponed consumption.

[1] Chap. v. § 5.

It is this consideration which gives the answer to the single sentence of J. S. Mill, which has been sometimes held to offer a complete refutation of the notion of an existing state of over-supply. "The error is in not perceiving that, though all who have an equivalent to give *might* be fully provided with every conceivable article which they desire, the fact that they go on adding to the production proves that this is not actually the case."[1] Here the present desire to consume either what is produced or its equivalent is assumed to be the only motive which can lead an individual to produce. The fact that people go on producing is regarded as proof that they are not "fully provided with every conceivable article they desire." If this were true it would be a final and conclusive refutation of the idea of over-supply. But if saving means postponed consumption, and the desire to save, as well as the desire to consume, is a *vera causa* in production, then the fact of continued production affords no proof that such production must be required to supply articles which are desired for consumption. Ultimately a belief that some one will consent to consume what is produced underlies the continued production of "a saving person," but, as we shall see presently, the belief of a competing producer that he can get a market for his goods, even when justified by events, is no guarantee against excessive production in the whole trade.

If, then, those who have the power to consume in the present desire to postpone their consumption they will refuse to demand consumptive goods, and will instead bring into existence an excess of productive goods.

§ 10. The diagram on next page may serve more clearly to indicate the quantitative maladjustment of Consuming and Saving which constitutes under-consumption, and exhibits itself in a plethora of machinery and productive goods.

A, B, C, D, E represent the several stages through which the raw material obtained from Nature passes on its way to the position of a consumer's utility. The five stages represent the five leading processes in production—the extractive process, transport, manufacture, wholesale and

---

[1] Bk. III., chap. xiv. § 3.

retail trade. The raw materials extracted at A, the wheat, skins, iron, timber, cotton, etc., obtained from various quarters of the globe, are gathered together in large quantities into places where they undergo various transformations of shape and character; they are then distributed by wholesale and retail merchants, who hand them over to persons who consume them as bread, boots, kettles, chairs, shirts. The extractive, transport, manufacturing, and merchant stages may of course be subdivided into many

MECHANISM OF PRODUCTION.

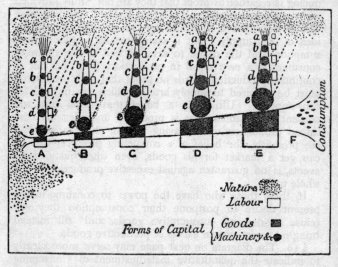

complex processes, as applied to the history of the more elaborately-produced commodities. But at each point in the process of production there must stand a quantity of plant and machinery designed to assist in moving the productive goods a single step further on the road towards consumption. This fixed capital is denoted by the black circles placed at the points A, B, C, D, E. But each machine, or factory building, or warehouse is itself the ultimate product of a series of steps which constitute a process similar to that denoted by the main channel of production. Consisting in raw material extracted from nature, the machinery and plant are built up by a number of productive stages, which correspond to A, B, C, D, E, into the completed shapes of fixed capital, adjusted to the positions where they can give the proper impulse to the main tide of production. Each productive stage in the production of plant or machinery requires the presence of other plant and machinery to assist its progress. Each of these secondary forms of fixed capital situate at *a, b, c, d, e,* has of course a similar history of its own. To represent the full complexity of the mechanism of industry thus suggested would be confusing and would serve no purpose here. It is sufficient that we recognise that at each point A, B, C, D, E, and at each of the points *a, b, c, d, e,* upon the perpendicular lines, stands a quantity of forms of fixed capital which are gradually worn out in the work of forwarding quantities of A to B, and quantities of B to C, and so on. Now if we turn to the point F, where goods pass out of the productive machine into the hands of consumers, who destroy them by extracting their "utility or convenience," we shall find in this flow of goods out of the industrial machine the motive-force and regulator of the activity of the whole machine.

Let us take an illustration from a single trade, the shoe trade. The number of boots and shoes purchased by consumers at retail shops and drawn out from the mechanism at the point F, determines the rate at which retailers demand and withdraw shoes from wholesale merchants, assuming for the sake of simplicity that all shopkeepers deal with manufacturers through the medium of merchant middlemen. If the number of sales effected in a given time by retailers increases, they increase their demand from the merchants, if it falls off they lower their demand. The quantity of goods which retailers will in normal conditions keep in stock will be regulated by the demand of consumers.[1] Thus the flow of shoes from D to E, and the

---

[1] The stock of a small retailer will not, however, in all cases vary proportionately with the aggregate sales of all classes of goods. A small shopkeeper, to retain his custom and credit, is often required to keep a small stock of a large variety of goods not often in request. If he sells them rather more quickly, he does not necessarily increase his stock in hand at any particular time.

quantity of shoes which at any given time are aι the point E, are determined by the demand of consumers—that is to say, by the quantity or pace of consumption. If, owing to miscalculation, a larger number of shoes stands in the retail shops than is required to satisfy current consumption, or if the flow from D to E is faster than the outflow from E, this excess ranks as an over-supply of these forms of capital. Now just as the demand of consumers determines the number of shoes which stand at E and flow from D to E, so the demand of the retailer determines the number of shoes which at any time constitutes the stock of the merchants at D, and the size and number of the orders they give to the manufacturers at C. Similarly with the earlier processes of production; the flow of leather from the "tanners" and the quantity of leather kept in stock are likewise determined by the demand of the manufacturers; and the transport of hides and bark, and the demand for these materials of tanning, will be regulated by the demands of the tanners. So the quantity of stock at each of the points A, B, C, D, E, and the rate of their progress from one point to the next, are dependent in each case upon the quantity demanded at the next stage. Hence it follows that the quantity of productive goods at any time in stock at each of the points in the production of shoes, and the quantity of productive work done and employment given at each point, are determined by the amount of consumption of shoes. If we knew the number of purchases of shoes made in any community by consumers in a given time, and also knew the condition of the industrial arts at the different points of production, we should be able to ascertain exactly how much stock and how much auxiliary capital was required at each point in the production of shoes. At any given time the flow of consumption indicated by F determines the quantity of stock and plant of every kind economically required at each point A, B, C, D, E. What applies to the shoe trade applies to trade in general. Given the rate or quantity of consumption in the community, it is possible to determine exactly the quantity of stock and plant required under existing industrial conditions to maintain this outflow of consumptive goods, and any stock or plant in excess of this amount figures as waste forms of capital or over-supply. F then is the quantitative regulator of A, B, C, D, E.[1] Nor is the accuracy of this statement impaired by the speculative character of modern trade. Speculative merchants or manufacturers may set up business at D or C and provide themselves with stock and machinery to start with, but unless they meet or create a growing demand of consumers their capital is waste, or else if they succeed in getting trade it is at the expense of other members of the trade, and their capital is made productive by negativing the capital of other traders.

§ 11. The truth here insisted on, that an exact quantitative relation exists between the amount of stock and plant, severally and collectively, required at the different points A, B, C, D, E, and that the amount economically serviceable at each point is determined by the quantity of current consumption, would seem self-evident. But though this has never been explicitly denied, the important results following from its recognition have been obscured and befogged by several conceptions and phrases relating to capital which have found acceptance among English economists.

Chief and foremost among these errors is the framing of a definition of capital so as to exclude the clear separation of productive goods and machinery, the economic means, from consumptive goods, the economic end. So long as a definition of capital is taken which includes any consumptive goods whatsoever, two results follow. One is a hopeless confusion in the commercial mind, for in commerce everything is capital which forms the stock or plant of a commercial firm, and nothing is capital which does not form part of such stock or plant. Secondly, to include under capital the food in the possession of productive

---

[1] It likewise determines the quantity of plant and stock at a, b, c, d down each of the perpendicular lines, for the demand at each of these points in the production of plant and machinery is derived from the requirements at the points A, B, C, D, E. The flow of goods therefore up these channels, though slower in its movement (since in the main channel only goods flow, while fixed capital is subject to the slower "wear and tear"), is equally determined by and derived from the consumption at F. The whole motive-power of the mechanism is generated at F, and the flow of money paid over the retail counter as it passes in a reverse current from F towards A, supplies the necessary stimulus at each point, driving the goods another stage in their journey.

labourers or any other consumptive goods is an abandonment of the idea of consumption as the economic end and a
substitution of production.

If we follow Böhm-Bawerk and the Austrian economists
in definitely refusing to include the consumptive goods of
labourers as capital,[1] we get a conception of capital which
is at once in accordance with the universal conception of
commercial men, and which enables us to realise the vital
relation between capital and consumption. We now see
Capital in the form of stock and plant at each point in the
industrial machine deriving its use and value from its contribution to the end, Consumption, and dependent for its
quantity upon the quantity of Consumption. We have
seen that a demand for commodities is the true and exact
determinant of the quantity of capital at each industrial
stage. It is therefore the determinant of the aggregate of
wealth which can function as useful forms of capital in
the industrial community at any given time. The aggregate
of plant and stock which constitute the material forms of
capital at the points A, B, C, D, E must in a properly adjusted
state of industry have an exact quantitative relation to the
consumption indicated by F. If F increases, the quantity of
forms of capital at A, B, C, D, E may severally and collectively
increase; if F declines, the useful forms of capital at each
point are diminished. Since we have seen that the sole
object of saving from the social point of view is to place
new forms of capital at one of the points A, B, C, D, E, it is
evident that the amount of useful saving is limited by the
rate of consumption, or financially, by the amount of "spending." Where there is an improvement in the general productive power of a community, only a certain proportion
of that increased power can be economically applied to
"saving"—*i.e.*, to the increase of forms of capital; a due
proportion must go to increased spending and a general
rise in consumption.

§ 12. This will hardly be disputed, except by those who
still follow Mill in maintaining that the whole of the current
production could be "saved," with the exception of what
was required to support the efficiency of labour, a doctrine

---

[1] Böhm-Bawerk, *Positive Theory of Capital*, p. 67. See Appendix
I. for conflict of opinion among English economists. Cossa stigmatises
the inclusion of labourers' consumptive-goods under capital as one of
"those well-known tangles of misconception which have proverbially
afflicted English economists." (Intro. to *Political Economy*, p. 360.)

to which even he could only give passing plausibility by admitting that the increased savings which resulted from an attempt to do this would take the shape of luxuries consumed by the said labourers—that is to say, would not be "savings" at all, but a transfer of "spending" from one class to another.[1] If capital be confined to commercial capital, and "saving" to the establishment of the forms of such capital, no one will deny that the quantity of "saving" which can be effectually done by a community at any time depends upon the current rate of consumption, or that any temporary increase of such saving must be justified by a corresponding future increase in the proportion of spending.[2]

This will be generally admitted. But there are those who will still object that production just as much limits and determines consumption as consumption does production, and who appear to hold that any increase in present saving, and the consequent increase of amount of plant and stock, have an economic power to force a corresponding rise of future consumption which shall justify the saving. This they urge in the teeth of the fact that in a normal state of industry in machine-using countries there exists more machinery and more labour than can find employment, and that only for a brief time in each decennial period can the whole productive power of modern machinery be fully used, notwithstanding the increasing blood-letting to which superfluous saving is exposed by the machinations of bogus companies, in which the "saving" done by the dupes is balanced by the "spending" of the sharps. Ignoring the fact that the alleged power of increased saving to stimulate increased consumption is not operative, they still maintain that there cannot be too much "saving," because the tendency of modern industry is to make production more and more "roundabout" in its methods, and thus to provide scope for an ever-increasing quantity of forms of capital.

Under modern machinery we see a constant increase in

---

[1] *Principles of Political Economy*, Bk. I., chap. v. § 3; see also Bk. III., chap. xiv. § 3.

[2] It should be noted that an increased amount of consumption in the future does not necessarily compensate for a disturbance of the current balance of saving and spending, for an *increased proportion of future income* will have to be spent in order to compensate.

the number of direct and subordinate processes connected with the forwarding of any class of commodities to its completion. A larger proportion of the productive labour and capital is employed, not upon the direct horizontal line, but upon the perpendicular lines which represent the making of subsidiary machinery. More and more saving may be stored up in the shape of machines to make machines, and machines to make these machines, and thus the period at which the "saving" shall fructify in consumption may be indefinitely extended.

Some of the labour stored and the capital established in the construction of harbours, the drainage of land, the construction of scientific instruments, and other works of durable nature and indirect service, may not be represented in consumptive goods for centuries. Admitting this, it may be urged, can any limits be set to present "saving" and its storage in forms of capital, provided those forms be selected with a due regard to a sufficiently distant future? The answer is that only under two conditions could an indefinitely large amount of present "saving" be justified. The first condition is that an unlimited proportion of this "saving" can be stored in forms which are practically imperishable; the second condition is that our present foresight shall enable us to forecast the methods of production and consumption which shall prevail in the distant future. In fact neither of these conditions exists. However much present "saving" we stored in the most enduring forms of capital with which we are acquainted—e.g., in the permanent way of railroads, in docks, in drainage and improvement of land, a large proportion of this "saving" would be wasted if the consumption it was destined to subserve was postponed for long.[1] Neither can we predict with any assurance that the whole value of such "savings"

---

[1] It must be borne in mind that many articles of utility and enjoyment must in their final processes be produced for immediate consumption. The "saving" of perishable goods is confined to a saving of the more enduring forms of machinery engaged in their production, or in some few cases to a storing up of the raw material. So likewise that large portion of productive work termed "personal services" cannot be antedated. These limits to the possibility of "saving" are important. No amount of present sacrifice in the interest of the next generation could enable them to live a life of luxurious idleness.

will not have disappeared before a generation has elapsed by reason of changes in industrial methods.

The amount of present "saving" which is justified from the point of view of the community is strictly limited. We cannot forecast the demand of our twentieth generation of descendants, or the industrial methods which will then prevail; we do not even know whether there will be a twentieth generation; there are certain large inevitable wastes in postponed consumption by reason of the perishability of all material forms of wealth, or the abstraction of them by others than those for whose use they were intended. Moreover, we do not believe it would be good for our descendants to have the enjoyment of excessive wealth without a corresponding personal effort of producing, nor would it be good for us to exert effort without some proximate and corresponding enjoyment. The limits of individual life rightly demand that a large proportion of individual effort shall fructify in the individual life.

Thus there are practical limits set upon the quantity of "saving" which can be usefully effected by extending the interval between effort and enjoyment. If the right period be exceeded the risk and waste is too great. The analogy of gardening adduced by Ruskin is a sound one.[1] By due care and the sacrifice of bud after bud the gardener may increase the length of the stem and the size of the flower that may be produced. He may be said to be able to do this indefinitely, but if he is wise he knows that the increased risks of such extension, not to mention the sacrifice of earlier units of satisfaction, impose a reasonable limit upon the procrastination. The proportion of "saving" which may be and is applied to establish late-fructifying forms of wealth, differs not only with the different developments of the industrial arts, but with the foresight and moral character of the race and generation. As our species of civilisation advances, and the demand for complex luxuries and the arts of supplying them advance, a larger amount of "roundabout" production becomes possible, and as regard for the future generations advances, more capital will be put into forms which fructify for them. But at the present in any given community there is a rational and a necessary

---

[1] Ruskin, *Unto this Last*, p. 145.

limit to the quantity of "saving" which can be applied to such purposes.

Secondly, we find that in fact the surplus "saving" over and above what is needed to provide the necessary forms of capital to assist in satisfying current consumption is not absorbed in making provision for distant future consumption by more "roundabout methods." Much of it goes into a mere increase of the number of existing forms of capital whose *raison d'être* lies in the satisfaction of present or immediately future wants. The multiplication of cotton-spinning-mills, of paper-mills, of breweries, ironworks, has gone on far faster than the growth of current consumption. This increase of productive machinery has not in fact been able to force such an increase of consumption as gives adequate employment to these new forms of machinery and to the labour which is at hand to work them.

§ 13. It is not therefore correct to say that the rate of production determines the rate of consumption just as much as the rate of consumption determines the rate of production. The current productive power of capital and labour places a maximum limit upon current consumption, but an increase of productive power exercises no sufficient force to bring about a corresponding rise in consumption. Just as in a particular trade—*e.g.*, the Lancashire cotton trade, an excess of "saving" may be applied to the establishment of mills and machinery which cannot be kept working because there is no market for their output, so it is with trade in general. It is not true that the inflation of capital in the Lancashire trade is due to a misdirection which implies a lack of capital in some other branch of industry. In a period of depression every other important branch of industry displays the same symptoms of excessive plant, over-supply of stock, irregular and deficient employment of labour, though not to the same extent. Nor is there any *à priori* reason why there should not be from time to time such general maladjustment.

It is universally admitted that from ignorance or mis-calculation too much new capital often flows into certain industries or groups of industry, and too little into others; some are congested, others starved. All economists allow that temporary over-production in certain fields of industry is thus caused, other fields being insufficiently fertilised with capital. This maldistribution of capital among the several occupations, they will likewise admit, involves a net waste of productive power: it is bad economy of production. But if this waste from misdirection in the application of capital at a given time is admitted as a natural occurrence, why is it unreasonable to expect that a general misdirection of capital, not as between one set of industries and another, but as between one period of time and another, may occur? In other words, is it unreasonable to expect that the saving and investing classes as a whole may be deceived as to the amount of new capital that can be economically absorbed by the industrial organism during a given period? Thus deceived, may they not be led from time to time to endeavour to put a larger amount of new capital into effective operation than is needed, in the actual condition of industry, to provide for the increased rate of consumption which will take place in the future? The same imperfect knowledge, the same short-sight which cause a local misdirection will also cause a temporary misdirection of capital: errors will arise as to the total quantity of saving that is economically desirable at a particular time.

The quantitative relations actually subsisting between the aggregate of "spending" and of "saving" do not rest upon any such basis of direct and accurately measured self-interest as will serve to keep a constant just balance, calling forth at each time exactly that amount of saving economically required to forward the progress of industry and provide for the actual needs of further consumption.

On the contrary, while it is the interest of every "saver" to put his savings into the most remunerative investment he can find, and he normally exerts some conscious effort in finding it, the question how large a proportion of his income he shall save does not in many cases form a subject of serious consideration. If every one saved with a keen eye to the rate of interest he was to get, increasing his saving when interest rose, decreasing it when interest fell, there would be a fairly effective economic check upon such over-saving and consequent over-production as we perceive takes place. But in fact a great deal of the "saving" is an automatic process by which surplus elements of income, over what is needed to maintain a customary class standard of consumption, save themselves. Much of the saving of the wealthy classes is of this nature. Even with regard to the saving of the less wealthy, much of it is done without regard to the rate of interest, and some sorts of saving, where the object is to secure a future income of a given size, are actually stimulated by a fall of interest.

Thus there exists no automatic check upon the proportion of saving to spending, so far as the general income is concerned. In certain conditions of distribution, where the automatic self-accumulation of the surplus incomes of the rich play a large part in the aggregate of saving, it is reasonable to expect the frequent recurrence of a tendency to congest industry with excessive capital. For consideration of the industrial organism shows that maladjustment in the relation of "saving" to "spending" can only lean one way. There cannot be too little saving to furnish current consumption, taking the industrial community as a whole, for it is impossible to increase the rate of consumption, F, faster than the increase of the rate of current production : any increase of the purchase of shop-goods by raising prices and circulating more money down the paths of production stimulates and strains the sinews of production, and if the existing machinery of production is inadequate it supplies a motive-power to increase " saving." In no case can a community consume faster than it produces. An individual can do so by living on his capital, a nation may do so for a time by living upon its capital, giving to other nations by means of an increased debt a lien upon its future wealth. But a whole industrial community can never live upon its capital, can never in the literal sense of the term " spend too much." This statement requires a single qualification. While a community can never by " spending " deplete its capital, while it cannot increase its " spending " without at the same time increasing its real capital,[1] it will doubtless be profitable to a progressive community to reduce its consumption for a while below the normal proportion in order to fully utilise new discoveries in the industrial arts which shall justify in the future increased consumption.

With this necessary qualification it is true that a community cannot exceed in the direction of spending. But the balance may lean the other way. A community may "save too much," that is to say, it may establish a larger

---

[1] This does not necessarily imply a stimulation of new saving. A fuller vitality given to existing forms of capital will raise the quantity of real capital as measured in money. Mills and machinery which have no present or future use, though they embody saving, have no value and do not increase real capital.

quantity of productive machinery and goods than is required to maintain current or prospective consumption. What is to prevent a community consisting of a vast number of individuals with no close knowledge of one another's actions, desires, and intentions, making such a miscalculation as will lead them to place at each of the points A, B, C, D, E, and in all or most branches of industry, a larger quantity of forms of capital than are required?

It is said that the harmony which subsists between the social interest and the self-interest of individuals will prevent this, or, in other words, that individuals would find that if they attempted unduly to increase the aggregate of capital beyond what was socially advantageous in view of the community's consumption, it would not pay them to do so. Is this true?

An individual working entirely for himself, whose capital lay in his tools and his raw or unfinished commodities, would never increase the latter unduly. A socialist community properly managed would never add to its stock of machinery or increase the quantity of its raw materials or unfinished goods, so as to leave any machines unused or half used, or any goods unnecessarily occupying warehouse room and deteriorating in quality. But when competition of individual interests comes in there is no such security.

It may pay individuals to build new factories and put in new machinery where it would not pay the community to do so, were it the sole owner of the means of production.

The knowledge that enough capital is already invested in an industry to fully supply all current demands at profitable prices has no power to deter the investment of fresh capital, provided the new investors have reason to believe their capital can be made to displace some existing capital owned by others. If the new-comer can, by superior business address, by successful advertising, by "sweating" his employees or otherwise, get hold of a portion of the business hitherto in the hands of other firms, it will pay him to build new factories and stock them with the requisite machinery, and to begin the process of manufacture. There may be in existence already more bicycle works than are sufficient to supply the consumption of the community.

But if a would-be manufacturer thinks he can withdraw from other makers a sufficient number of customers, he will set up works, and make new machines, though his methods of production and the goods he turns out may be no better than those of other makers. The same holds at every stage of production. In wholesale or retail distribution the fact that there are sufficient warehouses and shops in existence adequately to supply the current demand does not prevent any one from embarking new savings in more warehouses or shops, provided he believes he is able to divert into his own firm a sufficient amount of the business formerly held by others. In a district two grocers' shops may be quite sufficient to supply the needs of the neighbourhood, and to secure adequate competition. But if a third man, by an attractive shop-front or superior skill in the labelling or adulteration of his wares, can procure for himself an adequate share of the custom, it will pay him to put the requisite plant and stock into a shop, though the trade on the one hand and the community on the other are no gainers by his action.

There is indeed much evidence to show that it may be to the advantage of individuals to increase the machinery of production, even though there is no reasonable prospect of this machinery being worked at a profit. It is the unanimous testimony of business men that the Lancashire trade has been congested with mills and machinery in this way. As a result of an excessive desire to postpone consumption there are considerable sums of money which cannot find a safe remunerative investment. Here is the material for the company promoter. By means of the specious falsehoods of prospectuses he draws this money together; with him work a builder and an architect who desire the contract of putting up the factory; the various firms interested in manufacturing and supplying the machinery, the boiler-maker and fitters of various kinds, the firm of solicitors whose services are requisite to place the concern upon a sound legal footing, or to establish confidence, take up shares. It is to the interest of all these and many other classes of persons to bring into the field of production new forms of capital, quite independently of the question whether the condition of a trade or the consumption of the community has any need for them.

§ 14. These operations, which imply a conflict between the interests of individuals and those of the community, pervade all modern commerce, but are more prevalent in businesses where complex machinery plays a prominent part, or where specious advertising gives the outsider a larger chance of successful entry.

In each and all of these cases it is to the interest of the individual to place new "savings" in new forms of capital in branches of industry where sufficient capital already exists to assist in supplying the current demand for consumptive goods. So far is it from being true that the self-interest of individuals provides an economic check upon over-supply, that it is possible that at each of the points of production, A, B, C, D, E, and in all or the majority of industries at the same time, there should be an excess of forms of capital as compared with that which would suffice for the output, F. The automatic growth of bubble companies and every species of rash or fraudulent investment at times of depressed trade is proof that every legitimate occupation for capital is closed, and that the current rate of saving is beyond that which is industrially sound and requisite. These bubble companies are simply tumours upon the industrial body attesting the sluggish and unwholesome circulation; they are the morbid endeavours of "saving" which is socially unnecessary, and ought never to have taken place, to find investments. When one of these "bubble" companies collapses it is tacitly assumed by unthinking people that those who invested their money in it were foolish persons who might have sought and found some better investment. Yet a little investigation would have shown that at the time this company arose no opportunity of safe remunerative investment open to the outside public existed, every sound form of business being already fully supplied with capital.

At first sight it might appear that Consols and first-class railway and other stocks were open, and that the folly of the investors in bogus companies consisted in not preferring a safe 2½ per cent. to a risky 5 or 10 per cent. But this argument is once more a return to the unsound individualistic view. It was doubtless open to any individual investor of new savings to purchase sound securities at 2½ per cent., but, since the aggregate of such soundly-placed capital would not be increased, this would simply mean the displacement of an equal quantity of some one else's capital. A could not buy Consols unless B sold, therefore the community to which A and B belong could not invest any fresh savings in Consols. Any widespread attempt on the part of those who plunged into bogus companies to try first-class investments would obviously have only had the effect of further reducing the real interest of these investments far below $2\frac{1}{2}$ per cent. The same effect would obviously follow any effective legal interference with company-promoting of this order. The fact that Consols and other first-class investments do not rise greatly at such times is, however, evidence that the promoters of unsound enterprises succeed in persuading individual investors that their chance of success is not less than $2\frac{1}{2}$ per cent. In many instances the investor may be acting wisely in preferring a smaller chance of much higher profits, because a secure $2\frac{1}{2}$ per cent. may be quite inadequate to his needs. For it must be borne in mind that a knowledge that the new bank or new building society is unnecessary, because enough banks and building societies already exist, does not make it impossible or necessarily improbable that the new venture will succeed.

The objection, then, which takes the form that oversaving cannot exist, because the worst investments made with open eyes must be productive of more than that which could be obtained by investing in Consols, is not a valid one. It would only be valid on the supposition that capital were absolutely fluid, that the quantity of soundly-placed investments were indefinitely expansible, and that new forms of capital had in no case the power to oust or negative the use of old forms of capital. But this we have seen is not the case. If there existed absolute fluidity of competition in all forms of capital, the fact that interest for new investments stood above zero would be a proof that there was not excess of forms of capital. Capital appears to have this fluidity when it is regarded from the abstract financial point of view. A man who has "saved" appears to hold his "savings" in the form of bank credit, or other money which he is able to invest in any way he chooses. But, as we have seen, the real "savings," which represent his productive effort plus his abstinence, are of necessity embodied in some material forms, and are therefore devoid of that fluidity which appears to attach to them when reflected in bank money.

§ 15. The evils of trade depression, or excessive growth of the forms of capital beyond the limits imposed by consumption, are traced in large measure directly, but also indirectly, to the free play of individual interests in the development of machine-production. The essential irregularities of invention, the fluctuations of public taste, the artificial restrictions of markets, all enable individual capitalists to gain at the public expense. The added interests of its individual members do not make the interest of the community. All these modes of conflict between the individual and the public interest derive force from the complexity of modern capitalist production.

In fastening upon the uncontrolled growth of machinery the chief responsibility for that depression of trade which is derived from an attempt to devote too large a proportion of the productive power of the community to forms of "saving," two points should be clearly understood.

In the first place, it is the forms of capital and not real capital which are produced in excess. If there are 500 spinning-mills in Lancashire where 300 would suffice, the destruction of 200 mills would no whit diminish the amount of real capital. If 200 mills were burnt down, though the individual owners would sustain a loss, that loss, estimated in money, would be compensated by a money rise in the value of the other mills. The quantity of real capital in cotton-spinning is dependent upon the demand for the use of such forms of capital—that is to say, upon the consumption of cotton goods. If 300 mills are sufficient to do the work of supplying yarn to meet the demand of all manufacturers, the value of 500 mills is no greater than of 300; assuming that the 500 mills equally distributed the trade, it would simply mean that the real capital was thinly spread over 500 mills, which could only work a little over half-time without producing a glut of goods, instead of being concentrated upon 300 mills fully occupied.

Turning once more to the diagram,

$$a \quad b \quad c \quad d \quad e$$
$$\underline{\hspace{6cm}} < f \text{ (consumption),}$$

f (the current rate of consumption) determines the quantity of real productive power of capital that can be effectively employed at each point, a, b, c, d, e. The condition of the arts of industry, including the rates of wages and other conditions of the labour market, determines how many forms of capital (mills, warehouses, ironworks, raw material, etc.) at any given time are socially requisite to embody this capital. But though f has an economic power to force into existence the requisite minimum of these forms of capital, it has no power to prevent the pressure of individual interests from exceeding that minimum and planting at a, b, c, d, e more forms of capital than are required.

Secondly, over-production or a general glut is only an external phase or symptom of the real malady. The disease is under-consumption or over-saving. These two imply one another. The real income of a community in any given year is divisible into two parts, that which is produced and consumed, that which is produced and not consumed—*i.e.*, is saved. Any disturbance in the due economic proportion of these two parts means an excess of the one and a defect of the other. All under-consumption therefore implies a correspondent over-saving. This over-saving is embodied in an excess of machinery and goods over the quantity economically required to assist in maintaining current consumption. It must, however, be remembered that this over-saving is not measured by the quantity of new mills, machinery, etc., put into industry. When the mechanism of industry is once thoroughly congested, over-saving may still continue, but will be represented by a progressive under-use of existing forms of capital, that unemployment of forms of capital and labour which makes trade depression.

An increased quantity of saving is requisite to provide for an expected increase of consumption arising from a growth of population or from any other cause. Such increased saving is of course not over-saving. The proportion, as well as the absolute amount of the community's income which is saved, may at any time be legitimately increased, provided that at some not distant time an increased proportion of the then current income be consumed. If in a progressive community the proportion of " saving " to consumption, in order to maintain the current standard of living with the economic minimum of " forms " of capital, be as 2 to 10, the proportion of saving in any given year may be raised to 3 to 9, in order to provide for a future condition in which saving shall fall to 1 to 11. Such increased "saving" will not be over-saving; the forms of capital in which it is embodied will not compete with previously existing forms so as to bring down market prices. The efforts which take the form of permanent improvements of the soil, the erection of fine buildings, docks, railways, etc., for future use, may provide the opportunity to a community of increasing the proportion of its savings for a number of years. But such savings must be followed by an increased future consumption without a correspondent saving attached to it. The notion that we can indefinitely continue to increase the proportion of our savings to our consumption, bounded only by the limit of actual necessaries of life, is an illusion which places production in the position of the human goal instead of consumption.

§ 16. Machinery has intensified the malady of under-consumption or over-saving, because it has increased the opportunities of conflict between the interests of individuals and those of the community. With the quickening of competition in machine industries the opportunities to individuals of making good their new "savings" by cancelling the old "savings" of others continually grow in number, and as an ever larger proportion of the total industry falls under the dominion of machinery, more and more of this dislocation is likely to arise; the struggles of weaker firms with old machinery to hold their own, the efforts of improved machinery to find a market for its expanded product, will continue to produce gluts more frequently, and the subsequent checks to productive activity, the collapse of businesses, the sudden displacement of large masses of labour, in a word, all the symptoms of the malady of "depression" will appear with increased virulence.

It must be clearly recognised that the trouble is due to a genuine clash of individual interests in a competitive industrial society, where the frequent, large, and quite incalculable effects of improved machinery and methods of production give now to this, now to that group of competitors a temporary advantage in the struggle. It was formerly believed that this bracing competition, this free clash of individual interests, was able to strike out harmony, that the steady and intelligent pursuit by each of his own separate interest formed a sure basis of industrial order and induced the most effective and serviceable disposition of the productive powers of a community.

It now appears that this is not the case, and that the failure cannot in the main be attributed to an imperfect understanding by individuals of the means by which their several interests may be best subserved, but is due to the power vested in individuals or groups of individuals to secure for themselves advantages arising from improved methods of production without regard for the vested interests of other individuals or of society as a whole.

CHAPTER XII.

MACHINERY AND DEMAND FOR LABOUR.

§ 1. *The Influence of Machinery upon the number of Employed, dependent on "elasticity of demand."*

§ 2. *Measurement of direct effects on Employment in Staple Manufacturers.*

§ 3. *Fallacy of the Separatist Measure of Employment.*

§ 4. *Influence of Introduction of Machinery upon Regularity of Employment.*

§ 5. *Effects of "Unorganised" Machine-industry upon Regularity.*

§ 6. *Different Ways in which modern Industry causes Unemployment.*

§ 7. *Summary of General Conclusions.*

§ 1. In discussing the direct influences of machinery upon the economic position of the labourer we must distinguish its effects upon (1) the number of workers employed; (2) the regularity of employment; (3) the skill, duration, intensity, and other qualities of labour; (4) the renumeration of labour. Though these influences are closely related in complex interaction, it is convenient to give a separate consideration to each.

(1) *Effects of Machinery upon the number of Employed.*— The motive which induces capitalist employers to introduce into an industry machinery which shall either save labour by doing work which labour did before, or assist labour by making it more efficient, is a desire to reduce the expenses of production. A new machine either displaces an old machine, or it undertakes a process of industry formerly done by hand labour without machinery.

In the former case it has been calculated that the expenses incurred in making, maintaining, and working the new machines so as to produce a given output will be less than the corresponding expenses involved in the use of the old machines. Assuming that the labour of making and working the new machines is paid at no lower rate than the labour it displaces, and that the same proportion of the price of each machine went as wages and as profits, it must follow that the reduction of expenses achieved signifies a net displacement of labour for a given quantity of production. Since the skilled labour of making new machines is likely to be paid higher than that of making more old machines, and the proportion of the price which goes as profit upon a new invention will be higher than in the case of an old one,[1] the actual displacement of labour will commonly be larger than is represented by the difference in money price of the two machines. Moreover, since in the case of an old manufacturing firm the cost of discarding a certain amount of existing machinery must be reckoned in the substitution of new machinery for old will generally mean a considerable displacement of labour.

Similarly, when a new process is first taken over by machinery the expenses of making and working the machines, as compared with the expenses of turning out a given product by hand labour, will, other things being equal, involve a net diminution of employment. The fact that the new machinery is introduced is a proof that there is a net diminution of employment as regards a given output; for otherwise no economy would be effected.

What then is meant by the statement so generally made, that machinery gives more employment than it takes away —that its wider and ultimate effect is not to diminish the demand for labour?

The usual answer is that the economy effected by labour, saving machinery in the expenses of production will, through competition of producers, be reflected in a lower scale of prices, and this fall of prices will stimulate con-

---

[1] Against this we may set the possibility of a fall in the rate of interest at which manufacturers may be able to borrow capital in order to set up improved machinery. Where an economy can be effected in this direction, the displacement of labour due to the introduction of machinery may not be so large—*i.e.*, it will pay a manufacturer to introduce a new machine which only "saves" a small amount of money, if he can effect the change at a cheap rate of borrowing. (Cf. Marshall, *Principles of Economics*, 2nd edit., pp. 569, 570.)

sumption. Thus, it is urged, the output must be greatly
increased. When we add together the labour spent in
producing the machinery to assist the enlarged production,
the labour spent in maintaining and working the same, and
the labour of conveying and distributing the enlarged production, it will be found that at least as much labour is
required under the new as under the old conditions of
industry. So runs the familiar argument.

The following is a fair example of the argument which
has passed current, drawn from the pages of a competent
economic writer:—

"The first introduction of machinery may indeed displace and diminish for a while the employment of labour,
may perchance take labour out of the hands of persons
otherwise not able to take another employment, and create
the need for another class of labourers altogether; but if it
has taken labour from ten persons, it has provided labour
for a thousand. How does it work? A yard of calico
made by hand costs two shillings, made by machinery it
may cost fourpence. At two shillings a yard few buy it;
at fourpence a yard multitudes are glad to avail themselves
of it. Cheapness promotes consumption; the article which
hitherto was used by the higher classes only is now to be
seen in the hand of the labouring classes as well. As the
demand increases, so production increases, and to such an
extent that, although the number of labourers now employed
in the production of calico may be immensely less in
proportion to a given quantity of calico, the total number
required for the millions of yards now used greatly exceeds
the number engaged when the whole work was performed
without any aid of machinery."[1]

Now, turning from the consideration of the particular
instance, which we shall find reason to believe is peculiarly
unfortunate when we deal with the statistics of the cotton
industry, it must be observed that economic theory makes
dead against this *à priori* optimism. Ignoring, for the
sake of convenience, the not improbable result that an
economy of production may, at any rate for a time,
swell profits instead of reducing prices, it will be evident that the whole value of the argument turns upon

[1] Leone Levi, *Work and Pay*, p. 28.

the effect of a fall of price in stimulating increased consumption. Now the problem, how far a given fall in price will force increased consumption, we have found in our discussion of monopoly prices to involve extremely intricate knowledge of the special circumstances of each case, and refined calculations of human motives. Everything depends upon "elasticity of demand," and we are certainly not justified in assuming that in a particular industry a given fall of prices due to machine-production will stimulate so large an increase of consumption that employment will be given to as many, or more persons than were formerly employed. On the contrary, if we apply a similarly graduated fall of prices to two different classes of goods, we shall observe a widely different effect in the stimulation of consumption. A reduction of fifty per cent. in the price of one class of manufactured goods may treble or quadruple the consumption, while the same reduction in another class may increase the consumption by only twenty per cent. In the former case it is probable that the ultimate effect of the machinery which has produced the fall in expenses of production and in prices will be a considerable increase in the aggregate demand for labour, while in the latter case there will be a net displacement. It is therefore impossible to argue *à priori* that the ultimate effect of a particular introduction of machinery must be an increased demand for labour, and that the labour displaced by the machinery will be directly or indirectly absorbed in forwarding the increased production caused by machinery. It is alleged that the use of steam-hammers has displaced nine of the ten men formerly required, that with modern machinery one man can make as many bottles as six men made formerly, that in the boot and shoe trade one man can do the work five used to do, that "in the manufacture of agricultural implements 600 men now do the work which fifteen or twenty years ago required 2145, thus displacing 1515," and so forth.[1] Now in some of these cases we shall find that the fall of prices following such displacements has led to so large an increase of demand that more persons are

---

[1] Statement by Mr. Shaftoe, President of the Trades Union Congress, 1888; cf. Carroll D. Wright, *Report on Industrial Depressions*, Washington, 1886, pp. 80-90.

directly engaged in these industries than before; in other cases this is not the case.

The following quotation from a speech made at the Industrial Remuneration Conference in 1885 will present the most effective criticism upon Professor Leone Levi's position :

"In carpet weaving fifty years ago the workman drove the shuttle with the hand, and produced from forty-five to fifty yards per week, for which he was paid from 9d. to 1s. per yard, while at the present day a girl attending a steam loom can produce sixty yards a day, and does not cost her employer 1½d. per yard for her labour. That girl with her loom is now doing the work of eight men. The question is, How are these men employed now? In a clothier's establishment, seeing a girl at work at a sewing machine, he asked the employer how many men's labour that machine saved him. He said it saved him twelve men's labour. Then he asked, 'What would those twelve men be doing now?' 'Oh,' he said, 'they will be much better employed than if they had been with me, perhaps at some new industry.' He asked, 'What new industry?' But the employer could not point out any except photography; at last he said they would probably have found employment in making sewing machines. Shortly afterwards he was asked to visit the American Singer Sewing Machine Factory, near Glasgow. He got this clothier to accompany him, and when going over the works they came upon the very same kind of machines as the clothier had in his establishment. Then he put the question to the manager, 'How long would it take a man to make one of these machines?' He said he could not tell, as no man made a machine; they had a more expeditious way of doing it than that—there would be upwards of thirty men employed in the making of one machine; but he said 'if they were to make this particular kind of machine, they would turn out one for every four and a half days' work of each man in their employment.' Now, there was a machine that with a girl had done the work of twelve men for nearly ten years, and the owner of that machine was under the impression that these twelve men would be employed in making another machine, while four and a half days of each of these men was sufficient to make another machine that was capable of displacing other twelve men."

In cases like the above we must, of course, bear in mind that a diminution of employment in the several manufacturing processes directly and indirectly engaged in forwarding an industry, is not of itself conclusive evidence that the machinery has brought about a net displacement of labour. If the output is increased the employment in the extractive, the transport, and the various distributing processes may compensate the reduction in making goods and machinery.

§ 2. The industrial history of a country like England can furnish no sufficient data for a conclusive general judgment of the case. The enormous expansion of production induced by the application of machinery in certain branches of textile industry during the first half of this century indisputably led to an increased demand for English labour in trades directly or indirectly connected with textile production. But, in the first place, this cannot be regarded as a normal result of a fall of prices due to textile machinery, but is largely attributable to an expansion in the area of consumption—the acquisition of vast new markets—in which greater efficiency and cheapness of transport played the most considerable part. Secondly, assuming that the more pressing needs of the vast body of consumers are already satisfied by machine-made textile goods, we are not at liberty to conjecture that any further cheapening of goods, owing to improved machinery, will have a correspondent effect on consumption and the demand for labour. If England had been a self-contained country, manufacturing only for her own market, the result of machinery applied to textile industries would without doubt have been a considerable net displacement of textile labour, making every allowance for growth of population and increased home consumption. The expansion of English production under the rapid development of machinery in the nineteenth century cannot therefore be taken as a right measure of the normal effects of the application of machinery.

Neither in economic theory nor in industrial practice is there any justification for the belief that the net result of improved machinery is a maintenance or an increase of employment within the particular trade, or even within the group of the interdependent trades engaged in producing or supplying a class of commodities. Still less support is there

for this belief as applied to the trade of a particular locality
or national area. While the introduction of new labour-
saving machinery in type-setting and printing has been
followed by so large an expansion of business as to employ
increased numbers of workers, recent improvements in most
British textile mills, cotton, woollen, hemp, etc., have been
followed by an absolute reduction of employment.

The following figures[1] exhibiting the relative growth in
the consumption of raw cotton in Great Britain and the
number of persons employed in cotton manufacture from
1854 to 1891 affords a general indication of the influence
of improved machinery and methods of production upon
quantity of employment:—

				Consumption of Raw Cotton. Million Cwts.			Persons employed in Cotton and Lace Trades (including Dealers).
1854	...	...	...	6.9	...	...	627,819
1861	...	...	...	9.0	...	...	660,231
1871	...	...	...	10.8	...	...	647,633
1881	...	...	...	12.9	...	...	664,279
1891	...	...	...	14.9	...	...	682,075

The same economy of labour, though less marked, is
evidenced in the statistics of the relative growth of the consumption of iron in the United Kingdom and the number
of persons employed in iron and steel trades.

			Estimated Consumption of Pig Iron. Million Tons.			Persons employed in Iron and Steel Trades.
1854	...	...	2.8	...	...	110,408 (Census 1850)
1861	...	...	3.3	...	...	149,366
1871	...	...	5.6	...	...	223,448
1881	...	...	6.7	...	...	241,346
1891	...	...	6.6	...	...	245,847

Even if we take account of the industries subsidiary to
such particular manufactures and the transport and distributive employment of handling the larger quantities of
cheapened goods, we cannot conclude that the net effect of
certain improved machinery will not be a reduction in the
quantity of employment.

The statistics of employment given in Chapter XVI. point
to the conclusion that the further a nation advances in the

[1] Cd. 1761, p. 367.

application of labour-saving machinery to the production of those goods which satisfy the primary needs of the population, the smaller the proportion of the total employed class engaged in these productive processes. The best available statistics in various countries indicate that the proportion of employment afforded by the staple manufactures as a whole diminishes after modern machine methods are well established, and that the tendency is strongest in those manufactures engaged in supplying ordinary classes of textile, metal, and other goods in the home markets.

§ 3. In order to judge the net effect of labour-saving machinery upon the volume of employment a wider view is necessary. If the first effect is to cheapen goods, we need not look to the expansion of demand for this class of goods to absorb the labour which it is the object of the introduction of the machine to displace. We must look to the expansion of demand for other sorts of goods due to the application of the elements of income saved by the fall of prices in this first class of goods. If cotton goods are cheaper owing to improved methods of production, the chief result may be the increased demand for foods, other clothing, furniture, etc., due to the expenditure of a smaller proportion of the general income upon cotton goods.

A clear grasp of the interdependency of markets, through the law by which incomes are spent in securing the greatest aggregate utility of consumption-goods, exposes the fallaciousness of seeking to test the general effects of machinery upon employment by the separatist method.

This wider outlook enables us to conclude that though the effect of machinery may sometimes be a reduction of employment in a special trade or group of trades, the general result must be to maintain the same aggregate volume of employment as before, provided that the income liberated from a particular demand is applied to other demands for commodities. If a class of British consumers has been spending 10 per cent. of its income upon articles of food, or of clothing, and improved methods of production or of transport reduces the price of these goods by half, the saved 5 per cent. of this class income, expended upon other sorts of commodities, will afford as much employment for labour as has been saved in the food or clothing trades.

If, as may be objected, there is a simultaneous tendency to reduce the prices of most articles of ordinary consumption by applying machine methods of production and transport, the normal result would be to stimulate new wants, and so to create new channels of production yielding employment to displaced labour. That this is in fact the normal operation of economic forces in the world of industry, where this normal operation is not impeded by over-saving, no one can seriously doubt.

If the improvements of machine-methods were regular, gradual, and continuous in the several industries, no considerable effect in reducing the volume of employment would occur: the young labour ripening for the labour market would flow into the industries which were increasing their employment, and the decline of employment in other industries would be met by the normal mortality of the workers engaged in them, or by the slow transfer to other related trades.

But where industrial improvements are sudden, irregular, and incalculable, this natural adjustment is not possible. It is this irregular action of machine-development which has proved so injurious to large bodies of labourers whose employment is subjected to a sudden and large shrinkage. From time to time great numbers of skilled workers find the value of their personal skill cancelled, and are driven either to acquire a new skill or to compete in the unskilled labour market for a lower livelihood.

Where by a rigorous system of protection a trade is virtually restricted to the home market, these dislocations are larger, more frequent, and more injurious than where freedom of commerce affords more elasticity of foreign trade. This is a chief reason why, during recent waves of general industrial depression moving over the industrial world, the amount of unemployment has been greater in high-tariff nations, such as France, Germany, and the United States, than in Great Britain.[1]

This irregularity in machine-development, involving large temporary displacements of labour at certain times, is of course no inconsiderable factor in the problem of un-

---

[1] Cf. Memorandum on British and Foreign Trade, Cd. 2337 (Second Series, Board of Trade).

employment, though subsidiary to the main cause as defined in Chapter XI.

In an industrial society where the state of distribution of income was such that every saving in the general expenditure upon a particular commodity, due to improved machinery or other economy, automatically stimulated an increased expenditure upon other commodities, the brisk condition of general trade thus generated would quickly and easily absorb the labour displaced in the individual trade in question. If British trade remained normally in the condition of the year 1900 (as it might if the artificial stimulus then temporarily operative were replaced by a normal natural stimulus) no complaint of the influence of machinery in diminishing employment would be heard.

§ 4. Under actual conditions of industry, however, the disturbing influence of machine-economy upon regularity, as distinct from volume, of employment is very considerable. We have so little means of measuring the irregularity of employment before the industrial revolution that it is not possible to judge whether former leakages were as large as those in recent times: the waste due to sudden new methods of production was certainly less, but the limitations of and interferences with markets may have caused a net amount of waste quite as injurious to trade.

When agriculture was relatively so much more important a branch of industry than now, and manufactures were more dependent upon local supplies of raw materials, climatic and other natural disturbances must have occasioned great irregularity of employment.

Two points, however, are raised by Professor Nicholson which deserve consideration. He finds two laws or tendencies which operate to reduce the disturbing influence of machinery. He holds (1) that a radical change made in the methods of production will be gradually and continuously adopted; (2) that these radical changes—these discontinuous leaps—tend to give place to advances by small increments of invention.[1]

History certainly shows that the fuller application of great inventions has been slow, though Professor Nicholson

---

[1] J. S. Nicholson, *Effects of Machinery on Wages*, p. 33.

somewhat over-estimates the mobility of labour and its ability to provide against impending changes. The story of the introduction of the power-loom discloses terrible sufferings among the hand-weavers of certain districts, in spite of the gradual manner in which the change was effected. The fact that along with the growth of the power-loom the number of hand-looms was long maintained, is evidence of the immobility of the hand-weavers, who kept up an irregular and ill-paid work through ignorance and incapacity to adapt themselves to changed circumstances.[1] In most of the cases where great distress has been caused, the directly operative influence has not been introduction of machinery, but sudden change of fashion. This was the case with the crinoline-hoop makers of Yorkshire, the straw-plaiters of Bedfordshire, Bucks, Herts, and Essex.[2] The suddenly-executed freaks of protective tariffs seem likely to be a fruitful source of disturbance. So far as the displacement has been due to new applications of machinery, it is no doubt generally correct to say that sufficient warning is given to enable workers to check the further flow of labour into such industries, and to divert it into other industries which are growing in accordance with the new methods of production, though much suffering is inflicted upon the labour which is already specialised in the older method of industry.

Moreover, the changes which are taking place in certain machine industries favour the increasing adaptability of labour. Many machine processes are either common to many industries, or are so narrowly distinguished that a fairly intelligent workman accustomed to one can soon learn another. If it is true that "the general ability, which is easily transferable from one trade to another, is every year rising in importance relatively to that manual skill and technical knowledge which are specialised in one branch of industry,"[3] we have a progressive force which tends to minimise the amount of unemployment due to new applications of specific machinery.

Professor Nicholson's second law is, however, more specu-

[1] Babbage, *Economy of Manufactures*, p. 230.
[2] Cf. Thorold Rogers, *Political Economy* (1869), pp. 78, 79.
[3] Marshall, *Principles of Economics*, p. 607; cf. Cunningham, *Uses and Abuses of Money*, p. 59. See, however, *infra* Chap. ix.

lative and less reliable in its action. It seems to imply some absolute limit to the number of great inventions. Radical changes are no doubt generally followed by smaller increments of invention; but we can have no guarantee that new radical changes quite as important as the earlier ones may not occur in the future. There are no assignable limits to the progress of mechanical invention, or to the rate at which that progress may be effected. If certain preliminary difficulties in the general application of electricity as a motor can be overcome, there is every reason to believe that, with the improved means of rapidly communicating knowledge we possess, our factory system may be reorganised and labour displaced far more rapidly than in the case of steam, and at a rate which might greatly exceed the capacity of labour to adjust itself to the new industrial conditions. At any rate we are not at liberty to take for granted that the mobility of labour must always keep pace with the application of new and labour-disturbing inventions. Since we are not able to assume that the market will be extended *pari passu* with the betterment in methods of production, it is evident that improvements in machinery must be reckoned as a normal cause of insecurity of employment. The loss of employment may be only "temporary," but as the life of a working man is also temporary, such loss may as a disturbing factor in the working life have a considerable importance.

§ 5. (*b*) Whether machinery, apart from the changes due to its introduction, favours regularity or irregularity of employment, is a question to which a tolerably definite answer can be given. The structure of the individual factory, with its ever-growing quantity of expensive machinery, would seem at first sight to furnish a direct guarantee of regular employment, based upon the self-interest of the capitalist. Some of the "sweating" trades of London are said to be maintained by the economy which can be effected by employers who use no expensive plant or machinery, and who are able readily to increase or diminish the number of their employees so as to keep pace with the demands of some "season" trade, such as fur-pulling or artificial flowers. When the employer has charge of enormous quantities of fixed capital, his individual interest is strongly in favour of full and regular employment of labour. On this account, then, machinery would seem to favour regularity of employ-

ment. On the other hand, Professor Nicholson has ample
evidence in support of his statement that "great fluctuations in price occur in those commodities which require for
their production a large proportion of fixed capital. These
fluctuations in prices are accompanied by corresponding
fluctuations in wages and irregularity of employment."[1] In
a word, while it is the interest of each producer of
machine-made goods to give regular employment, some
wider industrial force compels him to irregularity. What
is this force? It is uncontrolled machinery. In the
several units of machine-production, the individual factories or mills, we have admirable order and accurate
adjustment of parts; in the aggregate of machine-production
we have no organisation, but a chaos of haphazard speculation. "Industry has not yet adapted itself to the changes
in the environment produced by machinery." That is all.

Under a monetary system of commerce, though commodities still exchange for commodities, it is an essential condition of that exchange that those who possess purchasing
power shall be willing to use a sufficient proportion of it to
demand consumptive goods. Otherwise the production of
productive goods is stimulated unduly while the demand
for consumptive goods is checked,—the condition which
the business man rightly regards as over-supply of the
material forms of capital. When production was slower,
markets[2] narrower, credit less developed, there was less
danger of this big miscalculation, and the corrective forces
of industry were more speedily effective. But modern
machinery has enormously expanded the size of markets,
the scale of competition, the complexity of demand, and
production is no longer for a small, local, present demand,
but for a large, world, future demand. Hence machinery is
the direct material cause of these great fluctuations which
bring, as their most evil consequence, irregularity of wages
and employment.

[1] *Effects of Machinery on Wages*, p. 66.
[2] An increase in the space-area of a market may, however, in some
cases make a trade more steady, especially in the case of an article
of luxury subject to local fluctuations of fashion, etc. A narrow silk
market for England meant fluctuating employment and low skill. An
open market gave improved skill and stability, for though silk is still
the most unsteady of the textile industries, it is far less fluctuating than
was the case in the eighteenth century. (Cf. Porter, p. 225.)

How far does this tend to right itself? Professor Nicholson believes that time will compel a better adjustment between machinery and its environment.

"The enormous development of steam communication and the spread of the telegraph over the whole globe have caused modern industry to develop from a gigantic star-fish, any of whose members might be destroyed without affecting the rest, into a μέγα ζῶον which is convulsed in agony by a slight injury in one part. A depression of trade is now felt as keenly in America and even in our colonies as it is here. Still, in the process of time, with the increase of organisation and decrease of unsound speculation, this extension of the market must lead to greater stability of prices; but at present the disturbing forces often outweigh altogether the supposed principal elements."[1]

The organisation of capital under the pressure of these forces is doubtless proceeding, and such organisation, when it has proceeded far enough, will indisputably lead to a decrease of unsound speculation. But these steps in organisation have been taken precisely in those industries which employ large quantities of fixed capital, and the admitted fact that severe fluctuations still take place in these industries is proof that the steadying influences of such organisation have not yet had time to assert themselves to much purpose. The competition of larger and larger masses of organised capital seems to induce heavier speculation and larger fluctuations. Not until a whole species of capital is organised into some form or degree of "combination" is the steadying influence of organisation able to predominate.

§ 6. But there is also another force which, in England at any rate, under the increased application of machinery, makes for an increase rather than a diminution of speculative production. It has been seen that the proportion of workers engaged in producing comforts and luxuries is growing, while the proportion of those producing the prime necessaries of life is declining. How far the operation of the law of diminishing returns will allow this tendency to proceed we cannot here discuss. But statistics show that this is the present tendency both in England and in the United States. Now the demand for comforts and luxuries

[1] *Op. cit.*, p. 117.

is essentially more irregular and less amenable to commercial calculation than the demand for necessaries. The greatest economies of machine-production are found in industries where the demand is largest, steadiest, and most calculable. Hence the effect of machinery is to drive ever and ever larger numbers of workers from the less to the more unsteady employments. Moreover, there is a marked tendency for the demand for luxuries to become more irregular and less amenable to calculation, and a corresponding irregularity is imposed upon the trades engaged in producing them. Twenty years ago it was possible for Coventry ribbon-weavers to "make to stock" during the winter months, for though silk ribbons may always be classed as a luxury, certain patterns commanded a tolerably steady sale year after year. Now the fluctuations of fashion are much sharper and more frequent, and a far larger proportion of the consumers of ribbons are affected by fashion-changes. Hence it has become more and more difficult to forecast the market, less and less is made to stock, more and more to order, and orders are given at shorter and shorter notice. So looms and weavers kept idle during a large part of the year are driven into fevered activity of manufacture for short irregular periods. The same applies to many other season and fashion trades. The irregularity of demand prevents these trades from reaping the full advantages of the economies of machinery, though the partial application of machinery and power facilitates the execution of orders at short notice. Hence the increased proportion of the community's income spent on luxuries requires an increased proportion of the labour of the community to be expended in their production. This signifies a drifting of labour from the more steady forms of employment to those which are less steady and whose unsteadiness is constantly increasing. A larger proportion of town workers is constantly passing into trades connected with preparing and preserving animal and vegetable substances, to such industries as the hat and bonnet, confectionery, bookbinding, trades affected by weather, holiday and season trades, or those in which changes in taste and fashion are largely operative.

Thus it appears there are three modes in which modern capitalist methods of production cause temporary unemployment. (1) Continual increments of labour-saving machinery displace a number of workers, compelling them to remain wholly or partially unemployed, until they have "adjusted" themselves to the new economic conditions. (2) Miscalculation and temporary over-production, to which machine industries with a wide unstable market are particularly prone, bring about periodic deep depressions of "trade," temporarily throwing out of work large bodies of skilled and unskilled labour. (3) Economies of machine-production in the staple industries drive an increasing proportion of labour with trades which are engaged in supplying commodities, the demand for which is more irregular, and in which therefore the fluctuations in demand for labour must be greater.

Most economists, still deeply imbued with a belief in the admirable order and economy of "the play of economic forces," appear to regard all unemployment not assignable to individual vice or incapacity as the natural and necessary effect of the process of adjustment by which industrial progress is achieved, ignoring altogether the two latter classes of consideration. There is, however, reason to believe that in an average year a far larger number of the "unemployed" at any given time owe their unemployment to a temporary depression of the trade in which they are engaged, than to the fluctuations brought about by organic changes in the economic structure of the trade.

The size and importance of the "unemployment" due primarily to trade depressions is very imperfectly appreciated. The following statistics[1] set forth the fluctuations of the last twenty years: a. in the general body of skilled trades; b. in a relatively unstable group of trades:—

Year.	Percentage for all Trade Unions.	Percentage for Engineering, Ship-building, & Metals.	Year.	Percentage for all Trade Unions.	Percentage for Engineering, Ship-building, & Metals.
1884	7.15	10.8	1894	7.70	11.2
1885	8.55	12.9	1895	6.05	8.2
1886	9.55	13.5	1896	3.50	4.2
1887	7.15	10.4	1897	3.65	4.8
1888	4.15	6.0	1898	3.15	4.0
1889	2.05	2.3	1899	2.40	2.4
1890	2.10	2.2	1900	2.85	2.6
1891	3.40	4.1	1901	3.80	3.8
1892	6.20	7.7	1902	4.60	5.5
1893	7.70	11.4	1903	5.30	6.6

[1] Statistical Tables, Cd. 2,337 (1904).

When it is remembered that these figures apply only to the well-organised trades unions, which, as a rule, comprise the best and most highly-skilled workers in the several trades, who are less likely than others to be thrown out in a "slack time," that the building and season trades are not included in the estimate, and that women's industries, notoriously more irregular than men's, are altogether ignored, it will be evident that these statistics very inadequately represent the proportion of unemployment for the aggregate of the working classes at the several periods. The *Report on Principal and Minor Textile Trades* deducts 10 per cent. from the normal wages to represent unemployment, though the year 1885, to which the figures refer, is spoken of as " fairly representative of a normal year."[1]

The injury inflicted upon the wages, working efficiency, and character of the working classes by irregular employment is, however, very inadequately represented by figures indicating the average of "unemployment" during a long period. In the first place, in such an estimate no allowance is made for the "short time," often worked for months together by large bodies of operatives. Secondly, in measuring the evil of "unemployment," we must look rather to the maximum than to the mean condition. If a man is liable to have his food supply cut off for a month at a time, no estimate showing that on the average he has more than enough to eat and drink will fairly represent the danger to which he is exposed. If once in every ten years we find that some 10 per cent. of the skilled workers, and a far larger percentage of unskilled workers, are out of employment for months together, these figures measure the economic malady of "unemployment," which is in no sense compensated by the full or excessive labour of periods of better trade.

§ 7. Our reasoning from the ascertained tendencies of machine-production points to the conclusion that, having regard to the two prime constituents in demand for labour, the number of those employed, and the regularity of employment, machinery does not, under present conditions, generally favour an increased steady demand for labour. It tends to drive an increased proportion of labour in three directions.

(1) To the invention, construction, and maintenance of

[1] Page xii.

machinery to make machines, the labour of machine-making being continually displaced by machines, and being thus driven to the production of machines more remote from the machines directly engaged in producing consumptive goods. The labour thus engaged must be in an ever-diminishing proportion to a given quantity of consumption. Nothing but a great increase in the quantity of consumption, or the opening of new varieties of consumption, can maintain or increase the demand for labour in these machine-making industries.

(2) To continual specialisation, subdivision, and refinement in the arts of distribution. The multiplication of merchants, agents, retailers, which, in spite of forces making for centralisation in distributive work, is so marked a feature in the English industry of the last forty years, is a natural result of the influence of machinery, in setting free from "making" processes an increased proportion of labour.

(3) To the supply of new forms of wealth, which are either (a) wholly non-material—i.e., intellectual, artistic, or other personal services; (b) partly non-material—e.g., works of art or skill, whose value consists chiefly in the embodiment of individual taste or spontaneous energy, or (c) too irregular or not sufficiently extended in demand to admit the application of machinery. The learned professions, art, science, and literature, and those branches of labour engaged in producing luxuries and luxurious services furnish a constantly increasing employment, though the supply of labour is so notoriously in excess of the demand in all such employments that a large percentage of unemployment is chronic.

So long then as a community grows in numbers, so long as individuals desire to satisfy more fully their present wants and continue to develop new wants, forming a higher or more intricate standard of consumption, there is no evidence to justify the conclusion that machinery has the effect of causing a net diminution in demand for labour, though it tends to diminish the proportion of employment in the "manufacturing" industries; but there is strong reason to believe that it tends to make employment more unstable, more precarious of tenure, and more fluctuating in market value.

CHAPTER XIII.

MACHINERY AND THE QUALITY OF LABOUR.

§ 1. *Kinds of Labour which Machinery supersedes.*
§ 2. *Influence of Machine-evolution upon intensity of physical work.*
§ 3. *Machinery and the length of the working day.*
§ 4. *The Education of Working with Machinery.*
§ 5. *The levelling tendency of Machinery—The subordination of individual capacity in work.*

§ 1. In considering the influence of Machinery upon the quality of labour—*i.e.*, skill, duration, intensity, intellectuality, etc., we have first to face two questions—What are the qualities in which machinery surpasses human labour? What are the kinds of work in which machinery displaces man? Now, since the whole of industrial work consists in moving matter, the advantage of machinery must consist in the production and disposition of motive power. The general economies of machinery were found to be two[1]—(1) The increased quantity of motive force it can apply to industry; (2) greater exactitude in the regular application of motive force (*a*) in time—the exact repetition of the same acts at regulated intervals, or greater evenness in continuity, (*b*) in place—exact repetition of the same movements in space.[2] All the advantages

[1] Cf. *supra*, chap. iii. § 2.
[2] Karl Marx ranks the chief economies of machinery under two heads—(1) Machinery supersedes the skill of men working with tools. "The machine, which is the starting-point of the industrial revolution, supersedes the workman, who handles a single tool, by a mechanism operating with a number of similar tools, and set in motion by a single motive power, whatever the form of that power may be." (2)

imputed to machinery in the economy of human time, the utilisation of waste material, the display of concentrated force or the delicacy of manipulation, are derivable from these two general economies. Hence it follows that wherever the efficiency of labour power depends chiefly upon the output of muscular force in motive power, or precision in the regulation of muscular force, machinery will tend to displace human labour. Assuming, therefore, that displaced labour finds other employment, it will be transferred to work where machinery has not the same advantage over human labour—that is to say, to work where the muscular strain or the need for regularity of movement is less. At first sight it will thus seem to follow that every displacement of labour by machinery will bring an elevation in the quality of labour, that is, will increase the proportion of labour in employments which tax the muscles less and are less monotonous. This is in the main the conclusion towards which Professor Marshall inclines.[1]

So far as each several industry is concerned, it has been shown that the introduction of machinery signifies a net reduction of employment, unless the development of trade is largely extended by the fall of price due to the diminution in expenses of production. It cannot be assumed as a matter of course that the labour displaced by the introduction of automatic folders in printing will be employed in less automatic work connected with printing. It may be diverted from muscular monotony in printing to the less muscular monotony of providing some new species of luxury, the demand for which is not yet sufficiently large or regular to justify the application of labour-saving machinery. But even assuming that the whole or a large part of the displaced labour is engaged in work which is proved to have been less muscular or less automatic by the fact that it is not yet undertaken by machinery, it does not necessarily follow that there is a diminution in the aggregate of physical energy given out, or in the total "monotony" of labour.

Machinery supersedes the strength of man. "Increase in the size of a machine, and in the number of its working tools, calls for a more massive mechanism to drive it; and this mechanism requires, in order to overcome its resistance, a mightier moving power than that of man." (*Capital*, vol. ii. pp. 370, 371.)

[1] *Principles of Economics*, 2nd edit., pp. 314, 322.

One direct result of the application of an increased proportion of labour power to the kinds of work which are less "muscular" and less "automatic" in character will be a tendency towards greater division of labour and more specialisation in these employments. Now the economic advantages of increased specialisation can only be obtained by increased automatic action. Thus the routine or automatic character, which constituted the monotony of the work in which machinery displaced these workers, will now be imparted to the higher grades of labour in which they are employed, and these in their turn will be advanced towards a condition which will render them open to a new invasion of machinery.

Since the number of productive processes falling under machinery is thus continually increased, it will be seen that we are not entitled to assume that every displacement of labour by machinery will increase the proportion of labour engaged in lighter and more interesting forms of non-mechanical labour.

§ 2. Nor is it shown that the growth of machine-production tends to diminish the total physical strain upon the worker, though it greatly lessens the output of purely muscular activity. As regards those workers who pass from ordinary manual work to the tending of machinery, there is a good deal of evidence to show that, in the typical machine industries, their new work taxes their physical vigour quite as severely as the old work. Professor Shield Nicholson quotes the following striking statement from the *Cotton Factory Times*:—" It is quite a common occurrence to hear young men who are on the best side of thirty years of age declare they are so worked up with the long mules, coarse counts, quick speeds, and inferior material, that they are fit for nothing at night, only going to bed and taking as much rest as circumstances will allow. There are few people who will credit such statements; nevertheless they are true, and can be verified any day in the great majority of the mills in the spinning districts."

Schulze-Gaevernitz shows that the tendency in modern cotton-spinning and weaving, especially in England, has been both to increase the number of spindles and looms which an operative is called upon to tend, and to increase the speed of spinning. "A worker tends to-day more than twice or nearly three times as much machinery as his father did; the number of machines in use has increased more than five-fold since that time, while the workers have not quite doubled their numbers."[1] With regard to speed, "since the beginning of the seventies the speed of the spinning machines alone has increased about 15 per cent."[2]

We are not, however, at liberty to infer from Schulze-Gaevernitz's statement regarding the increased number of spindles and looms an operative tends, that an intensification of labour correspondent with this increase of machinery has taken place, nor can the increased output per operative be imputed chiefly to improved skill or energy of the operative. Much of the labour-saving character of recent improvements, especially in the carding, spinning, and intermediate processes, has reduced to an automatic state work which formerly taxed the energy of the operative, who has thereby been enabled to tend more machinery and to quicken the speed without a net increase of working energy.

In the carding, slubbing, intermediate, roving, and spinning machinery there is in every case an increase in the amount of machinery tended. But carding machinery has been revolutionised within the last few years; the drawing frame has been made to stop automatically when there is a fault, thus relieving the tender of a certain amount of supervision; in the slubbing, intermediate, and roving frames certain detailed improvements have been effected, as is also the case in the spinning mules and sizing machines.

To some extent the increased quantity of spindles, etc., and increased speed may be regarded as set off by relief due to these improvements. Moreover, though there has no doubt been some general speeding up, any exact measurement is hardly possible, for the speed of machinery is very often regulated by the amount of work each process is made to do; for example, if a roving frame makes a coarse hank, the speed of the spindles does not require to be so great as when the hank is finer; in that case the mule draws out the sliver to a greater extent than when the roving is finer, or, in other words, the mule in one case does the work of the roving frame to a certain extent.

The general opinion seems to be that in the spinning

---

[1] *Der Grossbetrieb*, p. 120.   [2] *Ibid.*, p. 117.

mills, roughly speaking, 75 per cent. of the increased out-put per operative may be imputed to improved machinery, 25 per cent. to increased intensity of labour in regard to quantity of spindles or "speeding up."

In the weaving processes more specific measurement is possible, though even there much depends upon the quality of yarn that is used. Here a reduction in the working day is followed by an increase in speed without any labour-saving improvements. Previous to the Factory legislation of 1878, the speed of looms was generally from 170 to 190 picks per minute during the ten hours' day. In the course of about two years after the reduction of hours (6 per cent.) the general speed had become 190 to 200 picks, without change in machinery or raw material, a growth which must have proportionately increased the intensity of the work of weaving. A deterioration in the quality of the raw material used for producing cotton cloth is also commonly assigned as a fact involving more care on the part of the weaver, and increased danger and disagreeability of work owing to the heavy sizing and steaming it has brought into vogue. It is not easy to argue much respecting increased intensity of labour from the increased average of looms attended, for, as was recently admitted in evidence before the Labour Commission, everything depends upon the class of looms and of goods they are manufacturing. "It is quite as easy to drive five looms of some classes as two of others."[1] But the prevalence of the "driving" system, by which the overlookers are paid a bonus on the product of the looms under their charge, has admittedly induced, as it was obviously designed to do, an increased intensity of labour.

Summing up the evidence, we are able to conclude that the shortening of working hours and the improvements in machinery has been attended by an increased effort per unit of labour time. In the words of an expert, "the change to those actually engaged in practical work is to lessen the amount of hard manual work of one class, but to increase their responsibility, owing to being placed in charge of more machinery, and that of a more expensive kind; while the work of the more lowly skilled will be intensified, owing to increased production, and that from

[1] Evidence given by Mr. T. Birtwistle.

an inferior raw material. I mean that to the operative the improvements in machinery have been neutralised by the inferior quality of raw material used, and I think it is fair to assume that their work has been intensified at least in proportion to the increase of spindles, etc."

The direct evidence drawn from this most highly-evolved machine industry seems to justify the general opinion expressed by Professor Nicholson, " It is clear that the use of machines, though apparently labour-saving, often leads to an increase in the *quantity of labour*, negatively, by not developing the mind, positively by doing harm to the body."[1]

§ 3. When any muscular or other physical effort is required it is pretty evident that an increased duration or a greater continuity in the slighter effort may tax the body quite as severely as the less frequent or constant application of a much greater bodily force. There can be no question but that in a competitive industrial society there exists a tendency to compensate for any saving of hard muscular, or other physical effort afforded by the intervention of machinery in two ways : first, by " forcing the pace "— *i.e.*, compelling the worker to attend more machines or to work more rapidly, thus increasing the strain, if not upon the muscles, then upon the nerves ; secondly, by extending the hours of labour. A lighter form of labour spread over an increased period of time, or an increased number of minor muscular exertions substituted for a smaller number of heavier exertions within the same period of time, may of course amount to an increased tax upon the vital energy. It is not disputed that a general result of the factory system has been to increase the average length of the working day, if we take under our survey the whole area of machine-production in modern industrial communities. This is only in part attributable to the fact that workers can be induced to sell the same daily output of physical energy as before, while in many cases a longer time is required for its expenditure.

---

[1] *Op. cit.*, p. 82. Babbage, in laying stress on one of the "advantages" of machinery, makes an ingenuous admission of this " forcing " power. " One of the most singular advantages we derive from machinery is the check it affords against the inattention, the idleness, or the knavery of human agents." (*Economy of Machinery*, p. 39; cf. also Ure, *Philosophy of Manufacture*, p. 30.)

Another influence of equal potency is the economy of machinery effected by working longer hours. It is the combined operation of these two forces that has lengthened the average working day. Certain subsidiary influences, however, also deserve notice, especially the introduction of cheap illuminants. Before the cheap provision of gas, the working time was generally limited by daylight. Not until the first decade of this century was gas introduced into cotton-mills, and another generation elapsed before it passed in general use in manufactories and retail shops.[1] Now a portion of nature's rest has been annexed to the working day. There are, of course, powerful social forces making for a curtailment of the working day, and these forces are in many industries powerfully though indirectly aided by machinery. Perhaps it would be right to say that machinery develops two antagonistic tendencies as regards the length of the working day. Its most direct economic influence favours an extension of the working hours, for machinery untired, wasting power by idleness, favours continuous work. But when the growing pace and complexity of highly-organised machinery taxes human energy with increasing severity, and compresses an increased human effort within a given time, a certain net advantage in limiting the working day for an individual begins to emerge, and it becomes increasingly advantageous to work the machinery for shorter hours, or, where possible, to apply " shifts " of workers.[2]

But in the present stage of machine-development the economy of the shorter working day is only obtainable in a few trades and in a few countries; the general tendency is still in the direction of an extended working day.[3] The full significance of this is not confined to the fact that a larger proportion of the worker's time is consumed in the growing monotony of production. The curtailment of his time for consumption, and a consequent lessening of the subjective value of his consumables, must be set off against such increase in real wages or purchasing power as may have come to him from the increased productive power of machinery. The value of a shorter working day

[1] Porter, *Progress of the Nation,* p. 590.
[2] Cf. Schulze-Gaevernitz, p. 115.
[3] For a fuller treatment of this subject, see the next chapter.

consists not merely in the diminution of the burden of toil
it brings, but also in the fact that increased consumption
time enables the worker to get a fuller use of his purchased
consumables, and to enjoy various kinds of "free wealth"
from which he was precluded under a longer working day.[1]
So far as machinery has converted handicraftsmen in the
manufacturing arts into machine-tenders, it is extremely
doubtful whether it has lessened the strain upon their
energies, though we should hesitate to give an explicit en-
dorsement to Mill's somewhat rhetorical verdict. "It is
questionable if all the mechanical inventions yet made have
lessened the day's toil of any human being." But when
rude forms of unskilled or low skilled muscular labour are
taken over by machinery the benefit to labourers is indis-
putable. Steam-diggers, coal-cutting machines, grain and
coal elevators, and the use of most agricultural machines
assuredly "lighten the day's toil." "As to the influence of
machinery on farm labour," writes an American expert,[2]
"all intelligent expert observation declares it beneficial.
It has relieved the labourer of much drudgery; made his
work easier and his hours of service shorter; stimulated his
mental faculties; and made the labourer a more efficient
worker, a broader man, and a better citizen."

But while this holds true where machinery is made a
servant of labour, this condition is not yet applicable to
most factory trades. At any rate we have as yet no security
that machinery, owned by individuals who do not themselves tend it, shall not be used in such a way as to increase
the physical strain of those who do tend it. "There is a
temptation," as Mr. Cunningham says, "to treat the machine
as the main element in production, and to make it the
measure of what a man ought to do, instead of regarding
the man as the first consideration, and the machine as the
instrument which helps him; the machine may be made
the primary consideration, and the man may be treated as a
mere slave who tends it."[3]

§ 4. Now to come to the question of "monotony." Is the
net tendency of machinery to make labour more monotonous or less, to educate the worker or to brutalise him?

---

[1] Cf. Patten, *The Theory of Dynamic Economics*, chap. xi.
[2] J. R. Dodge, "American Farm Labour," in *Rept. of Ind. Com.*
(1901), vol. x. 7, p. 111 (quoted Quintance, p. 74).
[3] *Use and Abuse of Money*, p. 111.

Does labour become more intellectual under the machine? Professor Marshall, who has thoughtfully discussed this question, inclines in favour of machinery. It takes away manual skill, but it substitutes higher or more intellectual forms of skill.[1] "The more delicate the machine's power the greater is the judgment and carefulness which is called for from those who see after it."[2] Since machinery is daily becoming more and more delicate, it would follow that the tending of machinery would become more and more intellectual. The judgment of Mr. Cooke Taylor, in the conclusion of his admirable work, *The Modern Factory System*, is the same. "If man were merely an intellectual animal, even only a moral and intellectual one, it could scarcely be denied, it seems to us, that the results of the factory system have been thus far elevating."[3] Mr. Taylor indeed admits of the operative population that "they have deteriorated artistically; but art is a matter of faculty, of perception, of aptitude, rather than of intellect." This strange severance of Art from Intellect and Morals, especially when we bear in mind that Life itself is the finest and most valuable of Arts, will scarcely commend itself to deeper students of economic movements. The fuller significance of this admission will appear when the widest aspect of the subject is discussed in our final chapter.

The question of the net intellectual effects of machinery is not one which admits of positive answer. It would be open to one to admit with Mr. Taylor that the operatives were growing more intellectual, and that their contact with machinery exercises certain educative influences, but to deny that the direct results of machinery upon the workers were favourable to a wide cultivation of intellectual powers, as compared with various forms of freer and less specialised manual labour. The intellectualisation of the town operatives (assuming the process to be taking place) may be attributable to the thousand and one other influences of town life rather than to machinery, save indirectly so far as the modern industrial centre is itself the creation of machinery.[4] It is not, I think, possible at present to offer

---

[1] *Principles*, p. 315.   [2] *Ibid.*, p. 316.   [3] Page 435.

[4] A similar difficulty in distinguishing town influences from specific trade influences confronted Dr. Arlidge in his investigation into diseases of employments. "It is a most difficult problem to solve, especially in the case of an industrial town population, how far the diseases met with are town-made and how far trade-made; the former almost always predominates." (*Diseases of Occupation*, p. 33.)

any clear or definite judgment. But the following distinctions seem to have some weight in forming our opinion.

The growth of machinery has acted as an enormous stimulus to the study of natural laws. A larger and larger proportion of human effort is absorbed in processes of invention, in the manipulation of commerce on an increasing scale of magnitude and complexity, and in such management of machinery and men as requires and educates high intellectual faculties of observation, judgment, and speculative imagination. Of that portion of workers who may be said, within limits, to control machinery, there could be no question that the total effect of machinery has been highly educative.

The growing size, power, speed, complexity of machinery, undoubtedly makes the work of this class of workers "more intellectual." Some measure of these educative influences even extends to the "hand" who tends some minute portion of the machinery, so far as the proper performance of his task requires him to understand other processes than those to which his labour is directly and exclusively applied.

So likewise consideration must be taken of the skilled work of making and repairing machinery. The engineers' shop and other workshops are becoming every year a more and more important factor in the equipment of a factory or mill. But though "breakdowns" are essentially erratic and must always afford scope for ingenuity in their repair, even in the engineers' shop there is the same tendency for machinery to undertake all work of repair which can be brought under routine. So the skilled work in making and repairing machinery is continually being reduced to a minimum, and cannot be regarded, as Professor Nicholson is disposed to regard it, as a factor of growing importance in connection with machine-production. The more machinery is used, the more skilled work of making and repairing will be required, it might seem. But the rapidity with which machinery is invading these very functions turns the scale in the opposite direction, at any rate so far as the making of machinery is concerned. Statistics relating to the number of those engaged in making machinery and tools show that the proportion they bear to the whole working population is an increasing one; but the rate of this increase is by no means proportionate to the rate of increase in the use of machinery. Moreover, an increased proportion of machinery production is for export trade, so that a large quantity of the labour employed in those industries is not required to sustain the supply of machinery used in English work. In repairs of machinery, the economy effected by the system of interchangeable parts is one of growing magnitude, and tends likewise to minimise the skilled labour of repair.[1]

Finally, it should be borne in mind that in several large industries where machinery fills a prominent place, the bulk of the labour is not directly governed by the machine. This fact has already received attention in relation to railway workers. The character of the machine certainly impresses itself upon these in different degrees, but in most cases there is a large amount of detailed freedom of action and scope for individual skill and activity.

Though the quality of intelligence and skill applied to the invention, application, and management of machinery is constantly increasing, practical authorities are almost unanimous in admitting that the proportion which this skilled work bears to the aggregate of labour in machine industry is constantly diminishing. Now, setting on one side this small proportion of intelligent labour, what are we to say of the labour of him who, under the minute subdivision enforced by machinery, is obliged to spend his working life in tending some small portion of a single machine, the whole result of which is continually to push some single commodity a single step along the journey from raw material to consumptive goods?

The factory is organised with military precision, the individual's work is definitely fixed for him; he has nothing to say as to the plan of his work or its final completion or its ultimate use. "The constant employment on one sixty-fourth part of a shoe not only offers no encouragement to mental activity, but dulls by its monotony the brains of the employee to such an extent that the power to think and reason is almost lost."[2]

The work of a machine-tender, it is urged, calls for "judgment and carefulness." So did his manual labour before the machine took it over. His "judgment and carefulness" are now confined within narrower limits

---

[1] Cf. Marshall, *Principles of Economics*, vol. i. p. 315.
[2] D. A. Wells, *Contemporary Review*, 1889, p. 392.

than before. The responsibility of the worker is greater, precisely because his work is narrowed down so as to be related to and dependent on a number of other operatives in other parts of the same machine with whom he has no direct personal concern. Such realised responsibility is an element in education, moral and intellectual. But this gain is the direct result of the minute subdivision, and must therefore be regarded as purchased by a narrowing of interest and a growing monotony of work. It is questionable whether the vast majority of machine workers get any considerable education, from the fact that the machine in conjunction with which they work represents a huge embodiment of the delicate skill and invention of many thousands of active minds, though some value may be attached to the contention that "the mere exhibition of the skill displayed and the magnitude of the operations performed in factories can scarcely fail of some educational effect."[1] The absence of any true apprenticeship in modern factories prevents the detailed worker from understanding the method and true bearing even of those processes which are closely linked to that in which he is engaged. The ordinary machine-tender, save in a very few instances, e.g., watchmaking, has no general understanding of the work of a whole department. Present conditions do not enable the "tender" to get out of machinery the educational influence he might get. Professor Nicholson expresses himself dubiously upon the educational value of the machine. "Machinery of itself does not tend to develop the mind as the sea and mountains do, but still it does not necessarily involve deterioration of general mental ability."[2] Dr. Arlidge expresses a more decided opinion. "Generally speaking, it may be asserted of machinery that it calls for little or no brain exertion on the part of those connected with its operations; it arouses no interest, and has nothing in it to quicken or brighten the intelligence, though it may sharpen the sight and stimulate muscular activity in some one limited direction."[3]

The work of machine-tending is never of course abso-

[1] Taylor, *Modern Factory System*, p. 435.
[2] Cf. the comparison of conditions of town and country labour in Adam Smith's *Wealth of Nations*, Bk. I., chap. x., part 2.
[3] *Diseases of Occupations*, pp. 25, 26.

lutely automatic or without spontaneity and skill. To a certain limited extent the "tender" of machinery rules as well as serves the machine; in seeing that his portion of the machine works in accurate adjustment to the rest, the qualities of care, judgment, and responsibility are evolved. For a customary skill of wrist and eye which speedily hardens into an instinct, is often substituted a series of adjustments requiring accurate quantitative measurement and conscious reference to exact standards. In such industries as those of watchmaking the factory worker, though upon the average his work requires less manual dexterity than the handworker in the older method, may get more intellectual exercise in the course of his work. But though economists have paid much attention to this industry, in considering the character of machine-tending it is not an average example for a comparison of machine labour and hand labour; for the extreme delicacy of many of the operations even under machinery, the responsibility attaching to the manipulation of expensive material, and the minute adjustment of the numerous small parts, enable the worker in a watch factory to get more interest and more mental training out of his work than falls to the ordinary worker in a textile or metal factory. Wherever the material is of a very delicate nature and the processes involve some close study of the individual qualities of each piece of material, as is the case with the more valuable metals, with some forms of pottery, with silk or lace, elements of thought and skill survive and may be even fostered under machine industry. A great part of modern inventiveness, however, is engaged in devising automatic checks and indicators for the sake of dispensing with detailed human skill and reducing the spontaneous or thoughtful elements of tending machinery to a minimum. When this minimum is reached the highly-paid skilled workman gives place to the low-skilled woman or child, and eventually the process passes over entirely into the hands of machinery. So long, however, as human labour continues to co-operate with machinery, certain elements of thought and spontaneity adhere to it. These must be taken into account in any estimate of the net educative influence of machinery. But though these mental qualities must not be overlooked, exaggerated importance should not be attached to them. The lay-

man is often apt to esteem too highly the nature of
skilled specialist work.   A locomotive superintendent of
a railway was recently questioned as to the quality of
engine-driving.   "After twenty years' experience he declared
emphatically that the very best engine-drivers were those
who were most mechanical and unintelligent in their work,
who cared least about the internal mechanism of the
engine."[1]   Yet engine-driving is far less mechanical and
monotonous than ordinary tending of machinery.

So far as the man follows the machine and has his work
determined for him by mechanical necessity, the educative
pressure of the latter force must be predominant.   Machinery,
like everything else, can only teach what it practises.   Order,
exactitude, persistence, conformity to unbending law,—these
are the lessons which must emanate from the machine.
They have an important place as elements in the formation
of intellectual and moral character.   But of themselves
they contribute a one-sided and very imperfect education.
Machinery can exactly reproduce; it can, therefore, teach
the lesson of exact reproduction, an education of quantitative measurements.[2]   The defect of machinery, from the
educative point of view, is its absolute conservatism.   The
law of machinery is a law of statical order, that everything
conforms to a pattern, that present actions precisely resemble
past and future actions.   Now the law of human life is
dynamic, requiring order not as valuable in itself, but as the
condition of progress.   The law of human life is that no
experience, no thought or feeling is an exact copy of any
other.   Therefore, if you confine a man to expending his
energy in trying to conform exactly to the movements of a
machine, you teach him to abrogate the very principle of
life.   Variety is of the essence of life, and machinery is the
enemy of variety.   This is no argument against the educative uses of machinery, but only against the exaggeration of
these uses.   If a workman expend a reasonable portion of
his energy in following the movements of a machine, he may
gain a considerable educational value; but he must also
have both time and energy left to cultivate the spontaneous
and progressive arts of life.

§ 5.   It is often urged that the tendency of machinery is not

---

[1] *The Social Horizon*, p. 22.
[2] Cf. Veblen, *The Theory of Business Enterprise*, pp. 308-309.

merely to render monotonous the activity of the individual
worker, but to reduce the individual differences in workers.
This criticism finds expression in the saying : " All men are
equal before the machine." So far as machinery actually
shifts upon natural forces work which otherwise would tax
the muscular energy, it undoubtedly tends to put upon a
level workers of different muscular capacity. Moreover, by
taking over work which requires great precision of movement, there is a sense in which it is true that machinery
tends to reduce the workers to a common level of skill, or
even of un-skill.

" Whenever a process requires peculiar dexterity and
steadiness of hand, it is withdrawn as soon as possible
from the cunning workman, who is prone to irregularities
of many kinds, and it is placed in charge of a peculiar
mechanism, so self-regulating that a child can superin-
tend it."[1]

That this is not true of the most highly-skilled or qualitative work must be conceded, but it applies with great force
to the bulk of lower-skilled labour. By the aid of machinery
—i.e., of the condensed embodiment of the inventor's skill,
the clumsy or weak worker is rendered capable of assisting
the nicest movements on a closer equality with the more
skilled worker. Of course piece-work, as practised in textile
and hardware industries, shows that the most complete
machinery has not nearly abolished the individual differences between one worker and another. But assuming that
the difference in recorded piece wages accurately represents
difference in skill or capacity of work—which is not quite
the case—it seems evident that there is less variation in
capacity among machine-workers than among workers
engaged in employments where the work is more muscular,
or is conducted by human skill with simpler implements.
The difference in productive capacity between an English
and a Hindoo navvy is considerably greater than the difference between a Lancashire mill operative and an operative
in an equally well-equipped and organised Bombay mill.

But this is by no means all that is signified by the
"equality of workers before the machine." It is the
adaptability of the machine to the weaker muscles and

---

[1] Ure, *Philosophy of Manufactures*, chap. i. p. 19.

intelligence of women and children that is perhaps the most important factor. The machine in its development tends to give less and less prominence to muscle and high individual skill in the mass of workers, more and more to certain qualities of body and mind which not only differ less widely in different men, but in which women and children are more nearly on a level with men. It is of course true that considerable differences of individual skill and effort survive in the typical machine industry. " Machine-weaving, for instance, simple as it seems, is divided into higher and lower grades, and most of those who work in the lower grades have not the stuff in them that is required for weaving with several colours."[1] But the general effect of machinery is to lessen rather than to increase individual differences of efficiency. The tendency of machine industry to displace male by female labour is placed beyond all question by the statistics of occupations in England, which show since 1861 a regular and considerable rise in the proportion of women to men workers in most branches of manufacture where machinery is most fully applied.[2] Legal restrictions, and in the more civilised communities, the growth of a healthy public opinion, prevent the economic force from being operative to the same degree so far as children are concerned.

Those very qualities of narrowly restricted care and judgment, detailed attention, regularity and patience, which we see to be characteristic of machine work, are common human qualities in the sense that they are within the capacity of all, and that even in the degree of their development and practice there is less difference between the highly-trained adult mechanic and the raw " half-timer " than in the development and practice of such powers as machinery has superseded. It must be recognised that machinery does exercise a certain equal-ising influence by assigning a larger and larger relative importance to those faculties which are specific as com-pared with those which are individual.[3] " General ability" is coming to play a more important part in industry than specialised ability,[4] and though considerable differences

---

[1] Marshall, *Principles of Economics*, p. 265.
[2] Cf. *General Report of Census for 1901*, p. 86.
[3] Marshall, *Principles of Economics*, chap. x.
[4] Cf. Marshall, p. 265.

may exist in the "general ability" of individuals, the differences will be smaller than in specialised abilities.[1]

The net influence of machinery upon the quality of labour, then, is found to differ widely according to the relation which subsists between the worker and the machine. Its educative influence, intellectual and moral, upon those concerned with the invention, management, and direction of machine industry, and upon all whose work is about machinery, but who are not detailed machine-tenders, is of a distinctly elevating character. Its effect, however, upon machine-tenders in cases where, by the duration of the working day or the intensity of the physical effort, it exhausts the productive energy of the worker, is to depress vitality and lower him in the scale of humanity by an excessive habit of conformity to the automatic movements of a non-human motor. This human injury is not adequately compensated by the education in routine and regularity which it confers, or by the slight understanding of the large co-operative purposes and methods of machine industry which his position enables him to acquire.

[1] Cf. Marshall, *Principles of Economics*, p. 265.

CHAPTER XIV

THE ECONOMY OF HIGH WAGES.

§ 1. The theory of a "natural" rate of wages fixed at the bare subsistence-point which was first clearly formulated in the writings of Quesnay and the so-called "physiocratic" school was little more than a rough generalisation of the facts of labour in France. But these facts, summed up in the phrase, "Il ne gagne que sa vie," and elevated to the position of a natural law, implied the general belief that a higher rate of wage would not result in a correspondent increase of the product of labour, that it would not pay an employer to give wages above the point of bare sustenance and reproduction. This dogma of the economy of cheap labour, taught in a slightly modified form by many of the leading English economists of the first half of the nineteenth century, has dominated the thought and indirectly influenced the practice of the business world. It is true that Adam Smith in a well-known passage had given powerful utterance to a different view of the relation between work and wages :—" The liberal reward of labour as it encourages the propagation so it encourages the industry of the common people. The wages of labour are the encouragement of industry, which, like every other human quality, improves in proportion to the encouragement it receives."[1] But the teaching of Ricardo, and the writers who most closely followed him in his conception of the industrial system, leaned heavily in favour of low wages as the sound basis of industrial progress.

The doctrine of the economy of low wages in England scarcely needed the formal support of the scientific economist. It was already strongly implanted in the mind of the eighteenth century "business man," who moralised upon the excesses resulting from high wages much in the tone of the business man of to-day. It would be scarcely possible to parody the following line of reflection :—

" The poor in the manufacturing counties will never work any more time in general than is necessary just to live and support their weekly debauches. Upon the whole we may fairly aver that a reduction of wages in the woollen manufactures would be a national blessing and advantage and no real injury to the poor. By this means we might keep our trade, uphold our rents, and reform the people into the bargain." (Smith's *Memoirs on Wool*, vol. ii. p. 308.)

Compare with this Arthur Young's frequent suggestion that rents should be raised in order to improve farming.[2] So Dr. Ure, half a century later, notwithstanding that his main argument is for the " economy of high wages," both on the ground that it evokes the best quality of work and because it keeps the workman contented, is unable to avoid flatly contradicting himself as follows :—

" High wages, instead of leading to thankfulness of temper and improvement of mind, have, in too many cases, cherished pride and supplied funds for supporting refractory spirits in strikes wantonly inflicted upon one set of mill-owners after another throughout the several districts of Lancashire for the purpose of degrading them into a state of servitude." (*Philosophy of Manufacture*, p. 366.)

---

[1] *Wealth of Nations*, vol. i. p. 86.
[2] Cf. *Northern Tour*, vol. ii. p. 86.

So again (p. 298):—"In fact, it was their high wages which enabled them to maintain a stipendary committee in affluence, and to pamper themselves into nervous ailments by a diet too rich and exciting for their indoor occupation."

The experiments of Robert Owen in raising wages and shortening hours in his New Lanark mills failed utterly to convince his fellow-manufacturers that a high standard of comfort among the workers would bring a correspondent rise in working efficiency.

The history of the early factory system, under which rapid fortunes were built out of the excessive toil of children and low-skilled adult workers paid at rates which were, in many instances, far below true "subsistence wages," furnished to the commercial mind a convincing argument in favour of "cheap labour," and set political economy for half a century at war with the rising sentiments of humanity [1] Even now, the fear frequently expressed in the New World regarding the "competition of cheap labour" attests a strong survival of this theory, which held it to be the first principle of "good business" to pay as low wages as possible.

§ 2. The trend of more recent thought has been in the

---

[1] It is true that out-and-out defenders of the factories against early legislation sometimes had the audacity to assert the "economy of high wages," and to maintain that it governed the practice of early mill-owners. So Ure, "The main reason why they (i.e. wages) are so high is, that they form a small part of the value of the manufactured article, so that if reduced too low by a sordid master, they would render his operatives less careful, and thereby injure the quality of their work more than could be compensated by his saving in wages. The less proportion wages bear to the value of the goods, the higher, generally speaking, is the recompense of labour. The prudent master of a fine spinning-mill is most reluctant to tamper with the earnings of his spinners, and never consents to reduce them till absolutely forced to it by a want of remuneration for the capital and skill embarked in his business" (*Philosophy of Manufacture*, p. 330). This does not, however, prevent Dr. Ure from pointing out a little later the grave danger into which trade-union endeavours to raise wages drive a trade subject to the competition of "the more frugal and docile labour of the Continent and United States" (p. 363). Nor do Dr. Ure's statements regarding the high wages paid in cotton-mills, which he places at three times the agricultural wages, tally with the statistics given in the appendix of his own book (cf. p. 515). Male spinners alone received the "high wages" he names, and out of them had to pay for the labour of the assistants whom they hired to help them.

direction of a progressive modification of the doctrine of the "economy of low wages." The common maxim that "if you want a thing well done you must expect to pay for it" implies some general belief in a certain correspondence of work and wages. The clearer formulation of this idea has been in large measure the work of economic thinkers who have set themselves to the close study of comparative statistics. The work in which Mr. Brassey, the great railway contractor, was engaged gave him an opportunity of making accurate comparison of the work and wages of workmen of various nationalities, and his son, Lord Brassey, collected and published a number of facts bearing upon the subject which, as regards certain kinds of work, established a new relation between work and wages. He found that English navvies employed upon the Grand Trunk Railway in Canada, and receiving from 5s. to 6s. a day, did a greater amount of work for the money than French-Canadians paid at 3s. 6d. a day; that it was more profitable to employ Englishmen at 3s. to 3s. 6d. upon making Irish railways than Irishmen at 1s. 6d. to 1s. 8d.; that "in India, although the cost of dark labour ranges from 4½d. to 6d. a day, mile for mile the cost of railway work is about the same as in England;" that in quarry work, "in which Frenchmen, Irishmen, and Englishmen were employed side by side, the Frenchman received three, the Irishman four, and the Englishman six francs a day. At those different rates the Englishman was found to be the most advantageous workman of the three." Extending his inquiries to the building trades, to mining, and to various departments of manufactures, he found a general consensus of opinion among employers and other men of practical experience making for a similar conclusion. In France, Germany, and Belgium, where wages and the standard of living were considerably lower than in England, the cost of turning out a given product was not less, but greater. In the United States and in a few trades of Holland, where the standard of comfort was as high or higher than in the corresponding English industries, more or better work was done. In short, the efficiency of labour was found to vary with tolerable accuracy in accordance with the standard of comfort or real wages.

In his introduction to his work on *Foreign Work and*

English Wages, Lord Brassey gives countenance to a theory of wages which has frequently been attributed to him, and has sometimes been accepted as a final statement of the relation of work and wages—viz., that "the cost of work, as distinguished from the daily wage of the labourer, was approximately the same in all countries." In other words, it is held that, for a given class of work, there is a fixed and uniform relation between wages and efficiency of labour for different lands and different races.

Now, to the acceptance of this judgment, considered as a foundation of a theory of comparative wages, there are certain obvious objections. In the first place, in the statement of most of the cases which are adduced to support the theory reference is made exclusively to money wages, no account being taken of differences of purchasing power in different countries. In order to establish any rational basis, the relation must be between real wages or standard of living and efficiency. Now, though it must be admitted as inherently probable that some definite relation should subsist between wages and work, or, in other words, between the standard of consumption and the standard of production, it is not *à priori* reasonable to expect this relation should be uniform as between two such countries as England and India, so that it should be a matter of economic indifference whether a piece of work is done by cheap and relatively inefficient Indian labour or by expensive and efficient English labour. Such a supposition could only stand upon one of two assumptions.

The first assumption would be that of a direct arithmetical progression in the relation of wage and work such as would require every difference in quantity of food, etc., consumed by labourers to be reflected in an exactly correspondent difference of output of productive energy—an assumption which needs no refutation, for no one would maintain that the standard of comfort furnished by wages is the sole determinant of efficiency, and that race, climate, and social environment play no part in economic production. The alternative assumption would be that of an absolute fluidity of capital and labour, which should reduce to a uniform level throughout the world the net industrial advantages, so that everywhere there was an exact quantitative relation between work and wage, production, and consumption. Though what is called a "tendency" to such uniformity may be admitted, no one acquainted with facts will be so rash as to maintain that this uniformity is even approximately reached.

§ 3. There is, then, no reason to suppose that wages, either nominal or real, bear any exact, or even a closely approximate, relation to the output of efficient work, quantity and quality being both taken into consideration. But, in truth, the evidence afforded by Lord Brassey does not justify a serious investigation of this theory of indifference or equivalence of work and wages. For, in the great majority of instances which he adduces, the advantage is clearly shown to rest with the labour which is most highly remunerated. The theory suggested by his evidence is, in fact, a general theory of "the economy of high wages."

This theory, which has been advancing by rapid strides in recent years, and is now supported by a great quantity of carefully-collected evidence, requires more serious consideration. The evidence of Lord Brassey was chiefly, though by no means wholly, derived from branches of industry where muscular strength was an important element, as in road-making, railway-making, and mining; or from the building trades where machinery does not play a chief part in directing the pace and character of productive effort. It would not be unreasonable to expect that the quantitative relation between work and wages might be closer in industries where freely expended muscular labour played a more prominent part than in industries where machinery was a dominating factor, and where most of the work consisted in tending machinery. It might well be the case that it would pay to provide a high standard of physical consumption to navvies, but that it would not pay to the same extent to give high wages to factory operatives, or even to other classes of workers less subject to the strain of heavy muscular work.

In so far as the tendency of modern production is to relieve man more and more of this rough muscular work, it might happen that the true economy favoured high wages only in those kinds of work which were tending to occupy a subordinate place in the industry of the future. The earlier facts, which associated high wages with high productivity, low wages with low productivity, in textile factories and ironworks, were of a fragmentaɪy character, and, considered as evidence of a causal connection between high wages and high productivity, were vitiated by the wide differences in the development of machinery and industrial method in the cases compared. In recent years the labours of many trained economists, some of them with close practical knowledge of the industrial arts, have collected and tabulated a vast amount of evidence upon the subject. A large number of American economists, among them General F. A. Walker, Mr. Gunton, Mr. Schoenhof, Mr. Gould, Mr. E. Atkinson, have made close researches into the relation between work and wages in America and in the chief industrial countries of Europe. A too patent advocacy of tariff reform or a shorter working day has in some cases prevented the statistics collected from receiving adequate attention, but there is no reason to doubt the substantial accuracy of the research.

The most carefully-conducted investigation has been that of Professor Schulze-Gaevernitz, who, basing his arguments upon a close study of the cotton industry, has related his conclusion most clearly to the evolution of modern machine-production. The earlier evidence merely established the fact of a co-existence between high wages and good work, low wages and bad work, without attempting scientifically to explain the connection. Dr. Schulze-Gaevernitz, by his analysis of cotton spinning and weaving, successfully formulates the observed relations between wages and product. He compares not only the present condition of the cotton industry in England and in Germany and other continental countries, but the conditions of work and wages in the English cotton industry at various times during the last seventy years, thus correcting any personal equation of national life which might to some extent vitiate conclusions based only upon international comparison. This double method of comparison yields certain definite results, which Dr. Schulze-Gaevernitz sums up in the following words :—" Where the cost of labour (*i.e.* piece wages) is lowest the conditions of labour are most favourable, the working day is shortest, and the weekly wages of the operatives are highest " (p. 133). The evolution of improved spinning and weaving machinery in

England is found to be attended by a continuous increase in the product for each worker, a fall in piece wages reflected in prices of foods, a shortening of the hours of labour, and a rise in weekly wages. The following tables, compiled by Dr. Schulze-Gaevernitz, give an accurate statement of the relations of the different movements, taking the spinning and weaving industries as wholes in England:—

SPINNING.

	Product of yarn in 1000 lbs.	Number of workers in spinning mills.	Product per worker in lbs.	Cost of labour per lb.		Average yearly wages.		
				s.	d.	£	s.	d.
1819-21	106,500	111,000	968	6	4	26	13	0
1829-31	216,500	140,000	1546	4	2	27	6	0
1844-46	523,300	190,000	2754	2	3	28	12	0
1859-61	910,000	248,000	3671	2	1	32	10	0
1880-82	1,324,000	240,000	5520	1	9	44	4	0[1]

WEAVING.

	Products in 1000 lbs.	Number of workers.	Product per worker in lbs.	Cost of labour per lb.		Average yearly income.		
				s.	d.	£	s.	d.
1819-21	80,620	250,000	322	15	5	20	18	0
1829-31	143,200	275,000	521	9	0	19	18	0[2]
1844-46	348,110	210,000	1658	3	5	24	10	0
1859-61	650,870	203,000	3206	2	9	30	15	0
1880-82	993,540	246,000	4039	2	3	39	0	0

[1] *Der Grossbetrieb*, p. 132. In regarding the advance of recent average wages it should be borne in mind that the later years contain a larger proportion of adults. In considering the net yearly wages a deduction for unemployment should be made from the sums named in the table.

[2] Account must be taken of the depressed condition of hand-loom weavers, who had not yet disappeared.

The same holds good of the growth of the cotton-weaving industry in America, as the following table shows:—

	Yearly product per worker.	Cost of labour per yard.	Yearly earnings per worker.
	Yards.	Cents.	Dollars.
1830	4,321	1.9	164
1850	12,164	1.55	190
1870	19,293	1.24	240
1884	28,032	1.07	290

Of Germany and Switzerland the same holds. Every improvement of machinery increasing the number of spindles or looms a worker can tend, or increasing the pace of the machinery and thus enlarging the output per worker, is attended by a higher weekly wage, and in general by a shortening of the hours of labour.

A detailed comparison of England, the United States, and the Continent, as regards the present condition of the cotton industry, yields the same general results. A comparison between England and the United States shows that in weaving, where wages are much higher in America, the labour is so much more efficient as to make the cost of production considerably lower than in England; in spinning, where English wages are about as highly paid, the cost of production is lower than in America (p. 156). A comparison between Switzerland and Germany, England, and America, as regards weaving, yields the following results (p. 151):—

	Weekly product per worker.	Cost per yard.	Hours of labour.	Weekly wage.	
	Yards.			s.	d.
Switzerland and Germany	466	0.303	12	11	8
England	706	0.275	9	16	3
America	1200	0.2	10	20	3

The low-paid, long-houred labourers of the Italian factories are easily undersold by the higher paid and more effective labour of England or America. So also a comparison between Mulhausen and the factories of the Vosges valleys shows that the more highly-paid labour of the former is the more productive.

In Russia the better-paid labour in the factories near Petersburg and in Esthland can outcompete the lower paid labour of the central governments of Vladimir and Moscow.

Schulze-Gaevernitz goes so far as to maintain that under existing conditions of low wages and long hours, the Indian factories cannot undersell their Lancashire competitors, and maintains that the stringent factory laws which are demanded for India are likely to injure Lancashire,[1] instead of giving her an advantage. The most vital points of the subject are thus summarised, after an elaborate comparison of the cotton-spinning of England and of those parts of Germany which use English machinery :—

"In England the worker tends nearly twice as much machinery as in Germany; the machines work more quickly; the loss as compared with the theoretic output (*i.e.*, waste of time and material) is smaller. Finally, there comes the consideration that in England the taking-off and putting-on from the spindles occupies a shorter time; there is less breaking of threads, and the piecing of broken threads requires less time. The result is that the cost of labour per pound of yarn—especially when the work of supervision is taken into account—is decidedly smaller in England than in Germany. So the wages of the English spinners are nearly twice as high as in Germany, while the working day occupies a little over 9 hours as compared with 11 to 11½ in Germany." (P. 136.)

More recent investigations directed to a comparison between the efficiency of British and Continental labour confirm the conclusions of Schulze-Gaevernitz. German workers are still inferior to English in the cotton trade, though they have gained in efficiency during the last ten

[1] Here Schulze-Gaevernitz appears to strain his argument. Though official reports lay stress upon the silver question as an important factor in the rise of Bombay mills, there seems no doubt of the ability of Bombay cheap labour, independently of this, to undersell English labour for low counts of cotton in Asiatic markets. Brentano in his work, *Hours and Wages in Relation to Production*, supports Schulze-Gaevernitz.

years, a gain directly associated with higher wages and a better standard of living. The same is generally true of France, Switzerland, and Holland.

As regards the labour cost in India, we are told "The number of operatives required to manage a given quantity of machinery was five to eight times greater in India than in England, and now it is at least three times greater. It is the advantage of position alone which has enabled this native industry to oust foreign yarns, except a few the bulk of which are coloured."[1]

Later comparisons of the relative efficiency of American and English weavers are invalidated by the growing extent to which automatic looms and other improvements in machinery have been adopted in America. No quantitative measurement is possible between the efficiency of the best eight-loom weavers of Massachusetts, earning their 45s. or 50s. per week, and the best Lancashire weavers, with their smaller number of looms and lower wages. Alike in spinning and in weaving, the difference in the quality of the cotton goods further complicates the comparison. The higher average wages paid to cotton operatives in the Northern States is not, however, in the judgment of a recent professional observer,[2] compensated by a corresponding superiority of efficiency. As regards the efficiency of labour in Southern mills, there appears to have been a temporary economy in low wages; though to-day it is held that "in many instances the labour cost is actually higher in the South though the wages are so much lower."[3]

Some interesting testimony from Germany directly supports the economy of high wages in hard manual occupations. A Foreign Office report of 1898 on the coal industry of Rhenish Westphalia states: "Although wages are doubtless lower than in England, even in this district, where they stand higher than in any other part of Germany, I think it will still be found on the average that the working effect per coal-hewer and shift is only about half what it is in England, for the following reasons: because the English pitman lives better, works with more judgment and skill, and once he

[1] Brassey and Chapman, p. 152.
[2] Mr. Young.   [3] Brassey and Chapman, p. 181.

has made his conditions, gives his greater labour-power more freely; and last, not least, he is a trained hewer, timber-setter, or putter, as the case may be."

This is confirmed by the evidence of a German miner who worked for some time in Northumberland. "There is good reason why the English miner should be the stronger man of the two. He has time to rest properly, and he enjoys more meat than potatoes. Generally speaking, overstrain and under-feeding disable the German from competing with him."[1]

There exists a large amount of testimony, both of business men and of economists, in support of the favourable effect of the higher standard of comfort enjoyed by American workmen upon the output of labour. European workmen who have gone to work in the United States commonly admit that they give out a much larger amount of working energy. How far this is susceptible of physiological explanation, the better food converted into more work, may perhaps be questioned. Probably psychical factors play at least as important a part. The recognition of a career open to every talent, or at least a fair opportunity of distinct and appreciable improvement in the standard of comfort, has been a stimulus operative among all sections of American workmen, though recent conditions of the low-skilled labour market have diminished its effectiveness. The increase of the population of negroes and foreign immigrants, forming an unskilled class of labour kept in its place by a reduced demand for skilled labour relative to the supply, seems likely to reduce the energy of the American "stroke" to the level of the European. If, in addition to this, the real wage of unskilled labour falls, as it has in fact done since 1897, one great source of American industrial progress is perceptibly weakened.

§ 4. From the evidence adduced by Schulze-Gaevernitz, modern industrial progress is expressed, so far as its effects on labour are concerned, in seven results: (*a*) Shorter hours of labour. (*b*) Higher weekly wage. (*c*) Lower piece-wage. (*d*) Cheaper product. (*e*) Increased product per worker.

---

[1] *How the English Workman Lives*, Ernst Düchershoff (1899), quoted Brassey and Chapman, p. 48.

(*f*) Increased speed of machinery. (*g*) Increased number and size of machines to the worker.

All these factors must be taken into consideration before a full judgment of the net results of machinery upon the worker can be formed. The evidence above recorded, conclusive as it is regarding the existence of some causal connection between a high standard of living and high productivity of labour, does not necessarily justify the conclusion that a business, or a federation of employers, may go ahead increasing wages and shortening hours of labour *ad libitum* in sure and certain expectation of a corresponding increase in the net productivity of labour.

Before such a conclusion is warranted, we must grasp more clearly the nature of the causal relation between high standard of living and efficiency. How far are we entitled to regard high wages and other good conditions of employment as the cause, how far as the effect of efficiency of labour? The evidence adduced simply proves that *a b c*, certain phenomena relating to efficiency—as size of product, speed of workmanship, quantity of machines tended—vary directly with *d e f*, certain other phenomena relating to wages, hours of labour, and other conditions of employment. So far as such evidence goes, we are only able to assert that the two sets of phenomena are causally related, and cannot surely determine whether variations in *a b c* are causes, or effects of concomitant variations in *d e f*, or whether both sets of phenomena are or are not governed by some third set, the variations of which affect simultaneously and proportionately the other two.

The moral which writers like Mr. Gunton and Mr. Schoenhof have sought to extract, and which has been accepted by not a few leaders in the "labour movement," is that every rise of wages and every shortening of hours will necessarily be followed by an equivalent or a more than equivalent rise in the efficiency of labour. In seeking to establish this position, special stress is laid upon the evidence of the comparative statistics of textile industries. But, in the first place, it must be pointed out that the evidence adduced does not support any such sweeping generalisation. The statistics of Mr. Gould and Mr. Schoenhof, for instance, show many cases where higher money and real wages of American operatives are not accompanied by a correspondingly larger productivity. In such cases the "cheap" labour of England is really cheap.

Again, in other cases where the higher wages of American workers are accompanied by an equivalent, or more than equivalent, increase of product, that increased product is not due entirely or chiefly to greater intensity or efficiency of labour, but to the use of more highly elaborated labour-saving machinery. The difference between the labour-cost of making and maintaining this improved machinery, and that of making and maintaining the inferior machinery it has displaced, ought clearly to be added in, where a comparison is made between the relation of net labour-cost to product in different countries, or in different stages of industrial development in the same country. The omission of this invalidates much of the reasoning of Schulze-Gaevernitz, Brentano, Rae, and other prophets of "the economy of high wages." The direct labour-cost of each commodity may be as little, or even less, than in England, but the total cost of production[1] and the selling price may be higher. Lastly, in that comparison between England and America, which is in many respects the most serviceable, because the two countries are nearest in their development of industrial methods as well as in the character of their labourers, the difference of money and of real wage is not commonly accompanied by a difference in hours of labour.

The evidence we possess does not warrant any universal or even general application of the theory of the economy of high wages. If it was generally true that by increasing wages and by shortening working hours the daily product of each labourer could be increased or even maintained, the social problem, so far as it relates to the alleviation of the poverty and misery of the lower grades of workers,

---

[1] Mr. Gould's general conclusion, from his comparison of American and European production, is "that higher daily wages in America *do not mean a correspondingly enhanced labour-cost to the manufacturers*" (*Contemporary Review*, Jan. 1893). This he holds to be partly due to superior mechanical agencies, which owe their existence to high wages, partly to superior physical force in the workers. But Mr. Gould's evidence and his conclusion here stated, taken as testimony to the "economy of high wages," are insufficient, for they only show that high wages are attended by increased output of labour, not by an increase *correspondent* to this higher wage.

would admit of an easy solution. But though it will be generally admitted that a rise of wages or of the general standard of comfort of most classes of workers will be followed by increased efficiency of labour, and that a shortening of hours will not be followed by a corresponding diminution in output, it by no means follows that it will be profitable to increase wages and shorten hours indefinitely. Just as it is admitted that the result of an equal shortening of hours will be different in every trade, so will the result of a given rise in standard of comfort be different. In some cases highly-paid labour and short hours will pay, in other cases cheaper labour and longer hours. It is not possible by dwelling upon the concomitance of high wages and good work, low wages and bad work, in many of the most highly-developed industries to appeal to the enlightened self-interest of employers for the adoption of a general rise in wages and a general shortening of hours. Because the most profitable business may often be conducted on a system which involves high wages for short intense work with highly evolved machinery, it by no means follows that other businesses may not be more profitably conducted by employing low-paid workers for long hours with simpler machinery. We are not at liberty to conclude that the early Lancashire mill-owners adopted a short-sighted policy in employing children and feeble adult labour at starvation wages.

The evidence, in particular, of Schulze-Gaevernitz certainly shows that the economy of high wages and short hours is closely linked with the development of machinery, and that when machinery is complex and capable of being worked at high pressure a net economy of high wages and short hours emerges. In this light modern machinery is seen as the direct cause of high wages and short hours. For though the object of introducing machinery is to substitute machine-tenders at low wages for skilled handicraftsmen, and though the tireless machine could be profitably worked continuously, when due regard is had to human nature it is found more profitable to work at high pressure for shorter hours and to purchase such intense work at a higher price. It must, of course, be kept in mind that high wages are often the direct cause of the introduction of improved machinery, and are an ever-present incentive to fresh mechanical inventions. This was clearly recognised half a century ago by Dr. Ure, who names the lengthened mules, the invention of the self-acting mule, and some of the early improvements in calico-printing as directly attributable to this cause.[1]

But, admitting these tendencies in certain machine industries, we are not justified in relying confidently upon the ability of a rise of wages, obtained by organisation of labour or otherwise, to bring about such improvements of industrial methods as will enable the higher wages to be paid without injuring the trade, or reducing the profits below the minimum socially required for the maintenance of a privately conducted industry.

Our evidence leads to the conclusion that, while a rise of wages is nearly always attended by a rise of efficiency of labour and of the product, the proportion which the increased productivity will bear to the rise of wage will differ in every employment. Hence it is not possible to make a general declaration in favour of a policy of high wages or of low wages.

§ 5. The economically profitable wages and hours will vary in accordance with many conditions, among the most important being the development of machinery, the strain upon muscles and nerves imposed by the work, the indoor and sedentary character of the work, the various hygienic conditions which attend it, the age, sex, race, and class of the workers.

In cotton-weaving in America it pays better to employ women at high wages to tend six, seven, or even eight looms for short hours, than to pay lower wages to inferior workers such as are found in Germany, Switzerland, or even in Lancashire. But in coal-mining it appears that the American wages are economically too high—that is to say, the difference between American and English wages is not compensated by an equivalent difference of output. The gross number of tons mined by United States miners working at wages of $326 per annum is 377, yielding a cost of 86½ cents per ton, as compared with 79 cents per ton,

---

[1] Ure's *Philosophy of Manufacture*, pp. 367-369. Dr. Ure regarded mechanical inventions as the means whereby capital should keep labour in subjection. In describing how the "self-acting mule" came into use he adds triumphantly: "This invention comprises the great doctrine already propounded, that when capital enlists science in her service the refractory hand of labour will always be taught docility" (p. 368).

the cost of North Staffordshire coal produced by miners earning $253, and turning out 322 tons per head.[1] So also a ton of Bessemer pig iron costs in labour about 50 cents more in America than in England, the American wages being about 40 per cent. higher.[2]

It is, indeed, evident from the aggregate of evidence that no determinable relation exists between cost in labour and wages for any single group of commodities.

Just as little can a general acceptance be given to the opposite contention that it is the increased efficiency of labour which causes the high wages. This is commonly the view of those business men and those economists who start from the assumption that there is some law of competition in accordance with whose operation every worker necessarily receives as much as he is worth, the full value of the product of his labour. Only by the increased efficiency of labour can wages rise, argue these people; where wages are high the efficiency of labour is found to be high, and *vice versâ ;* therefore efficiency determines wages. Just as the advocates of the economy of high-wages theory seek by means of trade-unionism, legislation, and public opinion to raise wages and shorten hours, trusting that the increased efficiency which ensues will justify such conduct, so the others insist that technical education and an elevation of the moral and industrial character of the workers must precede and justify any rise of wages or shortening of hours, by increasing the efficiency of labour. Setting aside the assumption here involved that the share of the workers in the joint product of capital and labour is a fixed and immovable proportion, this view rests upon a mere denial of the effect which it is alleged that high wages and a rise in standard of comfort have in increasing efficiency.

The relation between wages and other conditions of employment, on the one hand, and efficiency of labour or size of product on the other, is clearly one of mutual determination. Every rise in wages, leisure, and in general standard of comfort will increase the efficiency of labour; every increased efficiency, whether due directly to these or to other causes, will enable higher wages to be paid and shorter hours to be worked.

---

[1] " No. 64 Consular Report " (quoted Schoenhof, p. 209).
[2] Schoenhof, p. 216.

§ 6. One further point emerges from the evidence relating to efficiency and high wages. According to Schulze-Gaevernitz's formula, every fall in piece wages is attended by a rise in weekly wages. But it should be kept in mind that a rise in time wages does not necessarily mean that the price of labour measured in terms of effort has been raised. Intenser labour undergone for a shorter time may obtain a higher money wage per unit of time, but the price per unit of effort may be lower. It has been recognised that a general tendency of the later evolution of machinery has been to compress and intensify labour. In certain classes of textile labour the amount of muscular or manual labour given out in a day is larger than formerly. This is the case with the work of children employed as piecers. In Ure's day (1830) he was able to claim that during three-fourths of the time spent by children in the factory they had nothing to do. The increased quantity of spindles and the increased speed have made their labour more continuous. The same is true of the mule spinners, whose labour, even within the last few years, has been intensified by increased size of the mule. Though as a rule machinery tends to take over the heavier forms of muscular work, it also tends to multiply the minor calls upon the muscles, until the total strain is not much less than before. What relief is obtained from muscular effort is compensated by a growing strain upon the nerves and upon the attention. Moreover, as the machinery grows more complex, numerous, and costly, the responsibility of the machine-tender is increased. To some considerable extent the new effort imposed upon the worker is of a more refined order than the heavy muscular work it has replaced. But its tax upon the physique is an ever-growing one. "A hand-loom weaver can work thirteen hours a day, but to get a six-loom weaver to work thirteen hours is a physical impossibility."[1] The complexity of modern machinery and the superhuman celerity of which it is capable suggest continually an increased compression of human labour, an increased output of effort per unit of time. This has been rendered possible by acquired skill and improved physique ensuing on a higher standard of living. But it is evident that, where it appears that each

[1] *Der Grossbetrieb*, p. 167.

rise in the standard of living and each shortening of the working-day has been accompanied by a severer strain either upon muscles, nerves, or mental energy during the shorter working day, we are not entitled to regard the higher wages and shorter hours as clear gain for the worker. Some limits are necessarily imposed upon this compressibility of working effort. It would clearly be impossible by a number of rapid reductions of the working day and increases of time wages to force the effectiveness of an hour's labour beyond a certain limit for the workers. Human nature must place limits upon the compression. Though it may be better for a weaver to tend four looms during the English factory day for the moderate wage of 16s. a week than to earn 11s. 8d. by tending two looms in Germany for twelve hours a day, it does not follow that it is better to earn 20s. 3d. in America by tending six, seven, or even eight looms for a ten-hours day,[1] or that the American's condition would be improved if the eight-hours day was purchased at the expense of adding another loom for each worker.

The gain which accrues from high wages and a larger amount of leisure, over which the higher consumption shall be spread, may be more than counteracted by an undue strain upon the nerves or muscles during the shorter day. This difficulty, as we have seen, is not adequately met by assigning the heavier muscular work more and more to machinery, if the possible activity of this same machinery is made a pretext for forcing the pace of such work as devolves upon machine-tenders.

In many kinds of work, though by no means in all, an increase of the amount of work packed into an hour could be obtained by a reduction of the working-day; but two considerations should act in determining the progressive movement in this direction : first, the objective economic question of the quantitative relation between the successive decrements of the working-day and the increments of labour put into each hour; second, the subjective economic question of the effect of the more compressed labour upon the worker considered both as worker and as consumer.

---

[1] *Vide supra*, p. 360. These wages, however, are the average of all the labour employed in the weaving-sheds, not of "weavers" alone.

There is not wanting evidence to show that increased leisure and higher wages can be bought too dear.

In drawing attention to this consideration it must not, however, be assumed that the increase of real wages and shortening of hours traced in progressive industries are necessarily accompanied by a corresponding increase in the compression of labour. In the textile and iron industries, for example, it is evident (*pace* Karl Marx) that the operatives has obtained some portion of the increased productivity of improved machinery in a rise of wages. Even where more machinery is tended we are not entitled to assume a correspondent increase in felt effort or strain upon the worker. A real growth of skill or efficiency will enable an increased amount of machinery to be tended with no greater subjective effort than a smaller amount formerly required. But while allowance should be made for this, the history of the factory system, both in England and in other countries, clearly indicates that factory labour is more intense than formerly, not, perhaps, in its tax upon the muscles, but in the growing strain it imposes upon the nervous system of the operatives.

The importance of this point is frequently ignored alike by advocates of a shorter working-day and by those who insist that the chief aim of workers should be to make their labour more productive. So far as the higher efficiency simply means more skill and involves no increased effort it is pure gain, but where increased effort is required the question is one requiring close and detailed consideration.

§ 7. Another effect of over-compressed labour deserves a word.

The close relation between higher wages and shorter hours is generally acknowledged. A rise of money wages which affects the standard of living by introducing such changes in consumption as require for their full yield of benefit or satisfaction an increase of consuming-time can only be made effective by a diminution in the producing time or hours of labour. When, for example, the new wants, whose satisfaction would be naturally sought from a rise of the standard living, are of an intellectual order, involving not merely the purchase of books, etc., but the time to read such books, this benefit requires that the

higher wages should be supplemented by a diminution
in the hours of labour in cases where the latter are unduly
long. But it is not so clearly recognised that such questions
cannot be determined without reference to the question of
intensity of labour. Yet it is evident that an eight-hours
day of more compressed labour might be of a more
exhausting character than a ten-hours day of less intense
labour and disqualify a worker from receiving the benefits
of the opportunities of education open to him more than
the longer hours of less intense labour. The advantage of
the addition of two hours of leisure might be outweighed
by the diminished value attached to each leisure hour. In
other words, the excess of intense work might be worse in
its effects than the excess of more extended work. This
possibility is often overlooked in the arguments of those
who support the movement towards a shorter working-day
by maintaining that each unit of labour-time will be more
productive. When the argument concerns itself merely
with alleging the influence of higher wages, without shorter
hours, upon the efficiency of labour, this neglect of the
consideration of intense labour has a more urgent importance. It may be gravely doubted whether the benefit of
the higher wages of the Massachusetts weavers is not over-
balanced by the increased effort of tending so large a
number of looms for hours which are longer than the
English factory day. The exhausting character of such
labour is likely to leave its mark in diminishing the real
utility or satisfaction of the nominally higher standard of
living which the high wages render possible. Where the
increased productivity of labour is largely due to the
improved machinery or methods of production which are
stimulated by high wages without a corresponding intensification of the labour itself, the gain to labour is clear.
But the possibility that short hours and high wages may
stimulate an injurious compression of the output of productive effort is one which must not be overlooked in
considering the influence of new industrial methods upon
labour.

§ 8. Duration of labour, intensity of labour, and wages, in
their mutual relations, must be studied together in any
attempt to estimate the tendencies of capitalist production.
Nor can we expect their relations to be the same in any two

industries. Where labour is thinly extended over an in-
ordinately long working-day, as in the Indian mills, it is
probable that such improvements of organisation as might
shorten the hours to those of an ordinary English factory
day, and intensify the labour, would be a benefit, and the
rise of wages which might follow would bring a double gain
to the workers. But any endeavour to further shorten and
intensify the working-day might injure the workers, even
though their output were increased. Such an instance,
however, may serve well to bring home the relativity which
is involved in all such questions. The net benefit derived
from a particular quantitative relation between hours of
labour, intensity, and earnings would probably be widely
different for English and for Indian textile workers. It
would, *à priori*, be unreasonable to expect that the working-
day which would bring the greatest net advantage to both
should be of the same duration. So also it may well be
possible that the more energetic nervous temperament of
the American operative may qualify him or her for a shorter
and intenser working-day than would suit the Lancashire
operative. It is the inseparable relation of the three factors
—duration, intensity, and earnings—which is the important
point. But in considering earnings, not merely the money
wage, nor even the purchasing power of the money, but the
net advantage which can be obtained by consuming what is
purchased must be understood, if we are to take a scientific
view of the question.

It should be clearly recognised that in the consideration
of all practical reforms affecting the conditions of labour,
the " wages" question cannot be dissociated from the
" hours " question, nor both from the " intensity of labour "
question ; and that any endeavour to simplify discussion, or
to facilitate " labour movements," by seeking a separate
solution for each is futile, because it is unscientific. When
any industrial change is contemplated, it should be regarded,
from the " labour " point of view, in its influence upon the
net welfare of the workers, due regard being given, not
merely to its effect upon wage, hours, and intensity, but
to the complex and changing relations which subsist in
each trade, in each country, and in each stage of industrial
development between the three.

But although, when we bear in mind the effects of

machinery in imparting intensity and monotony to labour, in increasing the number of workers engaged in sedentary indoor occupations, and in compelling an ever larger proportion of the working population to live in crowded and unhealthy towns, the net benefit of machinery to the working classes may be questioned, the growth of machinery has been clearly attended by an improved standard of material comfort among the machine-workers, taking the objective measurement of comfort.

Whatever allowance may be made for the effects of increased intensity of labour, and the indirect influences of machinery, the bulk of evidence clearly indicates that machine-tenders are better fed, clothed, and housed than the hand-workers whose place they take, and that every increase in the efficiency and complexity of machinery is attended by a rise in real wages. The best machinery requires for its economical use a fair standard of living among the workers who co-operate with it, and with the further development of machinery in each industry we may anticipate a further rise of this standard, though we are not entitled to assume that this natural and necessary progress of comfort among machine-workers has no fixed limit, and that it is equally applicable to all industries and all countries.

It might, therefore, appear that as one industry after another fell under machine-production, the tendency of machine-development must necessarily make for a general elevation of the standard of comfort among the working classes. It may very well be the case that the net influence of machinery is in this direction. But it must not be forgotten that the increased spread of machine-production does not appear to engage a larger proportion of the working population in machine-tending. Indeed, if we may judge by the recent history of the most highly-evolved textile industries, we are entitled to expect that, when machinery has got firm hold of all those industries which lend themselves easily to routine production, the proportion of the whole working population engaged directly in machine-tending will continually decrease, a larger and larger proportion being occupied in those parts of the transport and distributing industries which do not lend themselves conveniently to machinery, and in personal services. If this is so, we cannot look upon the evolution of machinery, with its demand for intenser and more efficient labour, as an adequate guarantee of a necessary improvement in the standard of comfort of the working classes as a whole. To put the matter shortly, we have no evidence to show that a rise in the standard of material comfort of shopmen, writing clerks, school-teachers, 'busmen, agents, warehousemen, dockers, policemen, sandwich-men, and other classes of labour whose proportion is increasing in our industrial society, will be attended by so considerable a rise in the efficiency of their labour as to stimulate a series of such rises. The automatic movement which Schulze-Gaevernitz and others trace in the typical machine-industries is not shown to apply to industry as a whole, and if the tendency of machine-development is to absorb a larger proportion of the work but a smaller proportion of the workers, it is not possible to found large hopes for the future of the working classes upon this movement of the earning of high wages in machine-industry.

§ 9. But though the individual self-interest of the producer cannot be relied upon to favour progressive wages, except in certain industries and up to a certain point, the collective interest of consumers lends stronger support to "the economy of high wages." We have seen that the possession of an excessive proportion of "power to consume" by classes who, because their normal healthy wants are already fully satisfied, refuse to exert this power, and insist upon storing it in unneeded forms of capital, is directly responsible for the slack employment of capital and labour. If the operation of industrial forces throw an increased proportion of the "power to consume" into the hands of the working classes, who will use it not to postpone consumption but to raise their standard of material and intellectual comfort, a fuller and more regular employment of labour and capital must follow. If the stronger organisation of labour is able to raise wages, and the higher wages are used to demand more and better articles of consumption, a direct stimulus to the efficiency of capital and labour is thus applied. The true issue, however, must not be shirked. If the power of purchase now "saved" by the wealthier classes passed into the hands of the workers in higher money wages, and was not spent by them in raising their standard of comfort, but was "invested" in various forms of capital, no stimulus to industry would be afforded; the "savings" of one class would have fallen into the hands of another class, and their excess would operate to restrict industry precisely as it now operates. Though we would gladly see in the possession of the working classes an increased proportion of those forms of capital which are socially useful, this simple act of transfer, however brought about, would furnish no stimulus to the aggregate industry. From the standpoint of the community nothing else than a rise in the average standard of current consumption can stimulate industry. When it is clearly grasped that a demand for commodities is the only demand for the use of labour and of capital, and not merely determines in what particular direction these requisites of production shall be applied, the hope of the future of our industry is seen to rest largely upon the confident belief that the working classes will use their higher wages not to draw interest from investments (a self-destructive policy) but to raise their standard of life by the current satisfaction of all those wholesome desires of body and mind which lie latent under an "economy of low wages." The satisfaction of new good human desires, by endowing life with more hope and interest, will render all intelligent exertion more effective, by distributing demand over a larger variety of commodities will give a fuller utilisation both of natural and human resources, and by redressing the dislocated balance of production and consumption due to inequality of purchasing power, will justify high wages by increased fulness and regularity of work. But it must be clearly recognised that however desirable "saving" may seem to be as a moral virtue of the working classes, any large practice of saving undertaken before and in preference to an elevation of current consumption, will necessarily cancel the economic advantages just dwelt upon. Just as the wise individual will see he cannot afford to "save" until he has made full provision for the maintenance of his family in full physical efficiency, so the wise working class will insist upon utilising earlier accesses of wages in promoting the physical and intellectual efficiency of themselves and their families before they endeavour to "invest" any considerable portion of their increased wages. Mr. Gould puts this point very plainly and convincingly: "Where economic gains are small, savings mean a relatively low plane of social existence. A parsimonious people are never progressive, neither are they, as a rule, industrially efficient. It is the man with many wants—not luxurious fancies, but real legitimate wants—who works hard to satisfy his aspirations, and he it is who is worth hiring. Let economists still teach the utility and the necessity of saving, but let the sociologist as firmly insist that to so far practise economy as to prevent in the nineteenth century a corresponding advance in civilisation of the working with the other classes is morally inequitable and industrially bad policy. I am not sorry that the American does not save more. Neither am I sure but that if many working-class communities I have visited on the Continent were socially more ambitious, there would not be less danger from Radical theories. One of the most intelligent manufacturers I ever met told me a few years ago he would be only too glad to pay higher wages to his working people, provided they would spend the excess legitimately and not hoard it. He knew that in the end he should gain thereby, since the ministering to new wants only begets others."[1] If there are theoretic economists who still hold that "a demand for commodities is not a demand for labour," they may be reminded that a paradox is not necessarily true. In fact, this particular paradox is seen to be sustained by a combination of slipshod reasoning and moral prejudice. The growing opinion of economic students is veering round to register in theory the firm empirical judgment from which the business world has never swerved, that a high rate of consumption is the surest guarantee of progressive trade. The surest support of the "economy of high wages" is the conviction that it will operate as a stimulus to industry through increased consumption. The working classes, especially in the United States and in England, show a growing tendency to employ their higher wages in progressive consumption. Upon the steady operation of this tendency the economic future of the working classes, and of industry in general, largely depends.

[1] E. R. L. Gould, *Contemporary Review*, January 1893.

CHAPTER XV

SOME EFFECTS OF MODERN INDUSTRY UPON THE WORKERS AS CONSUMERS.

§ 1. *How far the different Working Classes gain from the Fall of Prices.*

§ 2. *Part of the Economy of Machine-production compensated by the growing Work of Distribution.*

§ 3. *The Lowest Class of Workers gains least from Machine-production.*

§ 1. In considering the effect of machine-production upon a body of workers engaged in some particular industry we are not confined to tracing the effects of improvements in the arts and methods of that single branch of production. As consumers they share in the improvements introduced into other industries reflected in a fall of retail prices. Insomuch as all English workers consume bread they are benefited by the establishment of a new American railway or the invention of new milling machinery which lowers the price of bread; as all consume boots the advantage which the introduction of boot-making machinery confers upon the workers is not confined to the higher wages which may be paid to some operatives in the boot factory, but is extended to all the workers who can buy cheaper boots.

How far do methods of modern capitalist production tend to benefit the labourer in his capacity as consumer?

Economic theory is in tolerably close accord with experience in the answer it gives to this question. Each portion of the working classes gains in its capacity of consumer from improved methods of production in proportion to the amount by which its income exceeds the bare subsistence wage of unskilled workers. The highly-paid mechanic gains

most, the sweated worker least. The worker earning forty
shillings per week gains much more than twice as much as
the worker earning twenty shillings from each general
cheapening in the cost of production. There are several
reasons why this is so.

1. Where there exists a constant over-supply of labour
competing for what must be regarded at any particular time
as a fixed quantity of employment, wages are determined
with tolerably close reference to the lowest standard of
living among that class of workers, and not by any fixed or
customary money wage. This is particularly the case in
the "sweating" trades of large towns. Here such improvements in machinery and methods of industry as lower the
price of articles which fall within the "standard of living"
of this class are liable to be speedily reflected in a fall of
money wages paid for such low-skilled work. In other
words, a "bare subsistence wage" does not gain by a fall
in the price of the articles which belong to its standard
of comfort.

Even in the lowest kinds of work there is no doubt some
tendency to stick to the former money wage and thus to
raise somewhat the standard of real wages, but where the
competition is keenest this *vis inertiæ* is liable to be over-
borne, and money wages fall with prices. As we rise to the
more highly skilled, paid, and organised grades of labour,
we come to workers who are less exposed to the direct
constant strain of competition, where there is not a chronic
over-supply of labour. Here a fall of retail prices is not
necessarily or speedily followed by any corresponding fall of
money wages, and the results of the higher real wages
enjoyed for a time impress themselves in a higher habitual
standard of comfort and strengthen the resistance which is
offered to any attempt to lower money wages, even though
the attempt may be made at a time when an over-supply
of labour does exist.

In proportion as a class of workers is highly paid,
educated, and organised, it is able to gain the benefit
which improved machinery brings to the consumer, because
it is better able to resist the economic tendency to determine wages by reference to a standard of comfort independent of monetary considerations. So far as the lowest
waged and most closely competing labourers have gained

by the fall of prices, it has been due to the pressure of sentiment on the part of the better class of employers and of the public against the lowering of money wages, even where the smaller sum of money will purchase as much as a larger sum previously.

2. The smaller the income the larger the proportion of it that is spent upon commodities whose expense of production and whose price is less affected by machinery. Machine-production, by the fall of prices it brings, has benefited people in direct proportion to their income. The articles which have fallen most rapidly in price are those comforts and luxuries into which machine-production enters most largely. The aristocracy of the working classes, whose standard of comfort includes watches, pianos, books, and bicycles, has gained much more by the fall of prices than those who are obliged to spend all their wages on the purchase of bare necessaries of life. The gain of the former is manifold and great, the benefit of the latter is confined to the cheapening of bread and groceries—a great benefit when measured in terms of improved livelihood no doubt, but small when compared with the increase of purchasing power conferred by modern production upon the Lancashire factory family, with its £3 or £4 a week, and in large measure counterbalanced by the increased proportion of the income, which, in the case of town operatives, goes as rent and price of vegetables, dairy produce, and other commodities which have risen in price.

3. The highly-paid operatives generally work the shortest hours, the low-paid the longest. So far as this is not compensated by an increased intensity of labour on the part of those working short hours, it implies an increased capacity of making the most out of their wages. Longer leisure enables a worker to make the most of his consumption, he can lay out his wages more carefully, is less tempted to squander his money in excesses directly engendered by the reaction from excessive labour, and can get a fuller enjoyment and benefit from the use of the consumables which he purchases. A large and increasing number of the cheapest and the most intrinsically valuable commodities, of an intellectual, artistic, and spiritual character, are only open to the beneficial consumption of

those who have more leisure at their command than is yet the lot of the low-skilled workers in our towns.

§ 2. If we compare the statistics of wages we shall find that the largest proportionate rise of money wages has been in the highly-organised machine industries, and that the benefit which machinery confers upon the workers in the capacity of consumers falls chiefly to the same workers.

It must not, however, be assumed that improved methods of production yield their full benefit through competition to the consuming public. On the contrary, much of the economy of machine-production fails to exercise its full influence upon retail prices. There are two chief reasons for this failure. To one of these adequate attention has been already drawn, the growth of definite forms of capitalist monopoly, which secure at some point or other in the production of a commodity, as higher profits, that which under free competition would pass to the consumer through lower shop prices. The second consists in the abnormal growth of the distributive classes, whose multiplication is caused by the limitation which the economy of machinery imposes upon the amount of capital and labour which can find profitable employment in the extractive and manufacturing processes. A larger and larger number of industrial workers obtain a living by a subdivision of the work of distribution carried to a point far beyond the bounds of social utility. For, on the one hand, when competition of manufacturers and transporters is more and more confined to a small number of large businesses which, because their united power of production largely transcends the consumption at profitable prices, are driven into closer competition, a larger amount of labour is continually engaged in the attempt of each firm to secure for itself the largest share of business at the expense of another firm. On the other hand, shut out from effective or profitable competition in the manufacturing industries, a larger amount of capital and labour seeks to engage in those departments of the distributive trade where new-comers have a better chance, and where by local settlement or otherwise they have an opportunity of sharing the amount of distribution that is to be done. Hence a fall of wholesale prices is usually not reflected in a corresponding fall of retail prices, for competition in retail trade, as J. S. Mill clearly recognised, " often, instead of lowering prices, merely divides the gains of the high price among a greater number of dealers."[1]

§ 3. The wide difference between the economic position of the skilled mechanic and the common labourer shows how fallacious is that treatment of the influence of machinery upon the condition of the working classes which is commonly found in treatises of political economy. To present a comparative picture of the progress of the working classes during the last half century, which assigns to them an increase of money wages, obtained by averaging a number of rises in different employments, and reduces this increase to real wages without any reference to the different use of wages by different classes, is an unscientific and mischievous method of dealing with one of the most important economic questions. The influence of machine-production appears to be widely different upon the skilled mechanic and the common labourer considered both as producers and consumers, and tends to a wide difference in standard of comfort between the two classes. This difference is further enhanced by the indirect assistance which machinery and large-scale industry give to the skilled workers to combine and thus frequently to obtain wages higher than are economically requisite to secure their efficient work. On the other hand, growing feelings of humanity and a vague but genuine feeling of social justice in an ever larger portion of the public often enable the low-skilled worker to secure a higher standard of comfort than the operation of economic competition alone would enable him to reach. But after due allowance is made for this, the conclusion is forced upon us that the gain of machine-production, so far as an increase in real wages is concerned, has been chiefly taken by the highly-skilled and highly-waged workers, and that as the character of work and wages descends, the proportionate gain accruing from the vast increase of productive power rapidly diminishes, the lowest classes of workers obtaining but an insignificant share.

[1] *Principles of Political Economy*, Bk. ii., chap. iv. § 3.

CHAPTER XVI.

OCCUPATIONS OF THE PEOPLE.

§ 1. The most valuable source of information regarding the effects of modern industrialism is the study of the comparative statistics of occupations. Like every statistical inquiry, this is full of pitfalls, and much of the apparent precision which columns of figures and percentages suggest disappears when modes of collection and classification are subjected to detailed analysis. But while such errors invalidate many particular conclusions as to the nature and size of fluctuations, they do not affect to anything like the same degree the broader judgments based upon a large mass of cumulative statistical evidence.

Now there is a striking consensus of evidence which attests certain important tendencies towards the expansion or contraction of occupations under the pressure of modern industrial forces.

The summary tables of occupations in the last five censuses for England and Wales give the following enumeration of the employed population under general heads:—

ENGLAND AND WALES—SUMMARY TABLES OF OCCUPATIONS.

	1861.	1871.	1881.	1891.	1901.
I. Professional Class	481,957	684,102	647,075	926,132	972,685
II Domestic	1,367,782	1,633,514	1,803,810	1,900,328	1,994,917
III Commercial	623,710	815,424	980,128	1,399,735	1,858,454
IV Agricultural and Fishing	2,010,454	1,657,138	1,383,184	1,336,045	1,152,495
V Industrial	4,828,399	5,137,725	6,373,367	7,336,344	8,350,176
Total Occupied	9,312,302	9,927,903	11,187,564	12,899,484	14,328,727
Total Population	20,066,224	22,712,266	25,974,439	29,002,325	32,527,843
Percentage Increase of Population since last census	11.90	13.21	14.36	11.65	12.17

The main tendencies which appear in these summaries—viz., the relative and absolute decline of agricultural employment, the relative decline of domestic employment, the moderate increase of industrial and the very great increase of commercial and professional employment—are more profitably studied in the fuller analysis of the census of

1901,[1] stating the proportions per million employed in the principal sub-heads in the last three censuses, and distinguishing those which show an increase from those which show a decline.

The relative decline of agriculture, so far as employment is concerned, was not the sequel of the repeal of the Corn Laws. The census report of 1851 for England and Wales presents the following comparative table of percentages:—

						Agricultural.
1811 ...	...	...	...	...	...	35
1821 ...	...	...	...	...	...	33
1831 ...	...	...	...	...	...	28
1841 ...	...	...	...	...	...	22

To which we may add the later estimates derived from subsequent censuses, which, though computed on a somewhat different basis, exhibit the same general tendency:—

1851 ...	...	...	...	...	...	23.5
1861 ...	...	...	...	...	...	21.2
1871 ...	...	...	...	...	...	16.8
1881 ...	...	...	...	...	...	13.8
1891 ...	...	...	...	...	...	11.6
1901 ...	...	...	...	...	...	9.5

Turning to the professional class, we have first to note the growth of persons engaged in Governmental work, general or local, a growth of 37.3 per cent. during the last decennium, or more than three times greater than the growth of population. In the private "professions," the clerical and legal callings (except in their humbler branches) fail to keep pace with the occupied population; medicine grows faster, though its largest growth is in nurses and other medical attendants. The teaching profession and engineering show a moderate increase, somewhat faster than the aggregate of the occupied classes. By far the largest proportional advance is found under the heads of " Art, Music, and Drama," and "Exhibitions and Games," while the smaller group entitled "Literary and Scientific" also grows apace. In other words, the classes subsidiary to the liberal professions and the classes engaged in catering to luxuries and recreations grow fastest among the " professions."

---

[1] See Cd. 2174, p. 132.

25

Domestic service is declining in its proportionate employment, chiefly through the opportunities open to women to undertake industrial employment, partly also through the raising of the "school age." In the twenty years from 1881 to 1901 female domestic servants increased by only 8.2 per cent., while the entire population advanced 25.2 per cent.

One of the plainest and most considerable tendencies is the rapid growth of commercial occupations of almost every class. The "commercial" group in the English census consists almost entirely of clerks, accountants, brokers, agents, travellers, auctioneers, and persons engaged in banking and insurance. The main body of merchants, salesmen and buyers, and most retailers are relegated to the branches of "industry" which are concerned with the goods they handle. This prevents the census from affording exact or full measurement of the increase of commercial occupations. But in recent decades the rate of growth of this class has far exceeded that of the "industrial" class, giving a rate of increase of 42.8 per cent. for 1881-91, and 44.6 per cent. for 1891-1901. In ordinary commerce the growth of commercial clerks and travellers is respectively 47.1 per cent. and 46 per cent. during the last decade, or about four times as fast as the growth of the occupied population. Banking, broking, and finance agencies have increased during the same period 43.1 per cent., while insurance has grown no less than 79.4 per cent.

Although it is found impossible so far to separate dealers from makers as to present a faithful account of employment in retail trade, enough figures are available to make it certain that the retail trading occupations are growing faster than the "making" parts of the industries.

In his analyses of the censuses from 1841 to 1881 Mr. Charles Booth shows a very considerable advance in the proportionate importance of dealing:—

1841	...	...	...	...	5.3 per cent.
1851	...	...	...	...	6.5 ,,
1861	...	...	...	...	7.1 ,,
1871	...	...	...	...	7.8 ,,
1881	...	...	...	...	7.8 ,,

The recent census, making a cautious estimate of retail

trade, reaches the figure 9.5, giving the aggregate of 1,358,500 as covering the shopkeeping classes.

The census for 1891, comparing a number of retail trades where the dealers are separated from makers, showed an increase of 27.9, as compared with an increase of 15.1 for the whole occupied population.

Extracting from the comparative table of occupations for the last three censuses[1] such figures of retail dealers as are clearly distinguished under the several industrial sub-orders, we reach the following result, which may be taken as fairly representative, from the varieties of retail business it includes:—

	1881	1891	1901
Persons occupied	609,100	794,300	922,750

Regarding the commercial and industrial classes from the standpoint of the census, we perceive that the rate of growth of the former is considerably and persistently higher than that of the latter. If the retailers were taken out of the industrial class and put into the commercial, the more rapid growth of "dealers" or "distributors," as compared with "makers" or "producers," would be still more striking.

Turning now to the industrial group, which includes manufactures, mines, and the building trades, we find that though the whole class shows a considerable and continuous increase in proportion of employment, that increase is chiefly attributable to mining and building. Taking manufactures in the usual signification of that term, we do not find them gaining in the proportion of employment they afford during recent decades. Mr. Booth's recent investigations[2] show that, while the proportion grew up to 1861, it declined from that date to 1881.

His percentages for persons employed in manufactures are as follows:—

1841	27.1 per cent.
1851	32.7 "
1861	33.0 "
1871	31.6 "
1881	30.7 "

---

[1] Cd. 2174, Table 34.   [2] *Occupations of the People.*

Though recent census reports do not present the returns in a form which enables us to continue Mr. Booth's tabulation, a table comparing the censuses of 1881, 1891, and 1901 enables us, by extracting the distinctively manufacturing groups, to perceive that manufactures (whether building be excluded or included) do not engage any appreciable increase of the proportion of employed persons.

The percentages relative to the total population over ten years of age are as follows :—

	1881	1891	1901
Manufactures (excluding building)	21.54	21.89	21.73
Manufactures (including building)	25.50	25.49	26.18

If the dealing classes, included here, were left out, it seems probable that the decline shown by Mr. Booth to have taken place between 1861 and 1881 would be proved to have continued.

§ 2. A closer examination of the changes of employment in the several groups of manufactures shows that while manufactures as an aggregate are nearly stationary in the proportion of employment they afford, some sorts are advancing, others declining.

The orders which show the greatest decline are textiles and dress. While metal, ships, pottery, wood, food, etc., show a moderate advance, precious metals and instruments, vehicles, chemicals, printing, show a great increase. A still closer examination into the sub-orders of the census returns shows that the foundational and the staple processes of manufacture are stagnant or declining in importance, while those concerned with the finishing processes of manufactures, especially those concerned with the manufacture of more highly specialised articles, are increasing. In the metal trades, while the more fundamental and general branches, classed as "iron and steel," show an advance of only 10.3 per cent. in the employment they afford in the period 1891-1901, the sub-order engineering and machine-making shows an advance of 67.4 per cent.,[1] while the trades connected with the manufacture of brass, wire, and electro-plate goods, show large gains. Electrical apparatus and various species of scientific, surgical, and musical

---

[1] Some of this increase, however, must be imputed to greater precision in the census return.

instruments, together with the trades generally classed with jewellery, illustrate the same tendency in the metal industries for the finer and later processes to absorb a larger share of the occupation.

The order "paper, prints, books" shows the same tendency. The most rapid growth is in the processes of printing, lithography, bookbinding, etc.; the least rapid in the papermaking industry.

In the textile industry, amid a general decline of the staple branches of the spinning and weaving trades, the only group which holds its own is that employed on minor manufactures, "hemp, jute, cocoa fibre, rope, mat, canvas, sailcloth." The order "dress" would have shown a positive decline in the numbers employed between 1891 and 1901 had it not been sustained by the inclusion of various "dealing" and small miscellaneous manufacturing trades. All the staple trades here also show a marked decline in the rate of growth. In the "food" order, again, the most conspicuous gains are in confectionery, jams, pickles, spices, mineral waters, and in other trades where "making" is weighted by the inclusion of dealers. In "spirituous liquors, board, and lodging," the manufacturing processes fail to keep pace with the population in the employment they afford; the only real advances are in the mercantile and retail processes of distribution. Jewellery, printing, jam and pickles, motor cars, electrical apparatus, oilcloths, ginger-beer, india-rubber, drugs, explosives, housefittings and decorations are instances of rapidly-advancing manufactures from the standpoint of employment.

Two important groups of "making" trades which exhibit a most marked advance require separate notice.

First, the group of trades connected with houses, their building and furnishing. The greater mobility of the population, the increase of great towns, the demand for larger and better housing, the development of public buildings for educational and other public purposes have bred a great demand for building labour, while the comparatively meagre use of machinery and substitution of machine-formed for hand-formed materials has obliged this demand to be met by a great increase in the supply of labour. Though the figures of the last two censuses are vitiated for exact comparison by the exclusion in the former of large numbers of "general labourers" included in the latter, the fact that the number of houses, built or building, had increased by 15.5 per cent. between 1891 and 1901 is a sufficient testimony to the progress of this industry. Under the general head of building are also included "works of construction and roads," industries in large measure subsidiary to the transport trade.

The second of these great progressive groups of industry is that concerned with the manufacture of vehicles for land or water carriage. The growth of land vehicles, including, of course, the new cycle and motor car trades, greatly surpasses even the growth of the shipbuilding trades. The following figures show the increase of occupation per million of the population (over ten years of age) during the last two decades :—

	1881	1891	1901
Vehicles ...	3,280	3,694	4,679
Ships and boats ...	2,801	3,162	3,421

This great advance of the ship and vehicle industries serves to introduce one of the most significant movements of occupation, the enormous rise of the transport order. If we add to the conveyance heading of the census certain groups of workers engaged in or contributing to the railway service, we find that the percentage for the last three decades stands thus :—

1881		1891		1901	
4.4	...	4.9	...	5.5	
1851	...	...	...	4.1	per cent.
1861	...	...	...	4.6	,,
1871	...	...	...	4.9	,,
1881	...	...	...	5.6	,,

Each sub-order of the conveyance industries shows a signal advance in the amount of employment, except the sub-order "on seas, rivers, and canals," where there is a slight decline in absolute numbers during the twenty years. This decline of British employment, however, is attended by a considerable growth of foreigners employed in British ships, the total increase from 1887 to 1902 being considerably faster than the increase of tonnage.[2]

---

[1] Mr. Booth's different classification of transport in his analyses, 1851-81, includes elements omitted here.

[2] Statistical Abstract, Cd. 1727, p. 193.

§ 3. Statistics of occupations in the United States exhibit many of the same broad tendencies as those of Great Britain, a decline in the proportion of agricultural employment, a large advance in the professional classes, in commerce and the professions, a great development of mining, and during the last decade a stoppage of the earlier rise in the proportion of manufacturing and mechanical classes.

The following table marks the broadest lines of change:—

PERCENTAGES OF TOTAL EMPLOYED POPULATION.

	1880	1890	1900
Agriculture	44.3	37.7	35.7
Professions	3.5	4.1	4.3
Domestic and personal service ...	19.7	18.6	19.2
Trade and transportation	10.7	14.6	16.4
Manufactures and mechanical pursuits	21.8	25.0	24.4

Many of the more detailed changes resemble those which are occurring in England.

In the professions there is the same abnormal advance of the teaching, medical, and legal classes. The increase of the commercial classes is marked especially in employments connected with banking and insurance, and by an enormous rise in the number of clerks, bookkeepers, accountants, and commercial travellers. Most of the groups engaged in the conveyance of persons, goods, and news show an abnormal increase, especially those connected with street traffic, telegraphic and telephonic services. Traders, wholesale and retail, do not, however, advance so rapidly as in England.

In the manufacturing and other productive industries the most rapid recent advance is in the iron, steel, and machinery trades, in cotton, hosiery, and silk, in paper and printing, glass, oil, chemicals, and a few minor manufactures. Among the manufactures which decline in the proportion of employment they afford are many of the building and food trades, brewing and distilling, watch and clock-making, and precious metals, and various textile trades. An absolute decline in employment between 1891 and 1901 is recorded in boot and shoemaking and the general leather trade, in woollen and carpet manufacture, and in most of the lumber manufactures, bricks, tiles, and milling. Mining shows an immense increase, rising in ten years from 387,000 to 564,000.

The only available comparison of the movements of occupations in France, as afforded in the censuses of 1866 and 1896, exhibits the same general trend :—

Occupations.[1]	Numbers.		Percentages.	
	1866	1896	1866	1896
Agriculture	6,195,329[2] (7,200,000)	8,421,319	52	47
Industry	4,715,805	6,373,239	34	35
Commerce	572,816	916,532	4	5
Professions (various) and transport	488,630	971,433	3	5
Liberal professions ...	914,034	1,405,382	7	8

The rapid advance made by the "professional" classes, liberal or industrial, the commercial and transport classes, and in manufactures by the metal and food industries, is exhibited by a closer analysis of these general figures.

The change of occupations in Germany is exhibited in a comparison of the results of the two great industrial censuses of 1882 and 1895:—[3]

Occupations.	Numbers.		Percentages.	
	1882	1895	1882	1895
Agriculture and fishing	8,236,496	8,292,692	46.7	39.9
Industry and mining ...	6,396,465	8,281,220	36.2	39.9
Trade and transport ...	1,570,318	2,338,511	8.9	11.2
Domestic callings ...	397,582	432,491	2.2	2.07
Professions, military and civil	1,031,147	1,425,961	5.8	6.8
	17,632,008	20,770,875		
Unoccupied	1,354,486	2,142,683		

[1] Table compiled from the *Résultats Statistiques de Recensement,* Tome iv., 1901.

[2] In order to compare 1866 with 1896 about one million domestic employees must be accredited to the earlier year.

[3] *Statistiche Jahrbucher,* 1885 and 1904.

The detailed figures exhibit a striking parallel to the larger changes of occupations exhibited by our analysis of the English censuses, the same great advance in the mining, metal, building industries, in transport and dealing, in chemicals, printing and art trades, and in insurance; while textiles and clothing show a relative decline, and agriculture is virtually stationary in the absolute, and rapidly retrogressive in the proportionate, employment it affords.

By way of comparing the four largest and most advanced industrial countries with less developed countries, we may take the following official tables exhibiting the tendencies of occupations in Austria and Sweden :—

	AUSTRIA.	Percentages.	
		1890.	1900.
Agriculture		62.5 ...	58.2
Manufactures		21.2 ...	22.3
Trade and Commerce		6.2 ...	7.3
Official and Professional Service ...		10.1 ...	12.2
		100.0	100.0

	SWEDEN.	Percentages.	
	1880.	1890.	1900.
Agriculture and Fishing ...	71.87 ...	60.92 ...	55.32
Industry	14.71 ...	22.72 ...	27.08
Trade and Transport ...	5.06 ...	8.92 ...	10.47
Public Service, etc. (including professions) ...	8.36 ...	7.44 ...	7.13
	100.0	100.0	100.0

§ 4. In all these countries the statistics of occupations point to certain common tendencies :—

1. A relative decline in the importance of agriculture, a rapid positive decline in free-trade England with its earlier development of capitalistic industry and its dense population, a considerable relative decline in each of the other countries, irrespective of tariff policy, density of population, land tenure or manufacturing development. Agricultural protection, combined with a large retention of small land-owners as in France and Germany, the possession of a large export trade in agricultural produce, as in the United States, retard, but do not cancel, the operation of the tendency.

2. An abnormally rapid growth of the transport and distributive trades (wholesale and retail) with the building, car-making, electric, and other manufacturing industries subsidiary to transport and distribution.

3. Wherever large deposits of coal and iron exist a great development of employment in mines.

4. A relative decline of the staple or fundamental manufacturing industries, especially the textile and dressmaking, as compared with the manufactures of final commodities for consumption. Luxury trades, or trades subsidiary to the arts and professions, present an increasing proportion of occupation.

5. In almost every instance a large, rapid increase in the proportion of the occupied population engaged in public services, professions, and other branches of non-material production.

6. An increase in the proportion of the retired or unoccupied classes.

Now it is evident that these movements are in part the expression of the evolution of capitalism through improved economies of machinery and the attendant organisation of labour. Where machinery is most perfected and most generally applied, as in the leading branches of the textile and other staple manufactures, such as milling, we find everywhere a relative, in several instances a positive, decline in the quantity of occupation, notwithstanding the existence of a large export trade in these articles. The minor industries, especially those concerned with the supply of luxuries, and other articles, the demand for which fluctuates with fashion, season, or taste, or where rapid changes in the methods of production preclude the large use of expensive machinery, absorb a larger and larger proportion of the manufacturing classes. But manufacture, as a whole, does not advance at all, or at any rate not so fast as commerce and transport. This is evidently due in part to the fact that machinery and the routine economies of modern capitalism are less applicable to these latter industries. Commerce, wholesale or retail, employs a much smaller amount of fixed capital than manufactures, and although the proportion of fixed capital in the shape of machinery is very large in the main branches of the transport trades, only a comparatively small proportion of the employees in these trades are directly engaged in operating machinery, the great majority being occupied in subsidiary operations to which machine economy is but slightly applicable. The great proportionate increase of mining and building employment in most countries is also attributable in part to the comparatively small use of machinery in these operations, though it is possible that the use of coal-cutting and other machinery of digging and haulage for mining, and the use of prepared steel, wood, and other machine-made materials in the building trades, may reduce the growth of direct employment in these industries.

The rapid growth of the professions, and of most of the other classes engaged in producing "services" or non-material forms of wealth, is evidently due in large measure to the inherently individual economy of these modes of production.

The decline in the proportion of domestic service to the total of the occupied classes, exhibited in England and America, seems at first sight inconsistent with the attribution of so much importance to the capitalist economy. But reflection will show that while something may here be attributed to the reduction in supply for domestic services arising from the increased use of women in industrial and commercial occupations, a more direct source of the decline is the removal from the home, and the performance by machine-industry, of many of those processes of washing, cooking, cleaning, dressmaking, etc., which were formerly done at home. This is one of the most obvious economies of that city life which is lived by an ever larger proportion of our population.

§ 5. The positive or relative decline of agricultural occupations cannot, however, be adequately explained by the growth of machinery and scientific methods. Nor is it in the main attributable to dependence upon foreign countries for food supplies, for the United States, a great food exporter, and France, Germany, and Sweden, all of which are almost self-supporting in agricultural products, show rapid reduction in the proportionate employment in agriculture. Against the economies of machinery and of more scientific farming must be set the necessity of having recourse to less fertile lands to meet the growing demands of consumers.

In order to explain the decline of agricultural employment we must look not so much to changes in production as to changes in consumption. Every rise of the standard of consumption for a class or a nation is attended by a fall in the proportion which food and other products of the soil bear to the total of consumption. Whereas in the early decades of the nineteenth century food swallowed up almost the entire income of the poorer sections of the working classes, and was by far the largest factor in the expenditure of the upper working and lower middle classes, its present place in the standard of comfort of these classes, though important, is much smaller. If any accurate comparative statistics of consumption for the entire English nation were available, it is certain that the proportion of the general income of the nation expended upon food and other raw materials obtained by agriculture would show a rapid diminution during the last eighty years. What is true of food is also true of many sorts of manufactured goods, as the standard of comfort of large classes of a nation advances further. Though for the working classes the earlier advances of real wages from a bare subsistence economy may be taken almost entirely in demand for better and more various foods, and for larger quantities of furniture, clothing, and other manufactured goods, further advances exhibit a larger expenditure upon recreation, travel, education, professional services; and the middle and well-to-do classes spend a still larger share of their growing incomes upon non-material consumption and upon those more highly-finished or artistic forms of material wealth which derive a smaller proportion of their value from the extractive and mechanical processes. The paper and printing trades, as a half-way house between material and intellectual commodities, advancing in every country far faster than the occupied population, in spite of their great use of machine economies, may be cited as a convincing instance of the change in consumption. If improved education ever brings a better economy of reading, substituting a qualitative for a quantitative consumption, a diminution of the paper and print occupations may follow, accompanied by an increase of occupation in the higher non-material arts of literary and scientific interpretation, or even by a substitution of the non-economic art of thinking.

The rapid growth of the professional and commercial

classes is partly attributable to the fact that a larger number of people have more money to spend upon the services rendered by these less mechanical occupations. But partly the growth of these classes may be regarded as an artificial inflation, due to a combination of economic and social circumstances. The superior social consideration attaching to a professional career, or conversely the dislike of a life of manual or mental routine in manufacture or commerce among an increasing middle class, together with a great expansion of the means of professional education, leads to a congestion of many of the professions and to a growth of what is sometimes called an "intellectual proletariat," a struggling, ill-paid, and irregularly employed mass of qualified teachers, doctors, engineers, journalists, and other writers.

While a large increase of wholesale and retail dealers, agents, travellers, and other commercial classes is required for the improved distribution of the growing quantities of cheapened material products, the actual increase of many of these classes seems greatly in excess of this requirement. The increasing difficulty experienced in setting up for one-self with any prospect of success in a manufacturing busi-ness, as a farmer or other independent producer, drives larger and larger numbers of men into commercial pursuits, where with smaller and less specialised training they can struggle to earn a living by cutting into one or other of the distributive processes, as merchant, broker, retailer, or agent for some mercantile or insurance business. It is easier to enter the distributive competition with a chance of getting away some business from another firm than to enter a productive business. While therefore it is doubtless true that an excessive amount of productive power exists in many of our manufacturing industries, the waste is far less than is caused in the mercantile and retail processes by the reckless multiplication of distributors.

§ 6. The normal development of occupations for a nation passing through the era of modern capitalism would seem to be as follows:—Beginning at a point where the large majority of the population were occupied in or about agri-culture, and a small minority occupied exclusively in manu-facture or in commerce, it would proceed to provide more and more occupation in the mining and staple manufacturing industries, especially in the main textile and metal trades. Proceeding further it would effect great economies in the fundamental manufactures, or would become a large importer of the cruder manufactures, and would employ itself more largely in the final stages of manufacturing commodities for consumers, in novel industries concerned with special tastes and luxuries. Transport and commercial operations will then come to play a greater part, and the finance aspect of business life to engage an increased amount of energy. While "dealing" becomes relatively more important than "making" in regard to the occupation it affords, the production and distribution of non-material as compared with material goods grows apace—that is to say, the arts and professions (including the art of Government) engage a larger share of the population. When the general standard of consumption for the great mass of the people has reached a point where the more urgent needs of food, clothing, housing are satisfied, all further rises in the standard represent a larger proportion of demand for recreation, education, professional services and other immaterial forms of wealth. How rapidly a national economy will follow this line of progress depends largely upon special circumstances. Among these the most important are the relative power of the working classes to secure a share of the increased material wealth which capitalist methods tend to produce, and the freedom and expansibility of foreign markets. Where a large expansion of home markets for agricultural and manufacturing products is furnished by a rising effective demand on the part of the main body of the nation, and where at the same time a larger command of foreign markets is obtained, the proportion of employment in the productive arts may remain large for a considerable period. The rapidly expanding markets for British manufactures during the first two-thirds of the nineteenth century served to maintain a very large proportion of the people in productive occupations in spite of the great economies of labour effected by machinery. Where a rigorous protective policy prevails, as in the United States, Germany, and France, the rate of displacement of agricultural and manufacturing occupations by commercial and professional is considerably slower. These nations, not entering the era of machine economy for manufactures until half-a-century later than Great Britain, have been enabled to furnish occupation to a growing proportion of their populations in the manufacturing arts, in part displacing by home products the former imports from Great Britain, in part providing for the early increments of a material standard of comfort for their growing populations.

Where a nation enters the modern capitalist economy with a low standard of material comfort for the masses, a growing population and a protective system, it may postpone for a long time the diminution of agricultural and manufacturing occupation which is an inevitable tendency of an advanced economy.

§ 7. The bearing of this upon international trade is obvious. Although the number of wants common to members of different nations constantly increases, and an international standard of comfort thus established furnishes an ever-growing basis of international division of labour and exchange, very definite limits exist at any time to the kinds of national wealth really available for international trade. While improved and cheapened methods of storage and transport continually increase the quantity of foods, raw materials, and manufactured goods available for wide international distribution, an ever-increasing proportion of national energy is put into those final processes of preparing these material forms of wealth for consumers, and into the processes of distribution, which are of necessity confined to national industry. Again, every increase of the transport trades, and every growth in the proportionate importance of the arts, professions, and other branches of non-material production, further restricts the proportion of the national wealth adapted to international exchange. Where a nation is throwing an increasing proportion of its energies into these occupations, the proportion of its aggregate demands which is of a nature to be supplied from extra-national sources will diminish. It by no means follows that the volume and value of its imports is diminished either absolutely or in proportion to its total expenditure. Such a nation may, for a time at any rate, rely to an increasing extent upon foreigners for its supplies of food, raw material, and cruder manufactures. So long as it has large access to the markets of less advanced nations, it may displace its own agriculture and even its manufactures by imported goods consumed in rises of the material standard of comfort of the people, and paid for to an increasing extent by higher types of manufacture and by various sorts of services, commercial and financial.

While there is no theoretic limit thus assigned to the growth of an import trade which may more and more displace the more primitive home industries, it is to be expected that, as a diminishing proportion of the national consumption takes shape in cruder commodities, so in time the growth of the aggregate import trade will be checked, a diminishing proportion of the national income being expended upon buying foreign goods. This decline in the relative importance of foreign trade, so far from implying a fall of national prosperity, would imply an advance, signifying, as it would, that such a nation has become rich enough to spend a larger share of its income upon higher forms of wealth.

Great Britain is the nation which has gone furthest in this evolution. The history of her foreign trade during the nineteenth century shows her during the first half increasing the value of her import and export trade at a pace enormously more rapid than the growth of her aggregate income, foreign trade assuming an ever greater importance. About 1860 the pace of growth of foreign trade began to slacken, advancing at a pace which but slightly exceeded the growth of the aggregate income of the nation. After 1885 a slow decline in the rate of growth as compared with national income is discernible. It seems likely that Great Britain has already passed the turning-point in the development of foreign trade, and that in the future, while the volume and even the value of her imports (and therefore of her exports) will show a continual advance, those imports will constitute a slowly diminishing proportion of the annual aggregate of commodities and services consumed by the nation.

The statistics of occupations among other advanced industrial nations indicate that, though their later development may keep them for some time further in the era of rapidly expanding foreign trade, the time will come when they also will be subject to the same law, the aggregate of their national industry growing faster than their foreign trade.

CHAPTER XVII.

CIVILISATION AND INDUSTRIAL DEVELOPMENT.

§ 1. Modern industrial societies have hitherto secured to a very inadequate extent the services which modern machinery and methods of production are capable of rendering. The actual growth of material wealth, however great, has been by no means commensurate with the enormously increased powers of producing material commodities afforded by the discoveries of modern science, and the partial utilisation of these discoveries has been attended by a very unequal distribution of the advantages of this increase in the stock of common knowledge and control of nature. Moreover, as an offset against the growth of material wealth, machinery has been a direct agent in producing certain material and moral maladies which impair the health of modern industrial communities.

The unprecedented rapidity and irregularity of the discovery and adoption of the new methods made it impossible for the structure of industrial society to adjust itself at once to the conditions of the new environment. The maladies and defects which we detect in modern industry are but the measure of a present maladjustment.

The progressive adjustment of structure to environment in the unconscious or low-conscious world is necessarily slow. But where the conscious will of man, either as an individual or as a society, can be utilised for an adjusting force, the pace of progress may be indefinitely quickened. A strongly-rooted custom in a man yields very slowly to the pressure of changed circumstances which make it useless or harmful, unless the man consciously recognises the inutility of the custom and sets himself to root it out and plant another custom in its place. So the slowness of this work of industrial adjustment has been in no small measure due to the lack of definite realisation by the members of modern communities of the need and importance of this adjustment. A society which should bring its conscious will to bear upon the work of constructing new social and industrial forms to fit the new economic conditions, may make a progress which, while rapid, may yet be safe, because it is not a speculative progress, but one which is guided in its line of movement by precedent changes of environment.

Regarding, then, this conscious organised endeavour, enlightened and stimulated by a fuller understanding of industrial forces in their relation to human life, as a determinant of growing value in the industrial evolution of the future, it may properly belong to a scientific study of modern industry to seek to discover how the forces of conscious reform can reasonably work in relation to the economic forces whose operations have been already investigated.

In other words, what are the chief lines of economic change required to bring about a readjustment between modern methods of production and social welfare? The answer to this question requires us to amplify our interpretation of the industrial evolution of the past century, by producing into the future the same lines of development, that they may be justified by the appearance of consistency with some rational social end. The most convenient, and perhaps the safest way to meet this demand is to indicate, with that modesty which rightly belongs to prophecy, some of the main reforms which seem to lie upon the road of industrial progress, rendered subordinate to larger human social ends.

§ 2. So far as the waste of economic maladjustment consists in the excessive or defective application of various kinds of productive force at different points of industry, upon the existing basis of individual initiative and control, the reforms which are desirable must be considered as contributing to the more complete establishment of "free" competition in industry.

The complete breakdown of all barriers which impede the free flow of commerce and the migration of capital and labour, the fullest and widest dissemination of industrial information, are necessary to the attainment of the individualistic ideal of free trade. Perfect transparency of industrial operations, perfect fluidity of labour and of wealth would effect incalculably great economies in the production of commercial wealth. The free-trader, in his concentration upon the achievement of the latter economy, has generally failed to do full justice to the importance of the former. He has indeed to some limited extent recognised the value of accurate and extended industrial information as the intellectual basis of free trade. But, in common with most economists, he has failed to carry this consideration far enough. It is generally admitted that the increased pub-

lication of accounts and quotations of stock, springing out
of the extension of joint-stock enterprise, the growth of
numerous trade journals, the collection and dissemination
of industrial facts by government bureaux and private
statisticians, are serviceable in many ways. But the extreme
repugnance which is shown towards all endeavours to
extend the compulsory powers of acquiring information by
the state, the extreme jealousy with which the rights of private
information are maintained, show how inadequately the true
character of modern industry is grasped. In the complexity
of modern commerce it should be recognised that there is
no such thing as a "self-regarding" or a private action. No
fact bearing on prices, wages, profits, methods of production, etc., merely concerns a single firm or a single body
of workers. Every industrial action, however detailed in
character, however secretly conducted, has a public import,
and necessarily affects the actions and interests of innumerable persons. Indeed it is often precisely in the knowledge
of those matters regarded as most private, and most carefully
secreted, that the public interest chiefly lies. Yet so firmly
rooted in the business mind is the individualistic conception
of industry, that any idea of a public development of those
important private facts upon which the credit of a particular
firm is based, would appear to destroy the very foundation
of the commercial fabric. But, although in the game of
commerce a single firm which played its hand openly while
others kept theirs well concealed might suffer failure, it is
quite evident that the whole community interested in the
game would gain immensely if all the hands were on the
table. Many, if not most, of the great disasters of modern
commercial societies are attributable precisely to the fact that
the credit of great business firms, which is pre-eminently an
affair of public interest, is regarded as purely private before
the crash. As industry grows more and more complex, so
the interest of the public and of an ever-wider public in
every industrial action grows apace, and a correspondingly
growing recognition of this public interest, with provision
for its security, will be found necessary. So far as the
natural changes of industrial structure in the private business fail to provide the requisite publicity, the exercise of
direct public scrutiny must come to be enforced. The
reluctance shown alike by bodies of employers and of

workers to divulge material facts is in large measure due to the false ideas they have conceived as to the nature of industrial activity, which education can do something to remove, but which, if not removed, must be over-ruled in the public interest.

§ 3. It must not, however, be supposed that the most thorough transparency of industry, any more than the removal of the political barriers which prevent Free Trade, would tend to bring about the desirable adjustment between the healthy social organism and the environment of machine-production. Full free trade would supply, quicken, and facilitate the operation of those large economic forces which we have seen at work : the tendency of capital to gravitate into larger and fewer masses, localised where labour can be maintained upon the most economical terms : a corre-spondent but slower and less complete organisation of labour in large masses : the flow of labouring population into towns, together with a larger utilisation of women and (where per-mitted) children for industrial work : a growing keenness of antagonism as the mass of the business-unit is larger, and an increased expenditure of productive power upon aggressive commercial warfare : the growth of monopolies springing from natural, social, or economic sources, con-ferring upon individuals or classes the power to consume without producing, and by their consumption to direct the quantity and character of large masses of labour.

The complete realisation of full free trade in all directions has no power whatever to abate the activity of these forces, and would only serve to bring their operation into more signal and startling prominence.

For the waste of periodic over-production visible in trade depression, for the sufferings caused by ever larger oscilla-tions in prices and great irregularity of employment of capital and labour, for the specific evils of long hours or excessive intensity of labour, dangerous and unwholesome conditions of employment, increased employment of women and children, and growth of large-city life, freedom of trade conjoined with publicity of business operations can furnish no remedies.

It has been seen that these injuries to individuals and groups of individuals, and through them to society, arise naturally and necessarily from the unfettered operation of the enlightened self-interest of individuals and groups of individuals engaged in obtaining for themselves, by the freest use of industrial means available, the largest quantity of money.

So far as these evils are in form or in magnitude the peculiar products of the last two centuries, they are in large measure traceable to methods of production controlled by machinery, and to the social estimate of machine-products which gives machinery this controlling power.

If this is so, such progress as shall abate these evils and secure for humanity the uses of machinery without the abuses will lie in two directions, each of which deserves consideration : (1) an adequate social control over machine-production ; (2) an education in the arts of consumption such as may assign proper limits to the sphere of machine-production.

§ 4. That machinery subject to the unrestricted guidance of the commercial interests of an individual or a class cannot be safely trusted to work for the general welfare, is already conceded by all who admit the desirability or necessity of the restrictive legislation of Factory Acts, Mines Regulation Acts, and the large growth of public provisions for guarding against economic, hygienic, and other injuries arising from the conditions of modern industrial life.

These provisions, whether designed directly to secure the interests of a class of employees, as in the case of Factory Acts, or to protect the consuming public, as in the case of Adulteration Acts, must be regarded as involving an admission of a genuine antagonism between the apparent interests of individuals and of the whole community, which it is the business of society to guard against.

All this legislation is rightly interpreted as a restriction of the freedom of individual industry under modern methods of production, required in the public interest. Uncontrolled machine-production would in some cases force children of six or eight years to work ten hours a day in an unhealthy factory, would introduce suddenly a host of Chinese or other " cheap " workers to oust native labour accustomed to a higher standard of comfort, would permit an ingenious manufacturer to injure the consumer by noxious adulteration of his goods, would force wages to be paid by orders upon shops owned or controlled by employers, would oblige workers to herd together in dens of infection, and to breed physical and moral diseases which would injure the body politic. The need of a growing social control over modern machine-production, in cases where that production is left in the main to the direction of individual enterprise, is admitted on every side, though the development of that control has been uneven and determined by the pressure of concrete grievances rather than by the acceptance of any distinct theory of public responsibility.

Other limitations upon individual freedom of industry imply a clearer recognition of the falsehood of the *laissez faire* position. The undertaking by the State or the Municipality, or other units of social life, of various departments of industry, such as the railways, telegraphs, post-offices, is a definite assertion that, in the supply of the common services rendered by these industries, the competition of private interests cannot be relied upon to work for the public good.

§ 5. The industries which the State either limits or controls in the interest either of a body of workers or of the consuming public may be regarded as passing from a private competitive condition to a public non-competitive condition. If therefore we wish to ascertain how far and in what directions social control of modern production will proceed, we shall examine those industries which already exhibit the collective character. We shall find that they are of two kinds—(1) industries where the size and structure of the "business" is such that the protection afforded by competition to the consuming public and to the workers has disappeared, or is in frequent abeyance; (2) industries where the waste and damage of excessive competition outweighs the loss of enterprise caused by a removal or restriction of the incentive of individual gain. As we have seen in the analysis of "trusts," these two characteristics, wasteful competition and monopoly, are often closely related, the former signifying the process of intense struggle, the object and ultimate issue of which is to reach the quiet haven of monopoly. Generally speaking, social control in the case of over-competing industries is limited to legislative enactments regarding conditions of employment and quality of goods. Only those industries tend to pass under public administration where the monopoly is of an article of general and necessary consumption, and where, therefore, a raising of prices considerably above the competition rate would not succeed in evoking effective competition. Since the general tendency of industry, so far as it falls under modern economies of machinery and method, is either towards wasteful competition or towards monopoly, it is to be expected that there will be a continual expansion of State interference and State undertakings. This growing socialisation of industry must be regarded as the natural adjustment of society to the new conditions of machine-production. As under the economies of machine-production the business-unit, the mass of capital and labour forming a single " firm " or " business," grows larger in size and more potent in its operations, the social disturbances which it can occasion by its private activity, the far-reaching and momentous results of its strain of competition, the probability of an anti-social exercise of "monopolic" power over the whole or part of its market-area, will of necessity increase. The railway and shipping industries, for example, in countries like England and the United States, have already reached a stage of industrial development when the social danger arising from an arbitrary fixing of rates by a line or a "pool" of lines, from a strike or lock-out of dockers or railway men, is gaining keener recognition every year. The rapidly growing organisation of both capital and labour, especially in the fundamental industries of coal, iron, and machine-making, in the machine-transport industries, and the most highly evolved manufactories, gives to a body of employers or employed, or to a combination of both, the power at any moment to paralyse the whole or a large portion of the entire trade of a country in pursuit of some purely private interest or resentment, or in the acquisition of some strategical position, which shall enable them to strengthen their competing power or gain a monopoly. Although the organisation of masses of capital and of labour may, as is often urged, make industrial strife less frequent, the effects of such strife upon the wider public, who have no opportunity of casting a vote for war or peace, are more momentous. Moreover, as these private movements of capital and labour proceed, the probability of combined action between employers and employed in a particular industry, to secure for themselves some advantages at the public expense, will be a factor of increasing importance in industrial evolution.

The Trade Union movement and the various growths of Industrial Partnership, valuable as they are from many points of view, furnish no remedies against the chief forms of economic monopoly and economic waste; they can only change the personality and expand the number of monopolists, and alter the character, not the quantity, of economic waste. Society has an ever-deepening and more vital interest in the economical management of the machinery of transport, and this interest is no whit more secure if the practical control of railways and docks were in the hands of the Dockers' Union or the Amalgamated Society of Railway Servants, or of a combined board of directors and trade union officials, than it is under present circumstances. On the contrary, an effective organisation of capital and labour in an industry would be more likely to pursue a policy opposed to the interests of the wider public than now, because such a policy would be far more likely to succeed.

§ 6. When it is said that modern industry is becoming essentially more collective in character and therefore demands collective control, what is meant is that under modern industrial development the interest of the industrial society as a whole, and of the consuming public in each piece of so-called private enterprise, is greater than it was ever before, and requires some guarantee that this interest shall not be ignored. Where the industry is of such a kind, and in such a stage of development, that keen competition without undue waste survives, this public interest can commonly be secured by the enactment of restrictive legislation. Where such partial control is insufficient to secure the social interest against monopoly or waste, State management, upon a national, municipal, or such other scale as is economically advisable, must take the place of a private enterprise which is dangerous to society. This necessity becomes obvious as soon as the notion of a business as being purely "private" or "self-regarding" in its character is seen to be directly negatived by an understanding of the complex social nature of every commercial act. So soon as the idea of a social industrial organism is grasped, the question of State interference in, or State assumption of, an industry becomes a question of social expediency—that is, of the just interpretation of the facts relating to the particular case. In large measure this social control is to be regarded, not as a necessary protection against the monopolic power of individuals, but as necessary for the security of individual property within the limits prescribed by social welfare. Modern machine-evolution, as is seen, permits and encourages the wanton invasion and destruction of forms of capital by the competition of new savings employed in an anti-social way. It likewise tends to the frequent destruction of the value of that labour power which is the sole property of the mass of workers. "The property which every man has in his own labour, as it is the original foundation, so it is the most sacred and inviolable."[1]

There are certain wastes of economic power involved in all competition; there are certain dangers of monopoly attaching to all private conduct of industry. Collective control deals with these wastes and dangers, adjusting itself to their extent and character.

§ 7. To the question how far and how rapidly may this extension of collective control proceed, no more definite answer is possible than this, that as a larger and larger amount of industry passes into the condition of the most highly evolved machine-industries of to-day, and develops along with the corresponding economies, corresponding dangers and wastes, larger portions will pass under restrictive legislation or State management.

The evolution in the structure of capitalist enterprise, while it breeds and aggravates the diseases of trade depression, sweating, etc., likewise prepares the way and facilitates the work of social control. It is easier to inspect a few large factories than many small ones, easier to arbitrate where capital and labour stands organised in large masses, easier to municipalise big joint-stock businesses in gas, water, or conveyance. Every legislative interference, in the way of inspection or minor control, quickens the evolution of an industry, and hastens the time when it acquires the position of monopoly which demands a fuller measure of control, and finally passes into the ranks of public industry.

Thus it would follow that, unless proceeding *pari passu* with this evolution there was a springing up or an expansion

[1] *Wealth of Nations*, p. 110.

of other industries not so amenable to large machine production, and therefore not prone to the dangers and wastes which appertain to it, collectivism would absorb an ever-increasing proportion of industrial effort.

§ 8. At present it appears that there are several classes of productive work which are not amenable to machine-economy. There is much work which, though it could be performed by machinery so far as technical character is concerned, cannot economically be undertaken in factories so long as large quantities of very cheap hand-labour are procurable. This class comprises the bulk of what are commonly called the "sweating" trades, conducted for the most part in the homes of the workers, or in small workshops. Most of these trades are rightly regarded as cases of "arrested development," in the sense that they are kept out of the main course of industrial evolution by certain special circumstances relating chiefly to the supply of cheap labour. The wasteful working of the industrial system even in its best-ordered parts, the irregular and incalculable changes by which quantities of skilled labour are supplanted by new machinery, ill-directed migration of labour from country to town and from foreign lands, the diminution of domestic work for women in the home, these and other movements feed the large industrial centres with quantities of unskilled and untrained labour which can be bought so cheaply that in the lowest grades of many industries it does not pay the capitalist *entrepreneur* to incur the initial cost of setting up expensive machinery and the risk of working it.

Not only in the manufactures but in other occupations this existence of a permanent pool of low-skilled, inefficient labour presents a grave obstacle to the social and moral order of industrial nations. Large masses of "general" or casual labourers, dockers, cheap commercial clerks, shop-assistants, etc., offer by their presence in the labour market an unsurmountable obstacle to the better organisation of the occupations to which they adhere. The low economic calibre of these grades of workers, their lack of skill, education, their low standard of consumption, keep alive a number of small, irregular, loosely-managed businesses, retarding the legitimate evolution of organised capitalism, and sustaining the most wasteful and degrading sorts of competition.

Economic and social progress demands the destruction of these arrested developments: sanitary and other humanitarian legislation should harry the sweating den; technical and general education should implant more skill and evoke more wants; trade-organisation, where practicable, should make for higher wages and other improved conditions of employment; labour colonies and a more enlightened poor-law administration should assist to drain these malarial marshes. The retarded or discarded growths of "sweating" trades involve social surgery for their removal, and the governmental "interference" it involves should rightly be distinguished from the "socialism" which consists in the conversion of private normally grown monopolies into public undertakings.

§ 9. But apart from these degraded survivals of pre-capitalist business, there are other kinds of work which remain outside of capitalist production, because they are from their nature or the necessary conditions of their performance not amenable to machine industry. In branches subsidiary to the great routine industries we have seen that much work of final production and of repair remains in small businesses, that a genuine and healthy survival of hand-labour may exist in trades too dependent upon fluctuating demands to enable them to pass under factory rule, and that where the irregularity of the material or of the conditions of work preclude full use of routine methods, as over a large part of agriculture, an economy of small-scale production survives.

Certain recent tendencies of mechanical development favour, and may even extend, these types of small industry. The extension of small-power machines and the cheaper distribution of electric power, under public ownership or control, might give a new independence to small masters in some of our manufactures; while greater facilities and cheapness of transport might substitute co-operation of small farmers for the centralising process even in cases where the latter is at present predominant.

These genuine survivals of small businesses in agriculture and the manufactures, as also in certain departments of commerce, are, as we have seen, attributable to elements of personal care, skill, and interest, which, forming important conditions of success, are found to outweigh the economies of large-scale production. They are, in fact, elements which distinguish the business where they are found from mechanical industry, and stamp upon it the character of an art.

Wherever these individual mental activities of workers play a considerable part the art-economy displaces the machine-economy. Such arts or crafts may often be far removed in their end or purpose from the fine arts that are concerned with producing objects of which the utility consists in their "beauty"; sometimes they may be exercised merely in getting common forms of "standardised" goods out of irregular or otherwise intractable materials, or in the skilled use of climate, soil, and other natural conditions; at other times the individuality of the worker is directed to meet some special need or taste of the consumer that belongs to a narrowly utilitarian order. But wherever these characteristics of an industry attain importance, the direct stream of tendency towards large capitalism and machine-economy is checked or reversed.

Although, as has been pointed out, the indirect control of the capitalist system over the surviving forms of small handicrafts, farming, retail distribution, and even over the professions and the fine arts, is sometimes very considerable, the survival of these large and even growing departments of industry in small business forms vitalised by individual qualities of workmanship is a phenomenon of supreme significance.

If, therefore, we provisionally accept the view which regards the large routine-businesses, where mechanical methods are dominant, as tending towards a condition where competition disappears and public control, ultimately public administration, become necessary, we must clearly recognise the existence of even larger domains of industrial activity which, not conforming to this economy, remain in a state of competition and of private enterprise.

Accepting this method of interpretation, we shall be disposed to regard those large routine-industries, where public control is growing tighter, and which are striving ever more successfully to eliminate competition, and to establish forms of trade agreement or combination, as destined to pass into the form of public industries.

§ 10. Our examination of tendencies in the more advanced

industrial countries enables us to designate pretty clearly the general outline of this "socialistic" movement. A more definite re-assertion of public ownership of the land as the chief source of the material and the power of industry, as well as the basis of the home, is making its way in various forms into the work of modern government. While the present movement as regards agricultural and urban lands is chiefly directed to securing for the public by taxation an increased share of land-values, the growing recognition of the needs of city life imposes everywhere more restrictions upon the private use of lands and an increased public ownership of land for special public purposes. In modern democratic countries an increased availability of land for small settlers, embodying the principle of equal access to the natural resources of the soil, is rapidly advancing as a public policy. Legal restrictions upon large estates or upon other wasteful or extortionate uses of land are a chief line of governmental action. But the growth of city life in populous countries is pressing the demands for a more rigorous control over urban areas which makes for public ownership of city land as the final security for public hygiene, convenience, æsthetics, and finance. How far the interference with private contract, through the establishment of land-courts and the utilisation of public credit for converting tenants into owners, may turn out to be the preparatory stage of a process of public ownership of agricultural lands, occupied by tenants whose payment for their land may be regarded indifferently as a tax or a rent, remains a question for answer in the near future.

In regard to the primary uses of land, practicable socialism may confine itself to securing for the State as large a share of the annual value of the land as it can safely take, and to imposing more stringent conditions upon its uses, while abstaining from any large exercise of public ownership and administration. The greater interest imparted to the public by modern industry in the limited mineral resources of land, taken in conjunction with the appearance of cartels, trusts, and other combinations for the capitalist control of mining industries, places the latter in the category of those industries which appear destined to pass into public enterprise, and the fact that in certain countries they are so owned and administered favours this interpretation of the tendency.

If we follow the general line of development indicated by our earlier analysis, we shall ascribe to collectivism also the administration of the chief modes of transport by land, and probably by water, the main systems of national and international highways. The greater part of the railways of the world are already public industries, and it is extremely unlikely that Great Britain and America, the two important exceptions, will long resist the demand for nationalisation.

That local transport, especially in city areas, is passing from private into public enterprise, *pari passu* with other local routine services, is already sufficiently evident. Although the energy of private capitalist companies has at present secured this field for private profitable enterprise in most cities of the United States and many of Great Britain, they cannot long hold a position which a wider survey of the civilised world shows to be a gross anomaly.

How far the nationalisation of manufacturing industry is likely to go, we have at present insufficient data for prophecy. If the prevalence of tariffs encourages the growth of strong industrial trusts within national areas, the instinct or necessity of public protection against these monopolies may compel civilised states to substitute public for private monopoly, and to embark upon those fundamental metal, and other manufactures which are vital factors in national industry and consumption. Such a step would, however, be prefaced by a series of experiments in taxation and control, through restrictive legislation affecting prices and conditions of employment. But while there is no early probability of modern industrial states engaging in manufactures (except for special purposes of revenue or public security) there is more likelihood of a powerful, new, direct public control over manufacturing industries being exercised through public ownership of manufacturing power. As electricity becomes more and more the source of industrial power for manufacturing as well as for transport services, the ownership and distribution of this power will more and more be recognised as a function which municipalities, or other larger public areas of government, must undertake. Whether this new industrial power continue to be generated from coal, or in some other way, its safe and economical production and distribution over local areas cannot be long entrusted to private companies. This socialisation of manufacturing power is likely long to ante-date any considerable socialisation of concrete manufacturing processes, and may possibly become so potent an instrument of public control as to render unnecessary public ownership and working of specific manufactures.

How far municipal or other public enterprise is likely to invade the distributing trades depends, in part, upon the rate at which the carrying trades generally pass into public trade, partly upon the success or failure of the numerous experiments in inspection which are at present regarded as sufficient safeguards of the public interest in many trades. Where, however, strong control over prices by local rings exists, or where inspection is proved inadequate to secure the public health against diseased or adulterated wares, new invasions upon the domain of private trade will occur.

The public abattoirs which already exist in many European cities may turn out to be the first stage in a public meat supply; municipal dairies and bakeries may displace private trade in bread and milk; while the present extortionate practices of rings of coal merchants would hardly be likely to survive public ownership and management of railroads. Though the general machinery of credit and insurance still remains for the most part in private businesses, considerable encroachments in the shape of State insurance and public savings banks have been made. Here, as in many other departments, the forward movement in many countries takes shape in municipalism rather than in nationalism, and municipal insurance schemes, banks, and pawnshops are occupying places of increased importance in the development of public city life.

It is very germane to our present outlook to recognise the supersession of private by public enterprise which is taking place in that department of production which we term the professions. The assumption of education as a chief function of the State is of course the most conspicuous instance of this tendency. In most European countries, however, the socialisation of medical services and of general hygiene is advancing at a considerable pace. Even in Great Britain the majority of our hospitals and infirmaries are publicly supported and managed, and public dispensaries play an increasing part in the hygienic machinery of the country. Though the socialisation of law, in the sense of free access to public advice and administration of justice, is very far from completion, certain notable advances have been made in most countries within recent times. In Great Britain the extension of law to cover new areas of controversy, reforms of procedure, as in bankruptcy and in the administration of Public Companies Acts, gratuitous legal advice of magistrates, criminal defences paid out of the public purse, and various other movements illustrate this slow, uneven, but continuous advance towards the fuller nationalisation of justice.

The routine trades or professions engaged in supplying common forms of recreation are also becoming socialised, partly as appendages of public education or of public hygiene. Art galleries, free libraries, public parks and gardens are but a few of the embellishments of civic life which form important bases of public professions and industries.

§ 11. We now stand face to face with the main objection so often raised against all endeavours to remedy industrial and social diseases by the expansion of public control. Competition and the zest of individual gain, it is urged, furnish the most effective incentive to enterprise and discovery. Assuming that society were structurally competent to administer industry officially, the establishment of industrial order would be the death-blow to industrial progress. The strife, danger, and waste of industrial competition are necessary conditions to industrial vitality.

How much force do these objections contain in the light of the information provided by our study of industrial evolution? It should be recognised at the outset that the economic individualist is not a conservative, defending an established order and pointing out the dangers attending proposed innovations. Our analysis of the structure of modern industry shows the progressive socialisation of certain classes of industry as a step in the order of events, equally natural and necessary with the earlier steps by which

27

machine-industry superseded handicraft and crystallised in ever larger masses with changing relations to one another. The indictment against social control over industry is an indictment against a natural order of events, on the ground that nature has taken a wrong road of advancement. It is only possible to regard the legislative action by which public control over industry is established as "unnatural" or "artificial" by excluding from "Nature" those social forces which find expression in Acts of Parliament, an eminently unscientific mode of reasoning.

But though this growing exercise of social control cannot be regarded as "fighting against the constitution of things," [1] it may be considered by those who hold we have no guarantee of the future development of the human race, as one of the lines of action in which the advancing enfeeblement of man may express itself: the abandonment of individual strife in commerce may be regarded as a mark of diminishing vitality, which seeks immunity from effort and an equable condition of material comfort, in preference to the risks and excitement of a more eventful and arduous career. Order will be purchased at the price of progress: the abandonment of individual enterprise in industry is part of the decadence of humanity. This is the interpretation which Dr. Pearson, in his *National Life and Character*, places upon the socialistic tendencies of the age: the suppression of competitive industry in order to cure poverty, physical misery, and social injustice, will produce a society which is "sensuous, genial, fibreless." The validity of such a judgment rests upon two assumptions: first, that social control of industry necessarily crushes the spirit of individual enterprise and checks industrial progress; second, that extension of State control over capitalist industry necessarily implies a diminished scope of individual control in the production of wealth.

The first assumption is open to a number of criticisms which must be held to greatly modify its force, and which may be summarised as follows:—

(1) Much individual enterprise in industry does not make for industrial progress. A larger and larger proportion of the energy given out in trade competition is consumed in

---

[1] Spencer, *Contemporary Review*, March 1884.

violent warfare between trade rivals, and is not represented either in advancement of industrial arts or in increase of material wealth.

(2) History does not show greed of gain as the motive of the great steps in industrial progress. The love of science, the pure delight of mechanical invention, the attainment of some slight personal convenience in labour, and mere chance, play the largest part in the history of industrial improvements. These motives would be as equally operative under state-control as under private enterprise.

(3) Such personal inducements as may supply a useful stimulus to the inventive faculty could be offered in socially-controlled industry, not merely publicity and honour, but such direct material rewards as were useful.

Industrial history shows that in modern competitive industry the motive of personal gain is most wastefully applied. On the one hand, the great mass of intelligent workers have no opportunity of securing an adequate reward for any special application of intelligence in mechanical invention or other improvement of industrial arts. Few great modern inventors have made money out of their inventions. On the other hand, the *entrepreneur*, with just enough business cunning to recognise the market value of an improvement, reaps a material reward which is often enormously in excess of what is economically required to induce him to apply his " business " qualities to the undertaking.

(4) The same charges of weakened individual interest, want of plasticity and enterprise, routine torpidity, are in a measure applicable to every large business as compared with a smaller. Adam Smith considered them fatal barriers to the growth of joint-stock enterprise outside a certain narrowly-defined range. But the economies of the large business were found to outweigh these considerations. So a well-ordered state-industry may be the most economical in spite of diminished elasticity and enterprise.

But while these considerations qualify the force of the contention that state-control would give no scope for industrial progress, they do not refute it. The justification of the assumption by the State of various functions, military, judicial, industrial, is that a safe orderly routine in the conduct of these affairs is rightly purchased by a loss of elasticity and a diminished pace of progress. The arts of war and of justice would probably make more advance under private enterprise than under public administration, and there is no reason to deny that postal and railway services are slower to adopt improvements when they pass under government control.

It may be generally admitted that, as the large modern industries pass from the condition of huge private monopolies to public departments, the routine character will grow in them, and they will become less experimental and more mechanical. It is the nature of machines to be mechanical, and the perfection of machine-industries, as of single machines, will be the perfection of routine. Just in proportion as the machine has established its dominancy over the various industries, so will they increase in size, diminish in flexibility, and grow ripe for admission, as routine businesses, into the ranks of state-industry. If the chief object of society was to secure continual progress in military arts and to educate to the utmost the military qualities, it would be well to leave fighting to private enterprise instead of establishing state monopolies in the trade of war. It sacrifices this competition, with the progress it induces and the personal fitness it evolves, in order that the individual enterprise of its members may be exercised in the competition of industrial arts, inducing industrial progress and evolving industrial fitness. The substitution of industrialism for warfare is not, however, understood to imply a diminution of individual enterprise, but an alteration in its application.

If, starting from this point of view, we regard human life as comprising an infinite number of activities of different sorts, operating upon different planes of competition and educating different human "fitnesses," we shall understand how the particular phase of industrial evolution we are considering is related to the wider philosophic view of life. All progress, from primitive savagedom to modern civilisation, will then appear as consisting in the progressive socialisation of the lower functions, the stoppage of lower forms of competition and of the education of the more brutal qualities, in order that a larger and larger proportion of individual activity may be engaged in the exercise of higher functions, the practice of competition upon higher planes, and the education of higher forms of fitness.

If the history of past civilisation shows us this, there is an
à priori presumption that each further step in the repression
of individual enterprise and in the extension of state-control
does not mean a net diminution in individual activity or
any relaxation of effort in self-assertion, but merely an elevation of the plane of competition and of the kind of human
qualities engaged. This is, in fact, the philosophical defence
of progressive socialism, that human progress requires that
one after another the lower material animal functions shall
be reduced to routine, in order that a larger amount of
individual effort may be devoted to the exercise of higher
functions and the cultivation by strife of higher qualities.

To suppose that the reduction of all machine-industry to
public routine services, when it becomes possible, will imply
a net diminution in the scope of individual self-expression,
rests upon the patent fallacy of assigning certain fixed
and finite limits to human interest and activity, so that
any encroachment from the side of routine lessens the
absolute scope of human spontaneity and interest. If, as
there is reason to believe, human desires and the activities
which are engaged in satisfying them are boundless, the
assumption that an increase in the absolute amount of
state-control or routine-work implies a diminution of the
field for individual enterprise is groundless. The under-
lying motive, which alone can explain and justify each
step in progressive socialism, is the attainment of a net
economy of individual effort, which, when it is released
from exercise upon a lower plane of competition, may
be devoted to exercise upon a higher. If the result of
extending social control over industry were merely to bring
about a common level of material comfort, attended by
spiritual and intellectual torpor and contentment, the movement might be natural and necessary, but could hardly be
termed progress.

But such a view is based upon a denial of the axiom that
the satisfaction of one want breeds another want. Experience does not teach the decay but the metamorphosis of
individuality. Under socialised industry progress in the
industrial arts would be slower and would absorb a smaller
proportion of individual interest, in order that progress in the
finer intellectual and moral arts might be faster, and might
engage a larger share of life. To future generations of more

highly evolved humanity the peculiar barbarism of our age will consist in the fact that the major part of its intelligence, enterprise, genius, has been devoted to the perfection of the arts of material production through mechanical means. If it is desirable that more of this individual energy should be engaged in the production of higher forms of wealth by competition upon higher planes, this can only be achieved by the process of reducing to routine the lower functions. Higher progress can only be purchased by an economy of the work of lower progress, the free, conscious expression of higher individuality by the routine subordination of lower individuality. Industrial progress would undoubtedly be slower under state-control, because the very object of such control is to divert a larger proportion of human genius and effort from these occupations in order to apply them in producing higher forms of wealth. It is not, however, right to assume that progress in the industrial arts would cease under state-industry; such progress would be slower, and would itself partake of a routine character— a slow, continuous adjustment of the mechanism of production and distribution to the slowly-changing needs of the community.

§ 12. A most important misunderstanding of the line of industrial development arises from a conviction that all production of wealth embodied in matter tends to pass under the dominion of machinery, that an increasing number of workers in the future will become machine-tenders, and that the state-control of machine-industry would bring the vast majority of individuals into the condition of official machine-workers. This, however, is by no means a reasonable forecast. In competitive machine-industry, although it is to the interest of the individual business to "save" as much labour as possible, the play of competition causes to be made and worked a much larger quantity of machinery than is enough to maintain the current rate of consumption, and thus keeps in the ranks of manufacture a much larger quantity of labour than is socially necessary. Yet in a typical manufacturing country like England statistics show that the proportion of the working population engaged in machine manufactures is not increasing. If, then, by the gradual elimination of competition in the machine-industries, the quantity of machine-work were kept down to the social requirements of the community's consumption, the proportion of machine-workers would be less than it is, assuming the demand for machine-made goods continued the same.

But what, it may be said, will become of the increasing proportion of the workers not required by machinery? will they go to swell indefinitely the ranks of distributors? Will the number of merchants, jobbers, speculators, shopkeepers, agents, middlemen of various sorts, grow without limit? Assuming that the work of distribution were left to competitive enterprise, and that the quantity and quality of consumption remained the same as now, this result would seem necessarily to follow. The labour saved in manufacture would pass, as it does now, to intensify the competition of the distributive trades and to subdivide into needlessly small fragments the necessary but limited amount of distributive work. But these assumptions are not necessarily correct. If, as seems likely, the increased intensity of competition forced the growth of strong monopolies in certain departments of distribution, the anti-social power thus bestowed upon individuals would necessitate the extension of state-control to them also. The work of distribution would thus pass into routine-industry administered by the public for the public interest. Thus the area of socialised industry would extend until it absorbed one after another all industries possessing the machine-character and capable of administration by routine. It might thus appear that, after all, the forebodings of the individualist would be verified, the work of life would be reduced to a dull monotonous mechanism grinding out under bureaucratic sway an ever growing quantity of material comforts for a community absorbed in the satisfaction of its orderly behaviour.

This goal seems inevitable if we assume that no change takes place in the quantity and quality of the consumption of the community, that individual consumers save or try to save the same proportion of their incomes as now, and apply the portion that they spend to the purchase of increased quantities of ever-cheapening machine-made goods.

But are we justified in considering it necessary, or even probable, that consumption will in amount and character remain unchanged? In proportion as the large industries pass into the condition of monopolies, whether under private or public control, the area of safe and profitable investment for the average "saving" man will be more restricted. Thus some of the useless "saving" which takes the shape of excessive plant, machinery, and other forms of capital will be prevented. In other words, the quantity of consumption will increase, and this increase will give fuller employment to the machinery of production and to the labour engaged in working it and in distributing the increased product. If, however, increased consumption merely took the form of consuming increased quantities of the same material goods as before, the gain would be limited to the rise of material comfort of the poorer classes, and this gain might be set off by the congested and torpor-breeding luxury of the better-to-do. A mere increase in quantity of consumption would do nothing to avert the drifting of industry into a bureaucratic mechanism.

§ 13. It is to improved quality and character of consumption that we can alone look for a guarantee of social progress. Allusion has been already made to the class of artistic and intellectual work which cannot be undertaken by machinery. It must never be forgotten that art is the true antithesis of machinery. The essence of art in this wide sense is the application of individual spontaneous human effort. Each art-product is the repository of individual thought, feeling, effort, each machine-product is not. The "art" in machine-work has been exhausted in the single supreme effort of planning the machine; the more perfect the machine the smaller the proportion of individual skill or art embodied in the machine-product. The spirit of machinery, its vast rapid power of multiplying quantities of material goods of the same pattern, has so over-awed the industrial world that the craze for quantitative consumption has seized possession of many whose taste and education might have enabled them to offer resistance. Thus, not only our bread and our boots are made by machinery, but many of the very things we misname "art-products." Now a just indictment of this excessive encroachment of machinery is not based upon the belief, right or wrong, that machinery cannot produce things in themselves as fit or beautiful as art. The true inadequacy of machine-products for human purposes arises from the fact that machine-products are exactly similar to one another, whereas consumers are not. So long as consumers consent to sink their individuality, to consume articles of precisely the same shape, size, colour, material, to assimilate their consumption to one another, machinery will supply them. But since no two individuals are precisely similar in physical, intellectual, or moral nature, so the real needs of no two will be the same, even in the satisfaction of ordinary material wants. As the dominance of machinery over the workers tends to the destruction of individuality in work, obliging different workers to do the same work in the same way with a premium upon the mere capacity of rapid repetition, in the same way it tends to crush the individuality of consumers by imposing a common character upon their consumption. The progressive utilisation of machinery depends upon the continuance of this indiscriminate consumption, and the willingness of consumers to employ every increase of income in demanding larger and larger quantities of goods of the same pattern and character. Once suppose that consumers refuse to conform to a common standard, and insist more and more upon a consumption adjusted to their individual needs and tastes, and likewise strive to follow and to satisfy the changing phases of their individual taste, such individuality in consumption must impose a corresponding individuality in production, and machinery will be dethroned from industry. Let us take the example of the clothing trade. Provided the wearing public will consent to wear clothes conforming to certain common patterns and shapes which are only approximate " fits," machinery can be used to make these clothes ; but if every person required his own taste to be consulted, and insisted upon an exactitude of fit and a conformity to his own special ideas of comfort, the work could no longer be done by machinery, and would require the skill of an " artist." It is precisely upon this issue that the conflict of machine *versus* hand-labour is still fought out. The most highly-finished articles in the clothing and boot trades are still hand-made ; the best golf-clubs, fishing-rods, cricket bats, embody a large amount of high manual skill, though articles of fair average make are turned out chiefly by machinery in large quantities. These hand-made goods are produced for a small portion of the consuming public, whose education and refinement of taste induces them to prefer spending their money upon a smaller quantity of commodities adjusted in character to their individual needs, than upon a larger quantity of common commodities.

Assuming that industrial evolution places an increasing proportion of the consuming public in secure possession of the prime physical necessaries of life, it is surely possible that they too may come to value less highly a quantitative increase in consumption, and may develop individuality of tastes which require individual production for their satisfaction. In proportion as this happens, hand-work or art must play a more important part in these industries, and may be able to repel the further encroachments of machinery, or even to drive it out of some of the industrial territory it has annexed. But although the illustration of the present condition of the clothing trades serves to indicate the nature of the contest between machinery and art in the region of ordinary material consumption, it is not suggested that social progress will, or ought to, expel machinery from most of the industries it controls, or to prevent its application to industries which it has not yet reached. The luxury and foppish refinement of a small section of "fashionable" society, unnaturally relieved of the wholesome necessity of work, cannot be taken as an indication of the ways in which individuality or quality of consumption may or will assert itself, in a society where social progress is based upon equality of opportunity, and the power to consume has some just relation to ability and merit. It seems reasonable to expect that on the whole machinery will retain, and even strengthen and extend, its hold of those industries engaged in supplying the primitive needs of man—his food, clothing, shelter, and other animal comforts. In a genuinely progressive society the object will be so to order life as to secure, not merely the largest amount of individual freedom or self-expression, but the highest quality. If an undue amount of individuality be devoted to the production and consumption of food, clothing, etc., and the conscious, refined cultivation of these tastes, higher forms of individual expression in work and life will be neglected. The just economy of individuality will therefore relegate certain branches of production to machinery, in order that the energy saved by such routine-work may be set free for higher individual endeavour. The satisfaction of the primary animal wants—hunger, thirst, cold, etc.—are common to all; in these purely physical demands there is less qualitative difference in different men; as the needs are the same the consumption will be the same. The absence of wide individual differences of taste marks out the commodities for routine or machine-production. As individuals are nearest alike in their prime physical needs, so, as they gradually develop higher material wants, and, after these are satisfied, æsthetic, intellectual, moral wants, their individualism becomes more and more marked. It is therefore in the most highly developed, or, as they are sometimes called, the more "artificial" wants of man, that the diversity of individual nature shows itself most strongly, and demands a satisfaction peculiar to itself which only art can give. In a highly evolved society it is likely that many physical needs, and even some intellectual needs, will be common to all, and will engage little individual attention. These may be graded as routine wants, and may be satisfied by machine-made goods. As a society, safely ordered in the supply of ordinary physical comforts, continued to develop, a less and less diversity would show itself in the ordinary aspect of its material civilisation, because the individuality which once found expression there is raised to a higher plane of activity. The enrichment and enlargement of human life in such a society would undoubtedly manifest itself in a greater likeness between the individual members in the lower modes of life, but the extent of individual difference in the higher modes would be ever widening. The object of the levelling in the lower processes of life would be that higher individual differences might have opportunity to assert themselves. In a progressive society thus conceived, where socialisation and individuation grow inseparably related and reacting on one another, there is evidently no fixed limit to the progress of machinery. As each higher want is educated, some lower want will drop into the position of a routine-want, and will pass into the rightful province of machinery. But though a large proportion of material commodities would doubtless be made by machinery, it is not signified that art will be banished from what are commonly called the industrial arts. On the contrary, art may be in many ways the friend and co-operator of machinery, the latter furnishing a routine foundation for the display of individual taste and of individual satisfaction in the consumer. One of the most hopeful signs of the last few years is the growing intrusion of art into the machine-industries,—the employment of skilled designers and executants who shall tempt and educate the public eye with grace of form and harmony of colour. In pottery, textile wares, hardware, furniture, and many other industries, the beginnings of public taste are operating in demand for variety and ornament. May not this be the beginning of a cultivation of individual taste which shall graft a fine-art upon each machine-industry, apportioning to machinery that work which is hard, dull, dangerous, monotonous, and uneducative, while that which is pleasant, worthy, interesting, and educative is reserved for the human agent?

§ 14. Machinery is thus naturally adapted to the satisfaction of the routine wants of life under social control. The character of machine-production, as has been shown, is essentially collective. The maladies of present machine-industries are due to the fact that this collective character is inadequately recognised, and machinery, left to individual enterprise and competition, oppresses mankind and causes waste and commercial instability. In a word, the highest division of labour has not been yet attained, that which will apportion machinery to the collective supply of the routine needs of life, and art to the individual supply of the individual needs. In this way alone can society obtain the full use of the "labour-saving" character of machinery, minimising the amount of human exertion engaged in tending machinery and maximising the amount engaged in the free and interesting occupations. Engaged in satisfying the steady, constant needs of society under social regulation. machinery would no longer be subject to those fearful oscillations of demand which are liable unforeseen to plunge whole masses of workers into unemployment and poverty, and to waste an infinite amount of "saving." Where the fluctuations in consumption were confined to the region of individual taste, the changes of taste and growing variety of consumption would furnish the education of the artist, who will acquire skill and flexibility by freely following and directing the changing tastes of consumers.

In such a forecast it is of course useless to endeavour to

predict how far art will continue to occupy itself with industry, or how far, set free by machinery, it will be absorbed in the creation of finer intellectual or spiritual products, or in what are now termed the fine arts. This must depend upon the nature of the harmonious development of human capacities of effort and enjoyment under conditions of individual freedom, and the interaction of the free development of individuals in a society founded upon an equality of the material means of life. The study of the qualitative development of consumption in modern society is only just beginning to be recognised as the true starting-point of economic science, for although many of the older economists did verbal homage to the importance of this branch of study, it has been reserved for recent thinkers to set about the work.[1]

§ 15. It is hardly too much to say that the whole of social progress depends upon the substitution of qualitative for quantitative methods of consumption. In so far as individuals apply their growing ability to consume in order to demand increased quantities of the same articles they consumed before, or flash variety of fashionable goods in no wise adjusted to individual need or taste, they extend the dominion of machinery. In so far as they develop individual taste, delicacy rather than quantity of satisfaction, they give wider scope to work which embodies conscious human skill and deserves the name of art.

But there is another bearing of this point of equal significance. Political economists have a dismal formula called the Law of Diminishing Returns, which casts a dark shadow upon industrial progress as it is commonly conceived. The more food and clothing, fuel, and other material goods we require, the further we have to go for the material, and the harder it is to get: we must plough inferior lands yielding smaller crops, we must sink deeper shafts for our coal and iron. As our population grows ever larger, and this larger number wants more and more pieces of the earth to feed

---

[1] Professor Jevons' work upon this branch of Economics was marred by an attempt to treat it purely mathematically, that is to reduce qualitative to quantitative differences—an impossibility. Among recent writers, Professor Patten, of Pennsylvania University, has made by far the most important contributions towards a systematic treatment of the economics of consumption.

its machines and to turn out the increased quantity of goods, the drain upon natural resources is constantly increasing. The material world is limited; in time Nature will become exhausted, and, long before this happens, the quantity of human labour required to raise the increased supply of raw material in the teeth of the Law of Diminishing Returns will far exceed the economies attending large-scale machine-production.

This danger will also be found to result entirely from the quantitative estimate of human wealth and human life.

Confining our view for the moment to that branch of production which is engaged in providing food, to which the Law of Diminishing Returns is held to apply with special rigour, we can see without difficulty how, by a progressive differentiation of consumption, we can mitigate or even utterly defeat the operation of this law. If the inhabitants of a country persist in maintaining a single narrow standard of diet, and use the whole of their land for growing wheat and raising sheep, not merely do they waste all other fine productive qualities belonging to certain portions of the cultivated or uncultivated soil, but every increase in their narrow consumption drives them to worse soil, obliges them to put more labour into a quarter of wheat or a sheep, and increases the proportion of their aggregate product which goes as rent.[1] If, on the other hand, a community cultivates a varied consumption and seeks to utilise each portion of its soil for whatever form of food it can grow best, instead of grading its land exclusively according to its wheat or sheep-raising capacity, it is able to defeat the "niggardliness of nature" which asserts itself when the community insists upon a continual extension of the same demands. For land which may be very bad for wheat-growing or grazing, which may even be "below the margin of cultivation" for these purposes, may be well adapted for producing other commodities. A large variety of alternative uses will enable us to get the largest net amount of utilities out of Nature, and a community which, in lieu of an extension of demand for the same commodities, asserts its civilisation in the education of new demands and a greater complexity in

[1] Patten's *Premises of Political Economy*, chap. iv.

the standard of its comfort, may draw from the land an indefinite increase of wealth without putting forth more labour or paying higher rent. It is simply one more example of the economy attainable by division of labour and specialisation of function.

§ 16. What applies to food will equally apply to the use of the earth for providing the raw material of all other forms of material wealth. A people with growing variety of consumption is ever finding new and more profitable uses for slighted or neglected capacities of nature. The social progress of nations must be chiefly determined by the amount of their intelligent flexibility of consumption. Mere variety of consumption in itself is not sufficient to secure progress. There must be a progressive recognition of the true relations, between the products which can be most economically raised upon each portion of the soil, and the wholesome needs of mankind seeking the full harmonious development of their faculties in their given physical environment. A progressive cultivation of taste for a variety of strong drinks, though it might provide an increased number of alternative uses for the soil, and might enhance the aggregate market-values of the wealth produced, would not, it is generally held, make for social progress. That nation which, in its intelligent attainment of a higher standard of life, is able to thoroughly assimilate and harmonise the largest variety of those products for which their soil and climate are best adapted, will be foremost in industrial progress and in the other arts of civilisation which spring out of it.

The case is a simple one. A mere increase in the variety of our material consumption relieves the strain imposed upon man by the limits of the material universe, for such variety enables him to utilise a larger proportion of the aggregate of matter. But in proportion as we add to mere variety a higher appreciation of those adaptations of matter which are due to human skill, and which we call Art, we pass outside the limits of matter and are no longer the slaves of roods and acres and a law of diminishing returns. So long as we continue to raise more men who demand more food and clothes and fuel, we are subject to the limitations of the material universe, and what we get ever costs us more and benefits us less. But when we cease to demand more, and begin to demand better, commodities, more delicate, highly finished and harmonious, we can increase the enjoyment without adding to the cost or exhausting the store. What artist would not laugh at the suggestion that the materials of his art, his colours, clay, marble, or what else he wrought in, might fail and his art come to an end? When we are dealing with qualitative, *i.e.* artistic, goods, we see at once how an infinite expenditure of labour may be given, an infinite satisfaction taken, from the meagrest quantity of matter and space. In proportion as a community comes to substitute a qualitative for a quantitative standard of living, it escapes the limitations imposed by matter upon man. Art knows no restrictions of space or size, and in proportion as we attain the art of living we shall be likewise free.

§ 17. So far the consideration of reformed qualitative consumption has been confined to material goods. But a people moving along the line of progress, seeking ever a more highly qualitative life, will demand that a larger proportion of their energy shall be given to the production and consumption of intellectual goods.

This world likewise is at present largely under the dominion of Machinery and a Law of Diminishing Returns By making of our intellectual life a mere accumulation of knowledge, piling fact upon fact, reading book upon book, adding science to science, striving to cover as much intellectual ground as possible, we become mere worshippers of quantity. It is not unnatural that our commercial life should breed such an intellectual consumption, and that the English and American nations in particular, who have beyond others developed machine-production and the quantitative genius for commerce, should exhibit the same taste in their pursuit after knowledge. Pace, size, number, cost, are ever on their lips. To visit every European capital in a fortnight, see acres of pictures, cathedrals, ruined castles, collect out of books or travel the largest mass of unassorted and undigested information, is the object of such portion of the commercial life as can be spared from the more serious occupations of life, piling up bale after bale of cotton goods and eating dinner after dinner of the same inharmoniously ordered victuals.

Our schools and colleges are engaged in turning out year by year immense quantities of common intellectual goods.

Our magazines, books, and lectures are chiefly machine-products adjusted to the average reader or hearer, and are reckoned successful if they can drive a large number of individuals to profess the same feelings and opinions and adopt the same party or creed, with the view of enabling them to consume a large number of copies of the same intellectual commodities which can be turned out by intellectual machinery, instead of undergoing the effort of thinking and feeling for themselves. This danger, connected with the rapid spread of printed matter, is a grave one. Happily there are visible here also counteracting influences, forces that tend to individualise intellectual consumption and thus to stimulate the higher arts of intellectual production. In a progressive community it will be more fully recognised that it is not sufficient to induce people to give more time and attention to intellectual consumption; they must demand intellectual goods vitally adjusted to their individual needs.

§ 18. To the increased regard for quality of life we must likewise look to escape the moral maladies which arise from competition. For what is the cause of anti-social competition? It is the limitation of quantity. Two dogs are after one bone. Two persons wish to consume one commodity at the same time. Now, even in material goods, the more qualitative consumption becomes, and the more insistent each individual is upon the satisfaction of his peculiar tastes, the smaller will be the probability that two persons will collide in their desires, and struggle for the possession of the self-same commodity. Even in art-objects which are still bounded by matter, among genuine lovers of art the individuality of each stands out in mitigation of the antagonism of competition, for no two will have precisely the same tastes or estimates, or will seek with equal avidity the same embodiments of art. As we rise to purely intellectual or moral enjoyments, competition gives way to generous rivalry in co-operation. In the pursuit of knowledge or goodness the rivalry is no longer antagonism— what one gains another does not lose. One man's success is not another's failure. On the contrary, the enrichment of one is the enrichment of all. Both in the production and the consumption of the highest goods of Science, Art, and Virtue, social, not anti-social, motives are the chief stimulus. In the highest forms of consumption, the practice of the noblest arts of life, the enjoyment of the finest intellectual and spiritual goods, there is no purely selfish consumption. For though the highest individuality is then attained, the enjoyment of one individual requires the enjoyment of others. The attainment of the highest reaches of knowledge is impossible for the individual without the constant and increasing aid of other minds and the inspiring "spirit of the age"; the enjoyment of such knowledge is in an even wider communication. The practice and enjoyment of the arts of goodness are necessarily social, because the good life can only be lived in a good society. Spinoza has summed up the truth in saying—"The highest good is common to all, and all may equally enjoy it." So it appears that the highest goods are essentially at once individual and social, pointing once more the attainment of the higher synthesis in which the antagonism of the "one" and the "all," which shows itself in the lower planes of competing effort and enjoyment, disappears.

§ 19. One necessary condition of this progressive life cannot be ignored. Human life itself must become more qualitative, not only in its functional activities, but in its physical basis. The greatness and worth of a community must be seen more clearly to consist not in the numbers, but in the character of its members. If the number of individuals in a society continually increases, no reform in methods of consumption can prevent the constant increase in the proportion of human energy which must be put into the production of the prime material necessaries of physical life which are, and in spite of all improved methods of treating nature will remain, ultimately subject to a law of diminishing returns : so, less and less energy can be spared for the life of varied and delicate consumption, high individuality and intellectual and moral growth. Professor Geddes has well expressed the importance of this truth : "The remedy lies in higher and higher individuation— *i.e.*, if we would repress excessive multiplication, we must develop the average individual standard throughout society. Population not merely tends to out-run the means of subsistence, but to degenerate below the level of subsistence, so that without steadily directing more and more of our industry from the production of those forms of wealth which merely support life to those which evoke it, from the increase of the fundamental necessities of animal life to that of the highest appliances of human culture, degeneration must go on."[1]

§ 20. One final consideration remains.   Modern large-scale industry has enlarged and made more distinct an unnatural and injurious separation of the arts of production and the arts of consumption.   Work has become more and more differentiated from enjoyment, and in a twofold way. Modern machine-industry has in the first place sharpened the distinction between the "working classes," whose name indicates that their primary function is to labour and not to live, and the comfortable classes, whose primary function is to live and not to labour, which private enterprise in machine-industry has greatly enlarged.   The extremes of these large classes present the divorcement of labour and life in startling prominence.   But since work and enjoyment are both human functions, they must be organically related in the life of every individual in a healthy community.   It must be recognised to be as essential to the consumer to produce as for the producer to consume.   The attempt on the part of an individual or a class to escape the physical and moral law which requires the output of personal exertion as the condition of wholesome consumption can never be successful.   On the plane of physical health, Dr. Arlidge, in his book upon *The Diseases of Occupations*, points the inevitable lesson in the high rate of disease and mortality of the "unoccupied class" in that period of their life when they have slaked their zest for volunteer exertion and assume the idle life which their economic power renders possible.   The man of "independent means" cannot on the average keep his life in his body nearly so long as the half-starved, ill-housed agricultural labourer, from whose labour he draws the rents which keep him in idleness.   The same law applies in the intellectual world.   The dilettante person who tries to extract unceasing increments of intellectual or æsthetic enjoyment from books or pictures or travel, without the contribution of steady, painful intellectual effort, fails to

---

[1] **Professor Patrick Geddes,** *Claims of Labour.*   Cf. *The Evolution of Sex,* chap. **xx.** (Contemporary Science Series: Walter Scott Publishing Co.).

win an intellectual life, for the mere automatic process of collecting the knowledge of others for personal consumption without striving to enlarge the general stock, congests and debilitates the mind and prevents the wholesome digestion and assimilation.

The same necessary evil arises from the sharp separation of the processes of production and consumption in the individual life of the worker. Industry which is purely monotonous, burdensome, uninteresting, uneducative, which contains within itself no elements of enjoyment, cannot be fully compensated by alternate periods of consumption or relaxation. The painful effort involved in all labour or exertion should have linked with it certain sustaining elements of related interest and pleasure. It is the absence of this which condemns machine-tending from the human standpoint, it is the presence of this which distinguishes every art. Hence in a progressive society we must look to see not the abolition of machinery, but the diminution of machine-tending which attends the growing perfection of machinery, in order that the arts may be able to absorb a larger share of human exertion.

The arts of production and consumption will, in the evolution of a wholesome industrial society, be found inseparable : not merely will they be seen to be organically related, but rather will appear as two aspects of the same fact, the concave and the convex of life. For the justly ordered life brings the identification of life, a continuous orderly intake and output of wholesome energy. This judgment, not of "sentimentalism" but of science, finds powerful but literally accurate expression in the saying of a great modern thinker, "Life without industry is guilt, industry without art is brutality." Just in proportion as the truth of the latter phrase finds recognition the conditions which make "life without work" possible will disappear. Everything in human progress will be found to depend upon a progressive realisation of the nature of good "consumption." Just in proportion as our tastes become so qualitative that we require to put our own spontaneity, our sense of beauty and fitness, our vital force, into whatever work we do, and likewise require the same elements of spontaneity and individuality in all we enjoy, the economic conditions of a perfect society will be attained.

§ 21. This forecast of the social and industrial goal seems justified by a thoughtful interpretation of the tendencies visible in the development of modern industry. How fast may be the progress towards such an ideal, or how far such progress may be frustrated or impaired by the appearance of new or the strengthening of old antagonistic forces, lies beyond the powers of legitimate speculation. The endeavour to test industrial evolution by reference to the wider movements of human life brings into prominence two great tendencies whose operations, attested not dimly by modern history, are in close accord with the general trend of the development of social and individual life and the relations subsisting between the two.

As modern industrial societies develop they disclose certain material wants which are common to all or most members, and are less subject to fluctuations in quantity or quality of demand than others. These routine wants, representing that part of consumption which is common, can be supplied most economically by highly organised machinery and highly concentrated methods of production. But so long as the machinery for the satisfaction of the common wants remains outside the common control, and is worked for the benefit of sections of the community whose interests conflict, both with one another and with the general interest, an immense amount of waste and danger arises from the working of the machinery, and grave social maladies are engendered. These maladies evoke in the best ordered and most intelligent communities an increasing pressure of public control. This public control is strengthened and extended in proportion as the highly evolved structure of the industry enables its administrators to exercise powers of monopoly either in relation to the treatment of its employees, or in relation to the price or quality of the commodities it supplies to the public. Such industries as develop these economic powers of monopoly in the highest degree, and in relation to the supply of prime necessaries or comforts of common life, pass gradually into the condition of public industries organised for the public good. It seems likely that all the important machine industries engaged in satisfying common routine wants will gradually develop the monopolic characteristics which accrue to large production, and will pass by degrees through the different phases of public control until they become merged in public industry.

This so-called socialistic movement in industry represents the growing cohesiveness of modern societies. At all times there is a strong natural tendency to supply common wants by common efforts. So long as the common wants in their wider significance only extend to protection of the person and of certain forms of personal property, state-work is confined within these protective limits, and the work of producing common wealth, so far as it exists, is left to village communities or other small units of social organisation. As the elements of steady common consumption grow in number, the common organisation of activity to supply them will grow, and where the supply has at first been left to private enterprise, the abuse of power and growing inconvenience of competition will drive them into public industry. But since the very *raison d'être* of this increased social cohesiveness is to economise and enrich the individual life, and to enable the play of individual energy to assume higher forms out of which more individual satisfaction may accrue, more and more human effort will take shape in industries which will be left to individual initiative and control, the arts in which the freedom of personal spontaneity will find scope in the expression of physical or moral beauty and fitness and the attainment of intellectual truth. The infinite variety which these forms of artistic expression may assume, fraught with the individuality of the artist, will prevent them from ever passing into "routine" or "common" industries, though even in the fine arts there will be certain elements which, as they become part of the common possession, will become relatively void of individual interest, and will thus pass into a condition of routine activity. The idea of continuity in human progress demands this admission. But since each encroachment of routine upon the "finer arts" is motived by a prior shifting of the interest of the consumer into forms of higher refinement, there will be a net gain and not a loss in the capacity of individual exercise in artistic work. In every form of human activity the progress of routine industry will be the necessary condition of the expansion of individual freedom of expression. But while the choice and control of each higher form of "industry" will remain individualistic, in proportion as the moral bonds of society obtain fuller conscious recognition, the work of the "artist" likewise will be dedicated more and more to the service of his fellow-men. Thus will the balance of the social and individual work in the satisfaction of human wants be preserved, while the number of those wants increase and assume different values with the progress of the social and individual life.

SUPPLEMENTARY CHAPTER.

INDUSTRY OF THE TWENTIETH CENTURY.

PART I.

§ 1. *Growth of large Joint-Stock enterprises.*

§ 2. *The "Representative Business": its size and structure.*

§ 3. *The effect of limits of maximum efficiency in maintaining Competition.*

§ 4. *New Developments in Combinations, Cartels, and Trusts.*

§ 5. *Combinations in Post-War Britain.*

§ 6. *The Distribution of Occupations in Britain and the United States.*

§ 7. *Women's new place in Industry, Commerce, and Professions.*

§ 8. *Comparative Advance of Basic Industries of Capitalism in different countries.*

§ 9. *The Growth of International Trade.*

§ 10. *Export of Capital.*

§ 11. *Advance of America as a Creditor Nation.*

§ 12. *Effects of the War on Economic Strength of Nations.*

§ 13. *The New Electric Age.*

PART II.

§ 1. *The Revelation of Reserve Productivity in War Time.*

§ 2. *Waste in Productive and Distributive Processes.*

§ 3. *The Problem of Business Reconstruction.*

§ 4. *Relations of Capital and Labour.*

§ 5. *Socialisation of Fundamental Industries.*

§ 6. *State Provisions regarding Wages and Unemployment.*

§ 7. *National Economy and Key Industries.*

§ 8. *Constructive Economic Internationalism and its Problems.*

PART I.

§ 1. The increasing attention recently given by governments and private economists to statistics of production and of occupations enables us to trace with more certainty and exactitude the changes of business structure taking place in the industrially developed countries. The advance of capitalistic methods in the industry, commerce, and finance of such countries as the United States, Germany, and Japan enables us both to verify and to correct generalisations based too exclusively upon the example of Great Britain, and the experience of these later followers of capitalism has disclosed some new developments in economic structure.

The statistics of all these countries testify to the truth of the central law of the evolution of capitalism—viz., the movement of businesses engaged in the routine processes of manufacture, trade, transport, mining, and finance into large joint-stock firms, employing larger numbers of workers, turning out increasing outputs, and limiting free competition by various modes of regulation, co-operation and combination.

The continued growth of joint-stock enterprise in Great Britain is attested by the increase in the number of Registered Companies and the increasing aggregate of the capital invested in this form of business structure.

REGISTERED COMPANIES IN GREAT BRITAIN.

Year.	Number.	Capital.	
		Total. £ Millions.	Average. £ 000
1900 - -	29,730	1,623	56·3
1905 - -	39,616	1,954	49·1
1910 - -	50,137	2,133	42·6
1913 - -	58,882	2,377	40·4
1920 - -	77,021	3,438	42·6
1923 - -	87,930	4,265	48·5

(Figures for Ireland omitted after 1905.)

If we accept the rough estimate made by the *Final Report of the Census of Production* (p. 36) of the total capital employed in the manufacturing, mining, transport, and distributing trades as amounting in 1907 to a figure between £4,200 million and £5,000 million, we shall come to the conclusion that a little less than half of the total business of the country had by that time passed into the joint-stock form. When due allowance is made for the depreciated value of sterling since 1913, we shall recognise that the number of Companies has grown considerably faster than the total paid-up capital, indicating that a growing number of family businesses of moderate size have taken on the Company form.

Perhaps the most striking testimony to the advance of joint-stock enterprise, and the consequent displacement of individual businesses and private firms, is given by the comparison of the results of recent Census investigation into the manufactures of the United States.[1] During the period 1914–1919, the proportion of the total number of manufacturing establishments under the control of Corporations increased from 23·6% to 31·5%. The proportion of wage-earners employed by Corporations increased from 70·6% to 86·6%. The proportion of the value of the manufacturing product turned out by Corporations grew from 73·7% to 87·7%. The value added by the process of manufacture (*i.e.*, the net product) increased from 70·1% to 87·0%.

Another interesting table in the same report bears even closer testimony to the concentration of capital in manufactures by showing the increasing proportion of (1) number of workers; (2) quantity of gross product; (3) quantity of net product, in the hands of large businesses with a " value of product " exceeding one million dollars.

	Per cent. of Workers.		Per cent. of Product.		Per cent. of Net Product.
1904	-	25·6	-	38·0	-	29·9
1921	-	48·4	-	59·0	-	62·3

§ 2. We have seen that the concentration of capital in the sense of the tendency of businesses to take larger shapes and to limit competition is not a law of universal application in the world of business. In agriculture, in mining, in manufacture, in trade, in

[1] *Statistical Abstract of the U.S.A.*

transport, and even in finance, there are some business processes favourable to the maintenance of small businesses. Nor is this economy of the small or moderate-sized business confined to processes where expensive machinery and other capitalistic methods are inapplicable. Even in the great staple manufactures it is found that some limit exists at any given time to the net earning of the big business, at any rate as regards manufacturing establishments. In the textile, metal, and other staple manufactures in different countries, capital and labour tend to flow in to productive units of a more or less uniform size and composition, forming a representative or dominant type.

Among spinning and weaving businesses in Lancashire it has been shown that there is a representative type, in respect to number of spindles and looms, to which the industry tends to conform. That number is larger in 1925 than prevailed in 1889, but definitely, not indefinitely, larger. There is now in Lancashire a size or type for each branch of work beyond which it is evidently not profitable to lay out a business, unless some unusual circumstance favours a larger type. An extremely valuable statistical enquiry, by Sir S. J. Chapman and Mr. T. S. Ashton, into "The Size of Businesses mainly in the Textile Industries," [1] places before readers a large amount of well-sifted evidence regarding textile business in various countries.

Related to the question of the size of the representative business is that of the structure, and it is seen that not only are limits set upon the growth but also upon the specialisation of business types. There may, indeed, be more than one type of maximum efficiency in an industry. But there will always be some limit, however large, to the size, just as there will always be some law of the proportion of fixed to circulating capital, or of capital as a whole to labour employed. To those who grasp the conception of a business as an organic structure these conclusions will appear *a priori* reasonable. But the accumulation of evidence gives them a sound inductive foundation. It may here suffice to state in general terms the results of recent enquiries

[1] *Journal of Royal Statistical Soc.*, April, 1914.

in the summary which Sir S. J. Chapman and Mr.
T. S. Ashton append to their study:—

" Generally speaking, there would seem to exist in industries
or branches of industries, of adequate size, under given sets of conditions, typical or representative magnitudes to which businesses tend
to grow, typical proportions between their parts, and typical consti-
tutions. The number of spindles possessed by an exclusively spinning
firm, the proportion of spindles to looms in a combined firm, and
even their absolute numbers, the form of government originally, whether
autocracy, oligarchy, or elected directorate, all would seem to be
subject more or less to law, analogous to natural law. Indeed, the
growth of a business, and the volume and form which it ultimately
assumes, are apparently determined in somewhat the same fashion as
the development of an organism in the animal or vegetable world.
As there is a normal size and form for a man, so, but less markedly,
are there normal sizes and forms for businesses. Many variations about
the human type are to be found, according to variations in anteced-
ents and environments and in those unknown causes which for the
sake of convenience are termed chance. But a type will emerge in
any given time or place which results from the fundamental facts of
our nature. Roughly, a similar transformation may be expected in the
industrial world, according to the showing of our analyses of facts,
though more and greater variations are to be found in the case of
individuals." [1]

The determinant factors of sizes are partly objective.
Conditions relating to the provision of mechanical power,
available local supplies, the maximum workable size of
engines, the economy and waste of transmission, are
of leading importance. These objective conditions
determine the mechanical limit of maximum efficiency,
and limit the size of the single productive establishment. But modern organisation may place several or
many establishments under the same control and
management. The limit to the size of the business as
a financial and managerial unit is far more elastic, for,
though it is true that " A straitened supply of initia-
ting, organising, and directing ability, for instance,
is bound at some point to evoke decreasing returns
in a business," it is not easy to find these limits experi-
mentally. Modern business finance is continually
engaged in discovering new forms of co-operation or
federal union between formerly " independent " businesses which can raise the magnitude of " the subjective
units of maximum efficiency " towards a level which
gives it an effective control of the selling market.

[1] *Journal of Statistical Soc.*, p. 513.

§ 3. How far this admitted limitation of the productive efficiency of concentrated capital furnishes a natural check upon economic monopolies still remains a matter of acute controversy. In some lines of business the limit of maximum efficiency may not be reached until a substantial monopoly has been attained. The limit of productive efficiency may compel the survival of a considerable number of businesses in the textile and metal trades with the world for their potential market, but in railroading the maximum economy of working may not be reached until a single national railway system is adopted, and in banking or other branches of finance the business unit of maximum efficiency may be so large as to render effective competition impossible over many fields of enterprise. In Great Britain, as in the United States and wherever railroading has remained a private enterprise, the absorption of small and weak by large and strong companies has been continuous, and working and rate arrangements between formally competing lines have been more frequent and better maintained. In Great Britain, even before the war, railway companies fixing rates between competitive points had led to arrangements between single companies with a view to more economical working, and the merging of competing roads into four great systems, each with its unitary management and finance, is a marked achievement of concentrated capitalism.

In banking, where mere size secures a monopoly of certain large and profitable operations, the concentrative process has recently proceeded with great rapidity.

In 1890 the number of Joint Stock Banks in England and Wales was 104: in 1900 it had sunk to 77, and in 1914 stood at 38. The processes of absorption and amalgamation continued during and after the war, the number in 1924 being 18. During this same period, —i.e., from 1890 to 1924—the number of branches increased from 2,203 to 8,264, a continually increasing proportion of these branches belonging to the Big Five which have been absorbing a continually growing proportion of the increasing banking business of the country. In 1924 the five great Banks held 84 per cent. of the aggregate deposit and current accounts. The economies of this concentrative movement are illustrated by the statement that " The paid-up capital of the English Joint-Stock Banks has only risen from £61 millions in 1900 to £73·3 millions in 1924, while reserve funds have increased from £35½ millions to nearly £58¾ millions. During the same period deposits have risen from £587 millions to £1,813 millions." [1]

§ 4. But amalgamation, in the strict sense of the word, is not the only mode of limiting competition, securing economy of administration, and controlling markets. Too much attention has been accorded to a few dramatic instances of amalgamation along horizontal and vertical lines of movement, too little to the numerous experiments in associations, federal or other, short of amalgamation, which constitute the main trend of modern capitalistic combination. According to Mr. Macrosty's serviceable analysis,[2] the lowest or weakest class of business associations are " combinations for the settlement of terms upon which business shall be done," dealing with discount, terms of credit, payment for transport, etc., but not with selling prices. Price Associations form the next grade. They are largely unions of local manufacturers, or traders, meeting to arrange selling prices and price changes. They generally leave restriction of output alone. But the industrial combination is usually directed, not merely to price lists, but to that regulation of output which is essential to a control of prices. The essential feature of the Cartels or Syndicates which were conspicuous in the pre-war capitalism of Germany is the agreement as to quantities and proportions of supplies to be put upon the market. The general character of these Cartels has already been described.[3] But an interesting development of recent German experience has been the establishment of Sales Associations, whereby the members of the Syndicate form a Joint-Stock Company, which takes from the members their agreed product or output at an arranged price and sells it at a price

[1] *The Economist* Banking Supplement, May 9th, 1925.
[2] *The Trust Movement in British Industry* (Longmans & Co.).
[3] Chapter ix.

determined by the executive in accordance with the state of trade and of outside competition.

The general effect of the war has been to accelerate and strengthen in every belligerent country the movement towards consolidations, combines, and trusts, alike in their industrial, commercial, and financial structures. In Britain, Advisory Committees and Trade Associations were formed in all important industries, to control prices and regulate the conditions of industry. Many of these groups (virtually comprising all firms in a trade) retained the form and many functions of the Association after the war. Again, the restriction of new capital issues by Government, and the limitations upon export of capital, kept out new potential competitors, while large war profits enabled extensions of plant and the acquisition of weaker by stronger firms to proceed apace. When decontrol took place, an era of mergers and fusions followed, especially in the engineering, shipping, mining, and other war industries. The very processes of standardisation in technique and accountancy required by war economy facilitated combination afterwards.

§ 5. The war brought home more clearly than before to British business men and financiers the lesson, that if the nation was to hold its own in the new conditions of world manufacture and commerce, it must develop to the utmost the economies of co-ordination and amalgamation. It also brought home to the intelligent consumer the necessity of devising or extending public regulations to secure the purchaser against the possible or probable abuses of the monopoly powers thus brought into fuller play. The Report of the Committee on Trusts [1] records the existence in Britain of price-fixing Associations or other modes of combination in many branches of the metal and machine-making trades, in chemicals, textiles, and the building trades, and expresses the following judgment :—
"We are satisfied that Trade Associations and Combines are rapidly increasing in this country, and may within no distant period exercise a paramount control over all important branches of the British

[1] Published 1919.

trade." [1] Mr. Hilton's study, prepared for the Committee, thus summarises the extent of the movement:—
" It may be taken that there are considerably more than five hundred Associations, all exerting a substantial influence on the course of industry and price, in being at the present time in the United Kingdom." In regard to the building trades, he adds:—" The most painstaking enquiry yet undertaken into combination in any section of British industry is that made in respect of building materials, and the conclusion there reached was that 25 per cent. of the materials that go to the building of an average house are subject to full control, and 33 per cent. are partially controlled." [2]

The intensification of economic nationalism, with its more numerous and higher protective tariffs (especially in the Continent of Europe), its restriction of foreign investments, its subsidisation of home industries, evidently stimulates international combinations. There is also ripening everywhere a conscious policy of State control over prices, in order to safeguard the consumer against the danger of a trade with price-fixing powers.

The new protective policy in Great Britain is definitely altering the situation as it appeared to a pre-war observer, Mr. Herman Levy, who wrote that " The development of controls and trusts in English industries is restricted by three facts—the absence of a protective tariff, the comparative insignificance of freights, and the rarity of slowly reproduced mineral products likely to form national or international monopolies." [3]

But neither free trade nor protection is a solid or sufficient barrier to the development of international combines, which was taking place before the war and is already beginning to resume activities.

Writing before the war, Mr. Macrosty stated:—
" In one way or another the world's trade in rails, tubes, nails, screws, sewing-thread, bleaching-powder, borax, nitrates, and tobacco is, to a greater or less degree, brought under international control, while, at

[1] Report, p. 11.
[2] Report, p. 26.
[3] *Monopolies and Competition*, p. 304 (Macmillan).

least till lately, dynamite was so controlled, and repeated attempts have been made similarly to syndicate the whole steel trade." Some of the combinations are temporarily broken or weakened, but the combinatory economics are nearly all in force, and in certain trades (especially metals and engineering) the advantages of regulation of output and divisions of market are greater than before. In the meat trade and certain other food trades, foreign combinations, such as the American Meat Trust, are more powerful than before.

The growth of international combinations with price-fixing powers must in time evoke protective measures by agreement between Governments. The beginning of an economic international policy, already recognised in the work of the League of Nations and its related instrument the International Labour Bureau, must address itself with ever clearer intentions to this task of regulating the prices and distribution, upon equitable terms, of articles and services controlled by international capitalism.

Meanwhile, the perilous condition of finance and of trade, to which all great industrial nations have been recently subjected, is intensifying the process of combination. In Germany especially, and to a less extent in Britain and America, the looser associations of business in Cartels, confined to the marketing processes, are giving place to actual mergers.

§ 6. We have seen that modern capitalism brings in all developed countries certain definite changes in the proportionate importance of occupations. Agriculture, because its productivity gains less directly from capitalistic economies than other processes, generally dwindles, an increasing proportion of foods and materials coming in from outside commerce. The staple manufactures, except those engaged in supplying growing foreign markets, increase to a maximum, and then show a positive or relative decline, as measured by the employment they afford. On the other hand, the transport and other distributive trades engaged in moving and selling goods show a marked advance. So do the occupations providing professional, financial, official, and other services.

The British census of 1911 [1] shows these processes to be continuous. Agriculture shows a growth much below that of the population as a whole, the numbers being 1,128,604 in 1901, and 1,235,237 in 1911. Mining, on the other hand, shows an advance nearly three times as fast as the growth of the population—viz., 35·2 per cent. in the decennium. The conveyance trades increase by 13·1 per cent., the percentage for railway employees being at the higher figure of 16·7, albeit a much less rapid growth than in any of the preceding census returns. Of the manufacturing trade groups metals and machinery show a considerable rise, 20·5 per cent. in the case of men. This class, however, contains the shipbuilding and vehicle trades, inclusive of motors. "Precious metals," etc., shows an even larger increase, 23·7 per cent., largely accounted for by "scientific instruments, musical instruments, and apparatus for sports and games." "Wood, furniture, and fittings" increase by 22·7, chiefly accounted for by house and shop fittings and by dealers in art and furniture. This is in curious contrast to the building trade, which shows a decline of 9·3 per cent. in the decade, carrying with them a smaller shrinkage in the "brush, cement, pottery, glass group."

The other large proportionate advances of manufacture are in "chemicals, oil," etc., where the enormous rise of 38·2 is registered, and in "paper, prints, books, stationery," etc., where the increase is 24·8 per cent.

Textiles, after showing a relative decline of occupation during the preceding decade, again advanced slightly faster than the population, owing mainly to a recovery of male employment in the cotton trade. The woollen and dress trades lose ground, the latter groups registering a decrease of 1·5 for men, and an increase of only 3·8 for women among the "makers."

Wholesale trade, and retail, wherever the latter is distinguished from processes of manufacture, continue to absorb a largely increasing proportion of employees.

[1] Unfortunately the results of the 1921 Census are not comparable with earlier figures, owing to the adoption of entirely new modes of classification.

This is seen in the increase of the whole group " commercial," with a figure 34·3 per cent. Commercial travellers yield 31 per cent.; banking, 33·3 per cent.; insurance agents, 56·9 per cent. The group called " dealers " gives 23·8 per cent. for men, 54·2 per cent. for women. The boot and shoe trade presents an instructive contrast. For, whereas the makers show a decline of 7·9 per cent., the dealers show a rise of 52·9 per cent. Domestic and allied services continue to show a proportionate decline, especially indoor domestics, whose increase is only 1·3 per cent. Professions show a large continuous advance, though the rise of new subsidiary branches makes exact measurement difficult. The same qualification applies to the figures for general and local government, which include many persons " taken over " from private employment during the period. The actual and proportionate advance in public employment remains, however, a noteworthy fact. The increase is from 171,687 to 244,379, or 42·3 per cent. for males; from 26,500 to 44,882, or 69·4 for females.

The accompanying table indicates the rise or decline in the relative importance of the general classes of occupations of males during the decennium 1901–1911.

MALE OCCUPATIONS.

MALES PER 10,000 OVER 10 YEARS, ENGLAND AND WALES.

	1901	1911			1901	1911
I. General or Local			VII. Agriculture—			
Government	141	179	Farmers	167	153
II. Defence	139	151	Farm-workers	594	558
III. Professions	257	269	Others	121	124
			VIII. Mining—			
IV. Domestic—			Coal	528	647
Outdoor	148	166	Others	110	92
Domestic—			IX. Metals—			
Indoor, etc.	102	118	Machines	814	846
V. Commercial—			Ships	71	76
(a) Merchants,			Vehicles	95	128
Agents, Banking,			X. Building	859	693
etc.	184	222	XI. Wood	169	158
(b) Clerks	254	264	XII. Paper, Print	123	131
VI. Conveyance—			XIII. Textiles	331	343
(a) Rail	290	291	XIV. Dress	305	275
(b) Road	355	345	XV. Food, etc.	638	669

§ 7. In the recent evolution of economic forms and methods women have been taking a continually larger part. Not only have they followed into organised and specialised industry the various processes of spinning, weaving, and dressmaking, the preparation of food and drink, laundry, and other once domestic occupations, but they have entered in increasing numbers into a larger number of general occupations, many of which until lately were exclusively male in personnel. The most rapid and largest advances have been in certain branches of commerce, public service, and the professions. During the last half century the census figures show that in the class commercial clerks, women have advanced from 5 to 245 per 1,000 " persons so employed," the last decade alone being responsible for a rise from 153 to 245. The telegraph and telephone departments have now fallen predominantly into female operation, the rise being from 406 to 522 per 1,000 in the decennium. In the drapery, shoe, and certain other branches of distributive trade, women are displacing men rapidly.

On the other hand, in the manufacturing branches of the chief textile trades, which until recently had been passing predominantly into female hands, a certain definite reversal is discernible. The statistics for the cotton trades make this manifest.

	1901.	1911.	Increase per cent.
Persons Occupied -	529,131	605,177	14·4
Males - - -	196,898	233,380	18·5
Females - - -	332,233	371,789	11·9

The woollen trade figures run on the same line, showing that the total increase of employment, amounting to 6·2 per cent., is made up out of 9·0 per cent. for males and only 4·2 per cent. for females. In the dress manufactures women continue to gain on men, but these industries themselves show a rate of growth much below that of the occupied population as a whole.

Proportion of Females in Certain Occupations out
of every 1,000 Persons so Employed.

	1861.	1871.	1881.	1891.	1901.	1911.
Teachers - - - - -	725	741	727	740	745	727
Photographers - - - -	66	147	197	234	257	297
Laundry Service - - -	990	987	981	964	957	931
Commercial Clerks - - -	5	16	33	72	153	245
Telegraph and Telephone - -	82	76	236	291	406	522
Earthenware, etc. - - -	311	354	384	385	392	421
India-rubber Workers - -	206	200	275	391	398	370
Brush, etc. - - - -	321	346	382	389	431	440
Paper Manufacturing - - -	417	395	444	401	366	312
Stationery, etc. - - -	345	380	531	600	643	653
Cotton - - - - -	567	598	620	609	628	614
Wool - - - - -	461	513	561	557	582	571
Silk - - - - -	642	676	691	667	702	693
Hemp and other Textiles - -	265	304	374	393	492	530
Hosiery - - - - -	468	468	533	629	713	735
Lace - - - - -	829	826	743	625	653	630
Carpet, Rug - - - -	183	312	362	440	517	544
Drapers, Mercers - - -	208	257	349	433	504	560
Straw Manufacturers - - -	921	926	903	814	737	666
Glover Makers - - -	864	882	854	769	761	731
Boot and Shoe Makers and Dealers - - - -	154	115	160	185	210	226
Tobacco - - - - -	221	296	435	548	601	596

The foregoing table, dealing with the occupations,
other than domestic service, in which women take a
prominent place, sheds important light upon the
advance of women into a larger number of trades and
manufactures. Earthenware, stationery, photography,
hosiery, carpets, shoes, brushes, chemicals, are prominent in this class. Not merely does domestic service
show a large relative shrinkage before the demand
of industry and commerce, but the predominant part
taken by women as teachers appears to have reached
its zenith and to be declining. This doubtless is due
to the larger number of occupations open to educated
women.

As the following table serves to indicate, the economic
system of the United States exhibits many of the same
tendencies with regard to the changes in the relative

importance of occupations—*i.e.*, the decline of agriculture and of domestic service, the large increase of clerical occupations, the increase in trade, transport, professions, and public service.

DISTRIBUTION OF POPULATION BY OCCUPATIONS IN U.S.A. (PERCENTAGES).

	1920.	1910.
Agriculture, Forests, Animals	26·3	33·1
Extract, Minerals	2·6	27·5
Manuf. Mechanical	30·8	6·8
Transportation	7·4	9·9
Trade	10·2	1·5
Public Service	1·9	4·2
Professions	5·2	9·4
Domestic and Personal Service	8·2	2·9
Clercial Occupations	7·5	4·6

The proportions of aggregate employment in gainful occupations according to sex run as follows:—

	Male per cent.	Female per cent.
1880	57·8	14·7
1890	60·2	17·4
1900	61·2	18·8
1910	81·3	23·4
1920	78·2	21·7

In America the changes in occupations of women and girls also follow the same general course as in Britain. The largest proportionate advance is in clerical occupations. Next come the professions, trade, public service. Manufactures and transportation show a considerable increase. Agriculture and domestic service show a tolerably large decline.

§ 8. The check which the Great War put upon the growth of industry in the world at large, and in the European belligerent countries in particular, is best attested in terms of reduced production of iron and steel and in shrinkage of foreign trade. The following tables of world production in pig iron and steel show that the world output for 1923, in both, lay considerably below the pre-war level of 1913. They also afford conspicuous proof of the supremacy of the United States in these basic industries, and of the collapse and slow recovery of Germany.

WORLD PRODUCTION OF PIG IRON

(In thousands of tons.)

COUNTRIES.	1913	1919	1920	1921	1922	1923
World Total ..	77,182	50,843	58,854	34,700	51,938	64,580
United States	30,655	30,579	36,401	16,506	26,851	39,500
Britain ..	10,260	7,398	8,035	2,616	4,902	7,860
France ..	5,126	2,374	3,380	3,308	5,147	5,000
Belgium ..	2,428	247	1,099	862	1,578	2,118
Germany ..	19,000	6,192	5,568	6,096	8,000	4,000
Italy	420	251	107	75	91	200

(Statistical Abstract of U.S.A., 1923, p. 270.)

WORLD PRODUCTION OF STEEL

(In thousands of tons.)

COUNTRIES.	1913	1919	1920	1921	1922	1923
World Total ..	75,019	57,111	67,145	42,487	63,098	72,573
United States ..	31,301	34,671	42,133	19,744	35,603	44,400
Britain ..	7,664	7,894	9,067	3,703	5,881	8,480
France ..	4,614	2,151	3,002	3,010	4,464	4,750
Belgium ..	2,428	329	1,233	780	1,539	2,185
Germany ..	18,631	7,648	6,624	8,700	9,000	5,000
Italy	918	763	762	672	600	800

(Statistical Abstract of U.S.A., 1923, p. 279.)

§ 9. The growth of economic internationalism strengthens the bonds of commercial intercourse between the different countries of the world, promotes a closer and more effective co-operation between the members of different nations in the exploitation of the resources of the world for the general good, and standardises the arts of production and consumption in all countries brought into this economic intercourse. This movement made notable advances in various districts, both extensively and intensively, during the opening years of the present century.

The absolute and the proportionate increase of import and export trade of the chief European countries before the war is contained in the following table.

It will be observed that every country showed an exceedingly marked advance, both in import and in export values. In every country except Russia a large, and for the most part a growing, surplus of import over export values was recorded. In Germany, for example, the surplus of imports rose from a little under 50 millions in 1901 to nearly 92 millions in 1912; in France, from 16 millions to 59 millions. In Austro-Hungary an export balance of 10 millions in 1901 passed into an import balance of 34 millions in 1912.

This condition of foreign trade attested, of course, a large growth of unseen exports in the way of shipping, financial, and other services, together with an increase of the aggregate of interest on foreign investments in the case of such countries as Germany, France, and Belgium. The balance, in the case of Italy and Austro-Hungary, was partly maintained by remittances from America sent by recent immigrants into those countries.

VALUE OF IMPORTS AND EXPORTS INTO AND FROM. Value £.

	1901.	1904.	1907.	1910.	1912.
	£	£	£	£	£
GREAT BRITAIN—					
Imports	521,999,198	551,038,628	645,807,942	678,257,024	744,640,633
Exports	347,864,268	371,015,321	517,977,167	534,145,817	598,961,130
RUSSIA—					
Imports (Special)	62,639,000	68,759,000	84,444,000	114,469,000	123,687,000
Exports	80,389,000	106,229,000	111,152,000	152,959,000	160,318,000
GERMANY—					
Imports (General)	281,578,000	330,444,000	470,550,000	468,809,000	568,962,000
Exports (General)	232,247,000	273,622,000	365,913,000	397,252,000	476,140,000
BELGIUM—					
Imports	145,626,000	177,058,000	244,952,000	262,066,000	—
Exports	129,578,000	153,904,000	207,646,000	227,786,000	—
FRANCE—					
Imports	224,248,000	228,860,000	314,984,000	364,104,000	411,744,000
Exports	208,788,000	229,780,000	290,244,000	324,196,000	352,956,000
ITALY—					
Imports	69,758,000	78,514,000	119,994,000	137,866,000	156,646,000
Exports	55,997,000	65,853,000	81,590,000	87,553,000	100,594,000
AUSTRO-HUNGARY—					
Imports (Special)	68,860,000	85,329,000	104,249,000	118,869,000	148,200,000
Exports (Special)	78,561,000	87,028,000	102,387,000	100,775,000	113,911,000

The significant fact, however, was the rapid growth of international trade. After making due allowance for the general rise of prices in recent years, that growth was considerably faster than accepted estimates of the growth of industry as a whole in the respective countries. Foreign trade had everywhere been growing faster than internal trade. Closer investigation will also show that the trade was more varied, as regards kinds of goods, and as regards the countries with which it was carried on. In civilised countries everybody had become increasingly dependent upon the production of a greater number of foreigners for the supply of an increased number of their daily needs.

The damages done by the war and the post-war situation in Europe to this international trade were grave and numerous. Disordered monetary systems operated to retard recovery of industry and to disturb security and confidence in trade. The setting up of new tariffs, shifts in trade routes, deficiency of purchasing power, embargoes and boycotts, war animosities, the dropping out of Russia from the comity of nations, disturbances in China and elsewhere, have all been obstacles to easy commercial intercourse between nations. Though some considerable recovery from the severance of trade relations during the war had been made by 1923, the following general comparison of world trade in 1913 and 1923 shows a very large actual shrinkage in volume, as distinguished from inflated values. It also sheds interesting light upon the growing share of world trade passing to the United States and the British Empire (in particular the other British countries).

Table from p. 667 of the *Survey of Oversea Markets*, published (1925) by the Committee on Industry and Trade (Stationery Office). 6s. net.

WORLD TRADE 1913 AND 1923. BRITISH, AMERICAN, AND FRENCH SHARE.

IMPORTS (SPECIAL) OF MERCHANDISE.

	Total Value.		Per cent. of Total.	
	1913 Million £	1923 Million £	1913	1923
World Total (157 Countries) ..	4305·3	5700·0	100·0	100·0
British Empire— United Kingdom ..	659·2	958·4	15·10	16·81
Other British Countries ..	518·0	788·4	11·87	13·85
Total British Empire	1177·2	1746·8	26·97	30·66
United States ..	361·0	829·0	8·27	14·54
France.. ..	333·9	430·5	7·65	7·55
All Other Countries ..	2493·2	2693·7	57·11	47·25

EXPORTS (SPECIAL) OF MERCHANDISE.

	Total Value.		Per cent. of Total.	
	1913 Million £	1923 Million £	1913	1923
World Total .. (157 Countries)	4034·8	5299·0	100·0	100·0
British Empire— United Kingdom ..	525·3	743·5	13·02	14·03
Other British Countries ..	494·7	853·5	12·26	16·11
Total British Empire	1020·0	1597·0	25·28	30·14
United States..	503·1	894·3	12·47	16·88
France.. ..	272·8	401·8	6·76	7·58
All Other Countries ..	2238·9	2405·9	55·49	45·40

Note 1.—In the tables of Imports and Exports (Special) of Merchandise given on the preceding page, conversions of foreign currencies to sterling have been made at the averages of the quoted rates. The figures for 1923 are available for about 91 per cent. of the imports and 89 per cent. of the exports, and the balance has been estimated from the 1922 records. For better comparison with 1913, the figures of trade of the United Kingdom in 1923 have been adjusted (reduced) to apply to the British Isles as a whole, and not to Great Britain and Northern Ireland only.

Note 2.—For an explanation of the meaning of " special " imports and exports, see p. 27.

§ 10. The most distinctive feature of modern economic internationalism, however, is not the growth of ordinary commerce across political boundaries, but the increasing investment of capital in foreign countries. This growth of export of capital (involving great complications in the general trade balances of the countries engaged in it) has been common to all the advanced industrial countries of Europe. The United Kingdom has gone furthest in this direction, both as to the amount of money invested abroad and the proportion of that sum to home investments. The investments from the United Kingdom are also more widely distributed over non-European countries than is the case with the foreign investments of other capital-exporting countries. Though no closely reliable measures of the flows of exported capital or of the flow of home investments are available, such indices as are to hand point to a large absolute and relative growth of foreign as compared with home investments on the part of the United Kingdom from 1905 to 1914. The earlier year first registers a large predominance in the total of capital absorbed in London for investment abroad, as compared with that subscribed for investment at home, and the figures for subsequent years up to 1914 emphasise this predominance. When allowance is also made for capital " subscribed partly on the Continent," but wholly subscribed through London, the comparative figures, compiled from the beginning of the century, run as follows:—

In Thousands of £.

Year.	For Investment in United Kingdom.	For Investment Abroad.
1900	100,121	26,069
1901	106,585	26,978
1902	75,124	62,214
1903	44,868	60,013
1904	50,083	64,616
1905	48,426	110,617
1906	39,314	72,995
1907	32,988	79,334
1908	50,052	117,871
1909	18,681	150,468
1910	60,296	179,832
1911	26,146	142,740
1912	45,335	144,560
1913	35,951	149,735

Though the actual proportions of subscribed capital for the several fields do not closely correspond with the figures of issues, while large volumes of savings pass into home issues by private processes of investment, the general tendency disclosed by such statistics is unmistakable.

This flow is into an expanding number of employments in an increasing number of countries. While the largest flow has been into Canada, the United States and Argentina, other South American countries have been large recipients; smaller though considerable sums have been found for South Africa, our other African colonies, and Egypt, while India and Australia have also taken a share. Russia within recent years had come to count as a borrower of British savings.

" The main purpose for which these gigantic sums are required is still railway construction in almost every part of the world. Docks, water and gas works, electric lighting, telegraphs, and tramways, form another important group of enterprises which are constantly demanding fresh capital. All of these activities are conducted both by Governmental Authorities —central or local—and by Joint-Stock Companies. In addition, there are mining concerns and plantations, land mortgage companies, banks, trust insurance and trading companies, all of which figured prominently during earlier periods of foreign investment. There is, however, a new characteristic visible in the course of foreign investment during the past few years—namely, a tendency to invest in manufacturing and industrial concerns." [1]

Statistics of issues on the French Bourses showed the same tendency to a larger volume and a wider distribution of foreign investments, and, though the proportion of foreign issues in the case of Germany was much smaller, the absolute amounts, inclusive of Government loans, were very considerable. Whereas, during the pre-war period, Great Britain had invested yearly sums varying from 100 to 200 millions in the colonies and foreign countries, the yearly flow of French money into foreign lands had been from 80 to 100 millions, that of German from 40 to 60 millions. Holland and Belgium were also contributors towards a stream of money furnished from Western Europe to the borrowing countries of the world, amounting to some 300 millions annually.

The actual amount of British capital invested abroad was estimated in 1914 to be approximately £4,000,000,000, while French capital was put at £1,800,000,000, and German capital at £1,200,000,000.

The financing of the Great War materially affected the flow of export of capital and its ownership. Germany disposed of the greater part of her foreign securities; Great Britain reduced her foreign holdings by £1,000,000,000 or thereabouts. A large proportion of French foreign investments in Europe disappeared. Since the war none of these nations has had large surplus funds available for outside investment, though Britain has made some recovery of her war sacrifices.

§ 11. One of the most significant effects of the war in its bearing on the relative position of nations in finance and commerce has been the rapid transformation of the United States from the position of a debtor into that of a creditor nation. Up to the opening of the twentieth century America was still drawing capital from Western Europe, chiefly through London, though the tide was beginning to turn before the war. The

[1] *The Export of Capital*, by C. K. Hobson, p. 159 (Constable), the fullest historical and statistical treatment of the subject up to 1914.

heavy advances to Europe during the war, chiefly through credit sales of supplies, is estimated to have left a balance of indebtedness in America's favour to the extent of some £600,000,000, omitting the loans to foreign Governments. Since the war, new capital loans, public and private, of large dimensions, have been made.

The situation as regards the amount and territorial distribution of foreign investments at the beginning of 1924 was thus presented by the Department of Commerce.

Region.	Government Obligations. $1,000.	Industrial Obligations. $1,000.	Total. $1,000.
Canada	750,000	1,750,000	2,500,000
Cuba	110,000	1,250,000	1,360,000
Mexico	22,000	1,000,000	1,022,000
Central America and W. Indies	48,000	100,000	148,000
S. America	430,000	800,000	1,230,000
Europe	950,000	350,000	1,300,000
Asia	190,000	250,000	440,000
	2,500,000	5,500,000	8,000,000

This sum, $8,000,000,000, does not take into account obligations of foreign Governments, owed since the World War, amounting to some $18,500,000,000. Against the $8,000,000,000, representing American investments abroad, may be set foreign residents' investments in America, estimated at some $3,000,000,000 at the beginning of 1924.

Consideration of the trade balance in recent years makes it evident that, apart from the continued investment of new subscribed capital, an automatic increase of American holdings in foreign countries must result from the pursuance of a tariff policy that disables America from receiving the annual interest payments due to her from her foreign creditors. The average recent annual surplus of America available for foreign advances is conservatively estimated by Mr. Dawes at £130,000,000, inclusive of " what might in the most favourable circumstances be paid to us under the full settlement of international indebtedness." If this sum were left (as under the present tariff restriction upon imports) to roll up at compound interest, it would amount in twenty years' time approximately to £325,000,000 per annum, without any extension of American foreign trade. But the large surplus of exports over imports, the medium of this new expansion of foreign investments, is unlikely to cease, unless the Government reverses its tariff policy; and with the constantly expanding productivity of mass production in the iron and steel and other standard manufactures, it is likely to increase. A very rapid expansion of American investments, at present chiefly in Europe and on the American Continent, but later to an increasing extent for the development of oil, rubber, and other raw materials in backward countries of Asia and Africa, may be expected.

This advance of America coincides with a decline in the position of Britain as a foreign investor. For, though Britain has made good since the war a large part of her war sacrifices of American and other foreign investments, her average annual surplus is considerably reduced, and even a fair recovery of world trade will not enable her to resume her prewar supremacy in the world market for investments. The same must apply with every greater stringency to the other large investing countries, France and Germany. Assuming that these countries pay off any considerable portion of their foreign indebtedness for loans and reparations, their surplus available for foreign investment is likely for some time to be little or nil. Indeed, it seems quite probable that any foreign investments they may make will be offset by fresh borrowing from America, and, to a less extent, from

Britain, these countries being paid their interest on past loans and instalments of reparations out of fresh credits which they themselves supply.

§ 12. The increased dependence upon large amounts of capital for the successful conduct of so many branches of industry and commerce, and the large part played by distant and intricate processes of commerce involving long periods of time for their accomplishment, have given immense importance to the machinery of banking and finance. The modern investment system, through joint-stock enterprise, has not only extended and depersonalised the modern business ; it has given a dominant and determinant place in the business world to little groups of men in the great monetary centres who control and regulate the flows of capital and the credit system by which an increasing proportion of modern business is conducted. The work of floating new enterprises by collecting from diverse sources the required capital, of converting private into public joint-stock businesses, of assisting to finance the concrete operations of industry and commerce by loans, discounts, and other financial aids, of undertaking risks and providing guarantees, of furnishing to stockbrokers and other dealers in '' paper '' the means to carry on their operations, has given a pivotal position in modern capitalism to the men and houses wielding this money power. The great joint-stock banks in most countries are the centres of this power. Most of these operations are conducted, or at least financed, by them.

The direct relations between the bank and industry have differed in different countries. In Germany and in the United States the direct financial dependence of great manufacturing and other business firms upon the banks has been much closer than in Great Britain. But in every advanced country the development of banking and insurance, both extensive and intensive, has been a marked feature of our time. Every town, every considerable village, has its branches and its agents of some large company. The savings of all classes are tempted into broader channels of investment, and cheques are everywhere playing a larger rôle as methods of payment.

What applies to internal trade applies also to foreign trade. Great capitalistic countries like Great Britain, Germany, Holland, extended their banking systems over the whole world, assisting to finance trade and to develop the resources of new or backward countries. Great Britain, with her great predominance in shipping and in foreign trade, took the lead. In the early twentieth century, however, the more adventurous German banks forced numerous openings. The United States banks, hitherto absorbed for the most part in financing their own great developing industries, also began to enter on the international field, the National City Bank being the pioneer in the establishment of foreign branches in Brazil, Argentina, Uruguay, and Cuba. A paper read by Professor Emery R. Johnson at the meeting of the American Economic Association (December, 1915) stated, on the authority of a well-known New York banker, that more than a hundred European banks had established branches in foreign countries, exceeding two thousand in number. "There are more than one hundred in South America, about three hundred in Asia, four hundred in Africa, and more than seven hundred in Australia, New Zealand, and the Pacific Isles."

The growth of foreign trade and investments has been closely related to this movement of international finance. It is the most fluid form of economic internationalism.

§ 13. The Great War will probably serve in history as a convenient landmark indicating certain important changes in the relative economic strength and progress of the several industrial nations, and of the classes or occupations within these nations. In other words (partly as a consequence of the war itself, but more largely as a resultant of many forces which were operating prior to the war, but which acquired greater momentum owing to war and post-war conditions), important changes have been taking place in the distribution of wealth as between different nations of the world and different sections of the nations.

The following table was compiled in 1919 by Sir Josiah Stamp:—

Table showing the estimated Wealth and Annual Income of various Countries at the outbreak of War in 1914, and the approximate accuracy of the respective estimates.

Country.	National Capital.				National Income.			
	Estimates based on the work of	Approximation to accuracy: Grade*	Amount in Million £	Amount per head of Population £	Estimates based on the work of	Approximation to accuracy: Grade*	Amount in Million £	Amount per head of Population £
United Kingdom	Stamp	I	14,500	318	Bowley, Stamp	I	2,250	50
United States	Official, King	II	42,000	424	Official, King	II	7,250	72
Germany	Helfferich, etc.	II	16,550	244	Helfferich	I	2,150	30
France	Pupin, Thery	III	12,000	303	Pupin	II	1,500	38
Italy	Gini	III	4,480	128	—	IV	800	23
Austria-Hungary	Fellner	III	6,200	121	—	IV	1,100	21
Spain	Barthe	IV	2,940	144	Barthe	IV	230	11
Belgium	Official	III	1,200	157	—	—	—	—
Holland	Stuart	III	1,050	167	—	—	—	1
Russia	Neymarck	IV	12,000	85	—	—	—	1
Sweden	Flodstrom, Fochlbeck	III	940	168	—	—	—	—
Norway	Gini	IV	220	90	—	—	—	—
Denmark	Gini	IV	500	176	—	—	—	—
Switzerland	Gini	IV	800	205	—	—	—	—
Australia	Knibbs	I	1,530	318	Official, Knibbs	I	258	54
Canada	Banker's Association	—	—	—	—	—	—	—
Japan	Stamp	II	2,285	300	Giffen	IV	300	40
Argentine	Bunge	III	2,400	340	Stamp	III	325	6

* Grade I. Estimate is not likely to be inaccurate to a greater extent than 10 per cent.
„ „   II.   „   „   „   „   „   „   „   20   „
„ „   III.   „   „   „   „   „   „   „   30   „
„ „   IV.   „   „   may be inaccurate   „   „   40   „

Though material is not available for estimating wealth and annual income ten years later, certain general statements may be made, indicative of the relative gains and losses in economic position. Though the United States may not have greatly increased her lead in the amount of capital per head, owing to the large proportion of her wealth vested in as yet undeveloped natural resources, her income must have increased faster than that of any other country, both in terms of money and of commodities. Indeed, of the belligerent nations she is the only one whose current productivity (1925) is not below the pre-war level. Possessing the greatest variety of natural resources in the largest, wealthiest, and best connected market, her production and distribution of wealth have been far less disturbed than in any European country. During the war she reaped immense gains from an artificially stimulated world trade, conducted on a high price level, and after the war the forces of mass standardised production have (as the statistics of iron and steel and power indicate) made great further advances. Britain and France are still operating a little below their pre-war level of productivity, though British productive power in capital and labour is fully capable of the pre-war output were markets available. France is hindered by bad public finance and lack of business initiative from assuming the position which her enlarged natural resources of coal and iron would render possible. Germany, well furnished with plant, labour, and business capacity, is crippled by lack of working capital and adequate markets. Of the broken Austro-Hungarian Empire, Czecho-Slovakia is the only section that has made a good recovery. Austria, even with her restored monetary system, conducts a struggle for bare subsistence, owing to the tariff walls set up by sections of her former free markets. Though financial difficulties and political uncertainty damage the full recovery of Italy, it is probable that industrial Italy, with Switzerland and Scandinavia, by reason of their newly available resources of industrial power, will take a larger place in capitalistic industry. Belgium and Holland are evidently advancing in wealth production.

Spain and Russia are economically enfeebled, though the large varied natural resources of the latter, coupled with her improved land tenure, might lead to a rapid economic progress, were world confidence in her finance restored, and an adequate system of economic incentives applied to evoke industrial efficiency.

The relative strength and growth in capitalist production of the various countries must, of course, be profoundly affected by their relative possession and availability of coal, oil, and water power, together with improvements in the technique of the generation and distribution of electric power. The dominating part played by electric energy, distributed from great generating stations over wide areas, may not only alter the relative position of the industrial nations in wealth, production, and commerce, but may have equally important reactions upon the conditions of work and life within the industrial countries.

The development of electric power will have four chief distinguishable uses : for industry, transport, agriculture, and domestic services. In each department it can be utilised so as greatly to reduce costs and increase productivity. If it is fully utilised, it is capable, with a reasonable rate of progress in technique, of increasing so largely the output of wealth as to raise the existing populations of industrial countries to a far higher level of material comfort and leisure than has hitherto been attainable. If, as seems probable, the established checks upon birth-rate still hold good, poverty in the old use of the term might be abolished, and the economic struggle might cease to dominate politics. Decent arrangements between capital and labour, employer and worker, might bring about an ease and security of life and work which would transform the social and moral fabric of civilisation.

How far these immense gains may be attained will largely depend upon how far the new power is made easily and equally available for all sorts and conditions of men and work. It is self-evident that unrestricted private capitalism affords no adequate security for the nation as a whole attaining the full benefits of the new economies of power. If areas for the marketing of

electric power were handed over to competing companies, with their separate services, the waste, insecurity,
and disturbance occasioned by such private enterprise
would be immense. On the other hand, to establish
private monopolies of power, in sole possession of large
markets and at liberty to rackrent consumers, would
be still more intolerable. If this be admitted, we are
thrown upon the alternatives of public administration
or public control. If, as is likely at any rate in Britain
and America, the latter policy prevails, at any rate in
the earlier period of development, much will turn upon
the principles as well as the efficiency of State control.
Should the operation of the industry be that of ordinary
business and finance (the capital and conduct of the
industry being left to the incentives of private enterprise,
checked only by price restrictions for the protection
of consumers, with, perhaps, an excess profit tax
to divert some of the monopoly value to the public
revenue), the social economic effects might be quite
other than those attendant on a public enterprise.
For, in the case of a public service, the supply of electric
energy would take a time and space economy widely
divergent from that of a purely profit making company.
It might, for example, adopt a policy of equal supply
prices, at any rate for certain important uses, over the
whole area of supply, following the analogy of postal
services ; while it might take a longer time range for
the development of certain services than would be
remunerative to private enterprise. It is easy, for
instance, to see that the State might regard the cheap
availability of electric power to stimulate agriculture
and strengthen rural industries with a more liberal eye
than would a private company looking to quick profits
as its criterion. For the State could not disregard
certain considerations of human welfare that lie not
only outside the profit making scheme, but outside
the economic field.

A power policy that might enable and encourage a
wider spacing out of population for work and living
is one of the obvious possibilities of the new electric
age. The State might go further in this human
economy than private enterprise could afford to do,

by making favourable rates for works more distant
from the generating centres, or, at any rate, for such
cheap transport as would encourage workers to live
at some distance from their workplace. Even if strict
business motives should at first prevail, the possibility
of transmission of power at moderate rates will reduce
the close concentration of the steam age, though the
main industries of the country would still lie in the
neighbourhood of the great coal-fields in countries where
coal remained the source of power.

An era in which electric power was available cheaply
and easily for most industrial, agricultural, and even
domestic routine services, might not only raise the
standard of comfort for the whole population and
enable them to live in a less crowded environment,
but it might transform the methods of work and the
character of whole classes of workers. When the
farm-worker, the navvy, the shoemaker, the house-
wife, shift more and more of their routine manual
labour on to electric machines, they assume more and
more the attitude of skilled operators. With the
change in the nature of their work, their mental attitude
towards the work is changed. The command and skilled
direction of mechanical power gives a new interest and
dignity to work, where it is not unduly narrowed in
its application. Rural life is already visibly changing
with the new power, and, taken in conjunction with
the other services of communication, education, and
amusement, which are breaking up the isolation of
country life, electricity may effect a liberation of the
rural mind fraught with noticeable reactions in political
and other fields of conduct.

Part II.

§ 1. This speculation into the coming electric age
may serve as a convenient introduction to two chief
economic lessons of the Great War.

The most imposing revelation from the experience
of British industry during the war was its quantitative

and qualitative adaptability to sudden new demands. After nearly three years, during which more than four million men (or nearly one-third of the adult able-bodied male population) had been drafted into the fighting services, while something like a million more had been added for the special requirements of the munitions trades, the ordinary trades of the country were still able to be carried on so as to supply the material requisites of life for the remaining civil population upon a level not appreciably lower than before the war.

It is true that larger supplies than usual were imported to supplement our internal production. But, when freights and other special costs are taken into account, it is probable that the actual quantity of imported foods and materials available for civilian use and consumption was not much above the normal. It is clear that the nation was able to draw upon internal reserves of productive power much greater than would hitherto have been believed to exist. The production of material wealth as a whole (inclusive of munitions and other material war requisites) did not appear to have been perceptibly diminished by the withdrawal of four million men.

How has this been possible ? Well, in the first place, not more than half this supply of men was taken out of labour employed in the direct production of material goods. Probably nearly half of the four millions was drawn from the leisured, the student, and the employing classes, the professional, distributive, and transport occupations, domestic and other personal services. Some half-a-million represent the emigration suspended during the war. Some of the luxury trades and recreations, especially those catering for the needs of the well-to-do male, fell into abeyance. But the fundamental material industries were reinforced from various sources, so that their aggregate output did not much diminish. The unemployed margin was absorbed, retired workers came back to work, children and young persons were taken from education into industry, great numbers of women were drawn into manufacture, commerce, and agriculture, a fuller week was worked, with much overtime and even Sunday labour, more labour-saving machines were introduced, and all machinery speeded up, "dilution" produced a more effective division of labour, and a suspension of trade union rules gave more elasticity and productivity to labour. While, therefore, the distributive and other services were much let down, the "productive" were well maintained. Mr. Hoover draws the same lesson from the shorter war experience of America. "Certain proof of our deficient normal production is shown when, with 20 per cent. of man-power withdrawn into the army, we yet produced 20 per cent. more commodities than we are doing to-day." [1]

Post-war experience in Europe, and not least in Britain, has sharpened the conscious need for an increased national output. Demands for higher wages and shorter hours on the part of labour, the higher rate of interest required by new capital, and the consequent difficulty in keeping costs of production low enough to maintain the pre-war share of the shrunken world market, press home in each industrial country the needs for improved technique, business organisation, and finance, in order to maintain full regular production.

§ 2. Waste signifies the failure to utilise the best available methods, not only by the several businesses but by industries taken separately and as integral parts of a national economy. Some of the largest wastes are found in the wrong disposition of economic resources. A leading example is the excess of energy absorbed in the distributive processes. This perhaps attains its maximum in the handling of food stuffs. Sir Charles Fielding, analysing the retail prices of wheat, milk, and meat in England in the year 1923, showed that between 50 and 60 per cent. of the prices of these home-grown products was absorbed in the processes of distribution and conversion into food. In the vegetable, flower, and fish trades the percentage is probably higher. The constant increase in the proportion of the population employed in the distributive trades

---

[1] *Industrial Waste*, New York, 1921.

attests the wastes of selling costs, partly attributable to excessive competition, partly to needless duplication of wholesale and retail handling.

But in the technique of manufacture Britain is hardly less wasteful. " It seems probable that if all the iron and steel works in this country adopted the most efficient methods, they could, on an average, improve their output by something between 50 and 100 per cent."[1] The huge waste of coal in almost all its uses is too well known to need specific evidence. This waste, so far as it consists in failure to apply the best machinery and methods, may be attributed partly to mental indolence, partly to a lack of risk-taking enterprise, partly to lack of capital needed for scrapping out-of-date plant and putting in new expensive plant. Already, before the war, British business men were waking up to the fact that they were outclassed in certain branches of manufacture by the superior " science " of Germany and the mass production of America. The greater use of machinery and mechanical power in many American plants, and the greater readiness of German businesses to avail themselves of chemical and physical laboratories, were beginning to act as stimulants to British business enterprise. But, though there is plenty of evidence to show that in many branches of the textile, metal, and other trades Britain leads in efficiency and quality of output, the statistical comparisons in output per employee in many staple processes in England and America indicate large economies either in methods or in human energy favourable to America.[2]

[1] Industrial Fatigue Research Board Report 5, p. 95.

[2] See, for some striking examples, an article by Professor Taussig in the *Quarterly Journal of Economics*, Oct., 1924.

Economic students in Britain, however, are so accustomed to hear references to the high productivity of American labour and machine production that it will surprise them to learn the grave testimony borne by American business men and economists to the wasteful working of American businesses. Mr. Stuart Chase (*The Tragedy of Waste*, ch. iii) has classified this waste under four categories :

(1) Waste in the technique of Production and Distribution ;

(2) Waste of natural resources ;

(3) Idle man power, or lost labour time ;

(4) Waste in consumption, or what may be termed detrimental produc-

This leads to the recognition of a defect in the general working of our economic system largely accountable for the restrictions of output to which both employers and workers in many of our productive industries are prone. The amount of recorded unemployment during periods of trade depression is a very inadequate measure of the waste due to a knowledge on the part of employers and workers that their productive capacity is normally in excess of their market. This is no place to open a discussion of the root causes of cyclical depressions, and of the existence in ordinary times of a capacity of supply in excess of effective demand. The point is, that this limitation of the market, operative in most industries at most times, keeps the productive power of the economic system functioning far below its full capacity. The fear of unemployment is constantly before the workers, and exercises a depressing influence upon their output. It is largely responsible for the " ca' canny," organised or customary in many trade unions, and for the similar tactics of employers in trade combines or associations. The industrial system works normally at low gear, lest high productivity should precipitate a crisis, display over-production, and herald in a period of trade depression. The prolonged depression, beginning in 1920-21 and felt throughout the world of industry in different degrees of intensity, focussed more attention upon this central defect of our system than ever before. Prevailing poverty in Europe led economists and politicians to fasten upon insufficiency of purchasing power as the source of this trouble, though this was only another

---

tion. Certain of these wastes are greater in America than in most European countries, and go far to offset the superiority o that country in standardisation and machine economy. The waste of natural resources is probably the heaviest loss. Oil, timber, coal, water power, the soil, and animal life have been operated in a recklessly extravagant way. The advertising industry, accredited with a turnover of $1,200,000,000, speculation and gambling in their various forms, quackery in medicine and hygiene, are also large contributors. Mr. Chase's general estimate of the economic waste in the current working of America's economic system is given as approximately 50 per cent. of the total available labour power (p. 270).

way of saying that markets were limited. But it
has led to innumerable discussions of the monetary
machinery of the economic system, and to many speculative policies for pumping in more purchasing power
by open or masked processes of inflation. This
concentration upon the monetary aspect of the trouble
served to divert attention from the kernel of the problem
—viz., the question why there normally exists more
capital and labour than is wanted. The constant tendency of production to outrun consumption, due to a
distribution of income that tends to more creation
of capital than can find adequate employment in
helping to produce saleable goods, is the inevitable price
of the prevailing inequality of economic opportunities,
which disables large sections of the community from
expressing their needs and desires through effective
demand for commodities, while it enables and induces
small wealthy sections to disorganise the economic
system by the irregular and wasteful methods of their
spending, at the same time leaving too large a surplus
to pour automatically into new investments for creating
more plant and other capital than can be fully employed.

§ 3. There is no remedy for this low gear operation
of the economic system except better distribution of
wealth and better opportunities. It is, of course, true
that even in a country relatively so prosperous as
America the productive power of great industry is
continually held in leash by "the price system." It
would be unprofitable for industry to let itself "all out."
Therefore, it is idle to point to the need for higher
productivity without perceiving that it can only be
justified by radical changes in the distributive system.

These issues were ripening before the war. The
detailed evidence of our Census of Production, together
with the later statistical analysis of Professor Bowley
and Sir Josiah Stamp, made it manifest that the British
output of wealth was not adequate to provide a satis-
factory standard of living for our whole population
even were it parcelled out equally among them. But it
was bad logic that led so many to draw the lesson
that insufficient production, not inequitable distribution,
was the sole source of trouble. For larger produc-

tion is unattainable without improved distribution, partly because of the "limited" market, whose limitations would not be thus removed, partly because the incentives to employers and employees to produce n ore will remain inadequate. Slowly the mind of social economic reformers is moving towards a clearer recognition of the intimate correlation of the problems of increased production, more equal distribution, and improved consumption of wealth. They are not three sets of problems, but one. The inter-relation may be presented in the following terms. A more equal (and more equitable) distribution of income, by which a larger share passes to the workers, while the share of the owners and employers is reduced (by cutting down the surplus elements in the shape of rents, high profits, and other emoluments which do little or nothing to stimulate production), will have important reactions both upon the quantity and quality of the wealth produced and consumed. As it is admitted that inequality of incomes is favourable to saving, inasmuch as a larger proportion of high incomes is saved than of lower incomes, the first effect of equalisation would be to reduce the proportion of the aggregate income that is saved, and to increase the proportion that is spent. But this need not and should not involve any absolute reduction in the quantity of saving and provision of new capital. For the enlarged proportion of spending will have its first effect in a fuller and more regular employment of the existing supplies of capital and labour. This larger demand for capital will in all probability require the existing supply of capital to be reinforced by a rate of saving even higher than that which formerly took place. In other words, both the rate of spending and the rate of saving will simultaneously be raised by means of the higher productivity rendered possible by the stimulation applied to consumption through the better distribution of income. The rate of spending, however, will be raised more than the rate of saving. As the increased spending will operate in raising the standards of living for the main body of the workers, and in cutting down the expenditure of large unearned incomes upon luxuries, greater regularity and security will be imparted to the general working of the industrial system —*i.e.*, a transference of employment of capital and labour from essentially useless, fluctuating, and degrading trades and services to more useful, regular, and wholesome ones. This implies a general rise in the human utility of consumption. A double gain would thus result from a better distribution. It would stimulate a higher productivity, and would impart a larger consuming value to each item of the product.

If this be the true inter-relation of production, distribution, and consumption, it appears that the desired increase of production and the desired improvement of consumption are dependent on better distribution. Many business men, who may not accept or understand this interaction, will readily admit that the increased productivity which they would like to see attained without any alterations in the existing business arrangements appears unattainable, because the workers refuse to give out in time, energy, and skill the increased productive power required to enlarge the output and to keep down labour costs.

§ 4. There has arisen, therefore, in many quarters a new willingness to consider and to try bolder experiments, both in private and public enterprise, than have hitherto been possible. To realise the needed condition of higher productivity, more pacific relations between capital and labour, employer and employed, are essential. The peril of a situation in which falling wages and unemployment on an unprecedented scale are leading features drives the more active-minded employers to make considerable concessions from the old capitalist autocracy. From the employers' standpoint the problem is one of devising adequate and reliable stimuli to draw from the workers a larger and more regular output of productive energy, a greater willingness to adopt and apply new mechanical and business methods, and, in general, to co-operate more effectively with the other factors of production. But, in order thus to get labour to realise its community of interest with capital, that community itself must be established on a firmer footing. Labour must be given a more

definite "interest" in the business and in its conduct,
so far as matters directly affecting labour are involved.
Hitherto, the business has "belonged to" the persons
who owned the capital ; it has been exclusively their
property. The "interest" of any worker in it has
been terminable by a week's notice, or less. Except
so far as grudging concessions have been made to
trade union pressure, the worker has had no voice
in regulating the "conditions of labour" in the factory,
mine, mill, or farm. Some more solid property in,
and control of, the business must be secured for the
workers in it. How to make that property and control
consistent with the maintenance of the supremacy of
the employer in the general conduct of the business,
its organisation, as a technical instrument, the determination of the lines and methods of production, and the
buying and selling processes, will be the great problem
of business reconstruction. But closely related to it is
the problem of securing to the workers a definite
pecuniary interest in the success of the business as a
whole. The wage system need not be displaced. The
workers cannot be called upon to share fully in the
risks and possible losses which the owners of the capital
undertake. For no chances of participation in profits,
however high, could secure the workers against the risks
of periods of "working at a loss." But the wage
system could be supplemented and strengthened by
participation in the gains, applied so as to stimulate
the greater efficiency of labour which should create
gains. The evident defects which have caused the
failure of most profit sharing schemes are being studied
and remedies sought for them. For if capital and
labour are to be brought into conscious harmony within
the business, they must be got to realise that they stand
to gain by effective co-operation. If the labourers,
through their credited representatives, had some better
understanding of the nature and methods of the business and of the factors contributing to success or failure,
had some control over the conditions of working, and
some definite interest in putting out the largest and
best product compatible with reasonable consideration
of their health and safety, the output of industry would

undoubtedly be greatly increased, and its distribution would be more socially beneficial.

But in all reform of business structure there is a third factor, the interests of which must be brought into harmony with those of capital and labour—namely, the market, the consumer. In freely competitive industry, the competition of rival businesses is considered to furnish a sufficient guarantee for the consumer's interest. But over a very large part of the fields of industry and commerce, combination has displaced competition, so far as the relations of producer with consumer are concerned. From top to bottom, from bank, insurance, and shipping rates to retail prices of milk and bread, the consumer's interests are jeopardised by more or less tight, widespread, and continuous arrangements between the members of a trade. The experience of the war disclosed many conspicuous instances of this organised oppression of the consumer.

Considerations of market open up a wide divergence of interests and of policy between those trades which are sheltered, by reason of the virtual monopoly of the home market which their goods or services command, and those working largely for export trade, or exposed to the competition of foreign goods entering these shores. The weakness of the latter section, containing many of the most highly developed capitalist industries, especially in metals and textiles, stands in the way of that general enforcement of a national minimum of wages and hours which is a more or less accepted principle of enlightened social thinkers. The economy of high wages and short hours has its limits, and international trade unionism has not gone far towards standardising labour conditions in the competing nations. The result has been that in almost every European country certain of the sheltered trades have been able to keep a larger share of the artificially inflated rates of pay due to the war and post-war emergencies than the other trades, emphasising the weakness of the latter by the high prices which their sheltered condition enables them to maintain. The discontent and unrest among these great bodies of organised labour can find no obvious relief. Neither protective tariffs nor public subsidies can furnish any remedy for trades unable to hold their own in external markets.

Under these conditions many business firms are inclined towards radical changes in business organisation, with a view to harmonising the interests of capital and labour and establishing better relations. This signifies an abatement of the two distinctive features of ordinary capitalism—viz., the absolutism of the management and the exclusive sway of the profit making motive. Labour is to be taken into consultation, is to have a " voice " in all matters in which its interests are concerned and in which its experience and judgment are useful, not merely for arranging wage rates and other "conditions" of labour and for settling " disputes," but for improvements in organisation and methods of work. The beginnings of industrial representative government are here to be found. Following the famous Whitley Committee's report, a number of industrial councils were established in English trades, with a network of district councils and workshop committees. In other staple trades where some machinery of consultation and conciliation has long existed, as in the leading textile and engineering trades, many firms have endeavoured to interest their employees in efficient co-operation with the management by schemes of bonus wages, profit sharing, or participation in ownership. There are those, especially in Britain and America, who claim that in co-partnership and the general spread of ownership and investment the real remedy for industrial unrest and " ca' canny " is to be found. If the main body of the workers in any firm or industry were shareholders, even on a small scale, they would, so runs the argument, be led to identify in their own persons the interests of capital and labour. Their position as shareholders would carry a measure of control over the conduct of the business, and would give them some insight into the difficulties and delicacies of managerial work. An actual share in profits would make them less insistent in attempts to raise wages at the expense of dividends. The considerable savings which well-paid skilled labour can secure in some branches of industry, especially in America and Britain, must tend to affect working-class psychology in the ways above described, making in some measure for harmony in the working of industry. But the evidence adduced in America[1] to show that considerable numbers of workers are small shareholders in some large corporation does not go far towards establishing the new economic harmony. The number of businesses in which the employees possess a considerable, not to say controlling, share of the capital is negligible. Workers for the most part do not invest such savings as they make in the shares of the business where they work, except where some profit sharing experiment or other special inducement is brought into play. A very large proportion of their savings is not for permanent investment, but for deferred expenditure. No doubt, while it is invested and is earning interest, it has some slight educative influence in abating "proletarian" feeling. Where, as in America, rich trade unions and their members experiment in Labour Banks, there opens up the possibility of a small labour capitalism, perhaps controlling mines, farms, factories, and distributive agencies of its own. But at present this has gone a very little way towards any general improvement of relations between capital and labour. Workers who may draw some small percentage of their income from investments, through some Provident Society or Trust Company, in some unknown business operations, are not likely to alter appreciably their labour attitude. The proportion of the total capital owned by working-class persons in Britain is very small. Even in America during the prosperity of 1918-19, data gathered by the Department of Labour in 92 industrial centres showed that the annual savings of the two-thirds of the family budgets which disclosed a surplus was only $155 per family, while against that must be set a deficit of $127 per family in the case of nearly one-quarter of the budgets. The average city worker's family income, amounting to $1513, as indicated by the same enquiry, could not in any case yield a rate of saving sufficient to effect materially the distribution of property in America. In Britain, where in 1919 "we get two-thirds of the

[1] See Robert S. Brookings *Industrial Ownership* (Macmillan & Co.)

wealth held by just 400,000 people and the top one-third by 36,000 people," [1] no recent British computation of total or average wages has appeared, but Dr. Bowley in 1913 estimated £770 millions as the earnings of $15\frac{1}{5}$ million wage-earners, a trifle over £52 per annum for the average worker. Assuming, as is not unlikely, this £52 be raised to £80, to allow for the new monetary situation, the margin for saving must remain very small. There is no reason to hold that by large changes in ownership of capital any appreciable improvement in the relations of capital and labour can be effected. We must look for other remedies for unrest and low productivity. There are those who, maintaining the necessity of private ownership and administration of industry, look for peace and efficiency to various steps which admit the workers to a larger share of the product, and to a clearer understanding of, and interest in, the efficient working of the business. To this school standard wages, publicity of accounts, the substitution of debenture for share capital (or the limitation of dividend upon share capital), are "the way out," accompanied in some cases by a division of any "surplus" income, after standard wages and profits are met, in a manner favourable to labour. There are many variants of the schemes for reconciling the interests of the two parties. The most radical is that which envisages the workers in a business engaging to pay the owners of the capital a fixed interest and undertaking to run the business themselves, with or without the assistance of the former managers ; in other words, the workers to take over the business, paying the owners an annual interest and perhaps a sinking fund for their rights. But there has been no marked disposition for groups of workers to embark upon business on their own account, hiring the necessary capital, and conducting the concern for their own profit. Where attempts have been made, as recently in England by Building Guilds, little success has accrued. The history of Productive Co-operation, in the strict sense of the term, does not encourage hopes of wide success.

[1] Sir J. Stamp, *Wealth and Taxable Capacity*, p. 102.

In Britain at any rate, during the last generation, the growth of orderly collective bargaining appeared to many the best available means of improving the conditions of labour and of avoiding disastrous conflicts. But though there is no decline in the use of machinery for collective bargaining, its limitations and drawbacks from the social standpoint have become more evident. It has not shown itself generally effective during this century for raising the real wages of labour, nor for preventing strikes and lock-outs which, from the very strength of the organisations engaged, have been increasingly damaging to other trades and to the community. Where collective bargaining is not accompanied by any compulsory arbitration or other judicial settlement, and when bargaining fails to win agreement, there is no security for industrial peace. Thus it has come about that the worker has been disposed to use his organised political power to supplement trade unionism, while the public, in its capacity of consumer, looks to the State to safeguard its interests against failures of necessary supplies and services when quarrels of employers and employed bring stoppages, or against extortionate prices when competition fails, and industrial peace inside sheltered trades is purchased at the cost of high profits and high wages.

§ 5. This being the situation not only in Britain and her Dominions, but in most industrial countries, the State is everywhere driven to take a more active and varied part in economic affairs. The hastily improvised State Socialism of the war, for the most part scrapped when peace ensued, has left a curiously mixed attitude of mind in most countries. Professed contempt for the inefficiency of Governmental machinery, as illustrated by war controls, is accompanied by an increased expectation of, and acquiescence in, State intervention for emergency situations and for protective measures in general. Business men, bitterly hostile to State interferences and trade union privileges, are engaged in seeking tariff protection, or subsidies, or diplomatic and financial aids in the development of trade, while workers look more and more to Government to help in securing standard conditions of wages and hours, with adequate provisions against unemployment, the competition of foreign sweated goods, etc. The public subsidies which, under various pressure, have been found in recent times for the railways and mines, for agriculture and for export trade, are less significant on their own account than as indications of a widespread new attitude towards government regarded as an instrument of economic defence and progress. This attitude, no doubt, is largely due to disorders and perils that are war sequelæ. Britain, so vitally dependent upon foreign trade, seeks from government and public policy aids to recovery which she envisages as purely temporary expedients. But, in point of fact, what is taking place is a growing conscious realisation of national, and to a less degree imperial, economy as an organised system, conservation, and development of national and imperial resources, in view of the dangers, political and economic, of the outside world. This is seen in the attention given by all political parties to the revival of agriculture and reduced dependence upon overseas supplies, discouragement of overseas investments, proposals for expenditure of public credit on development of electric power, improved transport, and insurance in all its branches. Many of the schemes are unsound and even fantastic, but their wide prevalence attests a new spirit of dependence on and confidence in the State. Though in Britain, as in every advanced industrial country except America, a powerful political party is formally committed to Socialism, the attitude here indicated can not admit so compact an interpretation. It is very far from seeking the overthrow of private capitalism and the substitution of a general Socialism, State or Guild, or other. It is much more opportunist, tentative, experimental, and compromising. But it brings State action into the business world in a great variety of ways. Dislike of centralised autocracy and certain deep-seated defects of that system make it unlikely that any Western nation will resort to public ownership and operation of industry upon a general scale. There will, however, be a steady, though perhaps not rapid, movement towards the displacement of private by public ownership in certain vital industries and services. The public ownership of the land, or at any rate of city sites and mineral areas, formally existent as a right of eminent domain, will become a reality in all well populated countries. The instruments for production and distribution of "power" for industry, transport, agriculture, and domestic uses, will tend to become public services, after costly and necessary experiments in private enterprise have disclosed their best economies of technique. The nationalisation of mines and of railways, already partially effected in many countries of the old and new world, will become general. No less clear is the trend towards common ownership in the departments of banking and insurance. Recent experiences in the operations of finance have convinced all men of the paramount importance of the money power. It will be urged, no doubt, that the gravest sinners in the economic department have been governments. And it is true that the acts of inflation, whose consequences have been so disastrous, are mainly governmental. But the chief impelling forces that made governments inflate were the preference of the great business classes for this dishonest way of raising public revenues over the honest way of direct taxation, and the opportunites which would credit operations afforded to the gamblers in the money markets. There is an increase of the census of opinion among economists and informing publicists that the issue and control of money need unitar remanagement, and cannot safely be left to individuals of corporations whose private profitable interests do not coincide with the public needs.

Insurance in many branches, especially as a provision against working-class emergencies, has in many countries passed under public operation or regulation. Outside the area of industrialism, education, hygiene, and medicine and law are passing more and more from the status of private crafts or mysteries into that of public services.

Summing up, it may be said that, apart from all theories of socialism and individualism, a general tendency is seen in civilised countries towards the assertion of public ownership, operation, or control of land,

power, transport, money, insurance, education, hygiene
and justice, regarded as necessary prerequisites of
liberty and equality of opportunity. A stoppage or
shortage in any of these services, due either to the fixing of excessive rates or prices, in order to earn high
profits for a trade or profession, or to conflicts between
employers and employed, inflicts such intolerable injuries upon the community, that the State is bound to
intervene. But casual intervention in an emergency is
no adequate method of safeguarding the public interests.
It is a medley of these different considerations that
directs the practical and partial socialism to which all
modern States at various paces are committing themselves.

§ 6. But it may be said that, in order to safeguard
the public interest, public ownership and operation may
be unnecessary ; public control may suffice. Even where
strong trusts or other combinations command the supply
of prime necessaries, or administer essential public
services, such as railroads, telephones, electric supplies,
or banking, several alternatives to complete socialisation are proposed and practised. Public ownership
may be combined with private business operation, the
State leasing out the enterprise to profit making corporations, and the public interest being safeguarded by
regulation of prices and other conditions of supply,
public participation in profits, and standard conditions
for employees. If it were always, and in all cases,
unreasonable to expect that the best public operation
can approach the efficiency of good private enterprise, a
strong case would exist for this line of advance, assuming that the State could exercise effectively the powers
of control entrusted to it. Another much discussed proposal is that of combining public ownership with a
scheme of representative government of the trade by
its members with some governmental guarantees for
public order and consumers' interests. This approaches
Guild Socialism, the central idea being that those who
perform the productive functions, manual and mental,
should regulate the business of industry, subject to
consumers' safeguards. Where public ownership of
the existing and prospective capital of the industry

was established, it is evident that the rights of self-government, accorded to the workers of hand and brain, must be limited by some final power vested in the Government, or, better perhaps, in some permanent expert Commission. But, within such limits, a great field for free self-government might be assigned to the active elements in the industry. It is not unlikely that in Britain experiments along these lines may take place in the coal-mining and railway industries, though perhaps with widely different representation of the managerial, technical, and manual workers, in the two cases. Other trades, affected by strong public interests, might, even though formed in trusts or price fixing combines, be left free from public regulation, other than the ordinary Factory and Workshops Acts and some standard regulation of pay and hours, the State taking toll of any surplus gains by an excess profits tax. Any such arrangement would involve an adequately ordered publicity of accounts. Standardised accountancy is, however, essential to any effective form of public control, whether by governmental action or the force of public opinion.

State control, adequate to secure the interests of the workers on the one hand and the consumers on the other, and with due regard to the needs of the public revenue, inevitably involves much regulation and inspection by officials. Those who prefer public control to public ownership and administration must be prepared to show that such control can be exercised with sufficient skill and honesty to achieve the public ends, and without any interference with private business administration that is vexatious and injurious. Many of the objections made against State Socialism are also valid against strong State control, and it is notorious that most champions of private enterprise are hostile to any control that is rigorous and inquisitive enough to be effective. But the present prevailing disposition in Britain is to favour various experiments in public control, carrying the early policy of factory legislation in new directions involving what would appear to the older school of economists interferences with "economic laws." Such is the policy of legal minimum wages, and of Unemployed Insurance Funds, founded upon compulsory contributions from employers, workers, and the national exchequers. Perhaps the most radical of recent experiments along these lines is the Trade Boards, originally designed in 1909 to deal with wages and other conditions in a few definitely " sweated " trades, and now (1925) extended so as to apply to forty-five distinct trades with about a million and a-half employees. While most of these trades are concerned with minor textile or clothes making processes, some large industries have within the last few years been brought under the Act—*e.g.*, sugar and confec' onery trades, laundries, tobacco manufacture, grocery and provision shops. The theory is that the structure and condition of these trades are such that it is unsafe to leave them to the ordinary processes of the labour contract. Hence the establishment of Boards, with equal representation of employers and employed, and a smaller number of members appointed by Government, wielding a statutory power to fix wages, where agreement cannot be got by mutual consent of the parties.

The processes by which wages are regulated in two such important industries as coal-mining and agriculture, though not precisely on all fours with the Trade Board procedure, indicates how far public opinion and public practice have departed from the old *laisses faire* attitude.

§ 7. The economic consequences of the war have involved many temporary or lasting excursions into closer forms of national economy. The most general forms have been the extension of protective tariffs, regulation or prohibition of exports (including gold), and a policy of subsidies for the development of natural resources or new industries, all with the view to cultivating more economic self-sufficiency. The war emergency familiarised us with the vague concept " Key Industries," which we must preserve and encourage at all costs for purposes of national defence. Foreign luxuries, taxed in war-time, for reasons, partly of national finance, partly of transport economy, together with a few manufactured articles (mostly of

German origin) were continued in the same restrictions after the emergency had passed. Partly by this
fragmentary protectionism, partly by subsidies, partly
by imperial preferences applicable both to imports and
to exports, Britain has been attempting to diminish
her dependence upon foreign trade. Though there is
an obvious conflict between the national self-contained-
ness of Key Industries and agricultural subsidies and
the wider imperial economy, such contradictions are
so frequent in " high politics " as to occasion little
disturbance of the public mind.

It is impossible to gauge the distance or the pace
of this movement towards conservation and development of national and imperial resources with a view
to self-sufficedness. But, so far as it goes, it involves
a reversal of the free internationalism of trade and
finance which for the best part of a century has been
the prevalent feature of our economic life. The contraction of our free trade and investments throughout
the world would not only reduce our commercial profits,
but would be attended by a shrinkage of our world
control of shipping and finance and of the large direct
and indirect gains accruing to our nation therefrom.
The national or imperial economy which would impose
these sacrifices will not be arguable on any other
ground than that laid down by Adam Smith in his
famous declaration that " defence is much more important than opulence." The restrictions of a national
or imperial economy would undoubtedly be represented
in a diminished volume of national and imperial wealth.
But of that diminished volume a larger quantity than
formerly would be required and taken for defensive
services. For in the dangerous world which is contemplated we should have to add to the supremacy
of the navy (which might then be called upon to take
into account the new rising naval power of America),
an army, and an air force maintained upon a Continental
scale. Such a sacrifice of opulence would not, however, afford security ; it would only mitigate the
immediate insecurity, and help to preserve the balance
of power which ensures a future war.

This situation would be, of course, eminently

unfavourable to economic progress. Industry and commerce would be consciously subjected everywhere to political and military motives, and such scientific and technical developments as took place would continually be directed more by military than by economic utility. The trend of thought and valuation in such a world would be hostile to free processes of human co-operation. Nor is that all. The autocratic and protective functions exercised by the State would inevitably be exploited by organised business interests to build up monopolies and to secure profitable dips into the public purse. The cry for economic self-sufficiency always means rising rents and high profits for protected trades, with a consequent depression in real wages.

§ 8. The only escape from the costs and perils of economic nationalism is by a fuller measure of economic internationalism, secured by improved political arrangements between the Powers. Underneath the racial, national, and sentimental grievances which have figured in the forefront of the stage of history as causes of war, the struggles of trading, manufacturing, and financial groups, using the "foreign policy" of there respective governments to push their private profitable interests, are easily discernible. Look behind the diplomacy in all the recent danger zones—Egypt, Persia, Transvaal, Tripoli, Morocco, Mexico, China, and the Balkans—the real grievances that rankle, the real aspirations and demands that formulate policy, are of a mainly economic character: the desire for access to trade routes and harbours, the push for markets, and, above all, the establishment of capitalistic control over the undeveloped resources of great backward countries with supplies of cheap labour, and weak or corrupt governments. If a durable peace is to be obtained, it can only be obtained by international arrangements directed primarily towards stopping the conflicts of business interests and the consequent political disputes which arise between advanced industrial and commercial nations for markets and lucrative investments. To expect that all the advanced countries will easily or quietly abandon their national protective tariffs and admit one another's goods freely, is unreasonable. But is it impossible that they should assent to an agreement to maintain or to establish equality of access to all markets in their colonies, protectorates, and spheres of influence, and equal opportunities to the members of every nation to take part in the profitable development of the resources of these dependencies ? Such an arrangement, could it be got, would remove most of the feelings of suspicion, jealousy, and resentment which underlie the policy of imperialistic competition. Free access to trade routes by land and water, equal rights for traders to enter, buy, and sell, together with international agreements for sharing upon equal terms the commercial and developmental opportunities afforded by backward dependent countries—these are the basic conditions of such an international arrangement.

It is in part the fuller application to foreign trade of the doctrine of *laisses faire*, *laisses aller*. But it is a positive, not a merely negative, application that would be required. The State could not simply leave its traders and investors to go where they liked and put their goods where they liked at their own risk. The Governments of the several States should agree to give equal protection to the rights of the members of all nations in their respective areas of political control. Not merely should they agree not to take separate political action to secure markets, concessions, or other economic privileges for their respective nationals. They should agree to take concerted action for the fair apportionment of economic opportunities in dealing with the governments and peoples of countries which, like China, were ripening for development, by the use of foreign capital and enterprise.

A purely *laisses faire* internationalism, which left individuals or groups of business men within each nation free to engage in any foreign trade they chose or to invest their capital in any foreign enterprise at their own risk, has never been practised, and is not practicable. The actual practice has been for business men to secure the assistance of their governments in pushing for markets, investments, and concessions outside their own country, in competing with business men of other nations similarly supported by their governments, and in bringing diplomatic or public pressure to bear upon the government or people of any weak country where their trading or other economic interests are threatened. It is this illicit and underhand use of foreign policy by private business interests which has converted economic internationalism into the peril it has shown itself to be. Since it is impossible for governments to take a disinterested attitude towards the business operations of their nationals in foreign lands, a more definitely responsible control of these operations is the only alternative. And, if this control is to avoid the dangers of the past, it must be exercised by the concerted action of the Powers. In other words, international economics must be supported and sustained by international politics. This forward movement in political and economic internationalism is the only escape from a reversion towards a reactionary nationalism which will at once diminish the " opulence " of each country without securing its " defence."

The system of Mandates established under the Covenant of the League of Nations, though unsatisfactory in its origin and in its partial application, is a beginning of that internationalisation of opportunity in backward countries which is a basic condition for a world economy. By its extension to colonies and protectorates in Africa and parts of Asia, a large step would be taken towards regulating that competition for tropical and other resources that has hitherto been the chief obstacle to peace between nations and to the development of the wealth of the world for the good of mankind.

REPLETE INDEX.

Brooke's Soap, 212
BROOKINGS, 482
BROWN, (see John Brown and Co.)
Bruges, 3
Brunner, Mond, and Co., 206
Bryant and May's Match Company, 212
BÜCHER, 61
Buckinghamshire, 327
Building Guilds, 483
Building Trade, 389-390
BULLOUGH, 82
BUNGE, 467
Bureaucracy, 423
Burma, 142
BURNLEY, 54, 73, 143
Burroughs and Wellcome, 211
Bury, 77, 78
Business and the "Speculative" Factor, 130
Business Men : their origin as a class, 6, 7, 24
Business Structure : its Differentiation, 141-142
Business : the Scale of its Operations, 138-140
Byzantine Empire, 6, 11

"CA' CANNY," 475, 481
Cadbury's Cocoa, 207
Cæsarea, 10
Calico Printers' Association, 208, 209
CAMMELL, 206
Canada, 111, 461, 463, 467
Canadian Bankers' Association, 467
Canals, 45
CANNAN, 258
Canterbury, 46
Cape, 266, 279
Capital, 67, 68, 88, 336
Capitalism : defined, 1, 26 ; first conditions of, 1-2 ; money basis of, 5 ; early accumulations of, 19 ; British priority in development of, 23 ; instruments of, 25-29 ; periods of, 75 ; order of national progress in, 94-112 ; concentration of, 113-140, 251, 262 ; trustified, 180-234 ; financial, 235-272

Cardiff, 161
CARNEGIE, 194. 224
Carnegie Steel Company, 194, 197
Carolina, 150
Cartels and Trusts, 180-215, 446. (See also Trusts)
CARTWRIGHT, 78, 80, 82, 96
Castle Line, 175. (See also Union Castle Line)
Catholic. (See Roman)
Cattle Trust, 179, 200, 216
Cattle Trust of the U.S., 216
Census of Production, 476
Central America, 12, 463
CERCHI, 8
Ceylon, 12
Chadwick and Co., 208
CHALMERS, 37, 43, 45
CHAPMAN, 91, 138, 143, 202, 362, 363, 443, 444
Chartered Companies, 38
CHASE, 474, 475
Chemistry, 26
Chicago, 152, 175, 190, 198
Chicago, Milwaukee, and St. Paul Railway, 259
Children's Labour, 350
China, 35, 142, 146, 155, 175, 231, 245, 263, 458, 491, 492
CHIOZZA-MONEY, 112
Chorley, 160
Christian Science Church, 211
Claims of Labour, 435
CLAPLIN, 191
Clarke and Co., 208. (See also Coats and Clarke Thread Trust)
Clearing House for Export, 184
CLEMENTS, 88
Cleveland, 190
Climate, 158
Clothiers, 62-63
Coal, 108, 111
COATS (see J. and P. Coats)
Coats and Clarke Thread Trust, 208, 211, 212. (See also J. and P. Coats)
Cockerell (see Rickett)
COLBERT, 35
Colchester, 46
COLLIER, 189
Cologne (see Köln)
Colorado, 190